The Handbook of Transcultural Counselling and Psychotherapy

Edited by

Colin Lago

Open University Press

Open University Press
McGraw-Hill Education
McGraw-Hill House
Shoppenhangers Road
Maidenhead
Berkshire
England
SL6 2QL

email: enquiries@openup.co.uk
world wide web: www.openup.co.uk

and

Two Penn Plaza, New York, NY 10121-2289, USA

First published 2011

A catalogue record of this book is available from the British Library

ISBN-10: 0 335 23849 1 (pb) 0 335 23850 5 (hb)
ISBN-13: 978 0 33 523849 1 (pb) 978 0 33 523850 7 (hb)
eISBN: 978 0 33 523851 4

Library of Congress Cataloging-in-Publication Data
CIP data has been applied for

Typeset by Aptara Inc., India
Printed in the UK by Bell & Bain Ltd, Glasgow

Fictitous names of companies, products, people, characters and/or data that may be used herein (in case studies or in examples) are not intended to represent any real individual, company, product or event.

MIX
Paper from
responsible sources
FSC
www.fsc.org
FSC® C007785

The McGraw·Hill Companies

Praise for this book

"With its diversity throughout including almost 40 authors from different therapeutic modalities, continents and professional fields the book indeed is both an 'invitation and challenge' and a means 'to aid transcultural therapists in conducting their work in a sensitive and informed manner'. It brings to mind a colourful and well stocked market comprising two parts. The first provides nourishing food for practitioners such as contributions to theory, use of interpreters, training, supervision, research and case studies. The second offers an outstanding exploration of the impact of different cultural backgrounds orchestrated by the editor, whose compilation from a UK perspective might be a useful example for other cultural and language areas. The involved reader will be delighted to have this inspiring handbook to hand."

Gerhard Stumm, Ph.D., psychotherapy trainer, Vienna

"Therapists pride themselves on cherishing the uniqueness of every client. This book offers a powerful challenge for it plainly demonstrates that a commitment to honouring uniqueness cannot be divorced from a sensitivity to the cultural, racial, spiritual and ethnic differences that clients present in an increasingly multicultural society. Here is an impressive compendium that illuminates the many clinical, training, relational and supervisory issues involved together with the widest range of contributions from diverse cultures that I have ever encountered in one volume. Colin Lago is to be congratulated on editing an invaluable resource which is both stimulating and disturbing in its implications"

Brian Thorne, Emeritus Professor of Counselling, University of East Anglia and Co-founder of The Norwich Centre

The F
Transcultural
Counselling and
Psychotherapy

059572

Contents

Part 2:   Heritage and identity formation: transition and identity transformation

The editor and contributors

Aileen Alleyne is a UKCP registered psychodynamic psychotherapist and clinical supervisor in private practice. She is a full member of FIP, BACP and Nafsiyat Intercultural Therapy Centre. Alongside her private practice, she consults to organizations on issues of difference and diversity in the workplace. Her academic career has included lectureships at several London colleges and universities, including the University of London, Goldsmiths College, for eight years. Aileen's doctoral research, examining black workers' experiences in institutional settings, highlights the concept of 'the internal oppressor'. It offers ways of deepening understanding of black people's psychological reactions to the negative impact of racism. Aileen is the author of several book chapters and journal papers exploring black/white dynamics, shame and black identity wounding.

Alison Barty was born in Uganda and came to the UK in 1963. She graduated in modern languages from Oxford University and after working at the University of Manchester and the UK Council for Overseas Student Affairs (now UKCISA), trained as a counsellor and subsequently as a Gestalt psychotherapist. She has worked as a student counsellor at the Central St Martins College of Art and Design, South Bank University and currently works at the School of Oriental and African Studies, University of London. Alison regularly trains university and college staff on issues relating to international students. Her publications include *Higher Education Institutions and International Students' Mental Health* for Young Minds (2006). With Colin Lago she co-produced *Bridging Our Worlds*, a training DVD for staff working with international students for UKCISA in 2007.

Anita Chakraborty is a counselling psychologist who completed her training at the University of Surrey. She is of Bangladeshi origin and grew up in the suburbs of London. Her research interest lies in the acculturation strategies and related levels of acculturative stress of South Asian groups. In addition to this, she has carried out research into how therapists view their ethnic minority clients. She has worked in a range of therapeutic settings helping individuals, couples and groups to make insights and changes. She is currently living in Sydney with her partner, where she practises at a psychotherapy centre and enjoys using psychodynamic theories to inform her work.

Divine Charura is a psychotherapist based in Leeds. He is of African (Zimbabwean) origin and is a lover of photography, food, art, music and outdoor pursuits. He has years of various work experience which includes working in diverse psychiatric/clinical and therapeutic settings, working with children, refugees and asylum-seekers and co-managing a drug/alcohol detox rehabilitation centre in Leeds. His psychotherapeutic interests are in working with difference/diversity, dynamics in relationships or families, issues of power, discrimination/prejudice and their impact on mental health. Divine has researched and written on the links between psychopathology, the client's experience and effective psychotherapeutic approaches when working with individuals, couples or families. Apart from his psychotherapy practice, he is a part-time and guest lecturer in psychotherapeutic studies and their psychosocial influences at Leeds Metropolitan University.

Tiane Corso Graziottin is a Brazilian psychologist with training and experience in the fields of counselling/psychotherapy, mental health, educational psychology, social psychology and organizational psychology. She left Brazil in 2003 to live in London, where she remained until the end of 2010 working in diverse contexts such as substance misuse and family support programmes. She has an MSc in counselling undertaken at the University of Strathclyde where she developed research entitled 'The ethics of the person-centred approach'. Tiane's main interests are directly related to human development, including inter- and transcultural influences, at individual and collective levels.

Harbrinder Dhillon-Stevens has a doctorate in psychotherapy and is a BPS and HPC registered chartered counselling psychologist, UKCP registered integrative psychotherapist and HPC registered child art psychotherapist. Currently she is senior lecturer in counselling, psychotherapy and counselling psychology at the University of Roehampton. She is also primary tutor at the Metanoia Institute on the doctorate in counselling psychology and psychotherapy (DCPsych). Harbrinder is training director for DhillonStevens Ltd, a specialist training and research company, has a private practice and undertakes expert witness assessment and treatment, supervision and therapeutic work with children, young people, adults and families. She is interested in anti-oppressive practice in psychological therapies and has undertaken research and produced publications in this area.

Riccardo Draghi-Lorenz runs a private psychotherapy practice in London and is the course director of the doctorate in psychotherapeutic and counselling psychology at the University of Surrey. His take on therapy is pluralistic and he has also published on the issue, although his research so far has focused on early socioemotional development and the processes underpinning awareness of self and others. He developed an interest in the effects of ethnicity on therapy following input from the co-authors of the chapter reported here and his own experiences of working with ethnically diverse clients, trainees and colleagues.

Simon du Plock is professor and head of the Post-qualification Doctorates Department at Metanoia Institute, where he directs research degree programmes in partnership with Middlesex University. He has developed a doctorate in psychotherapy by public works which provides senior qualified practitioners with an opportunity to undertake a reflexive audit of their stories of professional entrepreneurialism. He is also recognized internationally as a leading figure in existential-phenomenological psychology and psychotherapy.

Patricia Eschoe is senior cognitive behavioural psychotherapist at Barnsley PCT NHS Mental Health and teaches diversity and working with interpreters on the IAPT course at Sheffield University. Born in Jamaica her Afro-Caribbean heritage is an important and informing influence in both her personal and her professional life. She holds an MSc in cognitive behavioural psychotherapy, a diploma in person-centred counselling, is a trained CBT, IAPT and person-centred supervisor, accredited by BABCP and a member of BACP. She has worked as counsellor and CBP for asylum-seekers over several years and also as a counsellor/coordinator for ethnic minorities, a young people's counsellor/CBP and in other complex areas.

Farkhondeh Farsimadan is a chartered integrative counselling psychologist with over 12 years' experience of working for West London Mental Health NHS Trust in various secondary and tertiary mental health settings, including assertive outreach, cognitive behaviour therapy and psychotherapy departments. She is also the Trust's training coordinator and clinical supervisor for doctoral trainee counselling psychologists studying in various universities in London. She currently works in a psychiatric intensive care secure unit with clients experiencing severe and enduring mental health problems. She has a special interest in working with ethnic minority clients and their experiences in therapy as well as the effects of ethnicity on process and outcomes of therapy.

Delroy Hall currently serves as a pastor and bishop for the Church of God of Prophecy in England, serving as a regional overseer in the North East. He trained as a psychodynamic counsellor over 20 years ago and enjoys the challenge of using biblical themes with psychological and counselling knowledge. At present he is completing his doctoral studies at the University of Birmingham, examining intrapersonal conflict as a legacy of enslavement and colonialism on African Caribbean diasporan faith communities. He also works one day a week as a student counsellor at Sheffield Hallam University. Delroy is married to Paulette who currently is a 'thesis widow' and has twin daughters Saffron and Jordan who are 'doctoral orphans'.

Fiona Hall is a person-centred therapist, now living in Canberra. She moved to Australia from Cambridge in 2004 after practising therapy for 20 years in the UK. As well as conducting a private counselling practice and offering supervision, Fiona provides consultancy services to a homeless youth organization.

Addila Khan specializes in addiction, trauma and enduring mental health issues including personality disorder. She works for EACH, an agency that is particularly sensitive to the needs of ethnic minorities. She runs a private practice in London, which includes psychotherapy and expert witness work and practises within an integrative framework utilizing CBT, EMDR, schema therapy and psychodynamic approaches. She maintains a special interest in the field of pervasive development disorders and holds further expertise in applied behavioural analysis techniques. She works with children, adolescents and adults. Addila cooperates with the University of Surrey as an examiner and visiting lecturer. Her research interest was developed through personal experience and expanded during her training at Surrey University. It focuses on the effects of ethnicity on therapy and includes the difficulties encountered by ethnic minorities, in particular the role of culture-sensitive variables within the therapeutic relationship.

Indu Khurana is an accredited member of the BACP and registered as an integrative child psychotherapist with the UKCP. She is currently working within the NHS and CSF, as well as being in independent practice as a counsellor for adults, children and couples, and a clinical supervisor. She has contributed to books on politics in therapy, and the mind–body link. Her main areas of interest include natural health, the mind–body link, relationships and attachment, and issues of culture.

Colin Lago was director of the Counselling Service at the University of Sheffield from 1987 to 2003. He now works as an independent counsellor, trainer, supervisor and consultant. He is a fellow of the BACP, an accredited counsellor/psychotherapist and UKRCP registered practitioner. He was awarded a D.Litt (and an honorary professorship) in 2009, specifically in recognition of his contributions to and publications in transcultural counselling and psychotherapy. Deeply committed to transcultural concerns he has had articles, videos and books published, including: *Race, Culture and Counselling: The Ongoing Challenge* (2006), *Anti Discriminatory Practice in Counselling and Psychotherapy* (co-edited with Barbara Smith) (2010) and *Carl Rogers Counsels a Black Client* (co-edited with Roy Moodley and Anissa Talahite) (2004). Despite growing older, Colin enjoys (among other things) dancing and mountain running.

Courtland C. Lee is a professor in the Counselor Education Program at the University of Maryland, USA. He is the author, editor, or co-editor of five books on multicultural counselling and two books on counselling and social justice. He is also the author of three books on counselling African-American males. In addition, he has published numerous book chapters and articles on counselling across cultures. Dr Lee is the president of the International Association for Counselling and is also a fellow of the BACP and a fellow and past president of the American Counseling Association.

Yair Maman is a professor of education and psychology and the chair of postgraduate counsellor training at Touro College in New York. He has proactively shaped the fields of counselling and psychotherapy in New York and in the USA, through establishing counsellor training programmes that are primarily concerned with recruitment and training in underserved schools and communities across the New York metropolitan area. He devised unique mental health counselling and school counselling programmes that are the result of major organizational changes at Touro College.

Susan McGinnis came to the UK in 1984 as a professional musician and trained as a counsellor in 1992 in response to working at a summer programme for gifted young people, where she discovered that they liked talking to her. A long-time advocate of counselling provision for children and young people, Susan has been editor of the journal *Counselling Children and Young People* and is author/editor of the *Good Practice Guidance for Counselling in Schools* documents for the BACP. As a trainer, she has a particular interest in developing person-centred theory and practice with regard to counselling young people. More importantly, she is still a counsellor in a school.

Isha Mckenzie-Mavinga has been teaching transcultural workshops at Goldsmiths for last 20 years. She has a private practice and offers clinical supervision for individuals and groups and an ongoing transcultural supervision group. Isha set up therapy services for the African-Caribbean Mental Health Association in the early 1990s and developed therapeutic group work at the Women's Trust, with women affected by domestic violence. She has also worked as a student counsellor and senior lecturer at London Metropolitan University. Isha has published several papers and a training booklet from her doctoral study about the process of understanding 'black issues' in counsellor training. She has also co-authored an autobiography and contributed poetry to anthologies. Isha's book *Black Issues in the Therapeutic Process* was published in 2009.

Roy Moodley is associate professor in counselling psychology at OISE/University of Toronto. His research and publications include race, culture and psychotherapy, diversity issues in therapy, traditional healing, and gender and identity.

Renate Motschnig is a professor of computer science and head of the Computer Science Didactics and Learning Research Center at the University of Vienna, Austria. Renate has held positions at the RWTH Aachen in Germany, the University of Toronto, Canada, and regularly teaches at and cooperates with the Masaryk University in Brno, Czech Republic. She has participated in encounter groups and several events based on the person-centred approach. She is deeply interested in the multiple ways in which understanding and whole-person learning happen and is determined to foster a style in higher education that is based on person-centred attitudes, our co-actualizing potential and thoughtful support by web-based technology. She appreciates synergies between a multitude of (scientific) disciplines and cultures.

Sheila Mudadi-Billings is clinical lead coordinator at Rotherham Women's Counselling Service and specialist counsellor for the Asylum Seeker Mental Health Project, Sheffield PCT. Of African origin she has lived in the UK for over 25 years. During this time she has 'adapted' to and 'adopted' the western culture which complements her African heritage. Sheila initially trained as a person-centred therapist, gaining her BACP accreditation in 2005 and UKRCP accreditation in 2008. She completed a postgraduate diploma in person-centred supervision in 2008. She also has a certificate in 'Counselling from an Islamic Perspective' (2005) and a postgraduate diploma in the human givens approach (2008). She also volunteered with the Samaritans and Victim Support between 1993 and 1999. Married, Sheila has a son and enjoys walking in the countryside, cooking and entertaining.

GoEun Na is a doctoral student at the University of Maryland, USA. She has presented at a number of local and national conferences on multicultural counselling. She is the vice president of the Alpha Delta Chapter of Chi Sigma Iota, the International Counseling Honor Society, and has served as the webmaster of the Maryland Association for Counseling and Development. Her research interests include multicultural counselling, supervision and acculturation issues among immigrants and international students.

Seamus Nash works within end of life care at a hospice in West Yorkshire, leading the family care team. He is a UKCP registered psychotherapist with a background in both social work and community education. He is currently researching reflective practice and 'client-centredness' for his doctorate at the University of Huddersfield. Among other things, he is passionate about advancing the person-centred approach in both research and practice. He also loves music, guitars, talking, listening to and being with people, and spending time with his partner and all their children.

Bernie Neville is adjunct professor of education at La Trobe University, Melbourne, Australia. Since he first encountered Carl Rogers' theory and practice in the 1960s the person-centred approach has provided the framework for his teaching and writing in both counselling and education. He is editor of the recently published collection *As Others See Us: The Values Debate in Australia* (2008).

Yuko Nippoda is a UKCP registered psychotherapist and BACP senior accredited consellor with more than 20 years' experience in the fields of psychotherapy and counselling, in both Japan and England. As a bilingual psychotherapist and counsellor, she has worked with clients on a wide range of issues from many different cultures since coming to the UK in 1992. She is also a qualified supervisor and supervises other counsellors, psychotherapists and trainees. Her special interest is in cross-cultural issues, particularly the differences and commonalities between individualism and collectivism. She conducts research and has published many academic and professional papers on this subject. She has also appeared in the media to talk about cross-cultural issues. She is currently based in London.

Ladislav Nykl is external lecturer at the University of Vienna and at Masaryk University. He works on projects at both universities and conducts a private practice as a psychotherapist in Vienna where he works primarily with adults in individual and group therapy. He is the author of *Pozvánka do Rogersovské Psychologie* (*Invitation to Rogerian Psychology*, 2004), *Beziehung im Mittelpunkt der Persönlichkeitsentwicklung* (*Relationship in the Center of Personality Development*, 2005) and, together with Renate Motschnig, *Konstruktive Kommunikation* (*Constructive Communication*) which has been translated into Czech and will be published in 2011.

Judy Ryde is a co-founder of the Bath Centre for Psychotherapy and Counselling and the Centre for Supervision and Team Development. She is a UKCP accredited psychotherapist and works as a psychotherapist, supervisor and trainer. She leads a project which provides counselling and psychotherapy for refugees and asylum-seekers through BCPC. Her doctoral research, which was undertaken at the Centre for Action Research in Professional Practice at the University of Bath, was entitled 'Exploring white racial identity and its impact on psychotherapy and psychotherapy organizations', and her book *Being White in the Helping Professions: Developing Effective Intercultural Awareness* was published in 2009.

Antony Sigalas has been working as a psychotherapist with culturally diverse clients in a number of clinical settings funded by the NHS and in private practice. He is the clinical lead of Nafsiyat's 'breakthrough' project for newly arrived refugee families who have survived traumatic experiences. He trains and lectures on the themes of clinical assessment and the therapeutic effectiveness of intercultural therapy. His research interest is centred on how the culturally different experience is being approached in therapy both from a psychodynamic and from a phenomenological perspective. He is currently a member of the Equality and Diversity Board for the London borough of Enfield.

Patsy Sutherland is a counsellor and psychotherapist, and a PhD candidate in counselling psychology at the University of Toronto. Her research and publication interests span areas of cross-cultural counselling and psychotherapy, traditional healing and transgenerational trauma in the context of the colonial encounter and slavery.

Rachel Tribe is a professor at the School of Psychology at the University of East London. She is also a fellow of the British Psychological Society and an HPC registered counselling and organizational psychologist. She has undertaken training and consultancy work in a number of countries and has published numerous articles, book chapters and several books. Her research and clinical interests include transcultural psychology, trauma and working with interpreters in mental health. She co-edited a book on *Working with Interpreters in Mental Health* in 2003, co-wrote the guidelines on working with interpreters for the British Psychological Society in 2008 and has produced a DVD for the Department of Health in 2011.

Andrea Uphoff is a UKCP registered psychotherapist with licence to practise in Germany, and so divides her time between the two countries. She is currently engaged in PhD studies at Regent's College, London, where her dissertation research is focused on client experiences of touch in the psychotherapeutic relationship. Formerly convenor of BAPCA (British Association for the Person-Centred Approach), she currently serves on the board of NEAPCEPC (Network of European Associations for Person-Centred and Experiential Psychotherapy and Counselling). She has been a practitioner of Sahaj Marg meditation for over 10 years.

Valerie Watson works as a person-centred counsellor, supervisor and trainer in the UK. She has experience of working within the voluntary and independent sectors and has been involved in education as a teacher and lecturer for over 25 years. Val has a long-standing interest in ethnicity within the helping relationship, group work and the provision of community access to therapy in all its forms. More recently her interests have included investigating how knowledge and application of neuroscientific understanding might aid the work of therapists and exploring the therapeutic use of mindfulness and meditation.

Tony Wright originally trained as a counsellor in Liverpool's inner city with COMPASS, followed by an MA in counselling studies at Keele University. His formal training included person-centred, psychodynamic, narrative and existential counselling. Tony has maintained, within his counselling career, a balance between one-to-one counselling, training and, more latterly, supervision. The interrelationship between training, theory and practice remains central to his overall approach. He is currently working on understanding the diverse aspects of counselling survivors of torture. Tony has worked in a variety of settings encountering people living with HIV and AIDS, people who are blind and partially sighted, the general public, students and survivors of torture, while maintaining a small private practice.

Jin Wu was born and raised in China and has lived in the USA since 1991. She worked as a research assistant in developmental psychology in China, and co-authored two books on early intervention. On receiving her MA in clinical psychology at the Illinois School of Professional Psychology, she worked in the mental health and social service fields in the USA. She has presented on the subject of Chinese culture and client-centred therapy at various conferences, and has presented workshops on client-centred therapy and the psychology of sexual orientation in different parts of China. Currently she is a Psy.D student at Argosy University, Chicago.

Neelam Zahid is a BACP accredited counsellor and psychotherapist currently working as a student counsellor at Kingston University. She has specialist training in bereavement counselling, life coaching, online counselling and counselling adult survivors of childhood abuse. Neelam's particular area of interest is the cultural implications of race and culture within the counselling room and she has delivered a number of cultural awareness workshops for trained professionals at AUCC and BACP conferences as well as for trainees in various educational institutes.

Foreword

From the beginning, the question of how to make sense of cultural diversity has represented a critical challenge to the counselling and psychotherapy professions. There are probably three main factors that account for the difficulty that the therapy community has had in coming to terms with this topic. First, the founding figures in psychotherapy, such as Freud and Rogers, formulated their ideas at a time when awareness of cultural difference was not regarded as a factor that needed to be taken seriously by white people. Second, counselling and psychotherapy organized themselves around an over-psychologized concept of the person. With psychology as a starting point, the influence of culture on personal identity and behaviour can only ever be an external 'bolt-on' – it can never be truly accepted as a central aspect of what it means to be human. Finally, when counselling and psychotherapy were exported from Europe and North America to Africa and Asia, it was initially done in a spirit of missionary or colonialist zeal that largely silenced the voices of those who recognized and objected to its culturally encapsulated agenda. The result of these factors has been that theory and practice in counselling and psychotherapy have struggled to catch up with other professions, and with society as a whole, where significant achievements have been made around the affirmation of cultural pluralism and equality.

The Handbook of Transcultural Counselling and Psychotherapy makes a welcome and substantial contribution to the advancement of effective transcultural practice. It brings together a wide range of authors, reflecting many different cultural traditions and areas of therapy. These writers have been given permission to express themselves in a direct and authentic manner, drawing on personal experience as well as relevant theory and research. The topics that are covered open up multiple perspectives on transcultural therapy – training, supervision, the role of interpreters, the use of research, the needs of different client groups. The book invites the reader into the field of transcultural counselling and psychotherapy in a manner that avoids the risk of overwhelming him or her with a sense of how hard, or even impossible, it is to grasp the complexities and nuances of this area of work. Instead, the reader is offered a wealth of ideas, positive and down-to-earth strategies and ways of understanding that can be translated into action.

One aspect of this book that I particularly appreciate is the way that the idea of 'heritage' is used to convey a sense of different cultural traditions and how they may shape the process of therapy. The 'heritage' chapters are not written from a position of authoritative knowledge about the characteristics, values and lifestyles of people from different cultural backgrounds. The chapter authors write from the reality of their own lives, as if they have been asked to tell a sympathetic listener 'here's what you need to know about where I am coming from, in terms of my cultural roots'. The concept of 'heritage' inserts into the dialogue an implication of something that is there, and is important and unavoidable, but which is neverthe-less open to being used and interpreted by people in a selective and flexible fashion that takes into account the concrete reality of their present situation. It also im-plies, in an easy and straightforward way, the notion that for many people there are *multiple* heritages that have meaning for them in the conduct of their lives. In my view, ways of thinking and talking that thicken and deepen the stories that we tell about ourselves open up valuable possibilities around meaning-making and relationship-building. My hope is that a discourse of 'heritage' catches on within the counselling and psychotherapy literature, and that the heritage chapters in this book inspire other writers to try similar things.

Finally, my own experience of reading and reflecting on the contents of *The Handbook* have given me much to think about and act on, and also a desire to learn more about many issues that have perhaps only been touched on in its chapters, and deserve further exploration in their own right. The mark of any good book is that it leaves the reader wanting more. In this case, I certainly look forward with keen anticipation to whatever comes next from these authors, and from those colleagues who join them in the quest to allow culturally informed ways of working to take their place as ordinary and routine facets of everyday counselling and psychotherapy practice.

John McLeod
Professor Emeritus of Counselling
University of Abertay, Dundee

Acknowledgements

I'm currently writing these few words in the time period just after the various British and American film award ceremonies have taken place, and have been somewhat stopped in my tracks, temporarily, in composing this brief, but so important section, by a critical review I read of these ceremonies in one of the 'quality' newspapers. The journalist seemed very scathing of the emotionality and the expressed gratitude, by the various award winners, to parents, other family members, good friends and other significant people in their lives to whom they wished to acknowledge their respect and thanks. And yet I cannot think of who else I would wish to acknowledge in this book than all those who have supported me, influenced me, taught me and loved me, particularly in relation to this critical subject addressing the importance of transcultural understanding to health and well-being.

To all the chapter writers I owe a good deal of gratitude for their shared vision, commitment and industriousness in compiling the work contained in this book. I have enjoyed and valued our various conversations, electronic and live, related to producing their texts during recent months. I am grateful to John McLeod, a good colleague of many years, who supported the original proposal, and penned the foreword, and to Monika Lee and her colleagues at the publishers for accepting the vision of this handbook and then guiding me through the process.

My 'cultural teachers' have included children and young people at school in Jamaica, youth club members in a London borough, student clients at two universities, my first 'boss' in student counselling, Jean Clark, who taught me so much and with whom I shared initial forays into this professional endeavour, all members of the original 'RACE' sub-committee of the British Association for Counselling, and Joyce Thompson with whom I wrote several pieces, including the first edition of *Race, Culture and Counselling* (1996).

The general origins of my interest in this subject inevitably date back to incidents within my own childhood: from being an 'incomer' and an 'outsider' at school, to reading Angela Davies and Eldridge Cleaver in my late teens, from meeting others of different heritages, to experiencing painful moments (for others as well as myself) of my own cultural insensitivity and lack of understanding in such relationships.

Space, sadly, does not allow me to describe the nature and details of the relationships which have been so supportive and nurturing of my interest in and commitment to this subject. In addition, I fear that in acknowledging people by name I will inevitably end up not naming others who are equally to be valued. My gratitude and acknowledgements, then, go to all colleagues, friends, teachers, co-writers and supervisors who have influenced and taught me. I am grateful, also, to friends and colleagues who pay me the honour of regularly inviting me to work with their counselling students within the UK and in various other countries.

It is such a crass understatement to say that the world is a complicated phenomenon where powerful and competing pressures and systems seek to exist and coexist; where politics, riches and poverty, wars and natural disasters, religious beliefs and practices all impact profoundly upon individuals, families and communities. Transcultural counselling and psychotherapy, the subject of this book, is just one small but nevertheless important professional endeavour that seeks to contribute to the quality of people's lives. I deeply hope that you will find that the contents of this book contribute, in however modest a way, to the quality of your relating to others, whoever and wherever they are.

Finally, I must thank all my running and dancing friends for the sheer joy I have shared with them and my family who continue to be so supportive of this man who spends hours in the office, either with colleagues or trying desperately to write! My 2-year-old grandson, Luke, is my symbol for the future.

Colin Lago
Spring 2011

Part 1

Ensuring professional practice in transcultural counselling and psychotherapy

1 Introduction to Part 1: towards enhancing professional competence – from training to research to practice

Colin Lago

> *As a Black woman, with 3 children, it fills me with dread and concerns that my children might suffer with any form of mental problem . . . As a person who has had a mental health problem . . . I am continually treated by those working in the mental health field, in any capacity, as being incapable, useless, and inadequate and in some cases, ignorant.*
>
> *(Jenkin 2004: 10, 11)*

> *Marginalised voices actually matter a great deal to all of us. They hold a hidden wealth of tacit and explicit knowledge. They are able to teach the profession of psychotherapy about the powerful combined experience of profound invalidation, alienation from society, stigmatisation and minimal self-compassion . . . the amplification of disenfranchised voices brings new understanding of the importance of compassion.*
>
> *(May 2009)*

The above quotations eloquently display, from their very differing perspectives, the potential complexity of the transcultural counselling relationship and task. Each quote, in its own way, reveals to us the multifaceted world(s) in which both clients and therapists live. The first example opens up the huge arena of concerns that are connected to fear, power, oppression, majority–minority group relations, prejudice, stereotyping, projection, attitudes – to the 'other' and to mental health – stages of identity development and anxiety about the possible transgenerational implications of relations between social (ethnic, cultural etc.) groups.

Kathryn May acknowledges both the profound gift of listening to those whose life experiences may be substantially different from those of the therapist and the gift of receiving precious insights into personal worlds and the social world.

Working across cultural, gender, ethnic, linguistic, national and other differences demands so much of counsellors if they are to achieve the establishment of sensitive, 'good enough', anti-oppressive working practices with their clients of difference.

This book is divided into two parts. This first is concerned with the wide variety of issues that underlie and impact upon the delivered quality of professional practice in transcultural settings. The second part consists of a series of chapters exploring the impact upon persons of their cultural heritages.

Part 1 sets out to offer a contemporary view of current concerns, practices and research within the field of 'transcultural' therapy. This book has been written at a time when the UK government has turned more of its attention to mental health within society, and consequently, more specifically, to the services that support those in the community who suffer psychologically and emotionally. Such developments have included:

- The government's agenda for Increased Access to Psychological Therapies (IAPT) which includes a statement of intent to reduce the stigma associated with mental ill health.
- In addition, within the UK, there is current government legislation, funding and supporting practices nationally for the delivery of racial equality in mental health.

We might hypothesize that these government-led initiatives (and the resultant increased awareness of mental health treatments within society) will inevitably lead to an increased usage of psychological therapy services – a growth that has been steadily occurring in any case over the past two to three decades as counselling and psychotherapy have become more acceptable and accessible as valued therapeutic interventions. There is likely also to be a growth, therefore, in clients coming from a range of different ethnic, cultural and faith communities to attend counselling and psychotherapy services. The need for informed, sensitive 'transcultural' psychotherapeutic practice has therefore never been higher.

Anyone who has looked at the previous literature addressing the delivery of counselling and psychotherapy within transcultural settings will already have noted the very considerable contributions to theory and practice made by colleagues in North America (USA and Canada) for many decades. Indeed, the majority of literature and research upon this subject hails from there. The consequent challenge for mental health therapists in other countries has been, and continues to be, how to develop their own indigenous expertise and conceptualizations of transcultural work that is directly relevant to their political, demographic and sociocultural settings, informed but not overly determined by this existing literature. For example, as a therapist and an occasional trainer, I have in recent years been very influenced by the ethnic identity development models within the USA (see Chapter 5). These now represent a considerable range of theoretical approaches depicting patterns of identity development for members of that population. The impressive research subsequently carried out on these models and how they can inform 'transcultural therapy' practice, which is reported in Robert Carter's *The Influence of Race and Racial Identity in Psychotherapy* (1995) is of great value to therapists wherever they are, but the sociocultural origins of this work must also be borne in mind if they are not to be applied naively and simplistically to other societies. This handbook is therefore an attempt to 'catch' some of the most recent thinking in terms of training, practice and research within the international field of transcultural counselling and psychotherapy. By implication, also, I extend an invitation and challenge to mental health workers in all countries working with clients from diverse origins to seek to develop therapeutic practices that reflect the cultural settings and the needs of those clients who consult them.

'The world can come into our interviewing room'

In a recent chapter, Christodoulidi and Lago (2010: 231) wrote:

> The world of today is profoundly multicultural, multiethnic and multinational. Many millions of people worldwide are continually on the move to new cultures, new places to live, to work and to seek shelter. Indeed, it is estimated that one in every 35 people in the world today is an international migrant . . . Such 'geographic' moves are frequently chosen in the hope that a new life in another place will offer enhanced work and life possibilities. Others, sadly, are subject to forceful relinquishing of their countries of origin. Both categories of people, whether choosing or forced to migrate, have to face considerable personal, cultural, linguistic, social and spiritual challenges, which are rarely anticipated and rarely acknowledged in the public domain.

I am reminded of a phrase I frequently use in training sessions dedicated to exploring the delivery of counselling and psychotherapy with clients from differing ethnic, cultural, linguistic and faith origins which states: 'These days, the world (in the shape of a client) can come into our interviewing room'. The current demographics of our developed world indicate that nigh on every culture and nation is multicultural, multifaith, multiethnic, and comprises both majority and minority groups. In addition, therefore, patterns of relations between such groups can be powerfully determined by history and consequently, sadly, characterized by misunderstandings, tension, discrimination, violence and racism.

In addition, then, to the obvious need for transcultural therapists to develop their capacities for understanding difference in all its many facets, this book advocates a commitment and principled approach to the values of respect, equality and social justice between people and peoples. Given the sheer volume of research to support the thesis that discrimination is widespread across all social, judicial, educational, health and mental health systems (within the context of the UK as one example), what reassurance do we have that as psychological helpers we will not repeat these discriminations towards our clients that are manifested by a whole range of other professionals? What reassurances do we have that we will prove any different?

If the world can truly come into our room, then we, as therapists, need to be the best that we can be in order to be of most service to the wide range of clients that consult us. This requires a considerable commitment to our own ongoing personal and professional development, a matter I return to later in this chapter.

A note on terminology

There are a variety of terms used within this text that are worthy of clarification here. In spite of possible criticisms for non-specificity or oversimplification, I still find the following outline penned by Joyce Thompson and myself most useful:

> We have deliberately used various terms interchangeably within this book in relation to the helping or therapeutic process. We are cognisant of the current debate about differences between counselling and psychotherapy. Our concern here, whatever these differences are, is to address all who aspire, through the skills of listening, relating and dialogue, to assist others' suffering. We hope that the various terms used, e.g. counsellor, counselling, psychotherapist, therapist, psychotherapy etc. facilitate easy reading.
>
> There is also a range of terms used in the book to describe the activity of counselling a client from another racial or cultural background. In recent times these terms have included cross-cultural, intercultural, transcultural and multi-cultural. In most instances we have used the latter conventions of transcultural, a term increasingly popular in British literature and multi-cultural, a term current within the United States.
>
> Similarly we have used terms such as 'culturally different', 'racially different', 'black' and 'white' as variously descriptive of counsellors and clients. Where we have used the terms 'black' and 'white' we intend these to be interpreted in their political sense where blackness is used to describe those who are not the traditional power holders or members of a dominant group in a society.
>
> Language can age very quickly and connotative meanings may thus swing from having positive to negative effects. Consequently we have erred from giving precise definitions and interpretations of these terms but rather, encourage the reader to appreciate our attempts to address the lived complexity of such helping relationships, whatever the current definitions are.
>
> (Lago and Thompson 1996: xxiii)

Other terminology has become more popular in the intervening years since the above passage was written, including concepts such as 'diversity' and 'black and minority ethnic' (BME).

On developing transcultural competence

Elements of the journey towards transcultural competence are outlined in the chapters that follow. Commencing with the theme of training, to which three chapters are dedicated, there follows chapters on identity development and how it can impact upon therapy, ethnic matching, the use of interpreters, the implications of therapist identity, avoiding discriminatory behaviour, research findings, culturally sensitive supervision and finally two case studies of work with diverse clients.

Valerie Watson writes the first of the three chapters on training. Her own doctoral studies focused upon the experiences of students of counselling and psychotherapy courses from minority groups. Converting her research findings through the prism of current and impending government mental health provision, Val charts radical developmental ideas for the future training of transcultural therapists. Among other elements, she focuses on the necessary skills, knowledge and competences of those in training positions as well as indicating key areas of knowledge acquisition pertinent to transcultural therapy work. She commences her chapter with reference to the 'four forces' of counselling and psychotherapy: psychodynamic, cognitive behavioural, humanistic and multicultural – a conceptualization originating from the deliberations of the early multicultural counselling scene in the USA.

Both Val and Isha Mackenzie-Mavinga, the writer of the next chapter on training, refer to their concern about and the existence of silence and how it manifests itself (a) within a stance frequently assumed by minority group counselling students as a way to survive their courses and, (b) how multicultural issues generally can occupy a silence within training courses. Isha notes that the therapist's awareness of their attitude to diversity and the impact of oppressions on the client are paramount. She presents a multidimensional, anti-oppressive approach to trainer input and students' ability to work with diversity issues. Three tiers within the training curriculum that support the practice of cultural awareness, sensitivity and therapists' ability to work with a variety of needs and diverse cultural experiences are fully considered. These 'tiers' are:

1   teaching and learning;
2   developing a transcultural perspective to traditional approaches; and
3   the facilitation of student groups.

Isha provides insights into different learner and learning experiences before and during training, encouraging the exploration of diversity, sameness and oppression. She has coined the term 'recognition trauma' to name the powerful feelings that can be evoked in training discussions about racism. This notion is also used within the further term of 'continuous trauma' (Straker *et al.* 2004), a description of the resulting experience of black students having been cast into the 'black expert' role.

Chapter 4 describes a unique counsellor training programme that focuses on training in the community and which has successfully produced graduates who are proactive in their communities and committed to being change agents. The authors Yair Maman and Simon du Plock, through providing examples of how the training was initially developed in three unique communities, show how such an innovative approach to the recruitment and training of therapists can have relevance for all those involved in counsellor training. They also hope to illustrate how the role of the community can be expanded in most postgraduate programmes in the fields of counselling and psychotherapy for the enrichment of both academia and the communities served.

Courtland Lee and GoEun Na present a conceptual framework for understanding how racial/ethnic identity development impacts upon the working therapeutic alliance in Chapter 5. As the authors describe, 'one of the basic components of a transcultural counselling working alliance is an understanding of how the inner visions of both therapist and client impact upon the helping process'. A contemporary perspective on the concepts of race and ethnicity is followed by an analysis of the general process of racial/ethnic identity development. Vignettes are then presented to demonstrate the potential impact that racial/ethnic identity development can have on the working alliance in counselling or psychotherapy.

In Chapter 6, the authors present an overview of the research on the effects of ethnic matching (EM) between therapist and client on the therapy process and outcome, with the aim of clarifying contradictory conclusions from meta-analyses and previous reviews. To this end they review findings from: (i) old studies using analogue designs; (ii) large studies of archival data from actual clients; (iii) recent studies of process and outcome as measured over time; and (iv) new, in-depth qualitative studies of client experiences. Finally, they consider the research implications for therapy, training and policy.

Rachel Tribe opens Chapter 7 with a quote from *Lost in Translation*, a book by Eva Hoffman (1989: 123), later made into a very successful film. The lead character says: 'And in my situation especially, I know that language will be a crucial instrument, that I can overcome the stigma of my marginality, the weight of presumption against me, only if the reassuringly right sounds come out of my mouth'. Rachel notes that mental health services have been criticized for being inaccessible or inappropriate for members of black and minority ethnic communities. Culture, language, idioms of distress and explanatory health beliefs require consideration by commissioners, service and training providers and individual clinicians to ensure that services meet the needs of all members of the community. This chapter thus focuses on working with interpreters in a therapeutic context. The issue of whether interpreters should interpret purely the spoken words or consider contextual or cultural variables is reflected upon. The exact relationship between language and culture is contested but the two appear to be inextricably intertwined. Rachel also provides a most useful summary of the literature on interpreters in mental health.

Chapters 8 and 9 are dedicated to an enhanced understanding of the impact of a therapist's identity on the therapeutic endeavour. White people, including white counsellors, tend to see themselves as the 'human ordinary' (Dyer 1997) which leaves non-white people to carry the sense of 'difference'. Judy Ryde's chapter thus challenges white counsellors to understand the impact that white power and privilege have on their non-white clients and suggests ways of working with this dynamic. Working with the intersubjective field is suggested as an approach which can acknowledge the complexity of the field and encourage a sense of reflection.

In Chapter 9, Harbrinder Dhillon-Stevens subsequently addresses the complex challenge of being a black therapist with white clients, citing one research participant who says 'the impact of oppression is that you learn to manage it so no one knows'. She notes how displays of vulnerability in the training process between majority group and minority group trainees are different and therefore frequently misunderstood. Experiencing reflections from the majority group trainees such as 'you need to tone it down a bit' opens up the bizarre (and frequently occurring) contradiction that psychotherapy (and by implication, training) invites 'relational dialogue', yet within this context also invites judgementalism of certain statements made from particular points of view. Harbrinder also explores the complexity of negatively introjected values by minority persons, helpfully differentiating the aspects termed 'internalized oppression' (the ways in which black people allow the external beliefs and value systems of majority society to invalidate their authenticity and inhibit their personal agency) and the 'internal oppressor', that aspect of the self that becomes the 'inner tyrant'.

Chapter 10, by Aileen Alleyne, offers pragmatic guidance for counselling and psychotherapy practitioners who want to achieve an anti-racist and anti-discriminatory approach in their work. With the help of two personal case examples, the author has paid particular attention to avoiding the common pitfalls of discriminatory practice, with specific regard to race. The case material that Aileen provides interconnects profoundly with what many other authors are saying in this first part of the book. She has also offered a set of working guidelines on the broader issues within 'diversity'. These focus on the key values and principles which underpin good therapeutic practice in working with other areas of difference and diversity.

In the following chapter, Patsy Sutherland and Roy Moodley consider the current practices, complexities and challenges that confront transcultural counselling and psychotherapy research. They attempt to clarify some of the confusions that transcultural researchers indicate are problematic areas in this field, and attempt to highlight some of the newer and emerging themes. Lastly, they elucidate the ethical issue governing transcultural research. They begin with a review and critique of the current practice and research in counselling and psychotherapy with black and ethnic minority clients. They note that: 'In recent years the changes in the theory and practice of counselling and psychotherapy concerning diversity have made it much more difficult for researchers to engage in research, given the wide remit which diversity now encompasses'. This lack of research and paucity of knowledge, they assert, also creates a space where therapists tend to see all black and ethnic minority clients as homologous, offering them the same treatment irrespective of their gender, ethnicity, sexual orientation and the other diverse identities.

Chapter 12 explores the way that supervision can be usefully employed to reflect on the effect of cultural difference on the supervisee's work. Here, Judy Ryde encourages supervisors to explore the ways that the supervisee's race and culture impacts on the client rather than always focusing only on the client's ethnicity and culture. This includes inviting reflections on the power and privilege that is held in the role and culture of white supervisors and supervisees. By adapting and modifying ideas from Hawkins and Shohet (1996), Judy introduces the CLEAR and the seven-eyed models of supervision to show how every aspect of the work needs to be attended to from a cultural perspective.

Chapter 13 by Antony Sigalas focuses the work of the Nafsiyat Intercultural Therapy Centre in London, and Chapter 14 by Tony Wright reflects on his work within the Medical Foundation for the Victims of Torture. These concluding chapters of Part 1 provide us with accounts of the everyday experience of therapists working within these organizations and the complexities they have to deal with in striving to be of service to their clients.

Antony writes that Nafsiyat has strived to meet the needs of black and ethnic minority communities over a period of 28 years. He includes background historical and demographic information along with an attempt to describe, in short, the culturally sensitive approach used, illustrated with case examples of the clinical experience gained at the Centre. These clinical cases reflect on a variety of presenting realities, such as the language barrier, the experience of racism and that of seeking asylum in the host country after having survived severe traumas elsewhere, and the challenging culturally specific experience and the intergenerational conflicts of an immigrant family. A final thought addresses the importance of sustaining the provision of effective services for the culturally different population.

Tony Wright conceptualizes 'transcultural' as 'intercultural' when working with a specific client group: survivors of torture. The limits of western psychotherapeutic approaches are contrasted with a relational understanding of working interculturally. While subjective difference is acknowledged, typological elements to working interculturally are detailed in a tabular form. Featuring the story of a specific client, examples of various cultural elements of client and counsellor are explored. Tony proposes that understanding individual client torture narratives requires an appreciation of multiple complementing and competing discourses. Some detailed examples of these discourses are given: torture, trauma, asylum, human rights and medical. The implications for working interculturally with survivors of torture, who present in complex and intense ways, are presented in this chapter and include the important elements of counsellors' self-care and supervision needs.

Extending our empathic capacities

> *You must become the change you wish to see.*
>
> *Ghandi*

Following on from a lecture given in London, I later penned an article that attempted to delineate what I considered to be the desirable elements required within a programme of continuing professional development towards 'transcultural therapeutic competence' (Lago 2010). Each of the chapters contained in this first part of this book inevitably constitute some elaborations of the issues that I identified in this aforementioned article. Inevitably, this publication was just one in a line of previous aspirational statements probably originating with a key article by Sue *et al.* (1992). The importance of this mapping of multicultural competences is signalled by the fact that this original article was jointly and concurrently published by two leading professional journals in North America.

Conceived originally as a basis for outlining the need and rationale for a multicultural perspective in counselling, the Professional Standards Committee of the (American) Association for Multicultural Counselling and Development went much further in proposing the 31 multicultural counselling competencies defined by Sue *et al.* and urged the counselling profession in the USA to adopt these as accreditation criteria.

Two years later, Sodowsky *et al.* (1994) published their own version of a matrix in which they listed competencies under the terms 'skills', 'awareness', 'relationship' and 'knowledge'. More recently, Roy Moodley and Dina Lubin, from the University of Toronto, updated the original matrix by Sue *et al.* and this was published in the edited text by Palmer and Bor (2008).

My article proposed a set of seven interconnecting domains, which are reproduced in Figure 1.1. The overlapping interconnections that are depicted graphically are deliberate and follow the ideal of what is familiarly known as 'joined-up' thinking. That is, it seems absolutely vital that these various qualities (and indeed the various sub-elements depicted later in this chapter fitting within each category) operate seamlessly within the personality and practice of the therapist.

Figure 1.1 The seven domains

Each of the seven domains encapsulates a range of desirable qualities in terms of awareness, knowledge, skills and professional practice.

Personal and professional qualities (therapeutic relational competencies)

I have positioned these therapeutic relational competencies at the centre of the interconnecting domains. The quality of relationship is at the centre of our work as therapists and without this it is likely that very little therapeutic progress may be achieved. The following qualities are listed under this heading: acceptance, humility, humanity, compassion, encounter capacity, relational capacity, empathy and motivation.

Primary knowledge and understanding (understanding diversities, 'isms' and power)

This domain advocates the importance of understanding the complex societal mechanisms that perpetuate discrimination and oppression within society.

It seeks to encourage therapists to not only understand the operational nature of the different 'isms' in society (sexism, racism, 'disablism', and so on) but to understand how they, themselves, are affected and impacted by them. All of us, by virtue of being in society, are subject to these pernicious attitudinal forces, whether we apparently 'gain' or 'lose' from them. The elements of this domain include:

- understanding the 'isms' (see Ridley 1995; Willie *et al.* 1995);
- power/powerlessness (see Carotenuto 1992; Proctor 2002);
- black issues (see Mckenzie-Mavinga 2008);
- whiteness (see Tuckwell 2002; Lago 2006a, 2006b; Ryde 2008);
- 'race' (see Carter 1995);
- culture (see Hall 1959, 1966, 1976, 1983; Hofstede 1980);
- ethnicity;
- other diversities/identity intersections (see Moodley 2003);
- communication values (see Casse 1981);
- an understanding and appreciation of equal opportunities legislation.

Further knowledge and understanding (working with specific communities)

Within this third domain of professional development I have listed those aspects of behaviours and beliefs that are pertinent to the communities (probably geographically local to the counsellor/psychotherapist) from which the clients come. This domain therefore recommends the acquisition of awareness and knowledge of the relevant local communities to specifically inform and enhance the counsellor's own therapeutic capacity. This domain thus requires understanding of: culturally differing notions of 'wellness'; differing help-seeking behaviours; cultural and religious beliefs; as well as having access to and being prepared to use 'culturally relevant' referral resources and an awareness of different 'helping' interventions (e.g. traditional healers/herbalists etc.) Further elements include: knowledge of local politics in relation to community relations; specific cultural differences and preferences; majority/minority group relations (social exclusion factors and consequences); understanding 'culture shock' (Furnham and Bochner 1986); and understanding the impact of trauma and post-traumatic stress disorder (PTSD); histories/origins/settlement patterns/transitions/experiences etc; and an understanding of place-related, process-related and relationship-related perceptions of one's own sense of belonging in the world.

Awareness (of self, cultural origins, identity, communication style and outside influences)

This domain is a critical component in the modus operandi of the therapist. Working with clients presumes an ongoing commitment to one's own awareness and self-development combined with a continuous focused attention towards the client while holding relevant theoretical and cultural knowledge in mind. Helpful questions include: 'What are my stereotypes?' and 'Who am I, "culturally" speaking?' This domain includes:

- awareness of own ethnic identity and its development (see Carter 1995; Lee 2006) and 'whiteness' (see Frankenburg 1993);
- personal values (how do these compare with other 'world' values?) (see Kluckholm and Strodtbeck 1961);
- communication styles;
- openness to complexity and challenge;
- impact of the media (see Hartman and Husband 1974; Troyna 1981).

Professional competencies (therapeutic, groups, systemic, linguistic and theoretical)

The transcultural therapist requires a wide range of working competencies that extend way beyond those required within monocultural and monolingual circumstances. In addition to core therapeutic competencies, elements such as working with interpreters, accessing 'cultural' interpreters, learning appropriate language(s), greetings and key words, competency and comfort in group work and a capacity to critique their own theoretical model in relation to other value perspectives.

Professional commitment (learning, supervision, ethics, research and outreach)

This requires: ensuring ongoing learning and professional development; ongoing supervision; appropriate consultation; reviewing one's ethical stance in relation to ongoing work; commitment to the research process; supporting those in training; engagement with and support of development work in your agency; creation of personal/professional links to local communities and encouraging supporting the training of therapists from minority groups.

Context(s) (background, interview context, location, ritual, etc.)

There is considerable evidence to show how we are impacted (positively and negatively) by our environs, access to nature, colours, smells, aesthetics, space and so on. Yet, the nature of 'context' is little discussed in much of the psychotherapeutic literature. What are the effects and impacts of the environment upon people? How does the nature of agency location, internal décor, advertising etc. affect clients? How much attention do we give to constructing therapeutic environments?

Conclusion

There is a general tension, in the world of therapy, between a 'universalist' perspective – where therapists believe that 'The way I work therapeutically can be applied to working with all clients, whatever their origins or identity' – and a 'client-diversity' or 'client-in-context' approach, exemplified by the following stance: 'In working with a client from particular (and different) cultural, racial and ethnic groups' therapists need to bear in mind and be sensitive to:

- the many issues that impact upon their ways of being in the world, their history, their upbringing, their levels of acculturation etc.;
- the many aspects of their identity – many of which, to the outsider, could appear to be contradictory and confusing;
- their specific usage of language and their conveyance of meaning;
- how all these might relate (or not) to the therapist's own views, attitudes, prejudices and relationships;
- the therapist's identity(ies) (both as experienced by them as well as by the client);
- how these might impact upon the client;
- appreciating the cultural underpinnings and limitations of the therapist's theoretical stance.

The whole of Part 1 of this book is dedicated to the exploration and explication of this latter approach.

References

Carotenuto, A. (1992) *The Difficult Art: A Critical Discourse on Psychotherapy*. Wimetta, IL: Chiron.

Carter, R. (1995) *The Influence of Race and Racial Identity in Psychotherapy: Towards a Racially Inclusive Model*. New York: Wiley.

Casse, P. (1981) *Training for the Cross Cultural Mind*. Washington, DC: Society for Intercultural Education, Training and Research.

Christodoulidi, F. and Lago, C. (2010) Tortoises and turtles: Pittu Laungani, cultural transitions and therapeutic relations, in R. Moodley, A. Rai and W. Alladin (eds) *Bridging East West Psychology and Counselling: Exploring the work of Pittu Laungani*. New Delhi: Sage.

Dyer, R. (1997) *White*. London: Routledge.

Frankenberg, R. (1993) *White Women, Race Matters: The Social Construction of Whiteness*. Minneapolis, MN: University of Minnesota Press.

Furnham, A. and Bochner, S. (1986) *Culture Shock: Psychological Reactions to Unfamiliar Environments*. London: Methuen.

Hall, E.T. (1959) *The Silent Language*. New York: Anchor Press/Doubleday.

Hall, E.T. (1966) *The Hidden Dimension*. New York: Anchor Press/Doubleday.

Hall, E.T. (1976) *Beyond Culture*. New York: Anchor Press/Doubleday.

Hall, E.T. (1983) *The Dance of Life*. New York: Anchor Press/Doubleday.

Hartmann, P. and Husband, C. (1974) *Racism and the Mass Media*. London: Davis-Pointer.

Hawkins, P. and Shohet, R. (1996) *Supervision in the Helping Professions*. Buckingham: Open University Press.

Hoffman, E. (1989) *Lost in Translation*. London: Minerva.

Hofstede, G. (1980) *Culture's Consequences: International Differences in Work Related Values*. Beverly Hills, CA: Sage.

Jenkin, C. (2004) Black women's mental health, *Asylum*, 14(4).

Kluckholn, C. and Strodtbeck, F. (1961) *Variations in Value Orientations*. Evanston, IL: Row, Peterson.

Lago, C. (ed.) (2006a) *Race, Culture and Counselling: The Ongoing Challenge*, 2nd edn. Maidenhead: Open University Press.

Lago, C. (2006b) White counsellor racial identity: the unacknowledged, unknown, unaware aspect of self in relationship, in G. Proctor, M. Cooper, P. Sanders and B. Malcolm (eds) *Politicizing the Person-Centred Approach: An Agenda for Social Change*. Ross-on-Wye: PCCS Books.

Lago, C. (2010) On developing our empathic capacities to work inter-culturally and inter-ethnically: attempting a map for personal and professional development, *Psychotherapy and Politics International*, 8(1).

Lago, C. and Thompson, J. (1996) *Race, Culture and Counselling*. Buckingham: Open University Press.

Lee, C. (2006) Updating the models of identity development, in C. Lago (ed.) *Race, Culture and Counselling: The Ongoing Challenge*. Maidenhead: Open University Press.

May, K. (2009) Psychotherapeutic work with marginalised groups: demonstrations of reflexive activism, unpublished doctoral thesis, Middlesex University and Metanoia Institute.

Mckenzie-Mavinga, I. (2008) Understanding black issues in counsellor training, unpublished PhD thesis, Middlesex University and Metanoia Institute.

Moodley, R. (2003) Double, triple, multiple jeopardy, in C. Lago and B. Smith (eds) *Anti-Discriminatory Counselling Practice*. London: Sage.

Palmer. S. and Bor, R. (eds) (2008) *The Practitioner's Handbook*. London: Sage.

Proctor, G. (2002) *The Dynamics of Power in Counselling and Psychotherapy*. Ross-on-Wye: PCCS Books.

Ridley, C.R. (1995) *Overcoming Unintentional Racism in Counselling and Therapy*. London: Sage.

Ryde, J. (2008) *Being White in the Helping Professions: Developing Effective Intercultural Awareness*. London: Sage.

Sodowsky, G.R., Taffe, R.C., Gutkin, T.B. and Wise, S.L. (1994) Development of the Multicultural Counseling Inventory (MCI): a self-report measure of multicultural competencies, *Journal of Counseling Psychology*, 41: 137–48.

Straker, J. *et al.* (2004) Trauma and disconnection: a transtheoretical approach, *International Journal of Psychotherapy*, 7(2).

Sue, D.W., Arredondo, P. and McDavis, R.J. (1992) Multicultural counselling competencies and standards: a call to the profession, *Journal of Counseling and Development*, 70: 477–86.

Troyna, B. (1981) *Public Awareness and the Media: A Study of Reporting on Race*. London: Commission for Racial Equality.

Tuckwell, G. (2002) *Racial Identity, White Counsellors and Therapists*. Maidenhead: Open University Press.

Willie, C. *et al.* (eds) (1995) *Mental Health, Racism and Sexism*. Pittsburgh, PA: University of Pittsburgh.

2 Training for multicultural therapy: the challenge and the experience

Valerie Watson

Introduction

This chapter discusses how recent initiatives and trends within the field of counselling and psychotherapy might influence future training and affect clients' experiences of counselling. Future challenges for counselling training are proposed, indicating changes that could meet the needs of black and minority ethnic (BME) clients.

Beginnings

Multicultural counselling theory and practice, defined as the 'fourth force' (Ivey *et al.* 1997), was developed in North America in the 1970s to challenge the ethnocentric bias of the three major theoretical 'forces' in psychotherapy: psychodynamic, humanistic and cognitive-behavioural. Theorists and practitioners aimed to devise training and practice frameworks which would provide more culturally appropriate therapeutic services, thus meeting the needs of marginalized clients. Counsellors were encouraged to (a) acquire an understanding of the dynamic nature of their own culture and that of their clients, and (b) to recognize how socioeconomic and historical contexts can affect therapeutic relationships. Sue and Sue (1990) identified the skills, knowledge, attitudes and behaviours of 'the culturally skilled counsellor'. These qualities have been reviewed and elaborated upon by successive theorists and are seen as evidential criteria for assessment of cultural competence in the training of counsellors. Multicultural counselling theory and practice includes reference to the intersecting cultural factors of 'race', age, gender, socioeconomic status, disability, sexual orientation, religion and spirituality. The theory has been further developed by Sodowsky *et al.* (1994), Moodley and Lubin (2008), and with reference to the UK, Lago (2010).

Trainees in the UK and elsewhere have been encouraged to recognize the necessity of acknowledging the fundamental 'inter', 'multi', 'trans', or 'cross' cultural nature of all therapeutic relationships. D'Ardenne and Mahtani (1999) present a compelling argument for the use of 'transcultural' as the preferred term.

Highlighting the 'active' and 'reciprocal' nature of relationships, they propose going beyond acceptance of cultural difference and world views towards recognition of the mutability of cultural identity over time.

The impact of recent trends and initiatives on training

With its diverse range of theories, approaches and qualifications, counselling in the UK has inhabited a kind of 'multicultural' space as an occupation. Apart from small skirmishes and academic debates, the majority of counsellors in the UK have coexisted, practised and accepted the regulation and leadership of the British Association for Counselling and Psychotherapy (BACP) and the United Kingdom Council for Psychotherapy (UKCP).

Government insistence on the statutory regulation and registration of psychological therapies brings the likelihood of imposed standardization of training and practice, which will affect clients' experience of and access to therapy.[1] The accumulated evidence of government-commissioned reports (Department of Health 2005; Centre for Economic Performance 2006) highlights the mental health needs of BME and other socially excluded groups, identifying the effects of and solutions to inequalities of provision. The introduction of 'Increased Access to Psychological Therapies' (IAPT) aims to meet these needs through targeted training of therapists and widespread implementation.

The impact of population change

The continuing debates about 'multiculturalism', its contested premises and terminology (Moodley and Palmer 2006), policies and questionable practices (Nelson-Jones 2002), is a distraction from the demographic reality that the UK, a nation comprising many cultures, has a rising multiple-heritage population (Office for National Statistics 2005) constituting 14.6 per cent of the minority ethnic population. People who identify as being of 'multiple heritage' do not form a distinct community or group, having numerous allegiances and links based on parentage, distant lineage and social class, which may assign their ethnicity.

The Office for National Statistics notes that members of the multiple heritage population in the UK are more likely to be the victims of violent crime and have reported high rates of mental ill health. Counsellors will need to be aware of the needs of multiple heritage clients, their contexts and intersecting cultural affiliations. Providing training for counsellors to develop an understanding of the

---

[1]As this book was going to press the UK government published a report indicating that it does not intend to enforce regulation of counselling and psychotherapy directly and other mechanisms are currently under consideration. For further details please see: www.dh.gov.uk/prod_consum_dh/groups/dh_digitalassets/docu.

manifestations of internalized oppression within the multiple heritage community will become increasingly important, as clients embrace the meanings of their plural identities.

Speed is of the essence? The impact of technology

Globalization and advancing technology have led to the transcending of language, social and geographical barriers at extraordinary speeds through social networking, as well as promoting democracy and equality through information exchange. However, at times this speed, volume and breadth of social networking, mobile phone and computer technology, can lead to anxiety, and a sense of overload or threat, causing difficulties in relating and relationships. Demand for the fast cure of mental distress through the use of medication and/or therapeutic strategies has led to a growth in the training of body—mind techniques, which often synthesize elements of traditional healing practices and knowledge of neuroscience.

For clients, online counselling including cognitive-behavioural therapy (CBT) programmes, is hailed as a significant development, enabling increased personal access to therapy at the individual's convenience without the need of a therapist. The growth in distance learning counselling training opportunities has improved the chances of changing the socioeconomic profile of counsellors and challenges the existing counselling training paradigm, which places high value on the benefits of intense experiential contact for trainees. Inclusion of an enquiry into the utilization of communication technologies in counselling training could aid transcultural understanding and prepare counsellors for the additional administrative and research roles required of them.

Curriculum content

There is implicit agreement among leading counselling organizations (e.g. BACP and UKCP) about essential personal, social and professional skills and theoretical knowledge to be included in the curriculum (Randall 2008; BACP 2009). Despite nods to diversity through photo illustrations and claims in course prospectuses, research (Davies and Neal 1997; Lawrence 2003; Watson 2004) and anecdotal evidence from recently qualified counsellors indicates that the curriculum content of training courses has hardly changed over the past 20 years and that cultural issues continue to be marginalized. The efforts of those who have been critical or innovative (for instance, Lago and Thompson 2002; McLeod 2003; Mckenzie-Mavinga 2009) are notable, though their effect thus far appears patchy.

Reports from ex-trainees show that input on transcultural issues is usually delivered as a 'one-off' rather than as an integrated training programme, and attempts to address all matters of inequality and diversity, even if delivered over a longer period of curriculum time, still remain unsatisfactory, leaving newly qualified therapists feeling ill-prepared for working with issues of diversity. Moodley (2007) blames:

- a lack of research and sophisticated debate with its focus on critique;
- the creation of identity models; and
- a focus on superficial differences

as an explanation for the limited developmental influence of transcultural therapy on westernized approaches.

Curriculum sufficiency is unlikely to be the cause of this stagnation. I suggest that the continuing fear of evoking uncomfortable feelings in students may also play a part. As Jane Elliot's infamous 'Blue eyes, Brown eyes' exercise demonstrates, participants continue to be provoked and shocked by their racism, even when prepared for what is to come. Johannes and Erwin (2004) present the case for adaptation of existing theories and practices to preempt defensive and hostile reactions to transcultural training development. Another likely explanation is that although recruitment for trainees remains buoyant, the critical attention of influential counsellors and theorists is focused elsewhere, on other topics.

IAPT's nationally prescribed curriculum for prospective CBT therapists, sponsored by the government, heralds a change in counselling training. Training modules specify required learning, assessment outcomes and how qualifying competence will be demonstrated. The inclusion of a 10-day module on 'Values, policy, culture and diversity' for low and high intensity trainee therapists is an indication that addressing issues of culture, diversity and equality is not to be considered as optional extra. This stance could set the tone for all counselling training establishments, obliging them to demonstrate their commitment to provide training and appropriate assessment on cultural and diversity issues in a more systematic and transparent way.

Counselling trainees

The substantial long-term costs of training and continuing professional development (CPD) required by accrediting counselling organizations has tended to restrict training access to those most able to afford it: in the main, white, middle-aged, middle-class women. This profile is slowly changing as access routes have broadened and support for training fees has become more readily available. Although no data are available, it would seem that UK BME counselling trainees have tended to access counselling training through the voluntary sector and further or higher education routes, with smaller numbers training through private institutions or as post-professional qualifiers.

Although unintentional, the introduction of IAPT and statutory regulation may lead to a reduction in the number and variety of routes into counselling training, which will directly affect the recruitment of BME trainees, who are often drawn from a lower socioeconomic group. The funding for IAPT may mean reductions in funding available for community projects, which largely provide specialized services for BME and other minority groups. For some BME clients, traditional therapies and provision of targeted services are attractive and perceived as less stigmatizing and more holistic in their approach compared to some of the psychological therapies on offer within the statutory services.

There are indications that statutory regulation and the professionalizing process of counselling could transform it into a graduate-only occupation, excluding counsellors unable or unwilling to seek out such qualifications. This is likely to affect BME and minority group counsellors working within the voluntary and community project sectors and counsellors training or trained in traditional healing approaches.

The counselling trainer: a hitherto neglected area of research, concern and consideration

Whether acting in a facilitative or didactic capacity, the trainer's effect and function as a resource, role model and assessor are too important to be left unexamined, and yet the competence of the counselling trainer is often ignored in training and practice discourse. Sparse attention has been given at a national counselling organizational level to the training or monitoring of counselling trainers. The recent demise of the BACP trainer accreditation scheme in 2010 is a case in point. The lack of training opportunities for trainers is professionally unacceptable, in view of their role and importance in the lives of clients via their trainees.

Counselling trainers are appointed on the basis of their professional practice experience, seniority and/or academic output, none of which attest to their abilities as trainers nor indicate their willingness to review their skills as therapists. Trainers' academic credentials are not a reliable indicator of their ability *as trainers*, their knowledge and experience of working with clients from diverse backgrounds, or whether they have addressed their own cultural identity development issues. Their level of self-awareness and ability to continually monitor this is assumed.

Research findings by Watson (2004) revealed that counselling trainers often failed to recognize or meet the needs of black trainees (and it follows, white trainees), through their lack of knowledge or inadequate facilitation in group work on matters relating to cultural difference and 'race'. Few trainers were described as examining the political and social significance of transcultural counselling theory, the contexts of clients and the effects of internalized oppression on clients and training group members.

Although evidence of good practice exists (Charleton and Lockett 2004), poorly facilitated experiential group work methods used in counselling training and the use of unsuitable materials which were not regularly updated were mentioned as evidence of trainers' difficulties in addressing transcultural issues. It is likely that this experience is repeated for trainees who identify with other minority groups and thus for transcultural therapy training in general.

Training the trainer: the benefits

The lack of a regular forum for counsellor trainers where the delivery and content of counselling training is scrutinized and discussed at a national level is woeful. Training the trainers for transcultural therapy would lead to raised social and political awareness of current issues. Therapists and their trainers might be more motivated to be active social advocates for clients in all areas of the community, revisiting their understanding about cultural differences and inequalities in the light of changes at the local, national and international level.

Effect on clients' experience

It is known that the effects of poverty, poor living conditions, discrimination, racism and oppression contribute to mental ill health (Thornicraft 2006). (For a more general but profound analysis of these phenomena see Wilkinson and Pickett 2009.) Lack of recognition or inattention to the effect of these societal experiences can exacerbate clients' problems. Sewell (2009) describes mental health services as having a 'toxic effect' on black people. This view is upheld by existing data on black mental health, numerous independent and government reports of BME clients' experience (Department of Health 2005) and reports by campaign groups such as BMH UK (2009). Countless case studies show that these socioeconomic and emotional stressors feature in what BME clients bring to the counselling re-lationship, emphasizing the need to address the impact of societal disadvantage and oppression (external and internalized) in training.

Transcultural therapy: encounters in training, therapy and supervision

At a conference workshop on transcultural encounter the facilitator asked each participant to answer the following: Who are you? Why are you here? What do you want from me? Using our individual answers she declared whether a working relationship could be forged and proceeded to deny some participants access to further work with her. This dramatic, potentially humiliating and hurtful public selection process demonstrated the power of the facilitator (counsellor), our vul-nerability as participants (clients), and our need to feel worthy. Assumptions about entitlement, fairness and counsellors' willingness and ability to work with anyone were questioned. We noted that during the selection process the facilitator's be-haviour and methods were not openly challenged or rejected. Nor was there a protest to support and include those who had not been chosen. The pertinence and potency of the facilitator's three questions applies to any and all therapeutic relationships, some of which will be referred to below.

Who are you and why are you here?

The theory and practice of family and systemic therapy can offer some effective strategies for deepening cultural understanding in counselling training and practice. For example, the sensitive use of genograms can help to validate the cultural identity of BME clients, providing some context and understanding of their current predicament arising from their history, their individual story, knowledge of what ill health and mental ill health might mean and how it is understood. In her novel *Who is it that can tell me who I am?* Haynes (2009) describes her interior world, her systemic history as therapist and client, showing the interlocking worlds of the therapeutic relationship where client and counsellor learn together, though the therapist's learning is often hidden from the client. It is likely that the move towards knowing and being known is an effective start in relationships with BME clients and may be particularly important for clients of multiple heritage with a variety of cultural allegiances. This move also places emphasis on the client and counsellor as being part of a community, rather than seeing the client's problem as entirely located within them as an individual.

In his work with Maori clients, Grimmer (2007) notes the spiritual and physical importance of a designated sacred space (a *marae*) for Maori clients. Client–counsellor introductions involve mutual disclosure about family origins and personal history using genograms to 'populate the [therapeutic] encounter, metaphorically, with significant contemporaries, ancestors and offspring' (p. 22). Grimmer describes how his use of metaphor and knowledge and understanding of the historical and cultural context of his clients led to his successful adaptation of the cognitive-behavioural approach for the benefit of his clients.

What do you want from me?

For months, L (a counselling trainee) searched for a black counsellor. Arriving with a 'shopping list' of qualifying criteria she enquired about my experiences of working with minority group clients, my experience of and response to racism, my views about her other minority group identities and my training experiences. L was thorough and earnest. I hoped that she would get what she wanted from me. We learned from each other about the generational damage and mistrust that internalized oppression can cause; how the skewed, often racist, debate about ethnic matching ignores its value, its healing qualities and its challenges (questions are not ordinarily raised about ethnic matching of white clients with white counsellors).

Helping the client to articulate their needs is a dimension often overlooked in counselling training and practice when there is a shared language. When the counselling relationship requires the involvement of an interpreter or the use of a communication aid, knowing what the client wants from the relationship takes on additional layers of complexity, which could be usefully addressed in training programmes. Even when clients' needs are expressed and understood, some counsellors can feel constrained or prevented by the boundaries of their role to deny the needs of their clients, resulting in an ineffective therapeutic alliance (Century *et al.* 2007).

Angela West (2006), a white counsellor working with asylum-seekers, describes how she has adapted her ways of working to meet her clients' needs. This has involved forsaking the implicit norms and rules of western therapy to advocate for her clients in particular ways, such as writing a letter or giving advice. In doing this, she gained the trust of her clients and advanced the therapeutic relationship; her clients felt understood and their primary needs were met.

Future challenges

Exploration and study of power relations and the dynamics of transcultural relationships in training enables counsellors to understand how the sustained experience of discrimination for minority group clients has a detrimental effect on their mental health. What might be made less clear in training is how therapists can usefully respond holistically to their clients' experience of discrimination and suffering.

It is important that transcultural counselling training explores how counsellors can work to minimize or prevent the unintended re-enactment of the experience of oppression that many BME clients risk when seeking help. BME clients could still leave therapy feeling misunderstood despite their counsellors' intellectual understanding of the issues and good intentions derived from their training. Worse still, BME clients may believe that their counsellors see them as powerless victims. On leaving the therapy room they could feel saddled with their counsellors' guilt, anger, defensiveness and impotence.

Training for whom?

If transcultural counselling theory and practice is to develop and reflect the needs of BME clients then the recruitment and training opportunities for trainee counsellors needs to embrace diversity, making training affordable, accessible and feasible, and attractive to the widest range of the populace.

Training for what?

Current initiatives could lead to changes in the practice of counselling which might involve what West (2004) describes as the 'deconstructing of counselling' when he questions the 'one size fits all' approach of counselling and training. It may lead to genuine dialogue between therapists with differing orientations and approaches and an integration of ideas, including those identified as non-western, such as using the arts, music, drama, meditation and other psycho-spiritual methods, including self-hypnosis. To some extent this is already happening on a small scale. Training therapists in using stories and guided visualization (human givens) is a departure from a more westernized two-way concrete verbal approach to therapy. There are some clear links with the oral traditions of a number of cultures with elements of a more didactic and possibly directive approach to training and counselling.

Language, communication and interpretation

Counselling training and trainers rarely address the work that might be done with clients and their interpreters exploring the values of, for example:

- multilingualism for counsellors;
- their learning other community languages;
- how best to work with interpreters.

In training for transcultural therapy this added dimension to communication is of critical importance, especially for counsellors working with émigrés and/or asylum-seekers.

Preparing the client for counselling

There is a strong argument for counselling training to include ways in which therapists actively educate or induct clients into therapeutic methods, language and culture. For clients unfamiliar with counselling, the initial expectations and experience of a counselling relationship can be puzzling. Clients, who are already contending with language and communication issues, accessing help in a short-term contract of fewer than 10 sessions, need to be aware of the counsellor's way of working in order to make the most of what is on offer in the early stages.

Learning by osmosis and learning together

There is a transcultural training challenge in accepting the reciprocal co-creative nature of the counselling relationship. Learning from clients and trusting in their expertise and experience is inherent in person-centred practice and many other traditional healing practices. Anderson and Goolishian (1992: 38) state that:

> A therapeutic conversation is no more than a slowly evolving and detailed, concrete, individual life story stimulated by the therapist's position of not-knowing and the therapist's curiosityto learn. It is this curiosity and not-knowing that opens conversational space and thus increases the potential for narrative development of new agency and personal freedom.

Such an approach may not cohere with the current trend towards the medical positivist framework (Freeth 2007) which marks the therapist as the expert deriving their authority from an evidence-based approach. West (2004: 432) observes that cultural understanding is often best achieved by 'hanging out with people', being and learning in their presence and discovering by listening with care what works and what they need from therapy. This applies to considering where therapy takes place, how it should be accessed and how it should be resourced. This will involve being less wedded to single theories and orientations as therapists in training.

Moving the debate forward: training for the real world

Training for transcultural therapy involves recognition that BME clients are less likely to access counselling from independent practitioners. They may enter the statutory system of rationed therapy (e.g. through the NHS, an educational setting or even an employee assistance programme) that is often short-term with a target of returning individuals to economic productivity. Perhaps more of the counselling training curriculum should focus on the provision of therapy for community and statutory groupings and group work, and less on independent practice management issues. This would necessitate political and philosophical explorations of the place of evidence-based therapeutic interventions, and the dominance of the biomedical model alongside traditional healing methods in transcultural therapy training and would engage counsellors in the wider debate and research of mental ill health and the care thereof. Of equal importance is that traditional healing methods are not accepted or offered uncritically. Establishing what clients want and is effective as opposed to what they are assessed as being in need of may be a significant departure from the current medical model assessment that often deters BME clients.

The evidence from Newham IAPT (Wright 2010) is that there has been an increase in BME clients accessing therapy in part due to the destigmatization of therapy through clients' improved local access points in non-medical settings; learning more about therapy from sources such as churches, religious centres, community centres, mosques and advice centres; and being able to self-refer for therapy at an early stage, especially among BME men. Other important factors concern recruitment of culturally diverse staff, continual monitoring of cultural sensitivity and effective in-house transcultural training.

Addressing spirituality in training

Spirituality, religious belief and interests in ceremony and symbols should be given attention in transcultural counselling training. Many clients are able to sustain themselves in the face of adversity or disruptive life events by attending to their spiritual concerns, connecting with community networks and gaining valuable insights, support and sources of resilience. Often these are misunderstood or maligned as unscientific within secular practice.

CBT and BME clients

Anxiety and depression are identified as the most common community health problems in the UK, diagnosed in 10 per cent of the general population, 33 per cent of UK asylum-seekers and 60 per cent of the UK roofless. NICE (2009) concludes that CBT and interpersonal therapy (IPT) present persuasive scientific evidence of effectiveness with clients presenting with anxiety and/or depression. This is also the main focus of training for IAPT therapists. It is claimed that culturally responsive CBT, which has been adopted in Asia and Africa with success (Rajkumar 2010), strives to reflect the culture and world view of clients, and is proving effective with BME clients in the UK. Moloney and Kelly (2008) and others question whether provision of CBT and manualized therapies are useful for BME clients. They argue that CBT is coercive, may encourage distorted self-blame and does not promote social change or equality. Further, providing access to short-term therapy for the masses in this way still means that in-depth therapy is available only to those who can afford it.

The need for more research

The practice of counselling embodies a belief in healing and change, for client and counsellor. Most counselling/psychotherapy trainees enter the profession with the intent to be part of the healing and change process for their clients. Direct involvement of BME clients in the process of developing transcultural counselling training through their qualitative testimony, research evidence and active feedback in the training process is a reliable and effective way forward. This could be achieved, for example, through an assessed work-based learning requirement that a proportion of counselling training and CPD of trainers takes place within BME services.

References

Anderson, H. and Goolishian, H. (1992) The client is the expert: a not-knowing approach to therapy, in S. McNamee and K.J. Gergen (eds) *Therapy as Social Construction*. London: Sage.

BACP (British Association for Counselling and Psychotherapy) (2009) *Accreditation of Training Courses*. Lutterworth: BACP.

BMH UK (2009) Government mental health strategy out of touch with black communities, www.blackmentalhealth.org.uk/index.php?option=com_content&task=view&id, accessed 23 December 2009.

Centre for Economic Performance (2006) *The Depression Report: A New Deal for Depression and Anxiety Disorder*. London: London School of Economics, http://cep.lse.ac.uk/textonly/research/mentalhealth/DEPRESSION_REPORT_LAYARD.pdf, accessed 20 December 2009.

Century, G., Leavey, G. and Payne, H. (2007) The experience of working with refugees: counsellors in primary care, *British Journal of Guidance and Counselling*, 35(1): 23–40.

Charleton, M. and Lockett, M. (2004) Using videotapes of the sessions to examine ways of helping counsellors to work with the person-centred approach in a transcultural setting, in R. Moodley, C. Lago and A. Talahite (eds) *Carl Rogers Counsels a Black Client*. Llangarron: PCCS Books.

D'Ardenne, P. and Mahtani, A. (1999) *Transcultural Counselling in Action*. London: Sage.

Davies, D. and Neal, C. (eds) (1997) *Pink Therapy*, 2nd edn. Buckingham: Open University Press.

Department of Health (2005) *Delivering Race Equality in Mental Health Care: An Action Plan for Reform Inside and Outside Services and the Government's Response to the Independent Inquiry into the Death of David Bennett*. London: Department of Health Publications.

Freeth, R. (2007) Working within the medical model, *Therapy Today*, 18(9): 31–4.

Grimmer, A. (2007) Maori and the *marae* experience, *Therapy Today*, 18(9): 19–22.

Haynes, J. (2009) *Who is it that can tell me who I am?* London: Constable Robinson.

Ivey, A.E. *et al.* (1997) *Counselling and Psychotherapy: A Multicultural Perspective*, 4th edn. Boston, MA: Allyn & Bacon.

Johannes, C.K. and Erwin, G. (2004) Developing multicultural competence: perspectives on theory and practice, *Counselling Psychology Quarterly*, 17(3): 329–38.

Lago, C. (2010) On developing our empathic capacities to work inter-culturally and inter-ethnically: attempting a map for personal and professional development, *Psychotherapy and Politics International*, 8(1): 73–85, http://dx.doi.org/10.1002/ppi.213.

Lago, C. and Thompson, J. (2002) Counselling and race, in S. Palmer (ed.) *Multicultural Counselling: A Reader*. London: Sage.

Lawrence, D. (2003) Racial and cultural issues in counselling training, in A. Dupont-Joshua (ed.) *Working Inter-culturally in Counselling Settings*. Hove: Brunner-Routledge.

Mckenzie-Mavinga, I. (2009) *Black Issues in the Therapeutic Process*. Houndmills: Palgrave Macmillan.

McLeod, J. (2003) *An Introduction to Counselling*. Maidenhead: Open University Press.

Moloney, P. and Kelly, P. (2008) 'Beck never lived in Birmingham': why cognitive behaviour therapy may be a less helpful treatment for psychological distress than is often supposed, in R. House and D. Lowenthal (eds) *Against and for CBT: Towards a Constructive Dialogue?* Ross-on-Wye: PCCS Books.

Moodley, R. (2007) (Re)placing multiculturalism in counselling and psychotherapy, *British Journal of Guidance and Counselling*, 35(1): 1–22.

Moodley, R. and Lubin, D. (2008) Developing your career to working with multicultural and diversity clients, in S. Palmer and R. Bor (eds) *The Practitioner's Handbook: A Guide for Counsellors, Psychotherapists and Counselling Psychologists*. London: Sage.

Moodley, R. and Palmer, S. (2006) Race, culture and other multiple constructions: an absent presence in psychotherapy, in R. Moodley and S. Palmer (eds) *Race, Culture and Psychotherapy: Critical Perspectives in Multicultural Practice*. London: Routledge.

Nelson-Jones, R. (2002) Diverse goals for multicultural counselling and therapy, *Counselling Psychology Quarterly*, 15(2): 133–43.

NICE (2009) *The Treatment and Management of Depression in Adults (Depression CG90)*. London: NICE.

Office for National Statistics (2005) *Focus on Ethnicity and Identity*, www.statistics. gov.uk/socialtrends35, accessed 20 December 2009.

Rajkumar, B. (2010) Evidence-based psychological therapies for BME people, paper presented at the conference 'Psychological Therapy for Black and Ethnic Minorities . . . Does it Work?' Nottinghamshire Healthcare, 2 February 2010.

Randall, S. (2008) Benchmarks for training, *Therapy Today*, 19(8): 41–2.

Sewell, H. (2009) Mental health services need to face up to their 'toxic effect' on black people, *Guardian*, 22 June, www.guardian.co.uk/society/joepublic/ 2009/jun/22/mental-health-services-failing-black-people, accessed 25 June 2009.

Sodowsky, G.R., Taffe, R.C., Gutkin, T.B. and Wise, S.L. (1994) Development of the Multicultural Counseling Inventory (MCI): a self-report measure of multi-cultural competencies, *Journal of Counseling Psychology*, 41(2): 137–48.

Sue, D.W. and Sue, D. (1990) *Counseling the Culturally Different*. Chichester: Wiley.

Thornicraft, G. (2006) *Actions Speak Louder: Tackling Discrimination Against People with Mental Illness*. London: Mental Health Foundation.

Watson, V.V.V. (2004) The training experiences of black counsellors, PhD thesis, University of Nottingham.

West, A. (2006) To do or not to do: a difficult question, *Therapy Today*, 17(6): 10–12.

West, W. (2004) Pittu Laungani in conversation with William West, *British Journal of Guidance and Counselling*, 32(3): 419–35.

Wilkinson, R. and Pickett, K. (2009) *The Spririt Level: Why More Equal Societies Almost Always Do Better*. London: Penguin.

Wright, B. (2010) The secret of our success: making psychological services accessible for BME communities, paper presented at the conference 'Psychological Therapy for Black and Ethnic Minorities . . . Does it Work?' Nottinghamshire Healthcare, 2 February 2010.

3   Training for multicultural therapy: the course curriculum

Isha Mckenzie-Mavinga

Introduction

Multicultural therapy embraces an understanding and reflection of diverse and intercultural experiences. In this approach, consideration is given to origins and belief systems that mirror and influence identity, personal experience and the social impact of oppressions, within the therapeutic relationship. An awareness of Eurocentric frameworks that dominate traditional approaches to understanding psychological well-being is important. This chapter reflects on the benefits and challenges of engaging with a curriculum for training in multicultural therapy. I present an overview of the current training situation and comment on the development of a multicultural course curriculum.

The discourses of feminism, the black power movement and gay liberation helped raise individual and group consciousness about the negative emotional and social impact of patriarchy, racism and homophobia. Hence a greater understanding of gender, colourism and sexuality has led to equalities legislation and the challenging of institutional oppressions. Intracultural issues have been addressed to a lesser degree. The women's movement was accused of whitewashing women of colour, sexism was functioning within the black power movement, and both racism and sexism impacted gay and lesbian communities. Multiculturalism has arisen out of a need to understand and eliminate oppressions within and between different ethnic and minority groups and individual intersecting identities. The concept of internalized oppression[1] has thus become a feature of ongoing efforts to understand how the hurt of prejudice impacts on developing identities.

The importance of exploring attitudes to diversity, intercultural and intracultural influences, oppressions and internalized oppression in training must be recognized. Terms such as 'cross-cultural', 'intercultural' and 'transcultural' have been used to describe multicultural therapy. In this chapter I use the latter two more common terms interchangeably to describe the nature of multicultural therapy.

---

[1] Internalized oppression refers to destructive attitudes and behaviours resulting from the distresses caused by oppressions that have not been expressed and discharged from the mind and body. If not expressed, oppressions can be re-enacted causing low self-esteem and feelings of powerlessness.

Intercultural therapy became popular during the late 1980s with the work of Kareem and Littlewood (1992) and Fernando (1989), when psychiatrists and psychotherapists became involved with developing resources for individuals who were not accessing therapy and counselling. These individuals were generally from black and minority ethnic (BME) groups and were more likely to be sectioned under the Mental Health Act and more prone to the 'revolving door' of the mental health system. Intercultural therapy synchronized with the work of feminist writers such as Eichenbaum and Orbach (1982) who viewed women's liberation as key to their emotional well-being.

With a demand to recognize how oppression impacts on the psyche and therefore the therapeutic process, the term 'transcultural' was born. D'Ardenne and Mahtani (1989) and Eleftheriadou (1994) highlighted the cultural elements of the relational process between therapist and client and the impact of the therapist's attitude to diversity on the client. This approach emphasized an expectation of the therapist to re-evaluate their own prejudices and experiences of oppression in order to appreciate the client's experiences of diversity and oppression. Fanon (1986), Davies and Neal (1996), Lago and Thompson (1996), Fletchman Smith (2000), Dalal (2002), Tuckwell (2002) and Yellin (2004) explored the impact of specific areas of oppression in therapy, such as racism and homophobia. More recently there has been a growing awareness of unlearning prejudice towards people with disabilities. However, there continues to be a need to link awareness and understanding to practice. Integrating multiculturalism into the therapy training curriculum can support this.

Overview of the current situation

Specialist therapy projects continue to hold the torch for anti-oppressive practice (Dhillon-Stevens 2005). Within these organizations in Britain, choice of therapist and the importance of understanding and working with diverse experiences and minority groups is a priority. For therapists to emerge from training with multicultural competencies, their knowledge and understanding of diversity and oppression needs to be supported. Development of personal awareness and practice that includes social and cultural concerns as a competency for professional practice is a training responsibility. Therapists need to feel competent to address these complex issues in their practice and be supported by their clinical supervisors and respective organizations. In the first place trainers have a responsibility to re-evaluate their attitude and approach to teaching multiculturalism.

Hellmundt and Ryan (in Carroll and Ryan 2005) consider the need to reflect on multicultural ways of thinking in order to achieve an appropriate teaching approach. They review approaches to learning that have shifted from the expectation of international students to adapt to traditional learning styles to a more integrated approach that involves valuing different ways of thinking. Fox (1996) cited by Hellmundt and Ryan, argues that intercultural dialogue provides a means of 'building bridges across multiple realities and truths' (p. 14). Boride (1984), also cited by the above authors, describes the students' cultural knowledge as 'cultural capital'[2] and suggests that this element be used to maximize learning (p. 14).

Levels of cultural capital and the social elements of the diverse student population contain the primary elements of what Warner Weil (Warner Weil and McGill 1989) calls 'disjunction'.[3] Disjunction describes a sense of fragmentation involving both 'personal and social identity', influenced by the past. Assumptions about learning and understanding can evoke disjunction. This is apparent when using metaphor during a teaching session and students with English as a second language ask 'What do you mean?' This disjunction shows that attention must be given to facilitating students to understand information within their own linguistic codes and nuances. Such an opportunity can also provide a model for a multicultural approach to the therapeutic relationship, where the therapist is open to different ways of thinking and being, and to finding an appropriate language for sharing.

The ability to share and explore diversity can be enhanced through the learning process and carried through into competencies to affirm students' ability to work with cultural diversity. Trainers must use their own transcultural awareness to support students to develop their understanding and ways of reflecting on the transcultural process. By being explicit about engaging with the social and cultural elements of the training, trainers can greatly assist this process. If not addressed in training, transcultural skills may remain a secondary element of therapy.

Sometimes cultural components are approached as though they are just an 'add-on' to serve the course objectives of equalities in training, rather than as an essential component of the client's experience. Students are often tentative about the cultural aspects of dialogue because they are not rehearsed in addressing them. Dialogue about the racial context often raises vulnerabilities and fears among student groups. Due to these fears, some students, when presenting in clinical supervision, do not disclose cultural and racial information about their client's background unless prompted. Often, rigid belief systems prevent students from empathizing with clients of a sexual minority, and disabilities are sometimes denied for fear of offending. Students are quick to abandon clients whose cultural diversity they are unfamiliar with rather than face their prejudices and mistakes, and walk with the client.

Appropriate use of transcultural literature to support these concerns is important for the multicultural curriculum. It is not enough to add references and expect students to convert text into practice. Transcultural concepts tend to remain theoretical mysteries. They need discussion, elucidation and ways of integrating

---

[2]Cultural capital describes levels of support and encouragement, derived from family, peers and educators to build and maintain a confident cultural identity.

[3]Warner Weil relates this concept of miseducation with conditions that can undermine the overall sense of identity of a learner and sometimes lead to internalizing the experience. If teachers are aware of these circumstances and the power dynamics involved, they can manage them using a process of accountability.

them into practice. Multicultural literature does not always give suggestions about working with attitudes about diversity and oppression. Students claim that they want models of applying transcultural and intercultural therapy. Unlike the application of traditional models they may struggle with the cultural aspects of therapy and need support. In my 2005 study (Mckenzie-Mavinga 2005) students were asking 'How do you do it?' – meaning, 'How do you open a dialogue about the cultural and racial context of relationships?' Sometimes these students felt silenced in the process of reflecting on diversity. Tuckwell (2002: 138) asserts her understanding of silence:

> There is a silence generally within our profession concerning racism, but I believe also that a silence can too easily develop in the consulting room. It is a dangerous silence for the therapy because it contains too much background noise for it not to infect all other work we try to do. A frequent response by the black patient is to stop and leave therapy, often silently. Another response is not to enter in the first place, which is the loudest silence of all.

During training, the lecturer must facilitate and process this silence for a productive learning experience. De Vita, in Carroll and Ryan (2005: 81), advocates that reflection is necessary to assist students to make sense of diversity and understand other experiences and belief systems. Students are not always prepared for this type of reflection and this can sometimes provoke powerful feelings. Trainers therefore need to think ahead about ways they can use the curriculum to reflect diversity issues to students and support their learning in this area. This approach is essential for a multicultural curriculum and the development of cultural empathy.[4]

Cultural empathy

Cultural empathy develops from the therapist's ability to connect and explicitly address cultural experiences attached to the client's emotions, thoughts and behaviour. Students must be encouraged to achieve cultural empathy and maintain openness to address cultural issues and explore the challenges they face during this process, otherwise the cultural components of personal development and the therapeutic process become marginalized, mirroring the impact of oppression. When this happens students begin to question their worthiness. Students therefore need to be encouraged to achieve cultural empathy as a transcultural competency in their training. Transcultural work needs to be at the centre of therapy training as though it were a core component, like empathy.

A study by Hussain and Bagguley (2007) concluded that insufficient attention was paid to the impact of isolation, racism and Islamophobia upon students. In

---

[4]Cultural empathy requires the therapist to be open to connecting with and exploring the experiences and challenges of diversity and oppression in both their clinical practice and supervision.

addition, 'racism and homophobia in universities have all too often been brushed aside' (p. 144). This study corroborates the need for the development of a transcultural dialogue within the multicultural curriculum.

Developing the course curriculum

Not unlike therapy, it is important to be aware of the student's learning disposition and learning needs. Warner Weil and McGill (1989) advocate that teaching and learning should be open to different ways of being and communicating prior experience in the context of power. Warner Weil enquired into the meanings of different learner and learning experiences before and during the training experience. One student claimed: 'I never feel confident in a room full of whites, never relaxed, always on guard. Automatic. Immune to it. Unconscious. I speak in a particular manner. More passive in the way I present myself. Not if in a group of black people' (p. 123). Black students playing down their experiences creates a silence, a muting of their identities that could be considered a cultural discourse arising from the impact of oppression on learning and practice. Warner Weil describes this sense of fragmentation, involving both 'personal and social identity' as 'disjunction'. In this study the students managed their disjunction by engaging with significant peers both on the course and outside. Their determination to complete the course and the subsequent engagement with tutors created a constructive process that enhanced their education. The researcher acknowledges these students' engagement as needing 'a stable psychology' in order to derive maximum benefit from a learning situation (p. 124). She affirms that tutors who value the need for students to reflect on their learning with other black people are important to the curriculum and the enhancement of student education. The involvement of trainers in the learning derived from disjunction (so that students are not left to resolve these silences) is key to a curriculum for training in multicultural therapy. Lack of this type of involvement can create a risk of further disjunction between students and trainers, reinforcing this silence. Warner Weil suggests that students need to be encouraged to 'unlearn' the silences: 'In these accounts, from those who, not just in terms of age, but also in terms of gender, class and race, have traditionally been underrepresented in higher and continuing education, the complexities and struggles in "unlearning to not speak" become manifest' (p. 125).

Creating opportunities for cooperative intercultural enquiry

Dowd (2003), cited in De Vita (2005: 79) emphasizes the need for offering explicit tasks to explore cultural identities. Such tasks can open up dialogue on stereotypes that individuals harbour about others and promote greater understanding about diversity. This author encourages 'cooperative intercultural enquiry' to assist students to share the role of researcher and learner. In this approach it is important to understand the role of teaching and learning, as self-awareness and personal development are key elements of intercultural work.

Strategies for intercultural work in the student group can be applied to alleviate disjunction and address diversity issues that may cause silence or misinterpretation. These strategies can present personal development challenges for both students and trainers. A common challenge is the assumption that intercultural exercises are only about black people. This response, one that I call the 'hierarchy of oppressions', is important, because an understanding of other minority group experiences creates a greater understanding of how racism affects both the oppressor and the victim. The emotional content attached to facilitation of racial issues needs to be acknowledged and supported, allowing students an opportunity to experience the process of working through their personal development and understanding. I call the process of powerful feelings evoked by discussions about racism 'recognition trauma'.[5]

Students must be encouraged to explore the impact of their prejudices on clients. Exploring diversity issues can be an emotional experience, laden with students' own experiences of oppression.

Cultural capital

Byfield (2008) uses the term 'cultural capital' to describe how the background experiences of black boys predisposes them to failure or success in higher education. Men, as role models and as students, are the most obvious minority in therapy training. Black men are even less visible due to the impact of institutional and personal racism. Therapy training that does not draw on their cultural capital is therefore feminized and whitewashed in its over-reliance on Eurocentric theories.

Therapy training can model the usefulness of cultural capital by integrating knowledge from intercultural and transcultural literature. The training environment needs to be a place where students can try out transcultural relationships, make mistakes and develop their learning process. To avoid a one-size-fits-all or colour-blind approach the transfer of cultural elements between training and practice needs to be explored. This requires trainers and professionals involved in therapy training to reflect on their own transcultural processes. Trainees need to have role models who demonstrate an open dialogue about cultural issues. This needs to be supported with a curriculum that includes trainees' contribution to transcultural practice. Particular attention should be given to minority group learning experiences, so that individuals from these groups are not placed in the expert role,

---

[5] Recognition trauma is 'A process where the emotions of individuals' relating to black issues either come to the fore or create a block' (Mckenzie-Mavinga 2009: 36).

with their own learning taking a secondary place. In Watson's research (2004: 47) a student said:

> Its harder work getting the issues taken seriously because it's down to ... it feels as though pressure is on you as the one Black person to represent all sorts of things or to raise all sorts of things whether you want to or not. Or if you don't then your silence is taken as agreement or collusion with the things that might happen.

The black student bearing the role of educator on training courses (the black expert role) may be forced to experience what Straker *et al.* (2004) viewed as 'continuous trauma' of their often-disempowered position in a white dominated society. Straker sees this trauma as an interruption in the ongoing process of self-development. In the role of the black expert the black trainee becomes distracted from their self-development and is burdened with white trainees' self-development and explaining about racism. For therapists this should only happen in the context of listening to clients.

Both trainers and students need to be open to the process of challenge and learning about minority oppressions and how to develop an anti-oppressive approach to practice. Dhillon-Stevens' model of anti-oppessive practice (AOP) (2005)[6] involves the therapist's exploration of their attitudes and internalized views, to create awareness of when these attitudes enter the therapeutic space. She presents three distinct areas for therapists to engage with (p. 51):

1   To demonstrate an understanding of discrimination and oppression in terms of a knowledge base.
2   To critically demonstrate that they can examine the impact of their values and beliefs (attitudes) on their work and be clear about moral and ethical principles and the management of ethical dilemmas.
3   To demonstrate concrete skills to work with a range of oppressed clients.

The AOP model is essential to a curriculum for multicultural therapy. Transcultural training must be ongoing and spread across the curriculum, not just included as a 'one-off' seminar so that students can fully explore the process of their transcultural learning alongside their development as therapists.

Teaching anti-oppressive practice

Lectures can deliver facts and models of a multicultural approach with well-defined learning outcomes that examine the 'connection between teaching, learning and assessment', a process described as 'constructive alignment' (Exley and Dennick

---

[6]AOP 'requires a fundamental re-thinking of values, institutions and relationships: therapists are seen as change agents and are proactive rather than reactive. Therapists accept that they can influence at individual-to-individual level but are also aware of their contribution at structural level in terms of institutional levels of the cultural norm' (Dhillon-Stevens 2005: 47).

2004). Since attending to diversity and equality is sometimes viewed as a problem, students should be offered space to engage with their personal challenges in
transcultural work. Their curiosity about how to apply a multicultural approach
to therapy needs to be encouraged lest they become passive recipients of knowledge and detached from their own personal connections with the theme. This
means that Eurocentric theory must be explored and challenged for its relevance
to particular cultural experiences.

Kareem, in Kareem and Littlewood (1992: 31), exemplifies the personal challenge and impact of Eurocentric training: 'It was a painful difficult battle not to
think what I was told to think, not to be what I had been told to be and not to challenge what I had been told could not be challenged and at the same time not to
become alienated from my basic roots'. The risk of becoming alienated from one's
basic roots is equal to the risk of becoming a *cloned therapist*; therefore the way students experience learning about multicultural therapy must be valued. If students'
learning experience is not valued, their cultural capital becomes diminished and
they may feel a loss of identity and the epistemological force of institutional oppression. A degree of flexibility is therefore needed to accommodate the diversity
of students' learning needs when exploring AOP.

When students discussed their learning needs in relation to the theme of black
issues, their prior knowledge and levels of relationship with the theme influenced
their responses. Those who lived in rural areas had little contact with black people.
Others formed opinions that relied on their personal relationships, their own ethnicity or experiences of urban communities in Britain (Mckenzie-Mavinga 2005).
Where previously there seemed to be a silence, facilitation of their different levels
of awareness supported a mutual learning process. This approach requires enthusiasm on behalf of the lecturer.

Developing an enthusiastic multicultural lecturer

What does it take to be an enthusiastic multicultural lecturer who models AOP
and implements a multicultural curriculum? Woods (1995, cited in Brookfield
2006: 16) proposed 'creative lecturing'. This approach relies on several principles
of effective practice that contribute to teaching learning transactions:

- *participation through choice* – helps students feel valued and respect individual levels of ability, self-worth and experience;
- *collaborative facilitation* – adults meeting equally and coping with diversity
  in learning and the employment market;
- *praxis* – the cycle of action and reflection which assists individual research
  and continuous building of knowledge incorporating past, present and
  future;
- *facilitation* – which fosters critical reflection on the social and historical
  context of learning, promoting hegemony; the aim of facilitation is to
  nurture self-directed, empowered, rather than reactive, adults.

These principles are not dissimilar to those of therapy and can be considered as a framework for training in multicultural therapy. Teaching methods can be adjusted to accommodate both the multicultural aims of the curriculum and the learning needs of students. Students can be encouraged to share their diversity and engage in facilitation of their intercultural and intracultural experiences.

Multicultural literature should be identified as essential reading to support therapy training. Students can be encouraged to examine multicultural case material that informs their learning development. It is important to develop a safe space for students to discuss their prejudices and the defences that impact on their listening skills and transcultural work. Consideration should be given to the process of understanding multiculturalism, thus making the learning process an enjoyable and inspiring experience. As a parallel to therapy, understanding an analysis of the learning process gives meaning to the relationship between student and lecturer. The lecturer's role in modelling an anti-oppressive approach is therefore key to a multicultural curriculum. Taking the above into consideration, I now present some ideas for engaging with a three-tier system to support training in multicultural therapy.

Tier one: student diversity and the social dynamics of oppression

Hellmundt and Ryan (in Carroll and Ryan 2005: 15) suggest that integrated methods that value different ways of thinking support a student-centred approach that creates space for their voices to be heard rather than marginalized. This represents a shift from the student as subject to student as co-researcher, being heard and listening to others in the process of learning. A parallel with therapy can be experienced. By valuing student diversity and contribution, the student as co-researcher can support teaching and learning in a more in-depth way. The authors suggest that this approach requires lecturers to model multiculturalism by not making assumptions about the way students learn because of their background or the way they look. The challenge to expect students not to respond to teaching in a passive way is set up. This approach calls for facilitation using a reflective approach to understand student experiences of learning and the cultural influences on that learning. The curriculum should demand that students' personal development in the light of their own diversity is considered. Engaging students in this process helps to challenge the one-size-fits-all approach and also assists students to consider working with diversity in their future employment. Trainers facilitating this process need to understand their personal attitude towards diversity.

In the transcultural approach, d'Ardenne and Mahtani (1989) emphasize the active and reciprocal process of therapy and require that professionals be 'sensitive to cultural variations and the cultural biases of their own approach' (p. 6.) The key words for a curriculum for multicultural therapy are 'active and reciprocal'.

This means that opportunities for discussion with students who are challenged by oppressions, language, disabilities and learning techniques that might otherwise be taken for granted, must be given. I will use an example from my own teaching to illustrate this.

A disabled student always placed her wheelchair by the classroom door as though she were constantly on the margins of the group. I asked whether this was her choice and she replied that the class always left a space for her in the same place. I invited her to decide whether she would like to take the same opportunity as other students and choose her place in the classroom. This was an enlightening process for the students, who from then on had a different view of how oppressions can operate for both the oppressed and the oppressor. While the other students felt empowered through their mobility to sit in different parts of the room they had colluded with this student's disempowerment. Opportunities for students in the oppressor groups to understand their role as oppressors and their own oppressions must be offered.

Tier two: the development of traditional approaches in a transcultural way

It is important that trainers are aware of how students can become dependent on traditional Eurocentric theory. Eurocentric concepts and interpretations need to be viewed as a framework for understanding client behaviour and relationships in a flexible way, and not used to homogenize individuals. The concept of the Oedipus complex, for example, may not apply to someone raised in or engaging in same-sex parenting or raised in an extended family. Lack of direct eye contact may not necessarily indicate an introverted personality. Symptoms and feelings need to be contextualized within the historical and cultural situation of the client. This means that therapists need to find a cultural language located in the client's heritage and the social influences of their development. Omission of this context may deny opportunities to explore cultural influences on personal development. The use of transtheoretical concepts can be helpful in bringing Eurocentric theory and the process together.

Empathy, for example, as a core condition and transtheoretical concept used in many therapies, helps to demonstrate emotional connection and understanding. This core condition can be supported in a cultural context. I have called this 'cultural empathy'. Competencies for multicultural therapy need to be evaluated for their usefulness. In talking therapies, empathy is usually evidenced as a competency for good practice. A multicultural curriculum is pointless if students are allowed to pass their training without evidencing their ability to address cultural issues. Cultural issues may not be deemed as an essential core condition of therapy, yet they present ethical and relational concerns for students and their clinical practice. Training courses therefore need to define and accept cultural competencies as important for qualifying therapists. When equalities are not followed through into teaching and learning assessments, power relations within learning institutions can become skewed and perpetuate marginalization of minority experiences. This is clearly a parallel to therapy. Ethnocentric frameworks that dominate approaches to learning must be challenged and trainers must create opportunities for intercultural sharing and understanding.

Tier three: facilitation of students' understanding and development of transcultural practice

I have discussed the need for a mutually reflective process that engages elements of students' past experience of learning, social and cultural experiences and oppressions. Training for multicultural therapy should be a collaborative process similar to the therapeutic process, with an emphasis on mutual respect and openness to challenge oppression. Trainers must reflect on their epistemological position when understanding the impact of institutional oppression and group dynamics. Facilitation of students' understanding and development of transcultural practice is key to a training curriculum for multicultural therapy. A reflective space in the curriculum creates an opportunity for disjunction. Below I have made some suggestions for integrating transcultural knowledge into training courses.

1   Trainers must model ways to open dialogue about oppressions.
2   Denial of social and cultural influences must be challenged in the training forum.
3   Traditional approaches or training models must be revised and strategies developed that include multicultural themes.
4   An anti-oppressive understanding of practice should be developed so as to avoid the perpetuation of oppression by exclusion or denial and lack of response to social and cultural themes.
5   Space should be provided to explore the historical and cultural impact of Eurocentricism.
6   The assessment process should be used to reflect students' levels of cultural capital.
7   The development of cultural empathy should be encouraged.
8   Personal development forums and supervision should be used to explore what it feels like to work with oppressions.
9   Opportunities need to be created to explore minority experiences and oppressions.
10 Dialogue about internalized oppression should be encouraged.

Student care and self-care is paramount in the process of exploring past and present, especially when oppressions are part of the discussions. The question of how trainers make a difference to individuals in the context of learning is a complex one, influenced by the impact of diversity and the reason for developing learning relationships that take this into account. Finally, I want to reiterate that a multicultural curriculum does not rely on the diversity within the student group and must not be taken for granted. It is primarily the responsibility of trainers to integrate and initiate facilitation of a training curriculum for multicultural therapy.

References

Brookfield, S.D. (1996) *The Skillful Teacher*. San Francisco: Jossey-Bass.

Byfield, C. (2008) *Black Boys Can Make It*. Stoke on Trent: Trentham Books.

Carroll, J. and Ryan, J. (eds) (2005) *Teaching International Students*. London: Routledge.

Dalal, F. (2002) *Race, Colour and the Process of Racialization*. Hove: Brunner Routledge.

d'Ardenne, P. and Mahtani, A. (1989) *Transcultural Counselling in Action*. London: Sage.

Davies, D. and Neal, C. (1996) *Pink Therapy: A Guide for Counsellors and Therapists Working with Lesbian, Gay and Bisexual Clients*. Buckingham: Open University Press.

De Vita, G. (2005) Fostering intercultural learning through multicultural group work, in J. Carroll, and J. Ryan (eds) *Teaching International Students*. London: Routledge.

Dhillon-Stevens, H. (2005) Personal and professional integration of anti-oppressive practice and the multiple oppression model in psychotherapeutic education, *British Journal of Psychotherapy Integration*, 1(2): 47–62.

Eichenbaum, L. and Orbach, S. (1982) *Outside In Inside Out: A Feminist and Psychoanalytic Approach to Women's Psychology*. London: Penguin.

Eleftheriadou, Z. (1994) *Transcultural Counselling*. London: Central Book Publishing.

Exley, K. and Dennick, R. (2004) *Giving a Lecture*. London: RoutledgeFalmer.

Fanon, F. (1986) *Black Skin, White Mask*. London: Pluto Press.

Fernando, S. (1989) *Race and Culture in Psychiatry*. London: Tavistock/Routledge.

Fletchman Smith, B. (2000) *Mental Slavery*. London: Karnac.

Hussain, Y. and Bagguley, P. (2007) *Moving on Up*. Stoke on Trent: Trentham Books.

Kareem, J. and Littlewood, R. (1992) *Intercultural Therapy*. London: Blackwell.

Lago, C. and Thompson, J. (1996) *Race, Culture and Counselling*. Buckingham: Open University Press.

Mckenzie-Mavinga (2005) A study of black issues in counsellor training, doctoral thesis, Metanoia Institute and The British Museum.

Mckenzie-Mavinga, I. (2009) *Black Issues in the Therapeutic Process*. Basingstoke: Palgrave Macmillan.

Straker, J. *et al.* (2004) Trauma and disconnection: a transtheoretical approach, *International Journal of Psychotherapy*, 7: 2.

Tuckwell, G. (2002) *Racial Identity, White Counsellors and Therapists*. Maidenhead: Open University Press.

Warner Weil, S.W. and McGill, I. (1989) *Making Sense of Experiential Learning: Diversity in Theory and Practice.* Buckingham: SRHE and Open University Press.

Watson, V.V.V. (2004) The training experiences of black counsellors, unpublished, PhD thesis, University of Nottingham.

Yellin, J. (2004) The changer and the changed: the therapist's transition in working with issues of transgender in a relational psychoanalytic therapy, paper presented at the 'Queer Analysis' conference, London, 15–16 October 2004.

4 Training for 'multicultural' therapy: the community role of the training department/institution

Yair Maman and Simon du Plock

Introduction

The role of the community in training counsellors and psychotherapists, whether within the confines of the academic world or when involving any other institutional training scheme, can be of great importance – especially when it comes to helping marginalized populations.

Based on my (Yair) experiences in training students to work with historically marginalized populations and also based on the extensive experience in therapist training of the second author (Simon) we try to convey in this chapter what training with 'community in mind' really means to us. In the course of relating three compelling stories based on the unique training one of us started to develop while working with underrepresented and underserved communities in New York City, we attempt to put forward a new approach that is founded on developing continuous relationships with a variety of people from all walks of life, including community leaders, politicians, programme directors, business people, students and many others.

I (Yair) consider myself a social entrepreneur. This can be seen in the ways I approached many of my projects. The project discussed here demonstrates how I devised a new approach to recruiting and training counsellors. It also suggests possible ways to replicate my training efforts. But a word of caution – any attempt to replicate these efforts requires elements of *flexibility* and *vision*.

Through professional entrepreneurialism I intended to utilize any available resources to advance the field of mental health care. My goal has always been to make a positive impact on society. The professional journey I undertook to re-conceive counsellor training, and to adopt new and innovative approaches, was therefore also a personal journey. I used funds, available facilities, social contacts and support systems to achieve my goals, but ultimately the success of such projects hinges on the ability to *connect* with people.

In addition to this unique strength, I have also worked very hard to achieve my objectives. In my experience not all people have the ability to effectively implement change. Many people who I worked with were incapable of being flexible and visionary; instead, they would focus on petty points and issues, such as certain administrative aspects that contributed no real value to the overall project. This is perhaps due to fear of change.

The process by which I have worked and continue to work with different communities is both very complex and very simple. However, most people are unwilling to understand issues as simultaneously multidimensional and simple, and this is where the difficulty lies in replicating my efforts. Those I encountered in academia and in practice preferred not to think and reflect on the interconnectedness of issues. Ultimately, this stemmed from an avoidance of social responsibility for anything that did not directly relate to their scope of accountability or practice.

Additionally, my approach could seem tedious, since it is founded on developing continuous relationships with an ongoing commitment to a variety of people from all walks of life. For social entrepreneurship to be truly successful there is a need to continuously interact with *all* the stakeholders, to learn about community needs and to have a deep understanding of community goals.

It is not a magical process. Making connections requires dealing with many small details and trying hard to understand people, their communities and their needs. This can be seen in the analogous example of attending a friend's social event. Through making a *connection* with someone you are invited to a wedding, bar mitzvah, baptism or other social event. This can lead to a sense of inclusion and trust in that specific community of people. These *connections* cannot be merely expressed on paper as ideas and concepts. People actually need to see you and interact with you, to feel comfortable with your company. This is, I believe, the main ingredient for effective social entrepreneurialism.

Training with community in mind

Like many clinicians who work in a multicultural environment, we realized that although mental health workers and trained clinicians were indeed skilled in many facets of psychotherapy and counselling, they were not trained to provide effective and efficient treatment of a specific community. For example, the treatment within communities such as the Hasidic community in Boro Park[1] requires an in-depth knowledge of the intricate issues facing that community. This is most evident in regard to the Hasidic community, where the therapist's lack of understanding about the culture, and in particular a thorough understanding of '*Halacha*',[2] may be detrimental to the client's ability to trust the therapist (Wieselberg 1992; Bilo and Witztum 1993).

---

[1]Boro Park is a neighborhood in Brooklyn, New York, which has the largest Hasidic population in the world.
[2]*Halacha* is Hebrew for the 'way of law', referring to the collective body of religious Jewish law, including biblical, Talmudic and rabbinical law.

The role of the community can be expanded in counsellor training. In most postgraduate programmes in the fields of counselling and psychotherapy that provide the necessary multicultural knowledge base there are two components that seem to be neglected in the curriculum: outreach to underrepresented groups and a tailored approach to each situation to offer the best possible chance for success.

Aten (2004) discusses how pastoral counsellor training programmes can use a ministerial approach when people from the community come to a college for counselling. The approach we discuss here comes from the other direction. We are suggesting a way to utilize the pre-existing network of counsellors in the community, recruiting those without academic training, but who are already involved in counselling on the ground.

We attempt to explain how a counsellor training programme facilitates a dynamic collaboration. In this mechanism the external processes are the main focus rather than the counsellor training programme aimed at serving underserved and/or underrepresented populations. In Figure 4.1, imagine that the middle circle does not exist. There will just be a dynamic collaboration between the students, faculty and community. The focus is on the dynamic collaboration, on the practical aspects of providing for community needs.

One objective is to train those who are already trusted in their community and familiar with the issues particular to that community. It will be obvious in our stories that all communities are affected by:

- a lack of public sympathy for the plight of those with mental disorders;
- a lack of funding; and/or
- a lack of public understanding of the serious consequences of inadequate funding, such as increased homelessness and crime.

Working with three New York communities

I (Yair) launched Touro College's Master of Science programme in Mental Health Counselling (MHC) in New York in 2003. The MHC programme was designed to meet new requirements set by New York State for licensure in the fields of counselling and psychotherapy (defined by the state as 'mental health counselling'). This licensure scheme was intended to protect the public from unlicensed practitioners who had provided counselling services in various communities. Seizing on this opportunity, I aimed to provide unique community-based counsellor training through the recruitment and training of counsellors to work with historically marginalized populations. A unique programme was then developed to meet the needs of diverse communities across the New York metropolitan area. Below are three examples of how the training began to develop in three unique communities (unique in that they represent the underserved and underrepresented in terms of mental health counsellor training). Based on a context statement, these stories surfaced in the course of undertaking a reflexive review of my achievements for

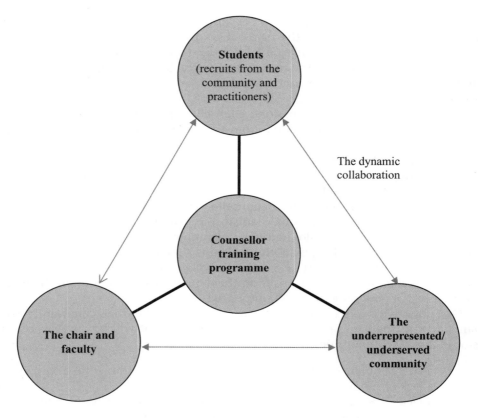

Figure 4.1 Facilitating a dynamic collaboration
Note: The bold lines represent the traditional connections sought by counsellor training programmes (they all seek to recruit students, seek qualified faculty and are affiliated with some community organization). The arrowed lines represent the dynamic collaboration between the three entities.

a 'first of its kind' Doctorate in Psychotherapy by Public Works in which supervision and a refinement of this training approach was provided by the second author (Simon).

Example 1: training in the Hasidic community

After I (Yair) tackled organizational change in this residential treatment system which culminated in my PhD dissertation (on this subject), I developed the necessary skills required for engaging academic leaders at Touro College. Organizational resistance was expected (since this was a new field in New York State) but I managed to introduce a new training programme.

The MHC programme consists of 60 semester hours of required coursework in the areas of assessment, diagnosis, intervention, report-writing and counselling. The programme may be completed in three years of full-time study or four or more years of part-time study. Some summer session coursework may be required. The MHC programme is designed to train students to work in a variety of mental health settings (e.g. clinics, hospitals, counselling centres, rehabilitation facilities, outreach programmes, after-care centres, private practice). The programme engages with the community to find ways that it can contribute and pass on this knowledge to our students. This usually takes the form of inviting prominent community members to guest lecture. Students are also encouraged to conduct independent outreach in marginalized communities.

I specifically set out to recruit from the community. The first community I approached was that with which I was most familiar, the Boro Park Hasidic community where I worked at the beginning of my career. I was there during the week of *Tisha B'av*, which symbolizes the saddest event in Jewish history, the destruction of the Temple in Jerusalem. During that week children were not in school and the streets were quiet. The sombre atmosphere left me with a sense of introspection and humility and I realized that I was standing at the threshold of an opportunity. I felt that if I did not take full advantage of this chance to fulfil Touro College's mission here of serving such an unrepresented community I would end up regretting it for the rest of my life. I decided that the best course of action would be to cast a wide net. I therefore needed to find out where people in the Hasidic community received different types of mental health services, including standard diagnostic tests for children, psychiatric services and social work services. Knowing that this was a very traditional community I also needed to find out the extent to which those services were provided by practitioners with a religious background.

In the first week of September 2003 I met two women who were both advocating for child welfare. They told me that they were aware of disturbing cases of child abuse that were 'swept under the rug' by school officials who were prominent religious figures in the community and did not want the problem exposed. Since they lived in Boro Park they were familiar with many families and many stories. They became two of my first students. These women were hopeful that my proposed programme would train them in their community and empower them to do something about the plight of children.

Other students also joined the programme. I targeted rabbis, realizing that they hold very powerful positions in the Hasidic community, as is the case with many communities where religious leaders are central to most social functions. The first step was to explain to them the advantage of receiving a licence for providing mental health counselling. There was a personal appeal for them in terms of the benefits of learning about different methods of treating people. Emphasis was placed on having people from the community who share the same values and traditions in a position of providing the treatment. Finally, there is a strong tradition of caring for the sick in a compassionate manner within the Jewish community and one of the cornerstones of MHC is the importance of using a humanistic treatment method.

In essence, there was a close fit between the values of this community in rela-tion to mental health care and the developing MHC programme. This provided a foundation from which the mental health care provided within the community would be enhanced to benefit all stakeholders.

Like many other marginalized groups of people, the members of the Hasidic community needed job opportunities. This community was excluded through their strange apparel and would also exclude themselves by keeping to themselves and rarely seeking communication with the world outside (beyond their narrowly-bordered neighbourhoods). There was a great need for them to support themselves and their families and the MHC profession can be a good way to both make money and contribute to society positively.

Example 2: training in the Hispanic community and the development of a more generalized training via the community feedback scheme

While trying to replicate what I (Yair) had accomplished in the Hasidic commu-nity in other communities was challenging, I was eager to take it on and engage with this vision as a piece of action research, with the Hasidic community as the first cycle. I decided that sensitivity and sensibility would be my approach. Being a 'street smart' New Yorker by now was very helpful. Knowing that New York has a large Hispanic population I decided to focus my efforts on this growing commu-nity. It was well known that this population required a unique cultural approach (Rogler *et al.* 1987). I also knew that it was the most rapidly growing population in New York and across the USA. However, a more universal template for approach-ing and contacting communities such as this was needed. Exploiting the internet as a research medium, I went online and conducted a general search for Hispanic community activities relating to outreach. I spent a long time researching to lo-cate activities in Hispanic communities across the New York metropolitan area. Although I began to find some interesting leads, I knew that one of my biggest obstacles was the language barrier. I was fortunate to have a few Hispanic friends that I could rely on in this regard.

Accompanied by Spanish-speaking colleagues, over the course of a few weeks I attended meetings at various locations, including intervention groups, local com-munity festivals and events that celebrate Hispanic heritage. I was a little discour-aged at first since I did not receive any positive responses regarding my enquiries about the needs of the Hispanic community, or any interest in my programme. I was not even able to interest community leaders in attending school functions and intercultural events. At this point it occurred to me that the reason I had such rapid success in the Hasidic community was because of my long-term association with that community, and, in a way, being part of that community. We believe that for any counsellor training approach to be truly successful there is a need to continuously interact with all the stakeholders, to learn about community needs and to have a deep understanding of community goals.

At this point there was, then, a need for a new approach. A method was developed whereby the programme was adjusted in response to the community feedback. First, the MHC curriculum committee now meets annually to discuss changes and adjustments to the courses taught on the programme. These changes are the result of responses from various sources, such as discussions with students after they start their internship, feedback from mental health providers at internships sites, and feedback from community centres that are affiliated with the programme. For example, one course was altered to focus more on the issue of obesity. This is an important and multifaceted issue and the course now includes a more thorough discussion of treatment methods, prevention and a variety of approaches, such as using a multidisciplinary team including a counsellor, a nurse and a caseworker. On another course, information was added about alcohol and drug abuse issues, and in yet another the issue of autism will now be included, with up-to-date information and treatment methods.

Second, some people in the community asked about ways to expand our programme so that graduates would be able to treat different age groups and a more varied population. As a result we tried to find ways to combine our programme with other degrees such as school counselling. This would allow our students to tackle community issues in relation to all age groups, such as school-aged children, and also provide more job opportunities. Now the MHC programme focuses on working closely with the newly designed school counselling programme (which will soon offer classes in high-need schools in the New York metropolitan area). We will also work to adjust our curriculum to fit with the English as a second language (ESL) degree programme, which is already offered at Touro. We have organized an exploratory committee to investigate the option of adding elective courses to the programme. These electives will offer the opportunity for students to obtain a certificate for three or four courses in a variety of subjects, while at the same time applying the courses towards the MHC degree.

Figure 4.2 illustrates the way changes occur in the curriculum. I am currently in the process of developing a comprehensive curriculum development handbook with the help of newly hired staff.

I continued my efforts for a few more weeks. When approaching the Hispanic community I had three main objectives: to encourage students from the community to enrol in my programme; to form relationships with religious leaders and other community leaders; and to find placements for future graduates of the MHC programme. In terms of attracting students, the ability to *connect* with people (discussed earlier) proved useful in offering at least a partial scholarship. In my talks with Touro College's president I stressed that we were alternating between providing tuition discounts of between 40 and 70 per cent, or providing full merit-based scholarships. He often waved his hand for me to stop talking and simply said, 'Do not worry; we will be helping those students'; which I interpreted as complete acquiescence to all my suggestions regarding scholarships and tuition reduction (a fortunate situation to be in).

As far as recruitment goes, in approaching those who were already involved in helping in the community, I put up such notices, both in Spanish and in English,

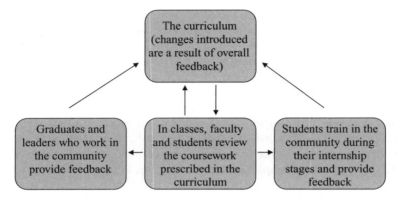

Figure 4.2 Enhancing the curriculum – a feedback loop
Note: Changes in the curriculum are based on feedback from all involved in the training process. Aside from input from faculty members, inputs from students and the community are factored in when faculty members meet with the chair to discuss curricular changes. It makes sense that counsellor training which emphasizes work with marginalized populations should involve empowerment for the students since they will eventually need to realistically 'empower' people on the margins of society. A counsellor trainee who is recruited from the community can introduce *real* change if he or she is already involved in changes to his or her training. Therefore the annual curriculum committee meetings are open to all faculty members, students and all community leaders involved in outreach activities.

on community bulletin boards. When attempting to form relationships with religious leaders and other community leaders I encountered a great deal of suspicion and mistrust. This was manifested in the comments made by many in the community who were accustomed to people trying to take advantage of funds, available to minorities, for personal gain. Here I was fortunate to have the assistance of several Hispanic community members. I started learning that it is very important to involve those who deeply care for their community. But, beyond such care for a community, the newly devised approach to training was the cornerstone for success. In many conversations with stakeholders in the community, who were often the prospective students themselves, I managed to get the right message across. What I was offering was not something the communities provide for themselves because:

- there were very few resources and money for scholarships for underrepresented communities; and
- there was very little communication between communities.

All of us involved in the MHC programme are aware that we cannot discard any possible approach that might work within a select population. This is evident in our approach of integrating spirituality, religion and mental health to care for the Hasidic community. We encourage the students to listen to and be aware of the needs of their communities and to be pragmatic. This means utilizing any method or person in order to provide effective mental health services.

One of the people who applied to the MHC programme became instrumental in finding placements for interns and graduates of the programme. As it happens, there was a huge shortage of mental health professionals in New York who were bilingual in English and Spanish. This particular person was always cheerful and energetic and instigated interesting conversations in class. He was an inspiration to many students, and not only those who were Hispanic. He was inspired by the approach that he found to 'focus on developing cultural sensitivity to the world view and behaviour paradigms that clearly manifest differently in every community'. He said those words to me following a class attended by a Hasidic man, three Hasidic women and one African-American woman. This new recruit was born and raised in the 1950s on the tough streets of Spanish Harlem, a predominantly Hispanic neighbourhood. One of his earliest recollections as a child was of his two older brothers, 18 years his senior, 'nodding out' on heroin. His mother raised the three of them on a very limited income.

Another memorable saying by this gentleman, after class, was, 'These children are manifesting the behaviours of their parents and their community. There is no way we can reach out to those children without reaching out to their parents at the same time.' He gained extensive counselling skills and broadened his perspective through shared experiences with students from other communities. When he finished the programme he said, 'Things are not always black and white. I learned that there are many grey areas and sometimes you have to reach out and help whenever you can and with whatever skills you have.'

Although I was hampered by my lack of knowledge of the Spanish language, I was still able to attend functions since many are conducted in English (the hosts tend to repeat in English what is said in Spanish for the benefit of non-Spanish-speaking guests). So I realized there was a need to closely liaise with colleagues at Touro College who were familiar with bilingual issues, in order to provide additional bilingual training to my students. When it comes to Hispanic populations it is also important to reflect issues relating to extended families. In much of the Hispanic world, the basic family unit extends beyond father, mother and children, to include grandparents, uncles, aunts and cousins.

Aside from the language issue the communities that were chosen as a recruitment ground were largely underserved. This meant that there were little or no mental health services available for these communities. State-funded social services were largely mistrusted by these populations.

Example 3: training in the African-American community

After I (Yair) began my involvement in the Hispanic community I decided to arrange several open houses at the college. I was not looking to recruit from any specific community in those events; they were intended to introduce the new mental health field to the general public. Many of the open houses were not successful in terms of participation numbers, probably due to the time of year and inclement weather. However, I was lucky that during one of those meetings some African-American students who were active in their communities were thrilled to learn about the nature of the MHC programme.

I saw an opportunity to reach out through them to the African-American community as a whole. I told them that, due to the demands on my time, I would arrange for a partial scholarship for them if they were willing to become involved in student recruitment in their spare time. I asked them to distribute flyers at churches and other community centres in their neighbourhood, which forms the largest African-American community in Brooklyn, extending from the East New York section to the Crown Heights section (where they live).

Within two weeks I began receiving many calls and soon started recruiting many students from the African-American community. By the end of 2007, I not only had the largest Hasidic and Hispanic student groups in a counsellor training programme in the New York area, but also the largest African-American group.

Conclusion

Based on the three communities discussed it is evident that it can be difficult to define what a particular group of people need in terms of mental health services and other special needs. Groups tend to congregate together to follow economic, religious or other goals. To define the mental health needs of children, or any other group, we need to first analyse those involved in the care of them: parents, educators and mental health professionals. Then there are issues relating to short- and long-term psychological treatment, and whether or not psychiatric medication is involved. It gets more complicated when cures are based on religious approaches. Consequently, I convey to faculty and students the importance of recognizing that it is not always possible to change behaviours. As a mental health practitioner it is hard, and at times impossible, to dispel beliefs that have been held for centuries and transmitted through generations. This is where, through community-based training, the MHC programme intends to create a bridge between academic training and mental health care delivery in the community.

Students need to be flexible and dynamic in order to respond to specific community needs. One community may need assistance regarding family therapeutic issues while another may need assistance with school-related issues and school-aged children. In some communities the counselling process will have to be more discreet whereas in others there is more openness and involvement.

The main mission of the MHC programme is to train counsellors to deal with not just one set of circumstances, but to address the different needs of each of the communities using the available resources within each community. From the outset I had very high standards and expectations and insisted that all counsellors trained within the programme adopt similar standards of excellence. Many mental health practitioners have low expectations of their clients because many times there are limited resources within an overworked and overtaxed bureaucracy. They often do not have the tools to effectively and efficiently deal with the needs of every separate community. There are usually just general approaches that do not take into account religion, culture and ethnic influences. Therefore the programme instructors are encouraged to think 'out of the box' in their teaching approaches, to use guest lecturers from the community, and to listen to the students to make sure that all issues are considered.

We both realize that the most important resources of the MHC programme (and any programme of this kind) are its staff and instructors, who are willing to use any and all means to train counsellors to understand not only the theories and practice of the profession but also the importance and usefulness of outreach activities. It is part of the MHC programme's goals to try to be creative and innovative in its teaching methods and approaches. Guest lecturers are invited to give brief presentations about their organizations and community involvements. A key ingredient towards the success of the programme is that it shuns formality and encourages both the student body and faculty to openly discuss important issues, especially those with cultural or communal significance.

A Hasidic man who graduated from the programme came as a guest to participate in a recent class discussion we had about drug use in the community. Most of the students in that class were of Hispanic background. After the class, one of the female students said: 'Everything that Rabbi Lebowitz refers to with regard to youth using drugs in his community can be applied in our community. The difference is that people seem to pull together more in his community − we should be doing more of that in our community.' We believe that this intercultural exchange is another key ingredient necessary to empower graduates towards positive change.

References

Aten, J. (2004) The College Campus Ministry Internship Site: interfacing religion and counseling, *Counseling and Values*, 49(1): 64.

Bilo, Y. and Witztum, E. (1993) Working with Jewish ultra-orthodox patients: guidelines for a culturally sensitive therapy, *Journal of Culture, Medicine and Psychiatry*, 17(2): 197–233.

Rogler, L.H., Malgady, R.G., Costantino, G. and Blumenthal, R. (1987) What do culturally sensitive mental health services mean? The case of Hispanics, *American Psychologist*, 42(6): 565–70.

Wieselberg, H. (1992) Family therapy and ultra-orthodox Jewish families: a structural approach, *Journal of Family Therapy*, 14(3): 305–29.

5 Identity development and its impact on the therapy relationship

Courtland C. Lee and GoEun Na

Introduction

A basic existential question which is common to all cultures is 'Who am I?' People all over the world, regardless of their cultural background, race or ethnicity are constantly attempting to develop an inner vision of themselves within a cultural context. It may be asked, 'Why is the answer to this question so important?' The response is that to understand who one is as a racial/ethnic being gives meaning to one's life and mediates one's relationship with self and others.

The struggle to answer the question 'Who am I?' has formed the basis of a number of psychosocial perspectives on how individuals form their identity. Developmental psychologists have considered the process of identity formation along a number of important dimensions. One of the most important of these is how people form an inner vision of themselves as racial/ethnic beings. Over the past several decades a number of racial/ethnic identity development models have emerged in the psychological literature which suggest that racial/ethnic identity formation is an important part of the psychosocial developmental process for people in any cultural context (Cross 1971; Phinney 1989; Helms 1990; Atkinson *et al.* 1993; Phinney and Ong 2007). Although the cultural context may vary given the emphasis placed on race or ethnicity in any given country, the process of forming a racial/ethnic identity is an important part of the psychosocial developmental process.

How a person views him or herself as a cultural being can have a profound impact on the counselling or psychotherapeutic relationship. This is true for both the counsellor/psychotherapist as well as the client. It also takes on a particular emphasis when the counsellor/psychotherapist and the client come from different racial/ethnic backgrounds. One of the basic components of a transcultural counselling or psychotherapeutic working alliance is an understanding of how the inner visions of both counsellor/psychotherapist and client impact the helping process (Carter 1995; Fischer and Moradi 2001; Cokley 2007; Helms 2007; Ponterotto and Park-Taylor 2007).

The purpose of this chapter is to present counsellors and psychotherapists with a conceptual framework for understanding how identity development impacts the working alliance. While there are many dimensions to identity development, given the multifaceted nature of culture, this chapter focuses on racial/ethnic identity development. Understanding how individuals develop an identity as a racial/ethnic being is a basic aspect of effective transcultural counselling and psychotherapy (Helms 1990; Atkinson and Thompson 1992; Carter 1995). The chapter begins with a contemporary perspective on the concepts of race and ethnicity. Next racial/ethnic identity are defined. This is followed by an analysis of the general process of racial/ethnic identity development. Two vignettes are then presented to demonstrate the potential impact that racial/ethnic identity development can have on the working alliance in counselling or psychotherapy.

Race versus ethnicity: a contemporary view

The terms 'race' and 'ethnicity' are generally used interchangeably. They are often both used to refer to groups of people who share similar physiological traits and/or personality characteristics. These traits and characteristics are either genetically transferred or have become reinforced through group association over long periods of time. However, these terms are not synonymous. Webster's dictionary defines *race* as, 'a category of humankind that shares certain distinctive physical traits'. These physical traits are things such as hair, eyes, skin colour, body shape etc. Whereas Webster defines the term *ethnic* in the following manner: 'of or relating to large groups of people classed according to common racial, national, tribal, religious, linguistic, or cultural origin or background'.

It can be argued that 'race' has become an archaic anthropological/biological classification of human differences that historically has been used as part of political, social, cultural and economic brutality and exploitation in many parts of the world. A classic example of this is Adolf Hitler's classifying Judaism (a religion and cultural experience) as a 'race' and perpetrating the Holocaust in the last century. This definition of race forms the core of the heinous phenomenon known as 'racism' (Lee 2001).

What is more important from a counselling/psychotherapeutic perspective, however, is not physiological/biological traits, but rather, personality characteristics among people that become reinforced through association over time. It is these long-standing dynamics of thinking, feeling and behaving that form the cultural aspects of nationality, religion and language. This makes implicit the significance of the concept of ethnicity as an important counselling or psychotherapeutic construct (Lee 2001).

While race and ethnicity are generally used interchangeably, they are qualitatively different in their meaning and emphasis. Throughout this chapter, both terms are used to examine the dynamics of identity development; however, implicit in this examination is an emphasis on ethnic identity development.

Racial/ethnic identity defined

Racial/ethnic identity refers to an individual's sense of belonging to a racial or ethnic group and the part of one's personality that is attributable to membership in that group. Racial/ethnic identity may be considered as the inner vision that a person possesses of him or herself as a member of a racial or ethnic group and as a unique human being. It forms the core of the beliefs, social forms and personality dimensions that characterize distinct racial/ethnic realities and world view for an individual (Lee 2006a). Racial/ethnic identity development is a major determinant of a person's attitudes towards him or herself, others of the same racial/ethnic group and others of different racial/ethnic groups (Atkinson *et al.* 1993; Sue *et al.* 1996).

Racial/ethnic identity development: a process

Racial/ethnic identity development occurs in a milieu characterized by complex social interactions among groups of people. Therefore, it is important to point out that most models of racial/ethnic identity development have been created in a context in which one group of people has been in a position of economic, political and social dominance while another group has been in a subordinate position. Specifically, one group has generally enjoyed privilege based on race/ethnicity and has been idealized and favoured in a common relationship with other racial/ethnic groups. This sense of racial or ethnic superiority has had an effect on both the racial/ethnic identity development of individuals within that group as well as those outside it. For example, whites have traditionally enjoyed racial privilege in their relationship with people of colour in many countries and cultural contexts (McIntosh 1989; Helms 1992). The privilege inherent in the dominant– subordinate relationship profoundly influences the attitudes of members of the dominant racial/ethnic group towards members of subordinate group(s). Likewise, the perceptions of this racial/ethnic privilege held by people from subordinate groups profoundly influences the attitudes they hold towards themselves and members of the dominant group (Atkinson *et al.* 1993; Helms 1995; Sue *et al.* 1996).

The dynamics of racial/ethnic identity development have traditionally been conceptualized as progressing through an evolutionary, linear stage process (Atkinson *et al.* 1993; Cross 1995) or, more recently, as a dynamic personality status process in which cultural information is simultaneously interpreted and internalized at a variety of levels (Helms 1995). Although theorists have presented different speculations about the specifics, the stages or levels of racial/ethnic identity development for people from racial/ethnic minority groups are theorized to progress in the following manner (Cross 1995; Lee 2006b):

- *Stage/phase 1*: this stage or phase of racial/ethnic identity development has been characterized as one of conformity on the part of people from racial/ethnic minority groups. A person at this stage will display a social and/or psychological distancing from their own racial/ethnic group. At the same time, a person will attempt a maximum social or psychological identification with a racial/ethnic group perceived to be in a dominant social position.

- *Stage/phase 2*: this stage has been characterized as a period of dissonance on the part of people from racial/ethnic minority groups. As a result of generally negative experiences or events with individuals from the dominant racial/ethnic group, a person begins to question the nature of his or her conformity and identification with this group.
- *Stage/phase 3*: at this stage people from racial/ethnic minority groups become involved in an immersion experience that brings them into direct contact with their own racial/ethnic cultural background. An individual generally embraces his or her own racial/ethnic sociocultural realities and attempts to fully relate to other members of his or her racial/ethnic group. This acceptance is often accompanied by a total rejection of the sociocultural realities of the dominant racial/ethnic group.
- *Stage/phase 4*: this stage is characterized by a period of reflection. An individual reflects on the meaning of him or herself as a racial/ethnic being. He or she generally questions the dichotomous nature of the complete acceptance of one's own racial/ethnic group and the categorical rejection of the realities of the dominant racial/ethnic group.
- *Stage/phase 5*: after the reflective process in stage 4, an individual engages in a transformative process of personality reintegration. The individual internalizes his or her awareness of self as a racial/ethnic being. This internalization is accompanied by an appreciation of one's own racial/ethnic group and a selective appreciation of the dominant racial/ethnic group.

Conversely, the process of identity development for individuals in dominant racial/ethnic groups seems to generally progress through the following stages or phases (Helms 1995; Lee 2006b):

- *Stage/phase 1*: at this stage an individual has limited awareness or appreciation of him or herself as a racial/ethnic being. A person is often oblivious to the realities of other racial/ethnic groups. At some level, a person feels that his or her race/ethnicity is superior to others. Key aspects of race/ethnicity are naively considered to be unimportant factors in human relationships (e.g. 'I don't see colour when I interact with people'). Also, because of inherent privileges that come with a dominant racial/ethnic social position, there is limited awareness of the sociopolitical influences regarding racism.
- *Stage/phase 2*: at this stage an individual's carefully constructed perceptions of race/ethnicity become unsettled due to events that challenge his or her privileged racial/ethnic position in society. Constructions of meaning concerning race/ethnicity disintegrate. The person often reacts with this disintegration with fear or confusion.
- *Stage/phase 3*: at this stage an individual often deals with the fear or confusion of the previous stage by distorting information about racial/ethnic diversity to enhance their own racial/ethnic status. The worst case scenario of this phase is characterized by extreme reactionary behaviour towards individuals from racial/ethnic minority groups.

- *Stage/phase 4*: an alternative way of distorting information about racial/ethnic diversity occurs at this stage. An individual champions the plight of those from racial/ethnic subordinate groups. However, this advocacy takes place at an intellectual level as opposed to their actually taking concrete action.
- *Stage/phase 5*: at this stage an individual attempts to move away from an intellectual perspective on issues of race/ethnicity. A major feature of this phase is an active attempt to change perceived racist attitudes and behaviours in one's own dominant cultural group. Guilt about one's privileged status leads to an attempt to immerse oneself in the realities of subordinate racial/ethnic groups. This is often accompanied by denigration of aspects of one's own racial/ethnic group.
- *Stage/phase 6*: an individual engages in an honest appraisal of him or herself as a cultural being in this stage. A person becomes introspective and assesses the categorical nature of his or her over-identification with subordinate groups and denigration of their own culture.
- *Stage/phase 7*: at this stage an individual develops new levels of understanding about him or herself as an autonomous racial/ethnic being. A person actively seeks true relationships with diverse racial/ethnic groups. He or she becomes fully aware of sociopolitical influences regarding racism and totally committed to eradicating systemic oppression.

While there may be significant variation in these stages or phases for those in both dominant and subordinate racial/ethnic groups, it is important to note that not everyone proceeds in a linear fashion through any racial/ethnic identity process. Environmental considerations, including family dynamics and general life experiences, make it possible that an individual may start their development at any stage or phase of this process. Additionally, as an individual progresses through the stages or phases of racial/ethnic identity development, it is possible that experiences with racism or other systemic factors of oppression may cause them to regress to an earlier level of development.

The impact of racial/ethnic identity development on counselling and psychotherapy relationships

The attitudes and perceptions that people develop about themselves and others as racial/ethnic beings have important implications for the counselling/psychotherapeutic relationship. An individual's racial/ethnic identity and one's attitudes about other racial/ethnic groups can significantly impact upon thoughts, feelings and behaviour. Therefore, racial/ethnic identity must be factored into the working alliance between counsellor/psychotherapist and client. An understanding of racial/ethnic identity development is an important aspect of the transcultural counselling and psychotherapy framework. The following two vignettes are presented to illustrate the impact of racial/ethnic identity development on counselling and psychotherapeutic relationships. Using a transactional analysis framework (Berne 1964), the impact of counsellor/psychotherapist and client stage/phase of racial/ethnic identity development on the working alliance will be explored.

Vignette 1

Figure 5.1 shows a statement by a black male client at the so-called immersion stage of racial/ethnic identity development for individuals from ethnic minority groups. This client comes to see a white male counsellor/psychotherapist for depression related to the inability to find a job. His anger appears to be related to his perception of racism in the employment process. Three possible responses from a white counsellor/psychotherapist are shown that would be reflective of

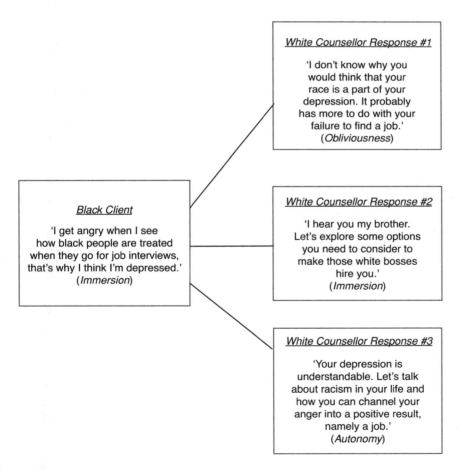

Figure 5.1 Vignette 1

three stages of racial/ethnic identity development on the part of the counsellor/ psychotherapist.

Response 1 would be indicative of a counsellor/psychotherapist who appears to be relatively oblivious to the racial realities that the client is experiencing. The counsellor/psychotherapist completely ignores both the client's anger and his perceptions of racism in the job-search process. These are not considered to be important from the counsellor/psychotherapist's point of view. It can be surmised that the counsellor/psychotherapist has a limited sense of his own racial/ethnic identity given the privilege that comes with his dominant racial/ethnic position in society.

It is obvious from this exchange that the client and the counsellor/ psychotherapist's levels of racial/ethnic identity development are not complementary or conducive to effective communication or counselling/therapeutic effectiveness. It can be speculated that the counsellor/psychotherapist's response will only serve to make the client angrier and, perhaps, validate his perceptions about racism.

Response 2 suggests that the counsellor/psychotherapist's level of racial/ethnic identity development has reached a stage of heightened awareness accompanied by a sense of advocacy for individuals in racial/ethnic minority groups. He attempts to develop an empathic bond with his black client based on a shared sense of anger about racism. While this interaction might be complementary and lead to an effective counselling/therapeutic outcome, the counsellor/psychotherapist runs the risk of being seen as overly familiar and possibly patronizing in his attempts to form a working alliance with the client. The client knows that the counsellor/psychotherapist is not his 'brother' and may take umbrage at this level of racial familiarity on the part of the counsellor/psychotherapist.

Response 3 is indicative of a counsellor/psychotherapist who is aware of himself as a racial/ethnic being and understands his role in the dominant social structure as a person with racial/ethnic privilege. His invitation to the client to explore racism and suggsestion as to how to channel his anger about it into a positive job search indicates the potential for complementary communication and a positive counselling/psychotherapeutic outcome. In such a situation, the client should feel that his anger and frustration regarding racism are being truly heard and understood while he is getting support for action that will ultimately lead to a job.

Vignette 2

Figure 5.2 shows a statement by a white male client who has been referred to counselling by a male physician who is concerned that the client's anger might lead to physical health problems. His statement suggests that there is fear and confusion regarding his perceptions of racial/ethnic reality. He fears that his privileged place in society is being threatened by those from racial/ethnic minority groups.

Response 1 suggests a counsellor/psychotherapist who displays a distinct distancing from his own racial/ethnic group and has a seemingly significant

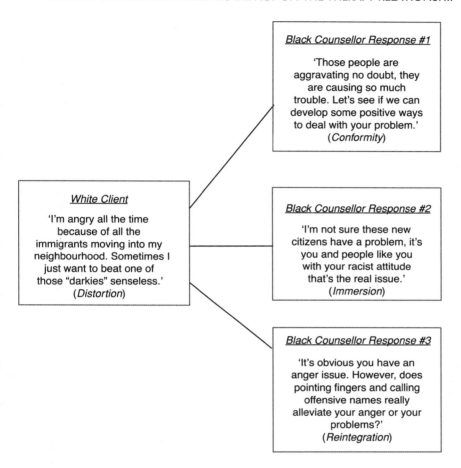

Figure 5.2 Vignette 2

over-identification with the client's racial/ethnic group. While the communication between counsellor/psychotherapist and client is complementary, the question must be asked: is the counsellor/psychotherapist helping the client or contributing to a larger systemic problem of racism?

Response 2 is indicative of a counsellor/psychotherapist whose racial/ethnic identity is strong with seemingly negative attitudes towards individuals in the dominant racial/ethnic group. It is evident that the communication in this exchange has the potential to develop into antagonism between the counsellor/psychotherapist and client that would jeopardize the possibility of a working alliance. From a racial/ethnic identity perspective, both the counsellor/psychotherapist and client are approaching this relationship from a place of anger.

Response 3 suggests a counsellor/psychotherapist who is comfortable with him-self as a racial/ethnic being and has developed a selective appreciation of the dominant racial/ethnic group. Rather than get angry at the client for his racist statement, the counsellor/psychotherapist is able to help the client channel that anger in a positive direction. The statement has the potential to facilitate comple-mentary communication because it diffuses the client's racial anger in a way that puts the onus on the client to direct his anger in more constructive ways.

What these vignettes make clear is that racial/ethnic identity development can significantly impact the therapeutic relationship. From a transactional analysis perspective, the levels of racial/ethnic identity of counsellor/psychotherapist and client can result in either complementary or crossed interactions. It is evident that the odds of a complementary cross-cultural interaction will be heightened if a counsellor/psychotherapist has achieved a level of racial/ethnic identity that is characterized by a strong inner vision of him/herself as a racial/ethnic being accompanied by an appreciation of racial/ethnic diversity. This will look differ-ent depending on whether the counsellor/psychotherapist is from a dominant racial/ethnic group or one that is in the minority. For a counsellor/psychotherapist from a dominant group, this entails developing new levels of understanding about him/herself as a racial/ethnic being and actively seeking true relationships with diverse racial/ethnic groups. It also involves becoming fully aware of the privilege associated with one's dominant racial/ethnic society. Conversely, for a counsellor/psychotherapist from a subordinate racial/ethnic group, this will involve internal-izing his or her awareness of self as a racial/ethnic being and developing a selec-tive appreciation of the dominant racial/ethnic group. It is from these levels of racial/ethnic identity development that complementary interactions with clients regardless of their level of racial/ethnic identity development will be assured.

Conclusion

One of the basic concepts to consider in a transcultural counselling or psychothera-peutic working alliance is understanding how the inner visions of both counsellor/psychotherapist and client impact the helping process. Knowledge of the devel-opmental process of how individuals develop an identity as a racial/ethnic being is a basic aspect of effective transcultural counselling and psychotherapy. Theo-rists and researchers have considered the impact of racial/ethnic identity on the working alliance for several decades (Carter 1995). The most important lesson for counsellors and psychotherapists that comes out of this scholarly consideration is that upon entering any therapeutic relationship one must ask oneself, 'Who am I as a racial/ethnic being and will my inner vision of myself affect the work-ing alliance?' The next question that must be considered is, 'How does my client appear to be making meaning as a racial/ethnic being?' These questions take on great significance when a client is from a different racial/ethnic background and the counselling/psychotherapeutic relationship becomes transcultural in nature.

References

Atkinson, D.R. and Thompson, C.E. (1992) Racial, ethnic, and cultural variables in counseling, in S.D. Brown and R.W. Lent (eds) *Handbook of Counseling Psychology*, 2nd edn. New York: Wiley.

Atkinson, D.R., Morten, G. and Sue, D.W. (1993) *Counseling American Minorities: A Cross-cultural Perspective*, 4th edn. Madison, WI: Brown & Benchmark.

Berne, E. (1964) *Games People Play: The Psychology of Human Relationships*. New York: Ballentine Books.

Carter, R.T. (1995) *The Influence of Race and Racial Identity in Psychotherapy: Towards a Racially Inclusive Model*. New York: Wiley.

Cokley, K.O. (2007) Critical issues in the measurement of ethnic and racial identity: a referendum on the state of the field, *Journal of Counseling Psychology*, 54: 224–39.

Cross, W.E. (1971) The Negro-to-Black conversion experience: toward a psychology of Black liberation, *Black World*, 20: 13–27.

Cross, W.E. (1995). The psychology of Nigrescence: revising the Cross model, in J.G. Ponterotto, J.M. Casas, L.A. Suzuki and C.M. Alexander (eds) *Handbook of Multicultural Counseling*. Thousand Oaks, CA: Sage.

Fischer, A.R. and Moradi, B. (2001) Racial and ethnic identity: recent developments and needed directions, in J.G. Ponterotto, J.M. Casas, L.A. Suzuki and C.M. Alexander (eds) *Handbook of Multicultural Counseling*, 2nd edn. Thousand Oaks, CA: Sage.

Helms, J.E. (ed.) (1990) *Black and White Racial Identity: Theory, Research, and Practice*. Westport, CT: Greenwood Press.

Helms, J.E. (1992) *A Race as a Nice Thing to Have: A Guide to Being a White Person or Understanding the White Persons in Your Life*. Topeka, KS: Content Communications.

Helms, J.E. (1995) An update of Helms's white and people of color racial identity models., in J.G. Ponterotto, J.M. Casas, L.A. Suzuki and C.M. Alexander (eds) *Handbook of Multicultural Counseling*. Thousand Oaks, CA: Sage.

Helms, J.E. (2007) Some better practices for measuring racial and ethnic identity constructs, *Journal of Counseling Psychology*, 54: 235–46.

Lee, C.C. (2001) Defining and responding to racial and ethnic diversity, in D.C. Locke, J.E. Myers, and E.L. Herr (eds) *The Handbook of Counseling*. Thousand Oaks, CA: Sage.

Lee, C.C. (ed.) (2006a) *Multicultural Issues in Counseling: New Approaches to Diversity*, 3rd edn. Alexandria, VA: American Counseling Association.

Lee, C.C. (2006b) Updating the models of identity development, in C. Lago (ed.) *Race, Culture and Counselling*. Maidenhead: Open University Press.

McIntosh, P. (1989) White privilege: unpacking the invisible knapsack, *Peace and Freedom*, 2: 10–12.

Phinney, J. (1989) Stages of ethnic identity development in minority group adolescents, *Journal of Early Adolescence*, 9: 34–49.

Phinney, J.S. and Ong, A.D. (2007) Conceptualization and measurement of ethnic identity: current status and future directions, *Journal of Counseling Psychology*, 54: 271–81.

Ponterotto, J.G. and Park-Taylor, J. (2007) Racial and ethnic identity theory, measurement, and research in counseling psychology: present status and future directions, *Journal of Counseling Psychology*, 54: 282–94.

Sue, D.W., Ivey, A.E. and Pedersen, P.B. (1996) *A Theory of Multicultural Counseling and Therapy*. Pacific Grove, CA: Brooks/Cole Publishing.

6 On ethnic matching: a review of the research and considerations for practice, training and policy

Farkhondeh Farsimadan, Addila Khan and Riccardo Draghi-Lorenz

Introduction

This chapter presents an overview of the research on the effects of ethnic matching (EM) between therapist and client on therapy process and outcome. Racial differences in therapy received some attention in the late 1940s but no systematic empirical study was carried out, and by the 1950s interest in the area had faded (Atkinson 1985). A review of the research carried out in the 1960s (Sattler 1970, in Sattler 1977) found only three relevant studies but, since then, enough research has been carried out for a number of reviews and meta-analyses to also be published.

Their conclusions, however, appear contradictory. Early reviews of studies exploring process variables (e.g. preference for therapist ethnicity, client self-disclosure, perceived therapist credibility and facilitative conditions) and outcome variables (e.g. client satisfaction and willingness to return, dropout rates and length of treatment) found either no significant effect of EM (Sattler 1977) or an even split between studies reporting an effect and those that did not (Harrison 1975; Abramowitz and Murray 1983; Atkinson 1983, 1985). Later reviews, instead, suggest that EM can be beneficial for both process and outcome. Sue *et al.* (1994), for instance, conclude that conditions such as EM, culturally responsive treatment and pre-therapy interventions are associated with effectiveness for at least some ethnic groups. Atkinson and Lowe (1995) also found that most ethnic minority clients preferred an ethnically similar therapist, and that some considered such a therapist more credible and also benefited more from seeing them than an ethnically dissimilar therapist. In a third review, Gray-Little and Kaplan (2000) suggest that, other things being equal, ethnic similarity may reduce the social distance and enhance the likelihood of shared beliefs and experiences between client and therapist, thus facilitating the therapeutic alliance and outcome. Nonetheless, in the latest review, Karlsson (2005) argues that 'the empirical support for ethnic matching is, at best, inconclusive and lacks a foundation of rigorous research designs' and that, as a result, 'the role of ethnic matching in therapy has been left essentially unexplored' (p. 124). Karlsson concludes that: 'Until such [valid] research findings have been generated, clinicians are left with making decisions regarding the need for ethnic matching based on unclear research findings and clinical lore, which hardly provides the information that is needed' (p. 125).

In our view, not only have studies using novel methodologies recently become available but the problems affecting the research on EM are also not different from those that affect much psychological research generally. In fact, we find Karlsson's conclusions curiously negative, for a careful analysis of the research actually suggests several *fundamental* practical considerations. Here we shall consider findings from: (i) old studies using analogue designs; (ii) large studies of archival data from actual clients; (iii) recent studies of process and outcome as measured over time; and (iv) new, in-depth qualitative studies of client experiences. Instead of reviewing individual studies, where possible we discuss reviews and meta-analyses, with a critical focus on Karlsson's paper. We will then consider the implications for therapy, training and policy in the conclusion.

Analogue studies

Like much of the social-psychological research from the 1960s to the 1980s, early studies on the effects of EM in therapy used primarily US college students as participants in analogue designs, with brief sessions either simulated using participants as clients or presented to participants via audiotapes, videotapes, vignettes or transcripts. Lopez *et al.* (1991) subdivided these studies into those that used a simple-choice method (preference paradigm) and those that used a paired-comparison method (perception paradigm). In the simple-choice method, participants are asked to express a preference for one of two or more simulations with ethnically matched/unmatched dyads. In the paired-comparison method participants are asked to rank their preference for therapist ethnicity but also other variables (e.g. therapist age, gender, level of education, similarity of values/attitudes).

In a large meta-analysis, Coleman *et al.* (1995) found that, overall, participants in analogue studies show a significant preference for – and more positive perceptions of – ethnically similar over dissimilar therapists, that paired-comparison studies tend to achieve a smaller effect size over simple-choice studies (d = 0.20 versus d = 0.73), and that the effect of ethnic differences is reduced when participants are affiliated to the therapist's culture. In his review, Karlsson (2005) dismisses analogue studies, arguing that: (i) results from simple-choice studies are inconsistent; (ii) those from paired-comparison studies show that, when given choice, participants rank other therapist characteristics higher than ethnicity; and (iii) in their meta-analysis Coleman *et al.* (1995) found a smaller effect size achieved with paired-comparison over simple-choice studies. However, these criticisms are puzzling. First, the effect sizes reported by Coleman *et al.* run counter to Karlsson's first point, namely that results from simple-choice studies are inconsistent, as these are precisely the studies reporting a particularly strong effect. Second, the observation that (in some studies) the effect of other background variables can be stronger than that of ethnicity is no ground to dismiss it. Third, a weakened effect of ethnicity in paired-comparison studies is precisely what to expect when considering it together with other significant variables.

Admittedly, because analogue studies only involve brief contacts between participants and hypothetical therapists and/or present participants with a snapshot record of a therapy session, they cannot represent the intricacies of preferences and perceptions that emerge with time in real therapeutic relationships. Karlsson is right to argue that these studies 'might inform us more about a person's perceptions, attitudes about race, and interpersonal attractions across race than about actual psychotherapy' (2005: 119). Nonetheless, it is reasonable to hypothesize that initial reduced preferences and negative perceptions in ethnically different dyads negatively affect process variables such as therapist credibility and the working alliance, which strongly predict outcome. Additionally, since analogue studies typically recruited US college students, who tend to be young, comparatively educated/acculturated, culturally conscious, liberal politically and non-racist, their findings may actually underestimate the strength of intraethnic preferences and interethnic negative perceptions in other sections of the population, not to mention of populations outside the USA.

Archival studies

Archival studies utilize existing records from the general client population and thus benefit from higher ecological validity than analogue studies. However, few services routinely employ direct measures of process (e.g. working alliance, perceived therapist credibility, client self-disclosure etc.) or actual outcome (i.e. difference between pre- and post-therapy functioning); by and large these studies use indirect measures such as premature termination, duration of treatment, post-therapy use of intensive services or overall post-therapy functioning.

Archival studies tend to show that, particularly when accompanied by linguistic matching, EM significantly increases therapy uptake and duration, and reduces early dropout. Flaskerud (1986), for instance, examined the case records of 300 African-American, Mexican, Asian-American and white clients treated in four community mental health centres and found that linguistic and ethnic match significantly reduced dropout and increased attendance (see also Flaskerud and Liu 1990). In another study, Flaskerud (1991) examined files from 1,746 Asian-American clients and found that both linguistic and ethnic match significantly increased attendance, and EM also significantly reduced dropout. In a study on 1,000 Asian-American women, Fujino et al. (1994) found that both ethnic and gender match were significantly associated with reduced dropout and increased treatment duration. In one of the few randomized controlled trials available, Mathews et al. (2002) examined the effect of EM among 5,983 inpatients by assigning African-Americans, Hispanics and Asian-Americans to three ethnically focused psychiatric inpatient units. They found that, for Asian-Americans and Hispanics, matching was associated with a significantly greater likelihood of accepting outpatient or residential treatment referrals and a significantly lower likelihood of referrals to locked facilities.

Archival data also suggest that EM may significantly improve outcome for some groups, again, especially when accompanied by linguistic matching. Analysing data from more than 13,000 outpatient service clients, Sue *et al.* (1991) found that for all the ethnic minority groups included (Asian-, Mexican-, African- and Caucasian-Americans) EM predicted notably longer treatment and, with the exception of African-Americans, substantially lower dropout. EM also predicted outcome (with pre-treatment functioning controlled for) for Asian-Americans and approached significance for Asian-Americans ($p < 0.06$), although effect sizes were small. In Asian- and Mexican-Americans who were non-native English speakers, instead, EM predicted outcome to a clinically relevant degree. Archival psychotherapy studies outside the USA lag behind but in Australia, Ziguras *et al.* (2003) examined the effects of matching clients from a non-English-speaking background with bilingual, bicultural clinicians for 2,935 psychiatric clients. They found that ethnic minority clients (Vietnamese, Greek, Italian, Macedonian) who were matched with bilingual clinicians had longer and more frequent contacts with community care teams and fewer and shorter contacts with crisis teams. Clients matched with a bilingual clinician also benefited from fewer and shorter hospital admissions than even Australian-born clients.

Similar effects of EM on outcome for some minorities are also reported in large US studies of young people. Examining data from 4,616 young Caucasian-, Mexican-, African- and Asian-American subjects, Yeh *et al.* (1994a) found that while EM did not significantly predict dropout, treatment duration and post-therapy functioning in children, it predicted dropout to a clinically significant degree in adolescents from all three minorities considered and also duration in Mexican- and Asian-American adolescents. By contrast, in a study of 4,695 African-, Asian- and Hispanic-American children and adolescents, Jerrell (1998) found that when ethnically matched they tended to stay longer in outpatient treatment and used less intensive services irrespective of age group. And in a study of 912 Asian-American children, Yeh *et al.* (1994b) found that those attending centres providing EM therapy (71 per cent of cases) benefited more from reduced dropout, increased service use and post-therapy functioning than those attending mainstream centres (8 per cent matching), also when social class and pre-therapy functioning were controlled for.

Perhaps because they tend to belong to the same mainstream linguistic and cultural group, EM may affect African-Americans and Caucasian-Americans less than other US ethnicities. In a recent meta-analysis of results for African-American and white clients drawn from 10 published and unpublished studies, Shin *et al.* (2005) found no significant effect of EM on: (i) dropout; (ii) total number of sessions attended; and (iii) overall functioning. However, the conclusion that EM is clinically irrelevant for African- and Caucasian-Americans would be incorrect. Shin *et al.* used random effects analysis, which yields a conservative measure of combined effects. A closer look at the studies from this very meta-analysis finds that the majority reported significant effects of EM on dropout and duration of treatment for both African-Americans and Caucasian-Americans, with effects ranging from weak to strong – i.e. suggesting that EM can affect dropout and treatment duration to a clinically significant degree. With regard to overall post-therapy functioning, the results from this meta-analysis lend themselves to many different interpretations. In addition, post-therapy functioning is not a good measure of outcome as it is most strongly predicted by pre-therapy functioning. The only study which used data on change in well-being over time (derived data from clients with severe diagnoses of psychotic or mood disorders) included Asian- and Latino-Americans and confirmed a clearer association between matching and positive outcome (as measured by therapist) for these groups over African- and Caucasian-Americans (Gamst *et al.* 2000). However, the authors argue that results for African-Americans were possibly affected by greater psychopathology over the other minorities and a paucity of African-American therapists, and conclude that:

> For African Americans matching may be more important for clients who embrace their racial identity and disparage White American values ... Without controlling for racial identity status (i.e. Afrocentrism) of African American clients during intake, preference and no preference clients are indiscriminantly lumped together to yield equivocal results (p. 562).

Although very few archival studies find no effect of EM on therapy (e.g. Martin 1994), Karlsson states that 'Unfortunately, archival studies have not produced consistent findings regarding the benefits of ethnic matching in psychotherapy (Sue *et al.* 1994)'[1] (2005: 116). Karlsson then refers to meta-analysis of 125 studies on psychotherapy dropout where Wierzbicki and Pekanik (1993) found that client ethnicity (white or non-white) was a weaker predictor of dropout than both socioeconomic status (SES) and level of education. He fails, however, to mention that these were the only three significant factors from an original pool of as many as 32 variables covering study characteristics, client and therapist demographics, psychological factors and type of therapy. Furthermore, while SES had a notably stronger effect ($d = 0.37$) than both level of education and ethnic background, these had comparable and clinically significant effects ($d = 0.28$ and $d = 0.23$ respectively).[2] Moreover, Wierzbicki and Pekanik not only employed a gross measure of ethnicity (white/non-white), collapsing together the effects of different ethnic backgrounds, but client ethnicity was also not a measure of EM. Because a proportion of therapists were non-white, their white clients were mismatched and their non-white clients matched (or mismatched with a therapist from a different ethnic minority), which could have reduced the dropout difference between whites and non-whites.

---

[1] Interestingly, Sue *et al.* actually argue that archival studies overall suggest that EM in therapy can be beneficial.

[2] The studies included were conducted between 1974 and 1990 and a meta-analysis including older studies by Garfield (1986) yielded very similar results.

Admittedly, Karlsson also relies on the results of a meta-analysis by Maramba and Hall (2002) of seven US archival studies on EM as a predictor of dropout, utilization and client's level of post-therapy functioning in either white or ethnic minority clients. This meta-analysis shows that for ethnic minority clients matching was significantly associated with reduced dropout ($p < 0.0001$) and increased attendance ($p < 0.0001$) but, as stressed by Karlsson, 'the effect sizes were so small that the authors ruled out EM as a clinically significant predictor of outcome' (2005: 116). In his conclusions on the validity of archival data, Karlsson also refers to Maramba and Hall's meta-analysis and states that: 'Finally, the effect sizes of archival studies are minimal, which may indicate that the significant results might be related to the enormous sample sizes in these studies' (p. 120). However, this conclusion relies on a small meta-analysis, published as a brief report and which, again, fails to consider the effects of: (i) averaging results from many individuals from the same group and, especially, (ii) lumping together results from different ethnic groups. Of the seven studies included in Maramba and Hall's meta-analysis (some of which are unpublished), two account for as much as 75 to 100 per cent of clients in each analysis. Most strikingly, overall these two studies (Sue *et al.* 1991; Yeh *et al.* 1994a) report clinically and statistically significant effect sizes for dropout and duration for all/most ethnic minorities and age groups considered. Because Maramba and Hall did not differentiate between these groups, in their meta-analysis these effects are lost altogether.

Eventually, even Karlsson admits that 'Findings from archival studies do suggest that ethnic matching is important' (2005: 120). In line with other reviewers (e.g. Sue *et al.* 1994), we conclude that archival studies show that EM tends to reduce dropout, increase retention and also facilitate positive outcome, at least for some ethnic groups and especially (but not only) when associated with language matching. Overall archival data also suggest that EM can be a factor of clinical relevance for many individuals from all groups, even when effect sizes for the group as a whole are not strong. Nonetheless, with some exceptions, archival studies fail to provide direct measures of outcome and, especially, process, which means that they cannot be used to test the idea that EM affects outcome because of its effects on process.

Studies using direct measures of process and outcome

To address these methodological shortcomings, some researchers have examined the effects of EM on direct measures of process and outcome over time. Ricker *et al.* (1999) examined ethnic similarity, working alliance and therapeutic outcome among 19 ethnically similar and 32 ethnically dissimilar therapeutic dyads engaged in brief therapy (maximum six sessions) at a university counselling centre. Outcome was significantly more positive in similar over dissimilar dyads but no relationship between ethnic similarity and working alliance was found; nor, surprisingly, was a relationship found between the latter and therapeutic outcome. This runs counter to what we know about the strong relationship between working alliance and outcome (e.g. Horvath and Symonds 1991; Horvath and Luborsky 1993) and it is possible that the small sample, the beneficial characteristics of college students highlighted above in relation to analogue studies and the brevity of therapy all limited differences in working alliance ratings.

In a similar but much larger study, Erdur *et al.* (2000, 2003) considered data from 4,483 African-American, Asian-American, Hispanic and white clients (students) and 376 therapists from 42 university/college counselling centres. Like other archival studies they found that ethnic mismatching was associated with fewer sessions attended. Surprisingly, they also found only a small relationship between outcome and working alliance (as rated by clients = 0.15) and no evidence that EM affected either the working alliance or outcome. These results are confusing but the final analysis was conducted on 2,154 dyads with only 70 ethnic minority matches (32 African-American, 1 Asian-American, 37 Hispanic) lumped together with 1,484 white matches, which may have over-run any positive effect of ethnic minority matching. Analyses of working alliance and outcome in individual minorities as a function of therapist ethnicity were also conducted but the numbers were then small. In addition, the brevity of treatment (four to six sessions) and beneficial characteristics of college students may have again weakened the relationship between working alliance and outcome and the effects of EM respectively.

Other studies employing direct measures of process and/or outcome conducted with young people from the general US population report rather different results. For instance, Wintersteen *et al.* (2005) examined the effects of gender and racial differences between therapist and client on the therapeutic alliance and treatment retention in a randomized trial with 600 adolescent substance abusers. They found that gender-matched dyads reported better alliances and were more likely to complete treatment, and that EM predicted greater retention and therapist-rated therapeutic alliance. In a study examining treatment outcomes of family therapy with 86 highly acculturated Hispanic and white substance-abusing adolescents, Flicker *et al.* (2008) found that whereas EM had no effects for white adolescents, EM Hispanic adolescents showed significantly greater reduction in their substance use than non-matched ones.

Some studies have also been carried out in western countries outside the USA. In the Netherlands, Knipscheer and Kleber (2004a) examined the contribution of ethnicity to perceived therapist characteristics and treatment satisfaction in 82 Turkish and 58 Moroccan clients. Clients generally considered clinical competence and compassion more important than EM and those seen by a native Dutch therapist reported similar satisfaction as those who were ethnically matched. However, while more than half of clients did not prefer EM, a substantial number of ethnic minority clients (especially Turkish clients) rated it as very important. In addition, because only 18 clients were ethnically matched against 92 who were not (and of 14 therapists only 2 were Turkish and 2 Moroccan), individual client/therapist factors may have overridden EM effects. In another study with 96 Surinamese migrants to the Netherlands, the same authors (2004b) found that while a considerable minority of clients reported compassion and expertise to be more relevant than ethnic background, the latter was a strong predictor for satisfaction in ethnic minority clients. Overall these results are consistent with the hypothesis that when EM affects outcome it is because of its effect on process.

To overcome some of the limitations in the available evidence, Farsimadan *et al.* (2007) examined the effects of EM on the working alliance, perceived therapist credibility and therapy outcome over time (difference between pre- and post-therapy global severity index) in 100 ethnic minority clients in London. All clients and therapists were South-Asian, Black-African, Black-Caribbean or Middle-Eastern; clients in matched dyads had expressed a preference for matching, and therapy was between 6 and 12 sessions. Outcome and process variables were significantly better in matched than in non-matched dyads, with notable effect sizes (adj. $R^2 = 0.194$ for outcome, 0.782 for working alliance, 0.768 for therapist credibility), whereas age, gender and length of therapy did not predict outcome or process. The two process variables were measured at different times in therapy but still almost perfectly correlated to one another, suggesting that process quality was established early on in therapy. Most importantly, however, the process variables were also found to fully mediate the relationship between EM and outcome, providing the strongest evidence to date that EM can affect therapy outcome because of its effect on process.

To test whether these results were not due to minority–minority mismatching, Khan *et al.* (in preparation) examined the dynamics between working alliance and therapy outcome in 236 dyads with white majority therapists and clients either from this majority or a South-Asian minority. Again, outcome and working alliance were significantly better in matched than in non-matched dyads, effect sizes were clinically as well as statistically significant (adj. $R^2 = 0.115$ for outcome, 0.56 for working alliance) and the working alliance fully mediated between matching and outcome. Age, gender and SES had no effect on process and outcome, and length of therapy (4 to 22 sessions) had a significant but weak effect on both. This study also considered five culture-sensitive characteristics that may negatively impact the process of therapy in mismatched dyads, namely pretence/secrecy with therapist, perceived stereotyping, self-concealment, social desirability and client change from their original culture. All these culture-sensitive factors significantly differentiated between the two groups of clients, predicted the working alliance and, with the exception of cultural change, also therapy outcome. Most interestingly, however, whereas culture-sensitive factors related to therapist–client dyads (pretence/secrecy with therapist, perceived therapist stereotyping) also moderated the relationship between ethnicity and working alliance, those related to client background characteristics (self-concealment, social desirability, cultural change) did not. This suggests that emergent relational dynamics, rather than South-Asian relational tendencies per se, contributed to working alliance problems in mixed dyads, and provides the first evidence to date that the effect of specific cultural differences contributes to the negative effect of mismatching on process.

Most of these studies were not available to Karlsson's review and he notes that: 'There are few actual studies of psychotherapy that investigate ethnic matching per se ... Of the few studies that are available, most suggest that ethnic matching does not affect the outcome of therapy' (2005: 124). Here he refers to four studies, of which two are the studies limited to US college students and reviewed above (Ricker *et al.* 1999; Erdur *et al.* 2003), one (Jones 1982) excluded clients who attended less than eight sessions (and by admission of its author might have thus selected out a proportion of its ethnic minority clients), and another was only published as a brief non-peer-reviewed letter and did not actually report any comparative results or data on EM (Littlewood *et al.* 1992).

We are not aware of any meta-analysis of studies involving direct measures of process and outcome. Karlsson duly notes that in their meta-analysis of therapy effectiveness, Smith *et al.* (1980) conclude that therapist–client similarity was related to positive outcomes. He then immediately adds, however, that in a meta-analysis of seven studies of the effect of EM on outcome, Lamb and Jones (1998) found effect sizes ranging from −0.09 to 0.68, with a very small overall effect size (d = 0.02), 'which they concluded could not support the singular concept of ethnic matching' (Karlsson 2005: 120). This is an unpublished manuscript and we cannot comment on its conclusions as reported by Karlsson. However, a range in effect size from −0.09 to 0.68 is fully consistent with data from archival studies, suggesting that matching can be unimportant for some groups/clients but very important for others.

In brief, like analogue and archival studies, published studies using direct measures of process and outcome tend to suggest that EM is a clinically as well as statistically significant factor, at least in brief or medium-term therapies, for most minorities considered thus far in large multiethnic western cities. In our published contribution, we could also confirm the widespread hypothesis that EM affects outcome because of its effects on process. In addition, in another study we found that while a number of culture-sensitive background and therapy-related factors differentiated between white and South-Asian clients (working with white therapists) and predicted process and outcome, only those inherent to the relation with the therapist contributed to the effect of matching on process. These findings are important and yet they only start to provide detail on the intricacies of the effects of EM/mismatching on the process and hence outcome of therapy.

Qualitative studies

Qualitative data are typically derived from small non-representative numbers of participants; however, when inserted within the broader picture sketched by quantitative data they afford a detailed understanding of how and why EM can affect therapy, which is very useful for practitioners.

Chang and Berk (2009) used a consensual qualitative analysis of interviews to compare the experiences of eight satisfied and eight dissatisfied clients from various Asian, Latino and mixed-race ethnic minorities in New York who saw a Caucasian-American therapist. Differences revolved around expectations met/unmet, emotional connectedness/disconnectedness with the therapist, happiness around therapy ending and interest/disinterest in continuing/resuming the relationship with the therapist. Discriminative therapist factors included: an active versus passive therapist role; self-disclosure; professionalism; attentiveness versus negligence; and acceptance versus criticism. Interestingly, therapist cultural competence did not really feature in the narratives of satisfied clients but cultural incompetence was prominent for dissatisfied ones. All satisfied clients stressed the importance of therapeutic skills and tasks over ethnic differences that, instead, were often described as irrelevant to the presenting problems. Nonetheless, some satisfied clients experienced alienation from their own ethnic group and most reported compartmentalizing ethnic differences out of therapy, efforts from themselves and therapists to bridge differences and some identification with their therapist. The authors conclude that despite the 'universality' of the core therapy processes 'the dynamics of racial/ethnic mismatches introduce unique challenges to the therapy relationship that may require attention and flexible adaptation of basic therapy skills' (2009: 532). They also warn against the possibility of therapist micro-aggressions due to cultural incompetence and note that 'whereas affective disconnection and premature termination are obvious consequences of failed efforts to negotiate cross-racial therapy interactions, the costs and benefits of client bridging strategies such as compartmentalizing race remain unclear' (p. 534).

To explore how ethnically matched clients may experience process and outcome, and the ways in which demographic similarities influence these variables, Farsimadan (2003) used interpretive phenomenological analysis of interviews with 12 matched clients from various ethnic minorities in London (West Indian, Indian, Pakistani, Iranian, Nigerian, Iraqi, Lebanese). All participants reported fairly positive experiences of therapy and the facilitative themes emerging from the analysis included: sharing the same ethnic/cultural background; empathic understanding and acceptance; same-gender experiences and understanding; therapist experience and maturity. Six participants argued that their presenting problems were related to race/ethnicity and only someone ethnically similar could understand them. Most black participants identified white culture/society as the source of their problem and cultural mistrust as the key determining factor in their choice of an ethnically matched therapist. For Asian participants, instead, family and relationship issues determined their choice in this sense. Three participants were matched by chance, of which two reported that, because of their experience, in future they would express a preference for EM.

In a study with mismatched dyads, Khan (2005) used the same methodology to explore the experiences of eight South-Asian clients in London who ended prematurely, with a white psychodynamic therapist. Themes identified included: secrecy and trust; a tendency to present a socially desirable self; negotiating/wrestling with own culture of origin; therapist empathy and understanding; expectations met/unmet; emotions about leaving therapy; own insecurities/transference/projections. Participants explained that issues related to these themes led them to withhold information for fear of being judged and stereotyped. All participants argued that their therapist ethnicity became particularly prominent for them when their problems were related to race/culture.

Conclusion

Conclusions from reviews and meta-analyses may appear contradictory but on close analysis the data actually paint a fairly clear picture. Analogue studies suggest that, along with other characteristics, people prefer an ethnically matched therapist. Archival data suggest that (other things being equal) this preference can have important clinical implications as ethnic dissimilarity is often associated with reduced therapy uptake, increased premature dropout, reduced duration and post-therapy functioning. Studies using direct measures of process and outcome confirm the hypothesis that mismatching can hinder outcome because of its negative effects on process. With some natural between-group and within-group variation, this picture holds across most ethnicities and age groups considered.

Clearly, when working with a client from a different ethnic background we should seriously consider the potential for added difficulties. But what should we look out for? Some authors (e.g. Karlsson) argue that it is not ethnic mismatching per se that may be problematic and point the finger at intervening factors such as language, levels of acculturation, affiliation to one's own culture of origin, client education, SES, the therapist's cultural competence etc. These factors, however, are not independent of ethnicity but, rather, its constituents. Were we to strip ethnicity of all linguistic, cultural, religious, educational and socioeconomic differences, there would be little left other than perhaps physical differences (in skin, hair, body and facial features) that in themselves really cannot affect therapy. In other words, differences in 'intervening variables' play a role because this is what ethnicity is about.

One may argue that when these differences are identified they may be also worked with, since process and outcome in many mismatched dyads are comparable to those in matched dyads. But what happens there? Next to quantitative results, qualitative ones suggest that when ethnic differences do not affect therapy it is because they do not interfere with basic conditions such as perceived acceptance, emotional connectedness, empathic understanding, genuineness, clarity of communication and, overall, a positive therapy process. Whether this follows the therapist's and/or in fact the client's skills and cultural competence, however, remains unclear. Quantitative data suggest that reduced differences in the constituents of ethnicity (e.g. language and culture) play an important role, and that often it is the client's acculturation — i.e. their competence in the host culture, that counterbalances therapist cultural incompetence. Qualitative data also indicate that clients who are struggling with aspects of their own culture (e.g. around sexuality or social/family roles) may particularly benefit from working with a white western therapist, and that to increase perceived similarity clients may also 'bracket out' issues related to ethnic differences and focus on other similarities within the dyad (e.g. of gender, sexuality, politics or world view). However, the research also indicates that, especially when differences are strong, clients in mismatched dyads often drop out prematurely, and when they stay they are less likely to benefit from positive process and hence outcome. This is striking since data are typically collected from therapists who work in multicultural cities, often for cross-cultural centres, and benefit from relevant training/experience, good intentions and open minds.

In our view there are at least three interrelated concurrent processes that can render therapy with ethnically different clients so difficult. First, clients may come to an ethnically similar/dissimilar therapist with a positive/negative assumption about being understood, which will self-fulfil in that they will be more or less open and trusting. Second, people naturally give prominence to aspects of reality that fit their assumptions, so that, in therapy, negative (and not necessarily conscious) stereotypes about the other's ethnic background would automatically block the development of a positive process. Third, but most importantly, clients and therapists may simply fail to understand each other, and not just because of their different cultural values and experiences. For instance, much affective information is exchanged, especially in the initial sessions, that makes the client and the therapist feel whether they can connect or not. Affective communication also tends to be non-verbal, implicit and deeply affected by cultural ways of relating to others, especially others of a given gender, age, social class, sexual identity etc. Cultures can also differ in the ways they deal with the same affects — for instance, in how and when they should be manifested, or the very meaning ascribed to their occurrence and manifestations. These differences develop in early interactions with significant others and continue to be affected by one's cultural milieu throughout development. As cultural idiosyncrasies they also operate automatically below one's immediate awareness and control and can thus generate misunderstandings in mismatched dyads that are difficult to avoid or sort out. A Caucasian male therapist may not hold any negative assumption about a South-Asian female client but still perceive her, say, secrecy and socially desirable self-presentation, as withdrawn and manipulative. She could then similarly perceive his ensuing uneasiness as withdrawn and also as expressing a negative judgement or even racist attitude.

Clearly, practitioners should gather as much information as possible on the cultural background of their clients. Special attention to the individual's culture, beliefs, values and needs (e.g. individuation versus collectivism, focus on family, respect for the elderly, how love and affect are expressed, etc.) is paramount. In addition, sensitivity and particular attention to the individual's mode of acculturation to the host culture (assimilation, integration, separation, marginalization — Berry 1980), their acculturative stress and cultural commitments are also important. However, how much knowledge of how many cultures and modes of acculturation is really possible? Knowing a culture well will require years of continued contact. Some comfort can be found in qualitative data suggesting that problems stem more from making assumptions than not knowing, as clients seem to note cultural incompetence more than cultural competence. Maybe, even when (we think) we understand someone's cultural background, an open attitude of not knowing (enough) may be best.

In summary, when working with ethnically different clients we should pay extraordinary attention to the therapeutic relationship and alliance, and facilitative conditions such as empathic understanding, respect for difference, positive regard, a seriously open attitude of not knowing, etc. A consistent finding within this review is support for similar therapeutic factors. Interestingly, these are shared across most therapeutic approaches and yet both quantitative and qualitative data indicate that, all too often, ethnic differences can still undermine a positive therapy process and outcome. Ultimately, therefore, the obvious way forward must be to offer more EM than is currently available. Universities and professional bodies in counselling and psychotherapy should make a concerted effort to recruit more ethnic minority trainees. Mental health services need to be more proactive and place a greater emphasis on recruitment and career promotion of ethnic minority professionals, to be able to offer optimal mental health services to people of all ages from this rapidly growing client group. Training therapists to work with clients from different ethnicities is an ethical duty and can only help, but the data suggest that this may not suffice. Needless to say, EM should be offered, not forced. Cultural categorization would do a disservice to the client and the therapeutic relationship. Nevertheless, the research is clear. Even though from the outset it may seem that EM may foster segregation and avoidance, adopting a colour-blind approach that denies the difference – i.e. the real world in which we live – is not the solution.

References

Atkinson, D.R. (1983) Ethnic similarity in counselling psychology: a review of research, *The Counselling Psychologist*, 11: 79–92.

Atkinson, D.R. (1985) A meta-review of research on cross-cultural counselling and psychotherapy, *Journal of Multicultural Counselling and Development*, 13: 138–53.

Atkinson, D.R. and Lowe, S.M. (1995) The role of ethnicity, cultural knowledge, and conventional techniques in counseling and psychotherapy, in J.G. Ponterotto, J.M. Casas, L.A. Suzuki and C.M. Alexander (eds) *Handbook of Multicultural Counselling*. Thousand Oaks, CA: Sage.

Berry, J.W. (1980) Social and cultural change, in H.C. Triandis and R.W. Brislin (eds) *Handbook of Cross-cultural Psychology: Social Psychology*, vol. 5. Boston, MA: Allyn & Bacon.

Chang, D.F. and Berk, A. (2009) Making cross-racial therapy work: a phenomenological study of clients' experiences of cross-racial therapy, *Journal of Counseling Psychology*, 56(4): 521–36.

Coleman, H.L.K., Wampold, B.E. and Casali, S.L. (1995) Ethnic minorities' ratings of ethnically similar and European American counselors: a meta-analysis, *Journal of Counseling Psychology*, 42: 55–64.

Erdur, O. *et al.* (2000) Working alliance and treatment outcome in ethnically similar and dissimilar client–therapist pairings, *Research Consortium of Counseling and Psychological Services in Higher Education*. Austin, TX: University of Texas.

Erdur, O. *et al.* (2003) Symptom improvement and length of treatment in ethnically similar and dissimilar client–therapist pairings, *Journal of Counseling Psychology*, 50(1): 52–8.

Farsimadan, F. (2003) Effects of ethnically similar therapeutic dyads on process and outcome of therapy: a review of the research, unpublished doctoral thesis, University of Surrey.

Farsimadan, F., Draghi-Lorenz, R. and Ellis, J. (2007) Process and outcome of therapy in ethnically similar and dissimilar therapeutic dyads, *Psychotherapy Research*, 17(5): 567–75.

Flaskerud, J.H. (1986) The effects of culture-compatible intervention on the utilisation of mental health services by minority clients, *Community Mental Health Journal*, 22: 127–41.

Flaskerud, J.H. (1991) Effects of an Asian client–therapist language, ethnicity and gender match on utilisation and outcome therapy, *Community Mental Health Journal*, 27: 31–42.

Flaskerud, J.H., and Liu, P.Y. (1990) Influence of therapy ethnicity and language on therapy outcomes of South-East Asian clients, *International Journal of Social Psychiatry*, 36: 18–29.

Flicker, S.M. *et al.* (2008) Ethnic matching and treatment outcome with Hispanic and Anglo substance-abusing adolescents, *Family Therapy Journal of Family Psychology*, 22(3): 439–47.

Fujino, D.C., Okazaki, S. and Young, K. (1994) Asian-American women in the mental health system: an examination of ethnic and gender match between therapist and client, *Journal of Community Psychology*, 22: 164–76.

Gamst, G., Dana, R.H., Der-Karaberian, A. and Kramer, T. (2000) Ethnic match and client ethnicity effects on global assessment and visitation, *Journal of Community Psychology*, 28: 547–64.

Garfield, S.L. (1986) Research on client variables in psychotherapy, in S.L. Garfield and A.E. Bergin (eds) *Handbook of Psychotherapy and Behavior Change*, vol. II. New York: Wiley.

Gray-Little, B. and Kaplan, D. (2000) Race and ethnicity and psychotherapy research, in C.R. Snyder and R.E. Ingram (eds) *Handbook of Psychological Change: Psychotherapy Processes and Practices for the 21st Century*. New York: Wiley.

Harrison, D.K. (1975). Race as a counsellor–client variable in counselling and psychotherapy: a review of the research, *The Counselling Psychologist*, 5: 124–33.

Horvath, A.O. and Luborsky, L. (1993) The role of the therapeutic alliance in psychotherapy, *Journal of Consulting and Clinical Psychology*, 64: 561–73.

Horvath, A.O. and Symonds, B.D. (1991) Relation between working alliance and outcome in psychotherapy: a meta-analysis, *Journal of Counselling Psychology*, 38: 139–49.

Jerrell, J.M. (1998) Effect of ethnic matching of young clients and mental health staff, *Cultural Diversity and Mental Health*, 4: 297–302.

Jones, E.E. (1982) Psychotherapist's impressions of treatment outcome as a function of race, *Journal of Clinical Psychology*, 38(4): 722–31.

Karlsson, R. (2005) Ethnic matching between therapist and patient in psychotherapy: an overview of findings, together with methodological and conceptual issues, *Cultural Diversity and Ethnic Minority Psychology*, 11(2): 113–29.

Khan, A. (2005) South Asian clients' accounts of their experiences of psycho-analytic/psychodynamic psychotherapy and the circumstances related to its premature ending: an interpretative phenomenological analysis, unpublished doctoral thesis, University of Surrey.

Khan, A., Farsimadan, F. and Draghi-Lorenz, R. (in preparation) Effects of ethnic dissimilarity and culture-sensitive relational factors on process and outcome of therapy by British white therapists with South-Asian clients, to be submitted to the *Journal of Counseling Psychology*.

Knipscheer, J.W. and Kleber, R.J. (2004a) A need for ethnic similarity in the therapist–patient interaction? Mediterranean migrants in Dutch mental-health care, *Journal of Clinical Psychology*, 60(6): 543–54.

Knipscheer, J.W. and Kleber, R. J. (2004b) The importance of ethnic similarity in the therapist–patient dyad among Surinamese migrants in Dutch mental health care, *Psychology and Psychotherapy: Theory Research and Practice*, 77(2): 273–8.

Lamb, W.K. and Jones, E.E. (1998) A meta-analysis of racial matching in psychotherapy, unpublished manuscript, University of California.

Littlewood, R., Moorhouse, S. and Sourangshu, A. (1992) The cultural specificity of psychotherapy, *British Journal of Psychiatry*, 161: 574.

Lopez, S.R., Lopez, A.A., and Fong, K.T. (1991) Mexican-Americans' initial preferences for counsellors: the role of ethnic factors, *Journal of Counselling Psychology*, 38: 487–96.

Maramba, G.G. and Hall G.C.N. (2002) Meta-analyses of ethnic match as a predictor of dropout, utilization, and level of functioning, *Cultural Diversity and Ethnic Minority Psychology*, 8: 290–7.

Martin, T.W. (1994) Community mental health services for ethnic minority adolescents: a test of the cultural responsiveness hypothesis, *Dissertation Abstracts International*, 55(7): 3018B.

Mathews, C.A. *et al.* (2002) The effect on treatment outcomes of assigning patients to ethnically focused inpatient psychiatric units, *Psychiatric Services*, 53: 830–5.

Ricker, M., Nystul, M. and Waldo, M. (1999) Counselors' and clients' ethnic similarity and therapeutic alliance in time-limited outcomes of counseling, *Psychological Reports*, 84: 674–6.

Sattler, J.M. (1977) The effects of therapist-client racial similarity, in A.S. Gurman and A.M. Razin (eds) *Effective Psychotherapy: A Handbook of Research*. New York: Pergamon Press.

Shin, S.M. *et al.* (2005) A meta-analytic review of racial-ethnic matching for African American and Caucasian American clients and clinicians, *Journal of Counseling Psychology*, 52(1): 45–56.

Smith, M.L., Glass, G.V. and Miller, T.I. (1980) *The Benefits of Psychotherapy*. Baltimore, MD: Johns Hopkins University Press.

Sue, S. *et al.* (1991) Community mental health services for ethnic minority groups: a test of the cultural responsiveness hypothesis, *Journal of Consulting and Clinical Psychology*, 59: 533–40.

Sue, S., Zane, N. and Young, K. (1994) Research on psychotherapy with culturally diverse populations, in A.E. Bergin and S.L. Garfield (eds) *Handbook of
Psychotherapy and Behaviour Change*. New York: Wiley.

Wierzbicki, M. and Pekanik, G. (1993) A meta-analysis of psychotherapy dropouts,
Professional Psychology: Research and Practice, 24: 190–5.

Wintersteen, M.B., Mensinger, J.L. and Diamond, G.S (2005) Do gender and racial
differences between patient and therapist affect therapeutic alliance and treatment retention in adolescents? *Professional Psychology: Research and Practice*,
36(4): 400–8.

Yeh, M., Eastman, K. and Cheung, M.K. (1994a) Children and adolescents in
community mental health centres: does the ethnicity or the language of the
therapist matter? *Journal of Community Psychology*, 22: 153–63.

Yeh, M., Takeuchi, D. T. and Sue, S. (1994b) Asian-American children treated in
the mental health system: a comparison of parallel and mainstream outpatient
service centers, *Journal of Clinical Child Psychology*, 23: 5–12.

Ziguras, S. *et al.* (2003) Ethnic matching of clients and clinicians and use of mental
health services by ethnic minority clients, *Psychiatric Services*, 54: 535–41.

7   Working with interpreters and bicultural workers

Rachel Tribe

And in my situation especially, I know that language will be a crucial instrument, that I can overcome the stigma of my marginality, the weight of presumption against me, only if the reassuringly right sounds come out of my mouth . . .
(Hoffman 1989: 123)

Introduction

Mental health practitioners need to be able to work effectively across cultures and languages if they are to ensure equity of service provision, meet the needs of a multicultural society and adhere to essential legal and professional rules and regulations. Legal requirements include national legislation such as the Race Relations Amendment Act 2000 and the Disability Discrimination Act 2005. Practitioners will also need to ensure that the services provided meet the requirements of the *Delivering Race Equality* (DRE) policy document emanating from the Department of Health (2005). Additionally, they will have to meet the codes of their relevant professional organizations.

Perhaps the most important goal is that of ensuring that clients who are not fluent in the English language can access therapeutic services when they are most needed, through the use of interpreters. Working in partnership with interpreters and bicultural workers will help ensure access to therapeutic services for clients who are not fluent in English. It may also enable any cultural variables to be considered more easily and thoroughly. In addition, it may lead to an expansion of the therapist's own repertoire of skills, a reconsideration of the therapist's cultural assumptions and the honing of a range of clinical skills. This chapter focuses on the issue of language and working with language interpreters in a therapeutic context. Clinicians need to be able to work effectively and comfortably with interpreters to ensure that non-English-speaking clients are not denied access to therapeutic services or that they find themselves only offered alternatives to talking therapies such as being prescribed medication (Fernando 2010). Implicit or institutional racism also needs to be considered.

Case scenario

You have been allocated a referral – Mr D, who has recently arrived in the UK from the Democratic Republic of Congo (DRC) – and you are due to see him in two days' time. You are informed that an interpreter, Ms C, has been booked for you. You have never worked with an interpreter before. What might your thoughts be in relation to this meeting? Spend a few minutes considering what Mr D might be thinking or feeling about your meeting and how this may impact on the meeting itself. He might be worrying about depending on an interpreter to voice and explain his emotions. He may even be unclear about why he is being asked to meet you and may have concerns about what seeing a psychotherapist in Britain means.[1]

Culture and language

> *Not being able to speak the language was like living in darkness . . .*
> *(Department of Health 2008)*

It is important to realize that culture is highly individualistic and while it will have been influenced by our country of origin and our heritage, it will also have been affected by any number of variables including our country of residence, religion, age, gender politics, family belief systems and individual life, as well as the many groups we are part of and our many life experiences. Each individual carries their own culture, beliefs and ways of doing things with them, although there may be some shared elements held by people from similar backgrounds. Some theorists have even described different professional training within mental health as 'sub-cultural influences' (MacLachlan 2006). Culture is not a monotheistic static entity but a dynamic and evolving one. Many clinicians have reported that they cannot work with certain clients, because they do not 'understand their culture', while others have worked hard to understand different cultures before working with clients from cultures different from their own. Yet, as Patel *et al.* (2000: 3) write, 'An individual practitioner may strive admirably to understand the contribution of their client's culture to the conversation created between them in therapy, but will rarely give the same scrutiny to the role of their own culturally determined belief systems'. An assumption that psychological theories, world views, explanatory health beliefs and idioms of distress developed in the West are generalizable across the world is simply incorrect and possibly racist. Issues of racism and assumed or implicit power differentials require constant consideration to ensure that therapy is a shared endeavour. Working cross-culturally, across language and culture, is likely to enhance all aspects of clinical work by encouraging active reflection

---

[1] All clinical material used in this chapter is based on fictitious people.

and an ongoing consideration of values held, thereby enriching the clinician's repertoire and reflective practice.

Language and culture are inextricably intertwined although the exact relationship between the two is contested. Anderson and Goolishian (1992) and Burr (1995) view language, with its culturally structured narratives, principles and 'norms', as conveying meaning while also constructing and shaping it to open up a particular range of realities at the individual and group level. Other theorists (e.g. Pinker 2007) argue that language is reflective of, as opposed to being essential in, forming the constructions held within a culture. Notwithstanding this, we can be sure that any language will appear to mirror, in some way, the culture from which it developed. Languages are not interchangeable but contain different constructions not only of grammar but also of meaning. Constructions of the self, of some behaviours including help-seeking behaviours, presentation of emotional distress and beliefs relating to causality and mental well-being are all located within our cultural frameworks (Maclachlan 2007; Fernando 2010). Words and phrases relating to psychological difficulties – for example, 'counselling/therapy', 'psychiatric, trauma', 'stress' and 'mental health' – may not exist or have the same meaning or resonance in other languages. Psychological theory has been developed in the West and is sometimes over-generalized and applied in ways which are not always meaningful (Patel *et al.* 2000).

An example of how language and culture can be intertwined is given by Hoffman (1989) who describes moving from Poland to Canada as a teenager. She describes her experience of learning about Canadian culture and language there:

> 'You're welcome' for example, strikes me as gaucherie, and I can hardly bring myself to say it – I suppose because it implies that there's something to be thanked for, which in Polish would be impolite. Even the simplest adjectives sow confusion in my mind: English kindliness has a whole system of morality behind it, a system that makes 'kindness' an entirely positive virtue.
>
> (Hoffman 1989: 106)

The need for interpreters

Case scenario

Dr J, an asylum-seeker from Iran, described feeling 'infantalized and ashamed' by her inability to speak for herself when she first came to England. Being reliant upon another person in some way appeared to replicate her experience of being detained in her country where she felt she had no voice or ability to change her circumstances. This was despite the fact that she was fluent in several other languages.

Difficulty in speaking the language of the country of residence has particular resonance when applied to therapeutic services, where language is frequently the primary method of communication and without which it may be extremely difficult to communicate or engage in therapeutic work (Tribe 2005). In addition, the notion of visiting a professional mental health worker in relation to an emotional difficulty or dilemma may be alien and not within the 'normal' help-seeking repertoire of many people (Bhui and Bhugra 2002; Lane and Tribe 2010). Help in such instances might have been sought in the past from an elder or religious leader or viewed as a community issue, rather than as an individual one (MacLachlan 2006). The Cartesian duality, or mind–body split, is based on western thinking and may be meaningless to many people and not represent how they would think about or present their own distress. Anyone working therapeutically across cultures needs to consider different idioms of distress and how they may incorporate these into their own therapeutic practice.

Thus, not only is language key when working therapeutically, but so is every individual's construction of the world which may be defined by their culture and will be ever-present in some form in the therapeutic space. Language will be the main lens through which this can be viewed or accessed. So working with an interpreter in an effective manner is a key skill which every mental health professional needs to possess. There is no doubt that it is crucial that both interpreters and therapists are trained to carry out their complex tasks (for the interested reader a possible training curriculum can be located in Tribe and Raval 2003). Several professional organizations now require training in working with interpreters to be part of their core curriculum.

Working with an interpreter is a qualitatively different experience from working without one, and recognition of this fact may go some way towards making the experience easier. Moving from a dyadic to a triadic consultation will change the dynamics in the consultation room (for further discussion of this issue see Tribe and Thompson 2009b).

Interpreting modes

Tribe (1998) outlines four different modes of interpreting, as shown in Table 7.1.

Regardless of which mode of interpreting is employed it is vital that the clinician and interpreter are clear about how they are going to work together and that this is agreed in advance – if it is not, the session is unlikely to work well.

Implications of using an interpreter

Some of the main implications of using an interpreter in a clinical setting, from the perspective of the client, the interpreter and the clinician/therapist are given below in Tables 7.2, 7.3 and 7.4. The implications may be experienced as

Table 7.1 Interpretation modes

Mode	Characteristics
Linguistic	The interpreter interprets word-for-word, is neutral and distanced. This is most applicable in a courtroom or medico-legal setting, when purely factual information is required and any psychological meaning or emotional resonance is seen as marginal or largely irrelevant. This mode assumes that to some degree languages are interchangeable codes which relate to a universal set of meanings; it minimizes the differences between languages and the ways they construct meanings (it favours a 'normative' etic position, which contends that a descriptive system exists that is equally valid for all cultures and languages).
Psychotherapeutic/ constructionist	The interpreter focuses on the meaning being conveyed rather than interpreting word-for-word, most helpful in a psychotherapeutic setting. This mode gives the interpreter more flexibility to manoeuvre in ensuring that the client's meaning is accurately conveyed but also requires a higher level of responsibility, expertise, training and trust between the client, mental health professional and interpreter. If this mode is to be used, all three members of the interpreting triad must feel prepared and comfortable with it. The interpreter is likely to require additional clarity and guidance on working in this way. It will be most suitable if there is to be a series of meetings rather than a one-off assessment (this mode is located more within an emic position which contends that psychological processes and language systems are often culturally constituted meaning systems).
Advocate/ community	The advocate or community interpreter is important in ensuring that a community or faith group with specific health or cultural views and needs are understood. The role is broader than those explained previously and might include empowering the client to negotiate or challenge the health care offered at the individual level as well as challenging at the service provision level. In Britain, health advocates or 'link workers' are employed in many parts of the NHS to try to ensure there is some equity of health provision and appropriate service provision regardless of the patient's language skills.
Cultural broker/ bicultural worker	A bicultural worker or cultural broker is concerned with interpreting cultural and contextual variables as well as words. This mode is based on the view that to understand the client's emotional world it is important to understand their context and cultural world view. The latter will be extremely useful when working within mental health and psychological well-being but it requires trust, open communication and shared responsibility between the client, interpreter and mental health practitioner, bearing in mind that culture is individual and shared meanings from culture must not be assumed. This mode of working is recommended when there is time to develop these characteristics; when the interpreter is experienced and the clinician has developed experience and expertise with working with interpreters and feels comfortable working in a more collaborative manner.

Table 7.2 The positive and negative implications of using an interpreter from the perspective of the client

	Positive	Negative
Client	Feels better understood and heard (Kline *et al.* 1980; Hillier *et al.* 1994; Mudaraki 2003)	May feel daunted by the presence of a third person in addition to the therapist
	Able to have a voice and make themselves understood (Patel 2003; Department of Health 2008)	May not trust the interpreter to accurately convey their words and feelings (Tribe and Morrissey 2004)
	Interpreter may be familiar with the meanings of the words used by the client and the cultural context (Qureshi *et al.* 2011)	Interpreter may assume an understanding of the meaning of the words and cultural context which is not actually shared (Qureshi *et al.* 2011)
	Clients using an interpreter have a higher return rate following assessment (Hillier *et al.* 1994)	Putch (1985) and Westermeyer (1990) describe situations where interpreters have actively dissuaded patients from disclosing important information that they believe might be seen as 'stigmatizing' their culture or religion by the clinician, although this may merely reflect a narrowness of vision or racism within the wider society
	Neutrality of interpreters seen as enhancing the work and maintaining appropriate boundaries for the client (Cushing 2003)	Neutrality by the interpreter seen as reducing the value of interpreters to service users and clinicians (Kaufert and Koolage 1984)
	Interpreter can function as a safe attachment figure (Alexander *et al.* 2004)	Presence of an interpreter can make the establishment of a therapeutic alliance more complex (Tribe and Thompson 2009b)
	Clients reported believing they had received better professional attention (Faust and Drickey 1986)	Issues of power need consideration – for whom is the interpreter working (Patel 2003)
	Blackwell (2005) highlights the additional value of interpreters in bearing witness in cases where human rights abuses or persecutions have occurred	May not be willing to talk about sensitive issues through a third party; there may be concerns about issues of confidentiality (Tribe and Thompson 2009a)
	Kaufert and Koolage (1984) argue that interpreters can usefully assist in establishing rapport and negotiating complex terminology and different explanatory models of health	Clients may feel that interpreters make it difficult for them to establish a 'direct' relationship with the clinician; dynamics will be altered (Blackwell 2005)
	Professional interpreters associated with improved clinical care compared to the use of ad hoc interpreters (Karliner *et al.* 2007)	May not be trained in mental health issues, so may be unaware of issues such as appropriate boundaries, confidentiality etc. (Razban 2003)
	Offers a non-English-speaking person the opportunity to access therapeutic services at the time of need (Patel *et al.* 2000)	Lack of support and supervision to assist with the stressful nature of the job (Granger and Baker 2003)

Table 7.3 The positive and negative implications of working with an interpreter from the perspective of the interpreter

	Positive	Negative
Interpreter	Drennan and Swartz (1999) note the many positive accomplishments of interpreters and cite several studies which emphasize interpreter initiative	Granger and Baker (2003) note the frustration of interpreters at not being accorded professional status/pay commensurate with their skills and expertise
	Acting as a positive role model for the client (Saxtroph and Christiansen 1991)	Possible errors of interpretation (omitting vital information, simplifying, adding information, replacing concepts (Vasquez and Javier 1991)
	The use of their considerable skills in the service of ensuring better care for a client (Tribe 1998)	Potential for vicarious traumatization (Salihovic 2008)
	The way in which language is used, often without thinking, is thrown into sharp relief, often with useful consequences (Raval 1996)	Issues of control, power, triangulation and accountability may arise; concerns about to whom the interpreter is accountable (Tribe 1998)
	Some practitioners say that working with an interpreter enables them to be more reflective in their work, and view this positively (Raval 1996)	Feel overwhelmed; might be uneasy about interpreting certain issues (e.g. child abuse, marital and sexual issues) (Kaufert and Koolage 1984; Raval 1996; Granger and Baker 2003)

positive, negative or indeed neutral by different members of the triad (Tribe and Thompson 2009b). What is experienced as negative by one may also be experienced as positive by another. The lists are indicative of current themes and not an exhaustive search of the literature. It is important to note that there is currently a dearth of literature written by interpreters from their own perspectives.

Dynamics and process issues

Process issues in therapy sessions can become complicated when three people (therapist, client, interpreter) rather than the usual two (therapist and client) are present in the room. It is not possible to do justice to this issue here, but the interested reader is referred to Blackwell (2005), Miller *et al.* (2005), and Tribe and Thompson (2009a, 2009b).

Table 7.4 The positive and negative implications of working with an interpreter from the perspective of the clinician/therapist

	Positive	Negative
Clinician/ Therapist	Farooq et al. 1997 found that use of an experienced interpreter did provide reliable data for diagnosis by the clinician	Have to negotiate two relationships at the same time (Tribe and Thompson 2009b)
	Opportunity to learn about and consider different idioms of distress/psychological well-being (Tribe 2007)	More likely to doubt own ability (Hillier et al. 1994)
	Allows the clinician to be more reflective (Raval 1996)	Interpreters frequently report they have a range of demands placed upon them by clinicians and clients that may exceed what they should resonably expect (Razban 2003)
	Can be an enriching and positive experience (Tribe and Morrissey 2004)	Clinician must be aware of and avoid using jargon, technical terms and sayings (Tribe and Morrissey 2004)
	Clinicians report a better quality of communication (Bischoff et al. 2003)	Have a lower opinion of effectiveness (Hillier et al. 1994)
	Can enhance all aspects of clinical repertoire (Tribe 2007)	Practitioners felt hostile if they believed that the interpreter went beyond the remit of the interpretation task (Kaufert and Koolage 1984)

Duty of care and vicarious trauma

> Interpreting in psychotherapy often entails an ongoing relationship with the client, and involves processing highly charged emotional material. The interpreter's knowledge of the intricacies and nuances of the language in which the client describes the trauma (the full potency of which may never reach the therapist due to distortion or omission), can make the interpreter more vulnerable to compassion fatigue (or vicarious trauma) than the therapist.
>
> (Salihovic 2008)

In addition to the consequences listed in Table 7.2 above, a clinician must also take into account that they owe a duty of care towards the *interpreter*, whether or not they are employed by an outside agency (Tribe and Thompson 2008). An interpreter is likely to hear extremely distressing material when interpreting within a mental health setting and has not had the training which the clinician has been through and frequently does not have the same access to a supervisor or support system. The possibility of vicarious, secondary trauma or compassion fatigue is a very real danger and the clinician and the employing agency need to monitor this. The interested reader is referred to Satkunanayagam *et al.* (2010) for a discussion on the differences between these developing terms. In addition, Salihovic (2008) conducted a study where he interviewed interpreters and clinicians working with survivors of traumatic events. He noted that greater empathic ability was associated with greater compassion fatigue only for clinicians. For interpreters, poor levels of social support, followed by exposure, were the best predictor of compassion fatigue. Thus therapists, health trusts and commissioners need to consider how they will provide ongoing support or supervision to interpreters.

Written translation and the use of psychometric tests

Any clinician should be extremely wary of using any psychometric tests in their work as the tests may not have been adapted for the population from which the client originates. It is not unusual to see tests that have merely been translated into a second language; however, without the psychometric properties being tested in an appropriate population, this may render them meaningless (Barrett 2005). For a psychometric test to have any meaning, adaptation must have included back translation (documents being translated from one language into another by one translator and then translated back to the original language by a different translator, the two versions then being compared). Also, measures of equivalence of construct, reliability, validity and 'norming' require attention.

Conclusion: best practice when using an interpreter

In order to work effectively with an interpreter in a mental health setting a number of issues need consideration. A set of guidelines developed by Tribe and Thompson (2008) for the British Psychological Society (BPS) on working with interpreters in mental health can be accessed at www.bps.org.uk/publications/guidelines-for-practitioners/guidelines-for-practitioners.cfm (scroll down to the bottom of the page). The need for training and support for all clinicians working with interpreters has been noted by the BPS, the Royal College of Psychiatrists (RCP) and the British Association for Counselling and Psychotherapy (BACP).

Working effectively with interpreters should be a skill that every clinician possesses. This is to ensure that equal opportunities are upheld and that certain groups are not denied access to psychological services. To achieve this aim, all clinicians should receive training in working with interpreters as a core part of their professional life. If this is not available within your trust or organization, it is

recommended that it is undertaken as part of your ongoing continuing professional development. Training courses are available in much of the country. To
conclude, the following good practice guidelines give an overview of the issues
that clinicians need to consider when working with interpreters to ensure that
they are able to be as effective as possible.

- Commissioners need to ensure that there are clear pathways to support for
  all members of their local community, including those who do not speak
  English.
- Undertake a language needs analysis for the population which your service
  covers and consider how you will best meet this need.
- If you have not undertaken training in working with interpreters, take a
  training course. If this is really not feasible as you will be working with an
  interpreter unexpectedly, read the guidelines and allocate time to consider
  the issues or discuss them with a more experienced colleague in advance
  of your first session with the interpreter.
- Check that the interpreter is qualified and appropriate for the consulta-
  tion/meeting.
- Allocate 10–15 minutes in advance of the session to brief the interpreter
  about the purpose of the meeting and to enable them to brief you about
  any cultural issues which may have bearing on the session.
- Be mindful of issues of confidentiality and trust when working with
  someone from a small language community as the client may be anxious
  about being identifiable and may be mistrustful of an interpreter's
  professionalism.
- State clearly that you alone hold clinical responsibility for the meeting.
- Create a good atmosphere where each member of the triad feels able to
  ask for clarification if anything is unclear, and be respectful to your interpreter – they are an important member of the team and make your work
  possible.
- Unless directed or indicated by the client, it is preferable for the same
  interpreter to be used with a client to allow the possibility of relationship
  development between all three members of the therapeutic triad and to
  create a contained and safe therapeutic environment.
- Match when appropriate for gender and age. Do not use a relative and
  never use a child.
- Be aware of the well-being of your interpreter and the possibility of their
  suffering from vicarious traumatization; consider what support they will
  be offered.
- At the end of the session allocate 10–15 minutes to debrief the interpreter about the session and to offer support and supervision as
  appropriate.
- All written translations used should have been back translated to ensure
  they are fit for purpose.

References

Alexander, C. *et al.* (2004) *Access to Services with Interpreters: User Views*. York: Joseph Rowntree Foundation.

Anderson, H. and Goolishian, H. (1992) Client as expert, in S. Mcnamee and K. Gergen (eds) *Therapy as a Social Construction*. London: Sage.

Barrett, K. (2005). Guidelines and suggestions for conducting successful cross-cultural evaluations for the courts, in K. Holt Barrett and W.H. George (eds) *Race, Culture, Psychology and Law*. Thousand Oaks, CA: Sage.

Bhui, K. and Bhugra, D. (2002) Explanatory models for mental distress: implications for clinical practice and research, *British Journal of Psychiatry*, 181: 6–7.

Bischoff, A. *et al.* (2003) Improving communication between physicians and patients who speak a foreign language, *British Journal of General Practice*, 53: 541–6.

Blackwell, D. (2005) *Counselling and Psychotherapy with Refugees*. London: Jessica Kingsley.

Burr, V. (1995) *An Introduction to Social Constructionism*. London: Routledge.

Cushing, A. (2003) Issues of language provision in health care services, in R. Tribe and H. Raval (eds) *Working with Interpreters in Mental Health*. London: Routledge.

Department of Health (2005) *Delivering Race Equality (DRE) in Mental Health Care*, www.dh.gov.uk/en/PublicationsandstatisticsPublications/PublicationsPolicy AndGuidance/DH_4100773, accessed 11 September 2009.

Drennan, G. and Swartz, L. (1999) A concept overburdened: institutional roles for psychiatric interpreters in post-apartheid South Africa, *Interpreting*, 4(2): 169–98.

Farooq, S., Fear, C. and Oyebode, F. (1997) An investigation of the adequacy of psychiatric interviews conducted through an interpreter, *Psychiatric Bulletin*, 21: 209–13.

Faust, S. and Drickey, R. (1986) Working with interpreters, *Journal of Family Practice*, 22: 131–8.

Fernando, S. (2010) *Mental Health, Race and Culture*. London: Mind Publications.

Granger, E. and Baker, M. (2003) The role and experience of interpreters, in R. Tribe and H. Raval (eds) *Working with Interpreters in Mental Health*. London: Routledge.

Hillier, S. *et al.* (1994) An evaluation of child psychiatric services for Bangladeshi parents, *Journal of Mental Health*, 3: 332–7.

Hoffman, E. (1989) *Lost in Translation*. London: Minerva.

Karliner, L.S., Jacobs, E.A., Chen, A.H. and Mutha, S. (2007) Do professional interpreters improve clinical care for patients with limited English proficiency? A systematic review of the literature, *Health Service Research*, 42(2): 727–54.

Kaufert, J.M. and Koolage, W.W. (1984) Role conflict among cultural brokers: the experience of native Canadian medical interpreters, *Social Science Medicine*, 18: 283–6.

Kline, F., Acosta, F., Austin, W. and Johnson, R.G. (1980) The misunderstood Spanish-speaking patient, *American Journal of Psychiatry*, 137: 1530–3.

Lane, P. and Tribe, R. (2010) Following NICE 2008: a practical guide for health professionals. Community engagement with local black and minority ethnic (BME) community groups, *Diversity, Health & Care*, 7(2): 105–14.

MacLachlan, M. (2006) *Culture and Health*. Chichester: Wiley.

Miller, K. *et al.* (2005) The role of interpreters in psychotherapy with refugees: an exploratory study, *American Journal of Orthopsychiatry*, 75(1): 27–39.

Mudarikiri, M.M. (2003) Working with interpreters in adult mental health, in R. Tribe and H. Raval (eds) *Working with Interpreters in Mental Health*. London: Routledge.

Patel, N. (2003) Speaking with the silent: addressing issues of dis-empowerment when working with refugee people, in R. Tribe and H. Raval (eds) *Working with Interpreters in Mental Health*. London: Routledge.

Patel, N. *et al.* (2000) *Clinical Psychology, 'Race' and Culture: A Training Manual*. Leicester: BPS Books.

Pinker, S. (2007) *The Stuff of Thought: Language as a Window on Human Nature*. London: Penguin.

Putsch, R.W. (1985) Cross-cultural communication: the special case of interpreters in health care, *Journal of the American Medical Association*, 254: 3344–8.

Quereshi, A. *et al.* (2011) Reconstructing Hermes: the messenger gets a voice, in D. Bhugra and S. Gupta (eds) *Migrants and Mental Health*. Cambridge: Cambridge University Press.

Raval, H. (1996) Systemic perspective on working with interpreters, *Clinical Child Psychology and Psychiatry*, 1(4): 505–11.

Razban, M. (2003) An interpreter's perspective, in R. Tribe and H. Raval (eds) *Working with Interpreters in Mental Health*. London: Routledge.

Salihovic, A. (2008) Compassion fatigue: interpreters and clinicians in trauma work, unpublished doctoral thesis, University of East London.

Satkunanayagam, K., Tunariu, A. and Tribe, R. (2010) A qualitative exploration of mental health professionals' experience of working with survivors of trauma in Sri Lanka, *International Journal of Culture and Mental Health*, 3(1): 43–51.

Saxtroph, V. and Christiansen, J. (1991) Working with refugee families from the Middle East in Denmark, paper presented at the third International Conference of Centres, Institutions and Individuals concerned with the Care of Victims of Organised Violence, Santiago, Chile.

Tribe, R. (1998) A critical analysis of a support and clinical supervision group for interpreters working with refugees located in Britain, *Group Work Journal*, 10(3): 196–214.

Tribe, R. (2005) The mental health needs of asylum seekers and refugees, *The Mental Health Review*, 10(4): 8–15.

Tribe, R. (2007) Working with interpreters, *The Psychologist*, 20(3): 159–61.

Tribe, R. and Morrissey, J. (2004) Best practice when working with interpreters in mental health, *Intervention: The International Journal of Mental Health, Psychosocial Work and Counselling in Areas of Armed Conflict*, 2(2): 129–42.

Tribe, R. and Raval, H. (eds) (2003) *Working with Interpreters in Mental Health*. London: Routledge.

Tribe, R. and Thompson, K. (2008) *Guidelines for Psychologists Working with Interpreters in Applied Settings*. Leicester: British Psychological Society.

Tribe, R. and Thompson, K. (2009a) Opportunity for development or necessary nuisance? The case for viewing working with interpreters as a bonus in therapeutic work, *International Journal of Migration, Health and Social Care*, 5(2): 4–12.

Tribe, R. and Thompson, K. (2009b) Exploring the three-way relationship in therapeutic work with interpreters, *International Journal of Migration, Health and Social Care*, 5(2): 13–21.

Vasquez, C. and Javier, R. (1991) The problem with interpreters: communicating with Spanish-speaking patients, *Hospital and Community Psychiatry*, 42(2): 163–5.

Westermeyer, J. (1990) Working with an interpreter in psychiatric assessment and treatment, *Journal of Nervous and Mental Disease*, 178(12): 745–9.

8 Issues for white therapists

Judy Ryde

Introduction

It is easy to overlook the effects that being white has on a therapeutic relationship. It seems so 'normal' to be white that there is not much to say about it. In illustration consider this: when I speak to groups which contain black and white therapists I sometimes ask the white therapists if they have been in therapy with a black therapist. Very few have. I then ask black therapists if they have been in therapy with a white therapist. Very few have not. This being the case, black clients will often talk about the issues they have about being black and black therapists will often talk about the impact of their blackness on the therapeutic relationship, but the issue of whiteness very rarely occurs in either situation. In this chapter I address myself to white therapists, though black therapists may be interested to read it too.

This ignoring of whiteness in intercultural therapeutic work, and indeed in any therapeutic work, may be because it is considered to be 'just normal' (Dyer 1997; Frankenberg 1999). Nevertheless, whiteness is beginning to be written and talked about and the issues involved are beginning to be addressed (Liebmann 1999; Tuckwell 2002; Jacobs 2005; Lago and Haugh 2006; Naughton and Tudor 2006; Ryde 2009). It has become clear that if white therapists are to really understand, and therefore be able to explore with their clients, the impact of their whiteness within a racial environment,[1] they need to understand what lies behind this dynamic.

So what are the special issues which face white therapists within this racial environment? I have chosen the following to explore in this chapter as they seem to me to be the most salient:

1 Whiteness as apparent normality.
2 Whiteness and privilege.
3 Whiteness and power.
4 Guilt and shame.
5 The impact of whiteness within the intersubjective field of therapy.
6 Common responses of therapists when working with black or non-white clients.
7 The needs of training and supervision.

---

[1] I say 'racial environment' here because human beings do still divide the world into 'races', even if this is a spurious classification and often deplored, so the meaning of 'race' within a therapy context is nearly always relevant.

Whiteness as apparent normality

Discovering that white people see themselves as 'normal' seems to be the major finding of those who research whiteness in the sociological discipline of 'white studies'. They find that whites regard others as 'having' a 'race' while white people are just the 'human ordinary' (Apple 1998). Dyer (1997: 2) says, 'there is nothing more powerful than being just human'. Nothing further needs to be asserted or explained or thought about. This brings about a habit of thought which makes reflecting on whiteness very difficult. In my book *Being White in the Helping Professions* (Ryde 2009) I describe how I found that focusing on being white feels like being magnetized strongly to a position which I can certainly pull away from but to which I inevitably get drawn back. The most I can say after engaging with this for many years is that the magnet is a little weaker than it used to be.

I have found that when I talk to white people that they often demur on this subject and point out that any group tends to think of itself as the 'normal' one – that it is human nature to do so. No doubt there is some truth in this, but when the apparent normality of white people is put together with the cultural power they have in contemporary society, then we are talking about a much more insidious phenomenon than the tendency of groups to be insular. Black people are less likely to see their groups as self-evidently 'normal' in the same way. If you have been described as 'other' both implicitly and explicitly for so long by a more powerful group, then it is hard not to think of yourself as 'other' as well, unless on reflection you want to angrily assert your normality.

If you are not sure you agree with this, think about the following points.

- Can white people be 'white' if they have a black ancestor? Those of mixed racial heritage are considered black, even if the black person was their grandparent or great grandparent – particularly if this 'blackness' shows in their features, skin colour or hair. If they look white then they just 'pass' as white. The blackness in them makes them 'other'.
- When thinking of courses or workshops about intercultural matters do you expect, as a white person, to be considering your own race? Until recently this would be very unlikely. You would be more likely to think you would be learning about black people and *their* needs. White values and tenets tend to be taken as the benchmark from which other approaches to life are measured, even if, as enlightened people, we can see that 'other' cultural norms have value. They are often characterized as norms we used to have, such as living within and valuing extended families. It is interesting that 'other' cultures are often characterized as 'old fashioned'.

Whiteness and privilege

So what kind of privilege does being white give us? It may seem, in the post-Obama election world, that white people are losing their privileged status. Certainly if a majority of Americans can vote for a black man then something must be happening. However, over 20 years ago McIntosh (1988) found 46 different ways in which she felt she was privileged by being white, most of which still apply. They demonstrate the easy, taken for granted way we as white people can negotiate life and expect to be accepted, valued and serviced. Here are 10 of them:

1   I have no difficulty finding neighbourhoods where people approve of our household.
2   Our children are given texts and classes which implicitly support our kind of family unit.
3   I can talk about the social events of a weekend without fearing most listeners' reactions.
4   I will feel welcomed and 'normal' in the usual walks of public life, institutional and social.
5   When I am told about our national heritage or 'civilization' I am shown that people of my colour made it what it is.
6   I could arrange to protect our young children most of the time from people who might not like them.
7   I can talk with my mouth full and not have this put down to my colour.
8   I can do well in a challenging situation without being called a credit to my race.
9   I am not made acutely aware that my shape, bearing or body odour will be taken as a reflection on my race.
10 I can be late to a meeting without having the lateness reflect on my race.

In workshops I often ask white participants to think of privileges they have and together we discover even more than McIntosh's 46. Maybe, since Obama's election as president of the USA, we could now add to the list: 'I can now become president of the United States without being thought a credit to my race'!

We, as white therapists, could also add that our psychological theory is based on the general mores and expectations of our cultural lives. Even when therapy tenets question or challenge these, the *basis* for this challenge is understood by all concerned. It means that most of our clients will accept our cultural standpoint without question and that if we go into therapy ourselves we can expect to easily find a therapist with more or less the same cultural or racial background as ourselves. The added privilege for therapists could therefore be: 'I can expect easily to find a white therapist who has similar cultural mores to myself and has underlying theories that I understand'.

Whiteness and power

So, being white makes us 'normal' and therefore privileged and this privilege, along with great wealth, has given us power. This power provides white people with the ability to develop and use very sophisticated technology, including for military ends, and to live within an environment which ensures that their cultural artefacts such as political and financial systems, languages, modes of dress, religion, music and other artistic endeavours etc. have predominance worldwide. Although 'whiteness' is a racial rather than a cultural issue, many white people have different cultures from each other, and some black people, particularly black people who have been born or raised in Europe or America, could be said to share a culture with white people. Nevertheless, whiteness does also, in a wider sense, have a cultural base within a globalized world. Even where this may at first glance seem not to be the case, such as when non-white people own multinational organizations, they play by white rules, within a white international culture.

In recent decades there have been attempts in 'western' countries to mitigate the effects of this power differential. Equal opportunities laws and policies have been designed to equalize the stakes between black and white (as well as other inequalities). On the surface we have much more tolerant and equal societies than previous generations. However, racial prejudice runs deep and cracks tend to reappear when under stress, such as when numbers of immigrants increase. When equal opportunities laws are rigorously applied there tends to be a backlash in which 'political correctness' is pilloried. In hard times, white people can feel that they are a 'minority', particularly those who are at the bottom of the social scale and where class inequalities also come into play.

These issues are evident within therapeutic contexts: along with the personal and interpersonal, sociopolitical issues follow both therapist and client into the room. Consider this in illustration: a colleague thinking of his different supervision groups for therapists working in intercultural settings, noticed among other things that it seemed as though the white therapists tended to be over-sympathetic to their clients, 'bending over backwards' to understand their plight. The black therapists, on the other hand, although affected by their clients' situations, seemed to demand more of their clients. My colleague and I reflected on this situation and wondered if the white therapists were affected by various and complex responses to being white in this situation, including a sense of guilt at their relative good fortune. The black therapists did not share this perspective, though may have other difficulties which affect them in being therapists to black clients within a white setting.

Although these issues may stay hidden in the corners, they make their effects known while not being directly addressed. These underlying or unconscious issues may be revealed through difficulties in the working alliance (Clarkson 1995: 43) or dreams and 'stories' that carry unconscious messages (Casement 1985: 72). This way of communicating when something is amiss is, of course, true in any therapy relationship but I have certainly found it to be true when race is a particular concern (Ryde 2009: 133). Addressing the impact of the power differential between therapist and client is both difficult but important if it is not to result in a therapy where underlying problems are not faced (Jacobs 2005: 1) and salient matters are never really addressed.

Guilt and shame

I have found in myself a deep feeling of guilt and shame about my own complicity in white privilege and, in my research, found that I was by no means alone in this (Ryde 2005). In a research group set up to explore these issues we found that our culpability for racism was not just about our own racist attitudes but the way we still benefit from racist policies of the past. We also found some resistance to this thought, both in ourselves and among our colleagues. I discovered that therapists I interviewed had a common feeling that, though we ourselves may have unconsciously or even consciously held prejudices against non-white people, we should not feel guilty about endemic or institutionalized racism. After all, they thought, we cannot affect this situation personally or the racist attitudes held by past generations which led to slavery and colonialism, as these were carried out before we were born by people we could not influence.

The more I reflected on this the more I felt that these attitudes were defensive and unhelpful. I showed in my book (Ryde 2009) that we are in fact still complicit in these more endemic forms of racism, especially as we are still benefiting from them. The wealth of the 'West' is built on past and present exploitation of other countries, often dubbed 'the third world'. The most gross forms of racism, such as believing that 'Negros' are more 'primitive' than Europeans, have been foresworn by most people, but underlying our apparent lack of prejudice more subtle attitudes remain, hardwired into our consciousness. For instance, I have found that, when meeting a black person, if I allow myself to catch my first thought, I tend to think they are dangerous or predatory. Normally I sweep these thoughts away before I have a chance to recognize them. In my research I discovered that I am by no means on my own in having these kinds of thoughts. I could regard them as merely evidence of my own personal racism but I also think they arise because I am, like everyone else, inevitably woven into the cultural attitudes of our society.

Because of the sense of guilt and shame that comes with this realization, and because I had noticed that many apparently well-meaning white people do feel ashamed of their racist attitudes, I did some research into this which I discussed in my thesis (Ryde 2005) and my book on the same subject (Ryde 2009). I found that, whereas it is not helpful to non-white people to express to them our feelings of guilt, these feelings do draw our attention to something being amiss and that reparation needs to be made:

> I could see that we need to develop a strong and flexible sense of self which can 'take' the narcissistic knock of understanding the harm we have done to others. A strong sense of self enables us to feel the pain of the guilt, gives us the ability to 'stay with' it, reflect on what it means to those harmed and the humility to own our culpability. Where a sense of self is fragile the pain is too much to bear and is likely to result in an attacking response to those who 'make' us feel guilty. Paradoxically, the more basic self-esteem we have, the more able we are to usefully respond to guilt. Without it we may either deny our guilt or be compulsively guilty which can lead to unproductive hand-wringing or a desire to be prematurely absolved.
>
> (Ryde 2009: 106)

I suggest that allowing ourselves to be aware of our sense of guilt and shame is part of a necessary process if we are to work towards a world in which white people are aware of their own place within the racialized environment and take that into account in their work and social lives. A strong enough sense of self may be necessary before we are able to bear the injury to our narcissism.

The impact of whiteness within the intersubjective field of the therapy

So what is the impact of our whiteness on our work with clients and how do we address it? This is not just an issue for our work with black clients – the fact of our whiteness can also impact on our work with white clients. As we are white then the issue of white privilege can be ignored within our relationships with white clients and the dominant cultural values and mores of white people can be shared between us without question. These shared values may lead to some areas which fall short of a wide understanding of emotional literacy such as the importance of valuing the communal. We stress instead individual and, possibly, narcissistic ends. In other words white therapy can emphasize individualistic gratification over the good of the whole as white values tend to err in this direction.

If the therapist is black and the client is white then the issue of race, along with racist thoughts and fantasies, will almost always arise in the client. I found myself expecting this recently when I referred a white friend to a non-white therapist. I explained that I had liked what this therapist had written (possibly to show that this therapist was intelligent and established in the profession) and that she spoke good English. No doubt I feared that my suggestion would be greeted with dismay.

When the therapist is white and the client is not, the issues of cultural and racial differences are more likely to be explored and the difficulties a therapist may have in understanding a client with a different cultural and racial background are often written about in books concerning intercultural therapy. It is, of course, self-evident that it is useful for the therapist to have some understanding of the culture and race of their client, particularly when they are different from their own. This is well recognized in other chapters of this book and can clearly help the therapist to have a better understanding of their client.

However, understanding and exploring the meaning of race, *including the whiteness of the therapist*, within their intersubjective meeting, can be paramount, if this relationship is not to be weighed down and overshadowed by a history of racism, including as far back as slavery and colonization. My own approach to the work of psychotherapy understands it to inevitably exist within an intersubjective context in which each participant co-creates their relationship (Stolorow *et al.* 2002). Whites and non-whites alike bring with them their personal histories, present philosophies, values and past histories including family and cultural ones. This rich mixture forms the context in which the meeting occurs and shapes and authors the story they make together. As we saw above, race, particularly the contribution of the white race, is often silent and not reflected on in this meeting.

I have a Muslim client who was brought up in Africa but since late adolescence had been living and educated in the West. She had apparently taken on western values and customs in a seamless way. At the time I am remembering she was very pressured with work and study and had several deadlines to meet. While this was happening her sister announced that she intended to come to stay. My client complained to me about the amount of time this would consume at such a difficult time and we started to look at how she might communicate this difficulty to her sister who would normally expect constant, undivided attention when visiting. I felt dismayed at the pressure this would put my client under. On having this thought I reflected that her sister's expectations were culturally based and that my client would have had, at least originally, the same cultural norm. Mine was very different. My own sister would not insist on coming to stay at a difficult time and I would have no problem in explaining that to her in a way which would not cause offence. I reflected to my client that maybe she herself was taking on a very western attitude in putting her own needs first and, maybe crucially, I wondered if she was doing that for my sake. This comment opened up a whole area of our relationship in which we had evidently combined to stress her 'western' side and downplay the part of her that would always drop everything to attend to a family member. In exploring this it became evident that, for her, family was always paramount and she had kept that from me, knowing or expecting that I was not able to understand or appreciate this value. The extent to which she had hidden this from me shocked me as I had regarded our relationship as intimate and open. Maybe a sense of betrayal had arisen in the intersubjective space – either myself or her family would have to be betrayed. Her western and non-western sides had to be held apart to survive in Britain, including in her therapy.

Common responses of therapists when working with black or non-white clients

Some readers may use the term 'counter-transference' for the phenomenon that I am terming 'therapist's responses' here, but, as this term is a technical one used specifically in psychodynamic therapy, I do not use it now. The phenomenon itself will be familiar to anyone who works in a therapeutic way, whatever their orientation, though they may have different ways of understanding and working with it.

What I want to discuss is the kind of unbidden response that comes to therapists when working with a client – the sensations, emotions, feelings, thoughts, fantasies, dreams etc. that arise within them. Some of these responses may be irrelevant and should be put to one side, but most do have a relevant meaning and can be taken into account during the work.

My own way of understanding these spontaneous manifestations is that they arise within the intersubjective field between therapist and client. This means that it is not, as is traditionally understood in psychoanalytic and psychodynamic work, solely material projected by the client towards the therapist. It arises in the work *together* and so is relevant to both therapist and client as well as their relationship, and is hence worth reflecting on and making sense of in these terms

(Orange *et al.* 1997: 87; Ryde 2009: 282). How much this reflecting is carried out explicitly with the client and how much remains the therapist's internal reflection is a judgement that needs to be made sensitively and thought about in supervision (see Chapter 12).

Of course when working as a white therapist with black clients some of these responses will not be specific to their racial differences, but crucially some will and it is these I focus on now. Having said that, it is always good practice to consider whether one's being white has any bearing on these responses. Common responses of this kind for white therapists working with black clients may include the following.

Guilt and shame

Maybe behind many of the therapist responses to black clients is a sense of guilt and shame – guilt at our relative good fortune in being white and shame at our failure to really address the issues of inequality, both in our lives in general and in the therapy. We may also not want to be accused of this and be at pains not to appear at fault.

A desire to please

In her paper 'For whites only' Jacobs (2005) says that she tends to want to be the 'nice therapist' who is 'not like the rest'. Maybe to stave off guilt and accusations of not being able to understand our clients, we do what we can to show how sympathetic we can be but, in doing so, may find that we are chasing our own agenda rather than being present for the client.

An avoidance of the negative

Related to the above may be an avoidance of any negative messages that black clients are giving us, just picking up on positive ones. This can insidiously encourage black clients to only give us more positive feelings, such as gratitude and admiration.

Physical withdrawal

An even more distressing response which might be hard to own, even to ourselves, is a physical withdrawal or even revulsion. This might include a dislike of clients' physical appearance or smell. Related to this is an exaggerated, apparent admiration of their physicality, telling ourselves that they are beautiful or sexy in a way that would not come to us with white clients. While these could of course be authentic responses, they can also be something of a reaction formation – 'thank goodness I can feel this. I mustn't physically reject this person' or 'look how lacking in prejudice I am, finding this person attractive'.

Judgement

A similar situation may occur with judgements made about our clients. We might feel judgemental, particularly regarding culturally-based attitudes, and then soft pedal on these and turn our back on them. Or we might make judgements and not adequately reflect on them and where they come from.

This is not a definitive list and, as I said above, any response, however apparently not connected with race or culture, can be reflected on to see if racial differences do have a bearing. The important thing is that such responses do not get pushed out of awareness, because they give us useful information for working honestly and meaningfully with our clients.

The need for training and supervision

Working as a white person within a multicultural situation is very challenging and requires a high degree of self-knowledge and commitment if we are to be any use to our clients. However, this aspect of the work often has a very low profile in training. To be covered adequately, intercultural and racial awareness needs to run throughout the training as well as at specific times when specific areas can be focused on. The training should therefore cover three basic areas.

An **understanding and awareness** of oneself within a racial environment

Work on one's own awareness of self is always important within therapy training and this is of course true when it comes to white therapists' awareness of their whiteness and its impact on therapeutic relationships.

Theory about white racial issues within a therapeutic context

An understanding of theories of white racial identity and its impact within a therapeutic racial environment will help to ground the work with clients.

Skill development to work therapeutically, as a white person, within a racial environment

As with all therapy training an awareness and understanding may not be enough to translate into effective work with clients. The training will need to develop ways of showing how theory relates to practice.

In order to be fully understood at a significant level, experiential as well as theoretical learning needs to take place. *Being White in the Helping Professions* (Ryde 2009) and Gill Tuckwell's *Racial Identity, White Counsellors and Therapists* (2002) have useful sections on training, as well as the relevant chapters in this book.

Similarly, the needs of supervision are particularly great if the complexity of this situation is to be unearthed and worked through. The added complexity of cultural and racial difference needs careful thought with great commitment to honest self-reflection and preparedness to share these thoughts with a supervisor. Supervisors need to be able to show supervisees that revealing all thoughts, feelings and fantasies will be received with an interest in understanding them rather than with judgement.

If the supervisee is white, the supervisor needs to bear in mind the question 'How does my supervisee being white affect the relationship with this client?' and, if they themselves are white 'How does my being white affect this three-cornered relationship?' In the complex intersubjective situation of supervision, the whiteness of the supervisor, if she or he is white, will affect the therapeutic relationship even if the other parties are both black. For more on this see Chapter 12 of this book, Chapter 8 of *Being White in the Helping Professions* (Ryde 2009), Chapter 8 of *Supervision in the Helping Professions* (Hawkins and Shohet 2006).

Conclusion

When working in a racial environment, it is important for white therapists to understand that they 'have' a race and that this race tends to be the most privileged within a racialized field – so privileged that white people can afford to ignore the issue of race completely. From this beneficial position white people have described and categorized the racial environment while absenting themselves from it (Bonnett 2000).

Once that is understood it is important for white therapists to understand and acknowledge the impact that this has in a racial environment. Just what this impact is needs to be addressed afresh with each new relationship so that it can be reflected on and taken into account within the intersubjective situation of each unique encounter.

References

Apple, M.W. (1998). Foreword in J.L. Kincheloe, S.R. Steinberg, N.M. Rodriguez and R.E. Chennault (eds) *White Reign*. New York: St Martin's Griffin.

Bonnett, A. (2000) *White Identities: Historical and International Perspectives*. London: Prentice Hall.

Casement, P. (1985) *On Learning from the Patient*. London: Tavistock.

Clarkson, P. (1995) *The Therapeutic Relationship*. London: Whurr.

Dyer, R. (1997) *White*. London: Routledge.

Frankenberg, R. (1999) *Displacing Whiteness*. London: Duke University Press.

Hawkins, P. and Shohet. R. (2006) *Supervision in the Helping Professions*. Maidenhead: Open University Press.

Jacobs, L. (2005) For whites only, in T.L. Bar-Joseph (ed.) *The Bridge: Dialogues Across Cultures*. New Orleans: Gestalt Institute Press.

Lago, C. and Haugh, S. (2006) White counsellor racial identity: the unacknowledged, unknown, unaware aspect of self in relationship, in G. Proctor, M. Cooper, P. Sanders and B. Malcolm (eds) *Politicizing the Person Centred Approach*. Ross-on-Wye: PCCS Books.

Liebmann, M. (1999). Being white: engaging with a changing world, in J. Campbell *et al.* (eds) *Art Therapy, Race and Culture*. London: Jessica Kingsley.

McIntosh, P. (1988) *White Privilege and Male Privilege: A Personal Account of Coming to See Correspondences Through Work in Women's Studies*. Belmont: Wadsworth.

Naughton, M. and Tudor, K. (2006) Being white, *Transactional Analysis Journal*, 36(2): 159–71.

Orange, D. *et al.* (1997) *Working Intersubjectively: Contextualism in Psychoanalytic Practice*. Hillsdale, NJ: The Analytic Press.

Ryde, J. (2005) Exploring white racial identity and its impact on psychotherapy and psychotherapy professions, PhD thesis, School of Management, University of Bath.

Ryde, J. (2009) *Being White in the Helping Professions: Developing Effective Intercultural Awareness*. London: Jessica Kingsley.

Stolorow, R.D. *et al.* (2002) *Worlds of Experience: Interweaving Philosophical and Clinical Dimensions in Psychoanalysis*. New York: Basic Books.

Tuckwell, G. (2002) *Racial Identity, White Counsellors and Therapists*. Buckingham: Open University Press.

9 Issues for psychological therapists from black and minority ethnic groups

Harbrinder Dhillon-Stevens

Introduction

In this chapter I hope to raise awareness from two perspectives, that of (i) being a black therapist and issues of training and the profession; and (ii) issues in the clinical setting. In the following pages I draw on theory, experience and my own doctoral research entitled *Healing Inside and Out: An Examination of Dialogic Encounters in the Area of Anti-Oppressive Practice in Counselling and Psychotherapy* (Dhillon-Stevens 2004a).

From the outset I think it is important to state that while I am aware of black issues in terms of structural, institutional and cultural contexts, I also see the individual and her uniqueness within such constructs. So while this chapter is meant to provide an overview of issues for black and ethnic minority groups, I do not see these groups as homogenous.

Defining terms

In terms of definitions I refer to 'psychological therapists'. This encompasses counsellors, psychotherapists and counselling psychologists. In order to proceed and clarify this discussion I feel it is important to define my use of certain other terms. I subscribe to the Multiple Oppression Model towards issues of difference (Dhillon-Stevens 2004b). This considers race, ethnicity, culture, gender, disability, sexual orientation, class, age, religion and language. In the Multiple Oppression Model it is important to recognize the differences as well as the similarities between oppressions. For example, while white working-class people are disadvantaged, black working-class people face discrimination not only because of class but also because of their skin colour (race). Anti-oppressive practice (AOP) works within this model as well as acknowledging structural and contextual issues of oppression. For a fuller discussion of AOP and the Multiple Oppression Model I refer you to Dhillon-Stevens (2004b).

Although I am alert to these issues of difference within this spectrum I am aware of how issues of race and racism have been excluded from psychotherapy training in favour of more cultural frameworks in the profession. How am I defining 'race'? In the British context I see 'race' in terms of black and white dynamics. 'Black' for me is a political term and encompasses people from Africa, the Caribbean and Asia, and ethnic minority groups, who experience racism. The experience of racism is a visible difference that profoundly affects experiences at various levels: psychological, emotional, cultural, economic, political, historical and internalized. I am coming from the perspective that white people do not experience racism. I also distinguish between culture and ethnicity (Dhillon-Stevens 2001). It is worth noting that some of these groups may not identify with such terms — for example, Asian groups.

Race in the British context creates different dynamics from other issues of oppression. I am not stating that race should be considered above or as more important than other issues of difference (gender, sexual orientation, class, disability, age etc.) but I am stating that the introduction of race is different from how other oppressions are understood and experienced by psychological therapists emotionally and psychologically. Race provides a different concoction in the dynamics and I am not entirely clear why. Bell's (2001) notion of 'infusing "race" into the dialogue' creates a difference. As she states, 'infusing is a technique of slowly introducing a new or uncommon ingredient to a dish. Infusing causes a subtle yet distinctive change in taste and sometimes the texture of the dish, giving layers of complexity' (p. 48).

Being a black therapist, issues of training, and the profession

Internal psychological challenges

In a research role play between a black therapist and a white client, the therapist introduced herself as an Asian woman, thereby creating an opportunity to discuss the power dynamics between herself and the white client. However, the client's response did not allow for such a discussion. The therapist understood the client's response as a message to her that stated, 'You are not allowed to be vulnerable. You need to be strong.' The therapist felt that had she worked longer with the client she would have returned to this issue.

In her recall (reflection) the therapist stated the choice point was to work either with the transferential relationship or the real relationship. In terms of the real relationship, 'there is a black therapist in front of the client'. This called into question the impact of the client's response to the black therapist. The therapist considered this and felt the transference was figural for the client and accepted this before she could work with the race material.

Below is a transcript with this black therapist in facilitating her to critically reflect on the experience in the research group.

HDS: [gently] How did you remain therapeutically available given that state-ment had an impact on you?

Therapist: I thought. I suppose . . .

HDS: What are you not saying? Where are you not going?

Therapist: [smiling as if recognizing some insight] I am not going there! Where it's too soft and vulnerable. This isn't the right space for it.

HDS: Okay, I hear that, just to acknowledge it had an impact and bring that to your awareness.

Therapist: It has an impact and what I am used to doing is putting it in a little space and talking about it in safer spaces.

This transcript demonstrates that where the therapist is black and the client white, and the therapist's race and ethnicity are considered insignificant by the client, the black therapist needs to hold two processes simultaneously: to be therapeutically available to the client and the client's material, while being aware of her own process and the reality of her experiences as a black woman, which are reinforced and triggered by the client. This is a difficult tension to hold in the real relationship. White therapists may not experience it.

The transcript also demonstrates that where the therapist is black the internal process she has to engage in with white clients is far more sophisticated and challenging of self and, I would argue, requires reflection in the midst of action. Trainers and supervisors need to be mindful that such processes impact on black trainees, and consider how they can be supported in a way that allows them to express these tensions and develop a coherent sense of self as a psychological therapist. I wonder if such processes are a reason why many black trainees find themselves leaving psychotherapy training or having to take a year out.

Furthermore, one needs to consider what is really happening regarding the contact boundary and the quality of the contact if the therapist has to put some part of herself 'away'. Although this is not the real relationship, neither should it be considered in terms of transferential material. These experiences are not located in the internal psyche of black therapists, as the psychoanalytical literature has stated, but are experiences of reality and living within the British construct. Thus for conscious black therapists these issues are more prevalent in training groups and clinical material.

In the light of this, the research group explored the following questions: 'Is there space for the therapist to bring this material into the real relationship or not?' 'How would such an intervention be viewed?' 'Would it be seen as the therapist's material or the therapist and client's material?' It was felt that non-aware therapists would view this as the therapist's material, and a boundary issue that should be dealt with in personal therapy. Aware therapists considered that the therapist would need to raise such issues with the client to work in the real relationship.

The material had an impact on the therapist and raising this could provide a useful discussion between client and therapist. Black therapists may need to engage in anti-racist awareness with white clients by the very nature of such dynamics. The issue is *how* this is done, which might be more in terms of an encounter in the dialogic than a 'tell' approach. We inform our clients if their sadness has impacted on us, and when such material impacts on therapists there needs to be a forum to address this. Otherwise therapists may do good work (as demonstrated by the role play) but the cost to themselves is greater and they struggle with processes that are not recognized or validated in training/supervision arenas. The enquiry concluded that such processes are in 'the in between' (Buber 1970) of therapist and client rather than the therapist's material. The therapist, in reflecting on the encounter, stated, 'The impact of oppression is that you learn to manage it, so no one knows.' This is just one example, out of many, of black enquirers' experience in the counselling and psychotherapy profession. The enquiry group highlighted this as an important area of which training institutions and bodies should be aware and that future research could pursue.

Distress

The notion of distress in a western context is about emotional expression. It is worth noting that the expression of distress for students may not be translatable into English or the therapy or group process. I remember being a client and struggling to describe my dream to my therapist. She remarked that normally I was very articulate and today I was having trouble with my words. It was at this point that I realized that I dream in Punjabi and was trying to translate my dream from Punjabi into English, hence my delayed process and incoherence. It was at this point that I realized language and my mother tongue is about my 'core being' and such experiences are difficult to translate.

Also, if we think about constructions of health in different cultural contexts, in mine, the ability to fulfil one's role is seen as healthy. Physical well-being is above emotional well-being and if emotional well-being is expressed, it is through physical terms such as 'my heart is heavy'; 'I have pains in my legs'.

In running training groups I am aware that this is a very emotive area. Overt displays of emotion can cause group observers to empathize with the trainee who is more emotionally upset. This dynamic needs further understanding if the white trainee is upset and the black trainee is not distressed in the same way. Black therapists too may be hurting, but given repeated experiences of oppression this feeling is displayed and engaged with differently. Black therapists develop different coping mechanisms that inform how they deal with distress. The display of vulnerability is held differently.

The need to tone down passion

In undertaking research in this area, the rage of two black therapists was seeping out and was not dealt with in an upfront manner or clean transaction. The message the participants were aware of was, 'It's full on, it's too much.' So in discussing oppression it was felt that psychological therapies encourage relational dialogue but the message to black trainees is, 'Don't be too honest, too direct, or else you'll be heard as too much.'

One of the black participants reported that she wanted to put her rage in a container and put the lid on. 'I don't do rage,' she said. The theme of black clients protecting white therapists from their rage and having to make their rage more palatable for others arose. It was felt by one black participant that her rage could annihilate others, in terms of the historical build-up of oppression as an everyday experience. The spontaneity of expression/passion may need to be quashed by black trainees in terms of having to tone this down and make comments more palatable for others in order to be heard and stay in some sort of alliance within groups/training. Again the cost to self and identity development is great.

Issues in the clinical setting with clients

Pre-transference and stereotyping

Black therapists have to deal with an awful lot of pre-transference (Curry 1964), and the stereotypes involved in such processes, before a working alliance can be formed.

A white Irish trainee phoned me to enquire about working with me in therapy. I am aware my presentation differs depending on the very use of my name. For example, Harbrinder, or Mrs Stevens, or Dr Dhillon-Stevens. My accent betrays I was born in India and I can move in and out of oppressive conversations and position myself differently in this sense more than I can in terms of more visible contexts. On the phone I was told, 'You speak English so well.' At our first meeting my client revealed, 'Gosh, I thought you would be wearing funny clothes and smell of curry.' Such comments are indeed a challenge in establishing the working alliance without having an immediate rupture. How am I supposed to react? How do I deal with such overt racism while being therapeutically available? My therapeutic stance involves using my self, and what I have to curb in the dialogue, as well as attend to, to be in relationship with my client. This is the tension for black therapists. How are such tensions processed in supervision? One needs to attend to the trainee as well as the client.

Black clients have intentional strategies as ways of engaging with therapists to find out if we can work constructively together. In my research, black therapists/ clients disclosed that they had a list of things that they would want to know from all therapists:

- How authentic can the therapist be about the issues that I might bring regarding difference?
- Is the therapeutic space going to be a safe space for me?
- Does the therapist have an awareness of my ongoing practical struggle outside the therapeutic space?

- Can I feel safe and trust the therapist?
- Is the therapist emotionally accessible to the kinds of things I might bring and have to deal with?

One client felt she had to work quickly to make a decision about whether to go ahead with a therapist. This showed that she had quite a few strategies in place regarding difference and that due to her experience of oppression she had constructs around issues linked to it and would explore how the therapist performed in relation to these constructs. The fact that black therapists as clients reported having strategies to see if therapists can attune to their black experiences raises the question of whose responsibility it is in the therapeutic space to raise issues of difference. As Kareem reminds us, 'from the point of view of the intercultural therapist, I believe that it is the responsibility of the therapist, from the very outset, to facilitate the expression of any negative transference which is based on historical context, and not leave the onus on the patient' (Kareem and Littlewood 1992: 23).

Education versus protection of the therapist

Black clients often report that in therapy they have to protect the therapist from dealing with what the issues were for them. Where therapists have little or no awareness of the issues for black clients, the potential for the client to use the therapy to its full extent is limited. Black clients often feel they have to spend a considerable amount of time in educating their therapists before there is trust and safety in the therapeutic space. Clients reported that if they want to leave the therapist they do so in a way that does not leave the therapist feeling terrible about herself. They do not want to damage the therapist. It is interesting to note the internalization process here of black clients.

In reflecting on a session the black client realized her statement: 'I feel lots of things' was a cop out. She was feeling scared and wanted to protect the therapist. 'I feel lots of things' was just a way of saying, 'This is all I can tell you.' The client feared the therapist would crumble if she were too direct about her true feelings. I remember in my own therapy I felt I did not want to disclose aspects of my cultural and religious upbringing that I disliked/rejected in case these reinforced my white therapist's views of Sikhs. So I, too, was mindful of holding the therapist and holding my own process in the therapeutic space. I am far more willing to engage with others in debates about difference if they have made attempts to educate themselves rather than expect me to.

Language

Language has immense power. The power to engage and empower or disintegrate and disempower, especially within the context of difference. Language use relates to personal awareness, understanding the theoretical discourses of oppression and a conscious commitment to understanding power dynamics, how these operate and how they are maintained by the use of certain terms by those in the majority.

In the clinical setting, use of terms is important — whether we use 'coloured' as opposed to 'black', 'mixed race' as opposed to 'half-caste'. Black clients have reported the intentional use of certain words to ascertain if they and the therapist are a good match. The use of language demonstrates the client's narrative of oppression.

Language is also related to awareness in terms of sociopolitical awareness. I notice in working with aware clients how my use of language is a facilitator in the working alliance and in the bond (Bordin 1979) between us. In working with non-aware clients I am aware how language becomes a barrier and how we struggle to see each other's perspectives and reach a platform from where we have enough of a working alliance to proceed. Language can also evoke transference and counter-transference reactions.

Self-disclosure

The notion of self-disclosure, I would argue, appears to be different in this arena. Self-disclosure is more within a spectrum that aids the therapeutic relationship when issues of oppression are present. Self-disclosure is a way in which clients of oppressed groups may test the therapist and her awareness of issues of oppression. For example, in working with a client with a disability, I named my awareness of being able-bodied and my potential to oppress my client and how I may do that in the therapeutic space. The client informed me that raising this issue demonstrated to her that it could be named and openly discussed. She felt we had a platform for working together and a commitment on my part to 'own my own fear' of disability.

I also notice in terms of my religious and cultural upbringing that there is a form of self-disclosure with clients who are black or from other ethnic groups. This is a form of etiquette in terms of the the nuances of getting to know and trust someone else. For example, I often disclose the village where I was born, whether I speak Punjabi or not, and whether I am married. Clients, especially from the Indian sub-continent, will ask me such questions as a way of establishing my trustworthiness and my values within a very short time frame. Having self-disclosed, clients are more willing to engage with me about personal aspects of who they are and what they feel are their current difficulties.

In terms of AOP and working with multiple issues of oppression I would say that a similar process needs to occur. For example, in working with white gay men I often talk about being heterosexual and the power dynamics of this, as well as acknowledging gender and race differences in the room. This opens up issues that I notice and am willing to take responsibility for, and allows me to engage in dialogue about such issues should they become figural in the therapeutic space.

The limitations of reflection as a skill in working with issues of oppression

In research between clients and therapists (Dhillon-Stevens 2004a), a black client reflected that the white therapist's sense that she was reflecting, clarifying and exploring (conventional therapist behaviour), was experienced very differently by the client. 'She was repeating what I was saying but all it did was push me back. Reflecting me to myself. Now I am a sophisticated client and I felt that wasn't appreciated here.' The client reported that she would have found it helpful if the therapist had talked more about the process and about her part in what was going on – the co-creation of the therapeutic relationship in which both parties participate. This is in line with intersubjectivity theory, which emphasizes 'reciprocal mutual influence' (Stolorow and Atwood 1992: 18).

It is also worth noting that the client later reported: 'I felt like I was banging my head a bit.' There comes a choice point where one considers whether to lose the therapist in the contact or to lose a part of oneself to remain in contact. As the client reflected, 'Every relationship I have, I have to test it. Are you going to meet me or have I got to get rid of something that makes you uncomfortable in order for me to meet you?'

A clinical example: in working with a Sikh woman who had one Sikh parent and one Muslim, I disclosed that I was a Sikh and wondered what the implications of this would be for our work. I said that I was thinking about a here-and-now context and in terms of a historical back-there context. My client asked me to say a bit more. I talked of the historical Sikh/Muslim feuds that resulted in war and hate and seeing the other as the enemy. In the here-and-now context I was aware how we might carry that history separately in terms of my being born in the Indian subcontinent and her being British-born with Sikh and Muslim parents.

The disclosure enabled my client to express that she felt I was able to hold all of her experiences. In the dialogue, I was saying I was aware that there might be parts of my history that oppressed her because she held two ends of the spectrum. I was also thinking of the potential for her to collude with me in terms of the Sikh polarity. I was naming transference, countertransference and pre-transference. This communicated something about my responsibility to the client, as opposed to me not naming it and asking her to tell *me*. Asking someone to tell me would be a very different power dynamic. I feel it is more helpful to say that I am going to share something that I know about and am wondering how will it impact our relationship from my perspective and yours, and how we will manage this in the therapeutic space.

However, in reflecting on this case further, the attunement to the client's issues of oppression without self-disclosure by the therapist would have been far more therapeutically affective. The therapist would still need to have the RIG (Representations of Interactions that have become Generalised) (Stern 1985) in terms of how to attune to and facilitate this in the therapeutic space. My research has clearly evidenced that in terms of power dynamics and other areas such as the one described above, therapists may or may not have such RIGs. In terms of power, therapists who have RIGs of being powerful and powerless (usually from oppressed groups) were more effective in working therapeutically than therapists who had no experience of power and operated in terms of the norm (Dhillon-Stevens 2004a).

Matching comfort and discomfort

Matching is an important issue. (See Chapter 6 in this book for an extended consideration of ethnic matching.) After sending out 140 questionnaires to psychological therapists, 41 completed questionnaires were returned (Dhillon-Stevens 2004a). The majority of respondents identified themselves as white, British, male, able-bodied, heterosexual, middle class and being born and brought up in England. The prevailing view was that the responding therapists were not in favour of matching. The significantly high 'not declared' response indicated ambivalence. The qualitative data indicated that therapists viewed the concept of matching as excluding them from working with difference as it meant 'sameness'. Given the homogenous group, matching would be seen to exclude this group. My impression was that matching was primarily seen in terms of race, culture and ethnicity, as various comments were made about 'not learning about other cultures'. In a Multiple Oppression Model I question what specific attribute is considered regarding matching. This further demonstrates for me that we may hold certain attributes in a hierarchical framework in our schemas (Beitman 1992). Matching was considered impractical, and the ambivalence in terms of that high percentage of 'not declared' responses showed there was little understanding about when or why matching may need to be considered. This issue may need to be looked at in training under the theme of assessments. As Kareem and Littlewood (1992: 12) state when discussing matching:

> I certainly think its position needs to be taken more sympathetically by its more liberal critics than previously, but it should be considered as one possible option, rather than 'the solution', one possible choice, analogous perhaps to women's therapy groups. It may present a safe space, but it may also be seen as the convenient excuse for white therapists not to confront their own implicit prejudice, and not to start working with black clients.

In this study respondents felt matching would not allow them to work with 'difference'. This raises the question of how difference is worked through if therapists have very little concrete experience of difference or have not explored their own prejudices. The authors further state:

> intercultural therapy should never be allowed to become some specialised psychotherapy, to be targeted at black people, but simply therapy which takes account of these issues... If I were black I would start by looking for a black therapist; not because of some inherent racial understanding, some shared mystique of consciousness, some hypostasised culture, but because, by and large, black therapists have actually given more serious consideration to these issues (p. 12).

The responses from individuals who were from minority/oppressed groups indicated more 'serious consideration' through concrete experiences, examples and personal experience in their responses.

Another important consideration concerning the responses was researched by Abramowitz and Murray (1983). They found that white reviewers tended to minimize the effects of ethnicity, while black reviewers tended to emphasize findings in which differences are found. Harrison (1975) showed in his work the existence of a general trend that people tend to prefer their counsellors to be of the same race. Who the therapist is and their experiences and understanding of the issues of AOP would be important in the matching debate.

This is an area that needs further research. In clinical practice my experience is that matching is important for black people. In working with a young Sikh woman she disclosed that when the counselling service she attended matched her up with me, another Sikh woman, she was pleased as well as feeling apprehensive. The apprehension was that I would judge her and think of her as disloyal to Sikh culture and that she was not a 'proper' Sikh. The pleased expression centred on feeling understood and working with someone who would understand concepts such as *izzat* which she did not need to explain. The result was my ability to comprehend the gravity of her experience.

'Internal oppressor'

It is worth noting the concept of internalized racism and how this affects black therapists, especially in having to survive cultural and institutional racism. Another concept that is also pertinent is that of the *internal oppressor*. Aileen Alleyne (2004: 49), in her research on workplace oppression, defines this as an aspect of

> [the] self that becomes the inner tyrant – and is distinct from internalised oppression. The latter is the way in which we allow external beliefs and value systems to invalidate our authenticity and inhibit our personal agency. The internal oppressor is in my view an aspect of the self that appears to carry difficult historical and intergenerational baggage across the generations. In terms of black/white relations, the internal oppressor seems to create a post-slavery/post-colonial mindset that colours our (black people's) dealings with the white Other. It influences our interrelational dynamics and attachment with this Other and may even collude unconsciously with the prevailing external difficulties. The internal oppressor seems to be ever present, but lies dormant for the most part. It is only when it is in contact with an external oppressive situation – real, perceived, or a mixture of both – that the historical memories are re-awakened, opening up old wounds that can lead to silent, invisible rewounding of the self and the nature of the internal oppressor appears to be the sum of these characteristics, which rest in the shadow of the self. The legacy of (our) black people's historical past, along with the burden of our internalised oppression, both seem to play a crucial part in shaping our pre-transference relationship and attachment patterns to the white Other.
> (Alleyne 2004: 49)

It is important for black therapists to be attuned to the concept of internalized oppression and the internal oppressor, both in ourselves and with our clients. Alongside this I would hold the notion of ongoing racism as a form of developmental trauma for clients in this area.

Conclusion

The notion of researching the experiences of black therapists in psychological therapy is one that is building momentum as more black therapists are involved in research and helping the profession understand the importance of such issues. Given that psychological therapies are still dominated by white therapists, it is vital we examine these issues in terms of training institutions, supervisors and therapists engaged in intercultural therapy with black clients.

References

Abramowitz, S. and Murray, J. (1983) 'Race affects in psychotherapy' in J. Murray and P. Abramson (eds) *Bias in Psychotherapy*. New York: Praeger.

Alleyne, A. (2004) The internal oppressor and black identity wounding, *Counselling and Psychotherapy Journal*, 15(10): 48–50.

Beitman, B.D. (1992) Integration through fundamental similarities and useful differences among the schools', in J.C. Norcross and M.R. Goldfried (eds) *Handbook of Psychotherapy Integration*. New York: Basic Books.

Bell, E.F. (2001) Infusing race into the US discourse on action research', in P. Reason and H. Bradbury (eds) *Handbook of Action Research*. London: Sage.

Bordin, E.S. (1979) The generalizability of the psychoanalytical concept of the working alliance, *Psychotherapy: Theory, Research and Practice*, 16(3): 252–60.

Buber, M. (1970) *I and Thou*, trans. W. Kaufman. Edinburgh: T. & T. Clark.

Curry, A. (1964) Myths, transference and the black psychotherapist', *Psychological Review*, 51(1): 7–14.

Dhillon-Stevens, H. (2001) Anti-oppressive practice in the supervisory relationship, in M. Carroll and M. Tholstrup (eds) *Integrative Approaches to Supervision*. London: Jessica Kingsley.

Dhillon-Stevens, H. (2004a) *Healing Inside and Out: An Examination of Dialogic Encounters in the Area of Anti-Oppressive Practice in Counselling and Psychotherapy*, doctorate in Psychotherapy by Professional Studies, Middlesex University.

Dhillon-Stevens, H. (2004b) Personal and professional integration of anti-oppressive practice and the multiple oppression model in psychotherapeutic education, *United Kingdom Association for Psychotherapy Integration (UKAPI) Journal*, 2: 47–62.

Harrison, D. (1975) Race as a counsellor–client variable in counselling and psychotherapy: a review of research, *The Counselling Psychologist*, 5(1): 124–33.
Kareem, J. and Littlewood, R. (1992) *Inter-cultural Therapy*. Oxford: Blackwell.
Stern, D. (1985) *The Interpersonal World of the Infant*. New York: Basic Books.
Stolorow, R.D. and Attwood, G.E. (1992) *Contexts of Being*. Hillsdale, NJ: The Analytic Press.

10 Overcoming racism, discrimination and oppression in psychotherapy

Aileen Alleyne

Introduction

To understand the very complex nature of racism, oppression and discrimination in psychotherapy, an interdisciplinary perspective incorporating research from social psychology, developmental psychology, sociology, cross-cultural psychology, counselling psychology and education must be taken into account. Such perspectives help broaden our understanding of individual and collective identity and other complex dynamics involving issues of power, powerlessness, the dominant and the dominated.

Many texts have covered these interdisciplinary perspectives. A few helpful examples particularly pertinent to the theme of race and psychotherapy are:

1 *Racism as splitting, projection and projective identification* (Dollard 1938; Money-Kyrle 1960; Hinshelwood 1989; Rustin 1991; Young 1992; Timimi 1996; Ward 1997; Gordon 2004). These texts represent arguments and counter-arguments for these concepts.

2 *Understanding the roots of racism through dynamics of the Oedipus complex* (Chasseguet-Smirgel 1990). Nazi genocide is referred to here as a clear example.

3 *Racism as an irrational process and therefore a form of neurosis if held onto* (Rustin 1991).

4 *Racism as sibling rivalry* (Sterba 1947) and *a way of understanding how and why black people are made to represent sibling rivals and then placed in situations to be infantilized.*

5 *Racism as a manifestation of sexual jealousy and associated with objectification of black people as primitive, the physical, shit and evil* (Berkeley-Hill 1924; Fanon 1968; Vannoy Adams 1996).

6 *Racism as a response to modernity* (Frosh 1989; Sarup 1996). Racism as a matter of cultural imperialism and exploitation and therefore *highlighting issues of power and powerless and the dominant and dominated.*

7 *Understanding racism from the perspective of boundaries and boundary drawing* – a way to fix the 'other', to assert and maintain a sense of absolute difference between self and 'other' (Gordon 2004).

8   *Understanding racial oppression in terms of its creation of a complex internal dynamic in black people.* The internal oppressor is an aspect of the self that contributes negatively and affects black attachment patterns and related-ness to the white 'other' (Alleyne 2004a, 2004b).

All the above writers provide different perspectives contributing to a compre-hensive theoretical understanding of racism, oppression and discrimination, and countless others offer further elaborations and variances on these topics.

I do not wish to regurgitate these well-worn texts. Rather, my aim is to offer a more pragmatic approach to the counselling/psychotherapy practitioner who aspires towards an anti-racist/anti-discriminatory approach in their work. To this end, particular attention is paid to avoiding common pitfalls of discriminatory practices with specific regard to race, thus enabling the practitioner to be more mindful of their own unconscious and semiconscious prejudices in this area. As anti-oppressive practices involve wider areas of difference and diversity other than race, a set of guidelines outlining values and principles underpinning good practice in working with other areas of difference and diversity is also offered.

Examples of 'subtle' racism in psychotherapy

Manifestations of very overt racism and other forms of blatant prejudice are in-creasingly rare in counselling and psychotherapy. In today's world, exhibiting such behaviour is considered unfashionable and singles out the perpetrator for public shame and ridicule. However, we should not become complacent and rush into thinking we can now celebrate a new post-racism era, where its negative effects have disappeared and therefore no longer exist. This would be naive and short-sighted.

A major challenge still remains for us to address virulent and quiet acts of racism that are more subtle, often hidden, and silent. These acts may not harm the body, but do violence to the soul.

The following are some common examples of subtle racism and hidden racial prejudice exhibited by practitioners in counselling and psychotherapy. I distin-guish racism as action and behaviour, and racial prejudice as thoughts, ideas and beliefs in response to difference.

- Holding negative or unfavourable pre-transference thoughts about clients based on their foreign-sounding names, and allowing this to influence 'actual' transference relationship development. For example, a new client presenting with the name Oye Ogunkoya, might lead a therapist to assume that she or he will be seeing someone who is foreign, male and African, with little ability in English, when in fact the client might be British born, female and public-school educated.
- Ignoring or not taking care to check out and pronounce unfamiliar sound-ing names correctly shows disregard for difference. Furthermore, suggest-ing that a foreign name should be shortened to make pronunciation easier, or worse, allocating your choice of a European name (e.g. 'Let's call you

Fred'), is seemingly inoffensive in nature, but can wound a person's sense of self.

- Failing to notice the client's race and falling prey to the *colour blind* syndrome ignores human diversity and uniqueness. The notion that *I don't see people's colour, everyone is a human being in my eyes* is a clear example of 'race avoidance' (Thomson and Jenal 1994), and is a failure to appropriately acknowledge and embrace important signifiers of someone's identity.
- Showing indifference in therapy can manifest as the therapist having no interest or engagement in the client's unique cultural and racial experiences. It can be felt at an individual level, affecting the client's own personal feelings, and on behalf of a collective, race or racial group as a whole. Indifference, as a form of intentional and unintentional racism, can leave the 'other' feeling invisible and a non-person.
- Assessing black minorities as not having the capacity to introspect or relate to symbolic forms of communication, and therefore not being eligible candidates for psychotherapy, is discriminatory. Such discrimination denies equality of treatment and falsely contributes to notions that black minorities can only respond to prescriptive forms of treatment, such as behavioural and brief solution-focused therapies.
- Assessing the client as resisting or avoiding in the therapeutic process because of their tendency to a focus more on family dynamics ('we' focus as opposed to 'I' focus), may suggest a Eurocentric bias in favour of the primacy of the individual. Such bias can disregard the importance of significant relationships within the 'collective' and represents a lack of creative synthesis between individualism and collectivism.
- Assuming all members of a racial group will adhere to all its cultural tenets and norms ignores individuality and uniqueness in cultural identity and is therefore discriminatory.
- Working from the premise that every black person *is scarred by the mark of oppression* and therefore engages life from this basic fault position is wholly presumptuous. Although no black person is spared the reality of the presence of racism, not everyone is scarred by its experience.
- Fixing the 'other' to assert and maintain a sense of absolute difference between self and 'other' is perhaps one of the more subtle examples of racism (e.g. a therapist innocently relating to a client thus: 'I don't expect you to know much about rural England, so it will be hard for you to...' or, 'Of course I won't expect you to be interested in English history and the Classics – that won't be your thing,' or, 'Let's guess, holidays for you must be going back to Pakistan or somewhere hot.') Such examples and tones in therapists' interventions can have the tendency of fixing the client in a stereotypical cultural box and creating distance between the white therapist and non-white client.

The above examples identify subtle forms of racism, which can be both culturally oppressive and infantilizing. Some may only be parked in the therapist's thoughts and never be verbalized. However, it is my view that, once present, such thinking carries the power of influencing interactive behaviours, attitudinal and interpretive responses. Clients pick up the 'vibes' and seek to protect themselves from further hurt. Black clients have been known to say, 'I think my white therapist is good, but when I talk about my black experiences, she tends to go quiet and slides over the subject,' or 'Therapy is helpful, but I feel I always have to explain and justify myself.' These examples highlight clients' ambivalent experiences in the working alliance. Therapists may be under the illusion of doing good work with their clients, and unaware that these powerful negative messages might be impeding the quality of trust and engagement in the alliance.

The following is a personal example of how a therapist's intervention in a difficult cross-cultural situation can appear seemingly inoffensive but have a most devastating and paralysing effect on the client and subsequent progress in the work.

A case example

In one of my past experiences of personal analytical therapy, I recalled being asked by my white therapist how I was feeling about a very painful and challenging situation I had recently negotiated in a psychotherapy training experiential group. It involved me, the only black student in a large predominantly white group, being the recipient of a white student's racist projection.

The incident followed a fairly healthy disagreement with a fellow student about a race matter that involved the whole group. My white colleague brought to the following group session a dream she declared she couldn't make sense of. She described her terror at being attacked by a big black gorilla that was chomping huge bits out of her arm. As she tearfully and dramatically spoke about her nightmare, all eyes were turned towards me, some darting, others lingering in an embarrassed and accusatory way. I felt very awkward and was left strangely irked and exposed in the group. The deafening silence that followed the telling of this dream made something unpleasant stick in the group. The facilitator's total lack of response in facilitating the unconscious elements in what I felt was a very revealing dream, and failure to deal with the group's reactions, left me feeling isolated and painfully alone.

I shared this difficult experience with my therapist and talked about the very upsetting feelings that were stirred up. The incident triggered and re-opened other painful experiences of being subtly targeted because of my race and it was as if I had been re-wounded in the same place. I shared with my therapist how difficult I felt it was for black students, and particularly the lone black student, to survive such training without sometimes feeling a casualty at the end of it. I let her know how worried I was for my position on the course and said that I felt I needed to guard against such a thing happening to me again.

Having by that time worked with my therapist for about nine months, I had naturally talked about my family history and those values and beliefs that were important to me. I shared with her that I had come from a culture and family home that valued education as being important to succeeding in life. Celebrating events that contributed towards this particular journey was customary. I let her in on some of the family sayings that I had introjected as a child and held dear, two of which were *education is power* and *you have to work twice as hard to make people notice you*. Such were their importance that all educational achievements were viewed as negotiating major rites of passage. My therapist was privy to learning how important this and many other cultural aspects of my life were to me, and I hoped she was developing a greater awareness of my Caribbean core within an adopted British identity. In other aspects of Caribbean life, she also learned that every significant achievement towards bettering oneself was an opportunity to celebrate – for example, traditionally pouring rum on the ground and thanking the gods. I underlined the fact that I was brought up in a family who believed these milestones were not to be forgotten, but rather to be marked in a very special way. Embarking then on my masters degree was an important and significant part of this personal journey.

In responding to my therapist's question of how I was feeling about the difficult experiential group situation, I shared with her that although I was a deeply affected by the unpleasant event, I had remained strong. I communicated that I was pleased with myself for being able to challenge the facilitator for his lack of intervention and not utilizing the situation to deal head-on with real underlying conflicts of race and cultural differences in the group. I described to my therapist a personal technique employed when faced with adversity – a tip from my dear mother, which is to call upon our ancestors to wrap their arms around you in times of need. I had used this method during the loneliest of moments in the group, where I felt I had no allies and no support. I let my therapist know about a family script that had helped me to remember that I was truly loved as a human being, and in remembering this, I was able to maintain a sense of equilibrium. I shared with her the fact that I did not allow myself to be pushed into responding rashly in the unpleasant group situation, which could have easily branded me the stereotypical *scary*, *angry*, *aggressive*, *threatening*, *difficult* black woman. I shared all of this in good faith and hoped the one place I would and could be held was in the haven of my twice-weekly psychotherapy sessions.

I felt I had built up a safe relationship in the nine months of working with my therapist, and was looking – at least initially – for a warm, empathetic and supportive reaction to my traumatic experiences in the training group. Instead, I received a bald and cold response which was: 'You clearly utilized a lot of mechanisms to shore yourself up . . . are we in danger of being a bit holier than thou?' I was stunned by this response and felt as if I'd been smacked in the face. In that instant my therapist had become one of the experiential group members. She was not with me or for me. I wondered whether she had really heard the importance of my personal and family history, and I silently questioned whether she had taken in what all that had meant to me. I felt disappointed by not receiving an unqualified acknowledgement of my fight for survival in a lonely and unfriendly situation, and above all, let down by the lack of a full acknowledgement of my transcendence over an undermining and destructive experience in the group. I had expected at least an initial uncomplicated response of support and empathy to convey a sense of attunement to the unpleasant hidden aspects of race that had surfaced in my group experience.

On reflection, I felt the therapist's perception of what she saw as my smugness in relaying back to her how I had coped with the uncomfortable group incident revealed two things. First, I think the unpleasant event highlighted obvious negative symbolizations which were awkward and uncomfortable to address head-on. Secondly, and perhaps more importantly, I was appearing not to need her, as I had first of all asserted myself in the group, and then called upon my mother, family and ancestors to protect and comfort me in spirit. My therapist, being analytically trained and choosing a hasty interpretation of my behaviour, was, in my view, giving primacy to the perceived effectiveness of a classical psychoanalytic intervention over a more straightforward humanitarian person-centred acknowledgement of my painful experience. I also concluded that the therapist's reference to my being a bit holier than thou was probably due to annoyance at my daring to blow my own trumpet – something that seems to be discouraged in sections of British culture. Identifying what I felt was the therapist's ungenerous streak led to an inhibition with regard to sharing other personal achievements and successes.

As the black client in this cross-cultural relationship, I was left feeling that it wasn't permissible to engage too proudly in positive reflections and indeed one's own affirmations. I wondered whether there was an expectation for me to focus only on tales of suffering and being blighted, beaten down and scarred by life's oppressive experiences. I reminded myself that a majority of black individuals will attest to the fact that being black was not their *raison d'être*, for the simple reason that, despite life's hardships, black people are still able to work well, play well, love well and expect well.

The ability to bounce back in the face of adversity is a notable quality of many minority groups and therefore raises the concept of *resilience* in cross-cultural work. This must be an important area of acknowledgement in counselling and psychotherapy, which should be fostered and celebrated.

Reflections on oppressive practice

In the above example, there is much to discuss and glean about the subtleties of oppressive practices. The therapist who rushes in to challenge a client's perceived or real experience of racism, or one who facilitates untimely rationalization of the client's feelings of discrimination, may unwittingly create mistrust in the alliance and set up *no go* areas in the work. The therapist will be experienced as lacking in empathy: not being able to bear witness to the client's feelings.

The paradox in the aforementioned case example is the therapist unwittingly contributing to feelings of oppression inside the work at a time when the client is seeking support and help with challenges of oppression outside. By adding this further burden to the client's experiences, a practitioner can unintentionally deny the individual a safe and helpful space to heal well.

In my own therapy, the ongoing alliance with my therapist was hampered and produced in me an unhealthy caution in our work. This was expressed by a silent dynamic where I felt pushed into relying on myself to be my own trusted caretaker. This very unfortunate choice of relating to the other points to a dynamic that may easily occur in dissatisfied and disgruntled clients who feel unsafe to *surrender* fully in the therapeutic process. I offer the following as a way of countering the pitfalls of this situation.

A state of grace

Dealing with subtle aspects of discrimination and oppression can be challenging for both client and therapist alike, but for the client who is affected and sometimes ground down by its damaging effects, the terror of losing one's sense of ontological security is great. In such situations, the battle-weary and battle-scarred can potentially stop learning. Facilitating hope and movement forward can be key tasks in helping the oppressed towards a state of grace. Grace in this context refers to the relief we experience when we understand how and why we have particular experiences, and then knowing how to do things differently so that the results are better.

The gift of this state of grace for black people is about engaging in the important work of living life in a more fully functioning and flourishing manner in spite of the scars of life's traumas. A state of grace is not just about surviving. It is about thriving and keeping alive the collective's distinct hybrid vigour, which is the process of delighting in *all* that makes us potent, resilient and powerful. Reclaiming our strengths and all of these positive aspects as part of the goal of therapy can only serve to repair, lighten and heal the soul.

The next account is a further experience of personal therapy, which highlights examples of subtle, quiet and hidden forms of racism in the cross-cultural encounter.

A second case example

In one of my much earlier experiences of seeking personal therapy, I chose a female therapist on the recommendation of my psychotherapy training body. The therapist happened to be white. I remember arriving at the therapist's home one dark autumn evening, feeling quite anxious about the unknown and unfamiliar process I was embarking on.

The first thing I noticed on getting there was the fact that the consulting room was in the basement of a very large building to which the entrance-way was very dimly lit. Getting to the front door was an undertaking in itself, as a steep flight of narrow concrete steps had to be negotiated in the semi-dark. The task was made treacherous because of wet, well-trodden autumn leaves that had become soggy and slippery. I remember having to hold tightly onto the cold steel railings so as not to lose my balance. My initial anxiety about starting therapy with a new person had now turned to irritation and I swore under my breath before re ̄ the consulting room door.

Meeting these external challenges even before any *actual* work had taken stirred my pre-transference thoughts and raised many questions. Was I goin held safely by this woman? Was she a trustworthy therapist? How could she allow her entrance-way to become like a death trap? Did she not care about her clients? Did she not use the entrance herself? How empathic was she? Could she empathize with me? Could I trust her? My pre-transference thoughts were running away with me and I was filled with negative feelings and doubts about this encounter.

On meeting my therapist following her delayed response to the doorbell, I, in typical and respectful Caribbean fashion, held out my hand. The therapist promptly ignored it and allowed hers to remain rigidly at her side. Instead, the bland 'hello' received only added to my sense of rejection, a feeling that was compounded by my early unwelcoming experiences. As I followed the therapist along a very narrow corridor to the consulting room, where only at that moment the room lights were turned on, I couldn't help thinking, 'What a cold welcome!' Not only was there the question of being held safely, I was now wondering about the therapist's capacities for warmth and generosity. These thoughts were heightened in the presence of an obvious race dynamic; her being white and clearly middle class, and me, the black client questioning whether I was not good enough to be properly received.

As the session began, I was struck by another disturbing observation. Opposite to where I was seated hung a painting depicting what appeared to be a farm scene. It caught my eye, as it was no ordinary farm scene. There were cotton fields worked by very dark, Lowry-like matchstick figures, industriously hunched over and picking away at clouds of white fluffy cotton buds. In the background stood an imposing shadowy image of a large grand house and a faint figure of a male dressed in khaki shorts, white shirt and sporting a large Panama hat. I soon realized I was looking at a typical slave plantation scene. I was very surprised at this and started to wonder whether the therapist had experience of working with black clients. I heard myself ask, 'Have you worked with any black clients before?' My therapist paused for a long moment, and then, meeting my gaze, said in a very exaggerated, ponderous, almost caricature psychoanalytic fashion, 'I wonder . . . how you would feel if you were to see the black side of me?'

I was left reeling from this question and puzzled by the therapist's use of the term *black* in an apparently very negative context. What did she mean? I was baffled by the choice of painting for a consulting room, and even more so by the previous off-putting experiences. Suffice it to say the stacking up of all of my previous negative pre-transference feelings on entering this brand new professional arrangement, coupled with my actual encounter with the therapist, all led to a clear decision to not carry on the work.

In this real case example, it would be true to say that the experiences with the unkempt and unsafe therapy entrance were straightforward issues of professional neglect and had absolutely nothing to do with race, racism or discrimination. The therapist's refusal of my greeting by offering a handshake can also be understood from the point of view of exercising personal choice and preference. No issues with that. However, when such factors are compounded by all the aforementioned personal experiences in this case example, they can offer useful insight into how we can avoid the impact of subtle racism, oppression and discrimination in the working and therapeutic alliance.

All that we expose (and don't) to our clients informs them about who we are as individuals and as therapists. A painting depicting an obvious slave plantation scene may have pleasing aesthetic value to a white therapist, but may re-open painful wounds and historical memories for a black client. Similarly, the negative or clumsy use of the term *black* may be viewed as innocent, an unfortunate choice of expression, and maybe even not minding the restraints of political correctness, but it is important to be mindful that it may have the potential of setting up barriers in the early stages of trust-building between therapist and client.

Establishing and building trust in the first meeting is essential in all therapeutic work. In the case example discussed, these elements are betrayed by the client's negative experiences on meeting the therapist for the first time. To harness them in order to show the cumulative impact on the client: there was the therapist's neglect in making the entrance-way to the consulting area safe and welcoming; this was followed by the delay in answering the doorbell, which created additional anxiety; the therapist's refusal to shake the client's outstretched hand at the initial meeting generated feelings of rejection and interfered with possible chances of fostering a warm connection; not having the consulting room lit beforehand indicated a possible tendency to withhold; the particular choice of painting for the consulting room and all the negative unconscious messages it screamed acted as a serious barrier to building confidence in the therapist's cultural/political awareness. Additionally, the therapist's apparent defensive reaction to the client's genuine enquiry about personal experiences in working with black people finally served to damage possible trust developing in the work between them.

What could have been particularly helpful in this scenario? On reflection, a reaction to the client's enquiry about the therapist's experience in working with black people could have been a straightforward reply such as, 'I am very happy to answer your question, but can we discuss what's inside or behind it?'; or, 'I sense you may have anxieties about working with me, a white therapist...would it be helpful for us to discuss this?' Either response might have been experienced as more holding, as opposed to the bald interpretation: 'I wonder...how you would feel if you were to see the black side of me?' What was *black* supposed to mean in this particular context? Was it stereotypical parlance meaning bad, ugly, wicked, cruel, and showing an absence of care? Or was it used figuratively to refer to one's shadow side or failings, for example, putting one's foot in it and getting it wrong? Whichever meaning is ascribed to the word, the message appears and remains pejorative.

Language therefore is of crucial importance to the cross-cultural encounter. For the practitioner, our words act as an essential and often key tool in the healing process, but they can also offend and hurt, and maybe even do damage to the soul.

Offering a guide to preventing prejudice and discrimination in counselling and psychotherapy cannot completely rid us of these tendencies. The fact remains that prejudice and discrimination are common phenomena and we are all prone to these attitudes and behaviours. However, we can only seek to decrease the potential for their negative effect by continually increasing our self-awareness and striving towards a cultural confidence in working with issues of diversity.

Values and principles underpinning good practice in working with issues of difference and diversity

> Remember, feedback should give value to the receiver not relief for the giver.

The following is a set of values and principles underpinning good practice in working with issues of difference and diversity. These can apply both to the practice of therapy and also to the work of clinical supervision. They are listed within specific categories of diversity for ease of consultation. Further pointers to other areas of diversity may be found in Lago and Smith (2010).

Working with lesbians and gay men

1   Acknowledge the existence of and work through external and internalized homophobic and heterosexist messages.
2   Maintain empathy by learning about and understanding lesbians' and gay men's identities and needs.
3   Affirm lesbians' and gay men's lifestyles as viable and legitimate alternative life-choices (e.g. that they can survive healthily and can enjoy legal and social recognition).
4   Validate lesbians and gay men by challenging clients, peers, colleagues and the organization for change.
5   Recognize the diversity of lesbians and gay men, and understand social and political issues which lead to feelings of powerlessness, systematic exclusion and marginalization for lesbians and gay men who are from black and other ethnic minority groups and those with disabilities.

Working with refugees

1   Acknowledge the fact that English may be the second language for refugee clients and that effective work with such individuals may require extra time allocation and the assistance of interpreters/translators.
2   Recognize the social, political and emotional problems for refugees. Endeavour to seek specialist knowledge to work with issues of cultural displacememt, homesickness, political torture, effects of war on the human psyche, culture shock, family disruption, isolation, housing and immigration problems.
3   Work with the effects of post-traumatic experiences which manifest mainly as loss, bereavement and mental distress.
4   Act appropriately as advocate when dealing with the *system* without taking away the client's responsibility and dignity.

Working with people with disabilities

1   Avoid the tendency to make decisions on behalf of the disabled person which deny them control over their own life.

2   Be aware not to reinforce 'medical' definitions of disability which focus on 'impairment' and 'special needs', and direct attention and approaches to these aspects of disability.
3   Acknowledge and address ways in which society and its institutions are organized to exclude people with disabilities from mainstream provision and employment.
4   Recognize that the 'problem' for people with disabilities lies not within individual bodies but with the ways society fails to organize its resources to include people with disabilities.

Working with black and Asian clients

1   Acknowledge and actively deal with racism operating at these levels: individual, institutional, intentional and unintentional.
2   Become aware of hidden feelings and subtle expressions of *indifference* (not caring, not being concerned or interested in the concerns of the racial 'other').
3   Take account of support structures within different communities (e.g. church, the role of religion, religious practices and rituals, the extended family and traditional family support structures).
4   Respect the need to include helping agencies relevant to different communities (e.g. spiritual healers, the shaman, the priest, elders and other specialist agencies).
5   Recognize the influence of the community.
6   Redefine and work appropriately with Eurocentric concepts of mental health.
7   Reappraise what psychological yardsticks are culturally relevant in determining psychic equilibrium and 'cure'.

Working with women

1   Be aware of the biological, psychological, cultural and social issues that have an impact on women in general and on particular groups of women in society.
2   Recognize and be aware of all forms of oppression and how these interact with sexism.
3   Increase ability of utilizing skills that are particularly facilitative to women in general and to particular racial and cultural groups of women.
4   Be aware of sexist language that may be unintentionally used in counselling, supervision, teaching, daily interactions and journal publications.
5   Do not engage in sexual activity with women clients under any circumstances. Be aware of the continuum of psychological covert and overt abuse which includes professional voyeurism, sexual gazes (covert), sexual remarks, unacceptable touching and more overt sexual contact.
6   Understand the effects of sex-role socialization on women's development and functioning.

Working with racism and the racist

1   Remember that those who remain silent to racist behaviour are likely to be colluding with its negative effects; therefore, maintain a proactive stance by challenging offensive, oppressive and all other forms of behaviour which excludes black people, Asians, Jews, Irish people and those people who represent the hidden white minority group (e.g., Greeks, Germans, etc.)

2   Failure to combat racism in any form is not just a simple act of racism; it is a perpetuation of racism. *If you are not part of the solution, you are part of the problem.*

3   Comment clearly on the offending behaviour (e.g. 'I did not find it funny when you mimicked the black cleaner's accent'). *Spell out the consequence of the behaviour* (e.g. mimicry in a racial context is *always* negative because its intention is to highlight an aspect of the person's identity for ridicule).

4   Spell out the positive consequences of the behavioural change to be made; people need to know the positive effects of the change before shifting from their position.

5   Use forms of communication that are appropriate for the individual and which take account of the need for privacy and respect. Remember, feedback should always give value to the receiver, not relief for the giver.

6   Support others actively to make a complaint about discrimination.

7   Deal with covert problems which undermine and affect personal morale by making these issues overt in individual supervision, staff meetings and, if necessary, special meetings to address the situation. Consider group consultancy if circumstances permit.

Working with yourself

1   Re-examine your own values and beliefs and how they have been influenced.

2   Be *willing* to learn new patterns of thinking, perceiving and behaving.

3   Be open to meeting the unknown and unfamiliar.

4   Be prepared to admit your shortcomings; there is strength in owning one's ignorance and naiveté about other cultures and showing a willingness to learn.

5   Stay with the *natural* discomfort stirred up by *difference* and allow yourself to become familiar with the new effects.

6   Do your own homework on *difference* and *diversity*. Do not expect the 'other' to feed you continuously in the process of learning.

7   Consciousness-raising on its own is not enough in working with cultural diversity; the priority should be to identify and change personal behaviour which limits open and effective interaction with others.

References

Alleyne, A. (2004a) Black identity and workplace oppression, *Counselling and Psychotherapy Research*, 4(1): 4–8.

Alleyne, A. (2004b) Race-specific workplace stress, *Counselling and Psychotherapy Journal*, 15(8): 30–3.

Berkeley-Hill, O. (1924) The 'color question' from a psychoanalytic standpoint, *Psychoanalytic Review*, 11: 246–53.

Chasseguet-Smirgel, J. (1990) Reflections of a psychoanalyst upon the Nazi biocracy and genocide, *International Review of Psychoanalysis*, 17.

Dollard, J. (1938) Hostility and fear in social life, *Social Forces*, 17: 15–25.

Fanon, F. (1968) *Black Skin, White Masks*. London: Pluto Press.

Frosh, S. (1989) *Psychoanalysis and Psychology: Minding the Gap*. London: Macmillan.

Gordon, G. (2004) Souls in armour: thoughts on psychoanalysis and racism, *British Journal of Psychotherapy*, 21(2): 277–94.

Hinshelwood, R.D. (1989) Social possession of identity, in B. Richards (ed.) *Crises of the Self: Further Essays on Psychoanalysis and Politics*. London: Free Association Books.

Lago, C. and Smith, B. (2010) *Anti-Discriminatory Counselling and Psychotherapy Practice*, 2nd edn. London: Sage.

Money-Kyrle, R. (1960) On prejudice: a psychoanalytical approach, *British Journal of Medical Psychology*, 33: 205–9.

Rustin, M. (1991) Psychoanalysis, racism and anti-racism, in *The Good Society and the Inner World: Psychoanalysis, Politics and Culture*. London: Verso.

Sarup, M. (1996) *Identity, Culture and The Postmodern World*. Edinburgh: Edinburgh University Press.

Sterba, R. (1947) Some psychological factors in Negro race-hatred and in anti-Negro riots, in G. Roheim (ed.) *Psychoanalysis and the Social Sciences*.

Thompson, C.E. and Jenal, S.T. (1994) Interracial and intraracial quasi-counseling interactions when counselors avoid discussing race, *Journal of Counseling Psychology*, 41: 484–91.

Timimi, B. (1996) Race and colour in internal and external reality, *British Journal of Psychotherapy*, 13(2).

Vannoy-Adams, M. (1996) *The Multicultural Imagination, 'Race', Color and the Unconscious*. London: Routledge.

Ward, I. (1997) Race and racisms: a reply to Sami Timimi, *British Journal of Psychotherapy*, 14(1).

Young, R.M. (1992) Benign and virulent projective identification in group and institutions, paper delivered to the First European Conference of the Rowantree Foundation on 'Projective Identification in Institutions', Wierden, Holland.

11 Research in transcultural counselling and psychotherapy

Patsy Sutherland and Roy Moodley

Introduction

As societies become increasingly diverse in terms of the 'Group of Seven' social identities ('Big 7': gender, race, class, sexual orientation, disability, age and religion) (see, for discussion, Moodley and Lubin 2008; Moodley and Murphy 2010), so too have the counselling and therapeutic needs of these diverse communities. While the practice of therapy appears to be growing exponentially in relation to the demographics of diversity, research on the other hand has not kept pace but seems to remain marginal, underfunded and not taken seriously by the mainstream counselling and psychotherapy research and professional community (Moodley 2003). In recent years the changes in the theory and practice of counselling and psychotherapy concerning diversity have made it much more difficult for researchers to engage in research given the wide remit which diversity encompasses, not least the confusions and complexities surrounding the concepts of race, ethnicity, culture and multiculturalism. This has made a difficult situation especially problematic when it comes to writing research proposals, defining the populations under study, applying for funding, selecting participants, data collection and analysis of the results (Moodley 2003), often leading many researchers in transcultural research to focus on particular ethnic groups (e.g. African-American, Asian, Latino/a, and so on). Meanwhile, mainstream research appears to be preoccupied with clinical issues that are central to the theory and practice of counselling and psychotherapy at a sophisticated level (see e.g. Toukmanian and Rennie 1992; Dryden 1996; Roth and Fonagy 1996).

Indeed, the lack of substantial research has ultimately resulted in a dearth of knowledge on many of the critical experiences of black and ethnic minority clients. At best, the consequences are misdiagnoses, poor treatment planning and high rates of premature termination. The lack of research and paucity of knowledge also creates a space where therapists tend to see all black and ethnic minority clients as homologous, and offer them the same treatment irrespective of their gender, ethnicity, sexual orientation and the other 'Big 7' multiple identities. Furthermore, the focus on race and culture as an exclusive feature of the client motivates therapists to gain cultural knowledge (the '3-S' effect – sari [ethic dress], somosas [ethnic food] and steel band [ethnic music]) rather than develop in-depth therapeutic approaches with black and ethnic minority clients.

In this chapter we consider the current practices, complexities and challenges that confront transcultural counselling and psychotherapy research. We attempt to clarify some of the confusions that transcultural researchers seem to indicate are problematic areas in research in this field, and attempt to highlight some of the newer and emerging themes. Lastly, we elucidate the ethical issue governing transcultural research. We begin with a review and critique of the current practice and research in counselling and psychotherapy with black and ethnic minority clients.

Review and critique of multicultural/cross-cultural counselling research

The practice of counselling and psychotherapy has evolved from being just culturally focused (ethnic minority) embracing all minoritized groups (gay, lesbian, disabled, and other stigmatized identities). This has taken almost 40 years in the making, and in the process its nomenclatures have changed accordingly – namely, 'cross-cultural', 'intercultural', 'transcultural', 'multicultural', and now 'diversity'. This in itself has created much confusion for researchers. A key argument made by multicultural counsellors is that issues of race, ethnicity and culture are further marginalized with the inclusion of diversity. For example, Carter *et al.* (1998) examined *The Counseling Psychologist*, the *Journal of Counseling Psychology* and the *Journal of Vocational Behavior* from 1982 to 1991 to determine counselling psychology's commitment or complacency with respect to race and ethnicity. The results indicated that issues pertaining to race and ethnicity were not addressed in the majority of articles (77 per cent); 9 per cent adequately focused on racial and ethnic issues, with the other 14 per cent only doing so superficially. What this analysis reveals is that researchers have only paid lip service when it comes to the inclusion and careful examination of race and ethnicity in counselling and psychology.

Over the past three decades an increased interest in multicultural/cross-cultural counselling has led to the proliferation of empirical research, particularly in North America, on numerous issues relating to black and ethnic minority populations in counselling and psychotherapy. While the focus has been on how culture impacts the therapeutic process, there has been a notable shift in increased efforts to understand, through empirical investigation, the possible influence of race and ethnicity on development and everyday human functioning, therapy outcomes and training strategies; other variables have also been examined. In reviewing 114 studies published in the *Journal of Counseling Psychology*, the *Journal of Counseling and Development*, the *Counseling Psychologist*, the *Journal of College Student Development*, the *Journal of Multicultural Counseling and Development* and *Cultural Diversity and Ethnic Minority Psychology*, Ponterotto *et al.* (2002) found that seven areas dominated cross-cultural counselling research. They are: acculturation, stress and coping, attitudes towards diverse populations and towards counselling, racial/ethnic identity development, multicultural competence and training, vocational and academic issues, and quantitative instrument development. At the same time, these studies are small when compared with the field as a whole, illustrating the marginal status of black and ethnic minority issues in counselling.

Although there is a long history of cross-cultural research in North America, the demographics or interest in this field is not reflected in the quality or quantity of publications. For example, a review of empirical articles published over the period 1990–9 revealed that racialized groups continue to be underrepresented relative to whites when compared to the overall US population (Delgado-Romero *et al.* 2005). Similar to counselling research in general, the career research literature from 1990 to 2007 also reflects this trend, leaving race/ethnicity as a variable that was either unexamined or assumed to not be relevant to career research (Wells *et al.* 2010). This ongoing problem is further compounded by the fact that the contributors, editorial boards and research samples for many of the leading journals, like the American Psychological Association (APA) publications, are for the most part American (Arnett 2008). Arnett further notes that 'By concentrating primarily on Americans, psychological researchers in the United States restrict their focus to less than 5% of the world's total population. The rest of the world's population, the other 95%, is neglected' (p. 602).

In addition to the problem of representation, cross-cultural researchers have been criticized for neglecting issues pertaining to the validity of measurements that are used with racial and ethnic populations and for their failure to account for social context where issues of racism, social status, intra-group differences etc. can have important clinical implications. We cannot ignore the fact that the theoretical foundations of many of the research methods, approaches and interventions that are used with ethnic minority groups were derived from white norms (Jones 1983; McLoyd and Randolph 1984; Ponterotto 1988; Atkinson and Thompson 1992; Graham, 1992). This in turn raises important questions about the usefulness and effectiveness of assessment, diagnoses and treatment when applied to ethnic minority populations and has led several multicultural advocates (see e.g. Carter *et al.* 1998; Spanierman and Poteat 2005) to question the counselling field's commitment to expanding the current narrow understanding of race, culture and ethnicity in counselling and psychotherapy. In fact, this may be an indictment of the profession itself for failing to seriously address the needs and validate the experiences of ethnic minorities. The problem is that, often, research conducted under the guise of objective study is, in essence, ideologically determined (Stanfield 1993). Consequently, who is researched and by whom is often dictated by those who fund research. This is hugely problematic given that the field is dominated by white researchers. This concern has been voiced by Guthrie (1976) and Holliday and Holmes (2003) who allege that the history of racism and oppression that characterizes counselling, psychology and psychotherapy has its underpinnings in the professional hegemony of white researchers. The result is a restricted and often dehumanizing conceptualization of racial and ethnic groups. Since, historically, black and ethnic minority people have always been connected to pseudo-scientific racist ideologies, research endeavours and researchers (white and black) are vulnerable to the insidious ways in which these beliefs can manifest, unconsciously or consciously (Moodley and Vontress 2006). Likewise, journal editors and reviewers, the gatekeepers of knowledge, are also accountable and play a critical role in providing more stringent guidelines for authors in delineating their sample groups (D'Andrea 2005, Delgado-Romero *et al.* 2005; Spanierman and Poteat 2005).

Clearly, greater efforts are needed to identify issues of racism and oppression in counselling research, to break the cycle of complacency and engage in meaningful efforts to stem racism in the field as a whole. An important step in this direction would be to gain insight, through empirical investigation, into the consciousness of white people; they too need to come to see themselves as racial beings in general, not simply in the context of cross-cultural exchanges (Parham 2001; Sue 2003). As Utsey *et al.* (2005: 569) aptly state, 'Whites often deny that race is a salient factor in a society in which racism is embedded and even deny that they are themselves racial beings'. If implemented, these strategies can go a long way in helping to counter some of the more sinister forms of racism that continue to adversely impact counselling and psychotherapy. Currently, many other issues are still being examined – for example, the intersections of multiple identities of race, gender, sexual orientation, class, age, religion and disability, multicultural counselling outcomes and multicultural counselling competences. Other emerging research areas are racism as trauma (Bryant-Davis and Ocampo 2005), white counsellors' cognitive and affective response to race and racism within the counselling context (Utsey *et al.* 2005) and the integrating of traditional healing practices into counselling and psychotherapy (Moodley and West 2005; Moodley and Sutherland 2010). These and other issues will no doubt raise a number of methodological problems which continue to plague transcultural research.

Methodology problems

The intrinsic methodological concerns that continue to haunt transcultural/multicultural/cross-cultural research are connected to some degree to the applicability of measurements and the notion that psychological meaning is consistent cross-culturally (Byrne *et al.* 2009) as well as to the methods that are used. A fundamental problem in transcultural research is that the instruments and models used are often those developed in a western context and used without any attempt to test their cross-cultural validity (see Fernando 1988). Since cultural research on psychopathology begins with particular kinds of meaning-making or interpretations of narratives which eventually culminate in their application across and within cultures, validation across cultures is critical (Draguns and Tanaka-Matsumi 2003). Moodley and Vontress (2006) argue that even if sociocultural and political factors feature as critical variables in psychotherapy, it is the treatment of these factors that will determine their effectiveness in bringing about therapeutic change. Indeed, there is widespread agreement among researchers on the need for culturally sensitive research, given its pivotal role in indentifying risk factors for psychopathology, as well as appropriate interventions (Rogler 1989). Nevertheless, what exactly comprises culturally sensitive or appropriate research instruments remains a highly contentious issue.

According to Netemeyer *et al.* (2003: 1), 'measurement is at the heart of virtually all scientific endeavors'. Likewise, research findings are also artefacts of the measurements and methodologies from which they were generated; if the methods and measures that are used lack integrity, so too will the results (Cokley 2007). There is no doubt that cross-cultural research is fraught with methodological challenges. This has led several writers to argue for a radical shift away from the conventional quantitative method of enquiry to more creative approaches in order to achieve a broader and more accurate understanding of cross-cultural concerns. For example, Canino *et al.* (1997) argue for the combination of an anthropological and epidemiological perspective. The aim of this approach is to elucidate the influence of sociocultural context on what appears to be universal psychopathologic phenomena; this approach guards against divorcing the client from his or her sociocultural and political milieu. Darcy *et al.* (2004) also propose a complementary (idiothetic) approach using a combination of top-down (normative) and bottom-up (idiographic) models in which both group and individual levels of analysis are introduced. They argue that 'Idiographic and idiothetic approaches give rich, in-depth, and highly individualized descriptions; these aspects have a particular advantage for counseling research and practice in which the focus is often on assessing individuals' constructions of self and experience' (p. 149).

In spite of the many important methodological advances in cross-cultural research, many challenges remain. In the following section, we discuss some of the difficult areas.

The 'difficult' areas in cross-cultural research

The lack of clear definitions, demographic recording, ethical issues and assessment and diagnosis are a few of the many areas that present 'difficulties' in cross-cultural research. We now turn to a discussion of these issues.

Definitions and demographics

Race, culture, ethnicity and multiculture are problematic terms to define, and so finding a coherent understanding within which meaningful research can be undertaken is also problematic. A general lack of consensus on the definition of race and ethnicity means that these constructs are frequently used interchangeably in research − for example, as Helms (1994: 297) notes, 'ethnicity is often used as a euphemism for race'. What ensues from this practice are general categories that are often applied uncritically to the study of racial and ethnic minorities, resulting in more ambiguity than clarification (Fish 1995), erroneous generalization of results (Delgado *et al.* 2005), a limited and distorted knowledge base which circumvents

the development of appropriate psychological interventions for racial and ethnic minority populations (D'Andrea 2005), and the supposition that racial and
ethnic minorities have some common psychological trait that is in some way connected to culture, which in turn is also related to personality and psychopathology
(Okazaki and Sue 1995). When researchers fail to elucidate the justifications for
their use of such categorical variables, it becomes impossible to make reliable in-
ferences about the constructs under study or their meanings, since these may vary
from one researcher to the next. According to Joseph Trimble (2007: 247), 'if we
scholars cannot come to an agreement on what the constructs mean, then we have
no business developing scales to measure them'.

Indeed, the complexities, inconsistencies and confusions surrounding definitions of race and ethnicity in research have stimulated much scholarly debate.
However, this ongoing debate may have inadvertently shifted attention away
from the real issue it was intended to address in the first place – namely, the
negative impact of racism on the psychological well-being of racial and ethnic
minority groups and the development of appropriate intervention and training
to deal with this (D'Andrea 2005; Delgado-Romero *et al.* 2005). At the same time,
Trimble (2007: 256) does not see the confusion in the field as a disincentive for
conducting ethical research. Rather, he states:

> The inconsistencies, incongruities, and confusion in the field should not
> deter or dissuade the scholar, scientist, and counselor from conducting
> further inquiry into the topic. Quite the contrary, the field is in des-
> perate need of structure and order. To accomplish orderliness and struc-
> ture, scholars and practitioners are challenged and encouraged to probe
> deeper into the topic to sort out and smooth over the discrepancies and
> incongruities.

Perhaps one of the most conspicuous flaws in transcultural research is the way in
which participants are selected, and racially and culturally described. Individuals
are often grouped according to broad categorical variables, with researchers using
previously constructed racial/ethnic checklists and no attempt made to interro-
gate existing racial and ethnic classification systems (Wells *et al.* 2010). Placing
individuals in racial or cultural boxes in this manner precludes any meaningful
examination of the complexities and fluidity surrounding self-identity, and rein-
forces popular notions of race and ethnicity as rigid, essentialistic and ahistorical
(Moodley 2007). For example, all individuals from Asia may be placed in a single category implying that they are culturally similar. Blacks are often assumed
to be descendants of American slaves in spite of the complexities surrounding
shifting definitions of the African diaspora. They are further homogenized into a
single category regardless of whether they are African, African-American, African-
Caribbean, black British, bi-racial or multi-racial. Even the diverse cultures which
make up the category 'white' are also made invisible (Moodley and Vontress 2006).
Given our knowledge of the differences that exist within groups, between groups,
and the intersection of multiple identities on people's development, the use of

such categorical classifications should no longer be considered feasible or ethical (D'Andrea 2005).

Admittedly, the prevalence of quantitative research designs and the need for large sample sizes mean that exploring within-group differences often becomes a monumental and costly endeavour (Fish 1995; Sue and Sue 2003). Many researchers overcome these issues by ignoring the rich diversity that exists within racial or ethnic minority populations and adhering to exceedingly broad categories and samples of convenience – predominantly white university students (Trimble 1991, 1995; Padilla and Lindhoiwt 1995). This kind of quasi-research results in significant misrepresentations of groups and begs questions regarding the generalizability of findings. In the absence of adequate explication of research samples, how can one begin to replicate a study or generalize the results? Based on their analysis of the research literature in cross-cultural counselling, Ponterotto *et al.* (2002) offer two suggestions: the implementation of a random sampling technique if college or university samples are used; and expansion of the research sample base to include research on children, the elderly and families.

Assessment and diagnosis

Although assessment and diagnosis are probably the most important aspects of counselling, the research has been negligent when it comes to issues of assessment and diagnosis of racial and ethnic minority populations. Moodley and Vontress (2006) argue that multicultural or transcultural counselling, in its role as a critique of western counselling and psychotherapy, has repeatedly pointed to the problems inherent in conventional assessment and diagnosis. This counter-cultural position is not just limited to the cultural impropriety or Eurocentric notions of health and psychopathology present in the *Diagnostic and Statistical Manual of Mental Disorders*, but is highly critical of all forms of assessment that do not account for race, culture and ethnic variables with black and ethnic minority clients. Nevertheless, the critique has not generated any new, appropriate or valid diagnostic procedures. The continued use of standardized diagnostic criteria drowns out cultural nuances and prevents the formation of relevant hypotheses important to culture (Canino *et al.* 1997). For example, Draguns and Tanaki-Matsumi (2003: 770) note that 'cultural research on psychopathology starts with the development of scales and other instruments of assessment. It culminates with their application across and within cultures', however, this application is problematized when no attempt is made to first establish cross-cultural validity (Kleinman 1977). To illustrate, although studies suggest that depression is likely to exist to some similar degree across cultures, one must be prudent when it comes to understanding the cultural nuances surrounding the condition. Research on cross-validation of depression measures suggests that many translated measures of depression are encouraging; however, the methods used to establish cross-cultural validity are inadequate (Fields 2010). Moreover, there is still the issue of finding a common clinical lexicon within which counselling can effectively make sense of the system of meanings of a particular client's personal and sociocultural experience. The lack of a common language can often lead to the pathologizing of cultural conceptualizations of psychological disorders. This is a view shared by Sue and Sue (1990: 21) on the North American position. They acknowledge that:

> The profession's preoccupation with pathology tends to encourage the study of personality deficits and weaknesses rather than strengths and assets. Racist attitudes may intensify this view, as minorities may be portrayed in professional journals as neurotic, psychotic, psychopath, parolee.

We must not forget that the ideologies and theoretical approaches of researchers will determine what gets studied and ultimately the findings that are obtained. Therefore, research is needed that focuses on the coping strategies that have been used by racial and ethnic minority communities for centuries, and the underlying mechanisms that lead to well-being. For many of these groups, conventional counselling and psychotherapy, with the focus on the individual, is a nascent and often peculiar approach to well-being. This is due in part to the way in which the notion of the self is conceptualized in many of these cultures – individuals see themselves as connected to others and hence culturally sanctioned beliefs regarding ailments, their cures and healthy psychological functioning are often inextricably linked to dense networks of family, friends, traditional healers, ancestors and spirits (Sutherland, in press). One area that we feel is beginning to show great potential for research in transcultural counselling is the examination and investigation of traditional healing practices and how these can be integrated into psychological treatment (see Moodley and West 2005; Moodley and Sutherland 2010).

Ethical issues

The issue of ethics, in spite of its importance, is another frequently unexamined matter in research with racial and ethnic minority populations (Ponterotto 1988). Given their history of abuse and exploitation by institutions – for example, the Tuskegee syphilis experiment and the more recently published The Immortal Life of Henrietta Lacks – racial and ethnic minority groups remain sceptical about engaging in research as subjects unless the benefits are obvious (Sanchez-Hucles and Jones 2005). To address this issue, researchers are encouraged to go beyond the research protocols established by institutional ethics review boards to observe the more advanced ideals of the Belmont principles which emphasize personal respect, transparency, justice and a commitment to engage in practices that would benefit the population under investigation rather than simply not to cause harm (see Bowman 1991). The ongoing lack of responsibility to ethnic minority groups and the use of research designs that fail to consider participants' points of view, principles and lived experiences have led several authors (e.g. Gordon 1973; Casas *et al.* 1986) to speak out about the impact of institutional-based research on these groups, arguing that the deluge of multicultural investigations has done nothing to improve the lives of the minorities being studied. More specifically, on the topic of general psychological research with the black community, Gordon (1973: 416) states:

> Black people are used indiscriminately as human guinea pigs to further the 'scholarly' ambitions and success strivings of white social scientists . . . Contracts, grants, degrees, consultantships, publications, tenures, prestigious appointments, careers and 'expert' reputations are carried home to suburbia on the backs of the poor and the black.

Conclusion

Any research in the context of multicultural, transcultural, cross-cultural or intercultural psychological experiences will be both limited and challenged by the factors mentioned above. The research investigation, data collection and the production of new knowledge(s), while evolving in spaces privileged for dominant discourses, will need to articulate newer meanings in the context of the psychosocial experiences of black and ethnic minority clients. If transcultural research is seen solely to be about analysing behaviour and psychopathology, and consequently predicting a set of treatment measures for black and ethnic minority clients, then it will do no more than reinforce prevailing and stereotyped notions about race and culture. Moreover, if transcultural research attempts to postulate a finite and essentialistic theoretical position imposing particular 'conditions of practice', epistemological definitions and ontological realities will also fail in the objective of engaging in knowledge production. Understanding these disclaimers is key to understanding the way in which research may need to be constructed with black and ethnic minority communities.

The lack of knowledge(s) about race, culture, ethnicity and psychotherapy has promoted a single-track treatment procedure for black and ethnic minority patients, often to the exclusion of these patient groups. Many, instead of being offered the opportunity to access counselling and psychotherapy, are given psychotropic medication. An ethical research engagement will contribute to the investigation and development of contemporary arguments surrounding the politics of multiple identities, multiple cultures and modernity. Such a process would engage in a discussion of the psychosocial, geopolitical and religiocultural constructs of power and 'self', in relation to ideas about freedom, oppression, justice and equality, thus positioning black and ethnic minority clients at the centre of counselling and healing.

References

Arnett, J.J. (2008) The neglected 95%: why American psychology needs to become less American, *American Psychologist*, 63(7): 602–14.

Atkinson, D.R. and Thompson, C.E. (1992) Racial, ethnic and cultural values in counseling, in S. Brown and S. Lent (eds) *Handbook of Counseling Psychology*. New York: Wiley.

Bowman, P. (1991) Race, class, and ethics in research: Belmont principles to functional relevance, in R.L. Jones (ed.) *Black Psychology*, 3rd edn. Berkeley, CA: Cobb & Henry.

Bryant-Davis, T. and Ocampo, C. (2005) Racist incident–based trauma, *The Counseling Psychologist*, 33(4): 479–500.

Byrne, B.M. *et al.* (2009) A critical analysis of cross-cultural research and testing practices: implications for improved education and training in psychology, *Training and Education in Professional Psychology*, 3(2): 94–105.

Canino, G., Lewis-Fernandez, R. and Bravo, M. (1997) Methodological challenges in cross-cultural mental health research, *Transcultural Psychiatry*, 34: 163–84.

Carter, R.T, Akinsulure-Smith, A.M., Smailes, E.M. and Clauss, C.S. (1998) The status of racial/ethnic research in counseling psychology: committed or complacent? *Journal of Black Psychology*, 24: 322–34.

Casas, J.M., Ponterroto, J.G. and Gutierrez, J.M. (1986) An ethical indictment of counselor research and training: the cross-cultural perspective, *Journal of Counseling and Development*, 64: 347–9.

Cokley, K. (2007) Critical issues in the measurement of ethnic and racial identity: a referendum on the state of the field, *Journal of Counseling Psychology*, 54: 224–34.

D'Andrea, M. (2005) Continuing the cultural liberation and transformation of counseling psychology, *The Counseling Psychologist*, 33(4): 524–37.

Darcy, M., Lee, D. and Tracey, T.J.G. (2004) Complementary approaches to individual differences using paired comparisons and multidimensional scaling: applications to multicultural counseling competence, *Journal of Counseling Psychology*, 51(2): 139–50.

Delgado-Romero, E.A., Galván, N., Maschino, P. and Rowland, M. (2005) Race and ethnicity in empirical counseling and counseling psychology research: a 10-year review, *The Counseling Psychologist*, 33(4): 419–48.

Draguns, J.G. and Tanaka-Matsumi, J. (2003) Assessment of psychopathology across and within cultures: issues and findings, *Behaviour Research and Therapy*, 41: 755–76.

Dryden, W. (ed.) (1996) *Research in Counselling and Psychotherapy*. London: Sage.

Fernando, S. (1988) *Race and Culture in Psychiatry*. London: Croom Helm.

Fields, A.J. (2010) Multicultural research and practice: theoretical issues and maximizing cultural exchange, *Professional Psychology: Research and Practice*, 41(3): 196–201.

Fish, J.M. (1995) Why psychologists should learn some anthropology, *American Psychologist*, 50: 44–5.

Gordon, T. (1973) Notes on White and Black psychology, *Journal of Social Issues*, 29(1): 87–95.

Graham, S. (1992) 'Most of the subjects were white and middle class': trends in published research on African Americans in selected APA journals, 1970–1989, *American Psychologist*, 47: 629–39.

Guthrie, R.V. (1976) *Even the Rat was White: A Historical View of Psychology*. New York: Harper & Row.

Helms, J.E. (1994) The conceptualization of racial identity, in E. Trickett, R. Watts and D. Birman (eds) *Human Diversity: Perspectives on People in Context.* San Francisco: Jossey-Bass.

Holliday, B.G. and Holmes, A.L. (2003) A tale of challenge and change: a history and chronology of ethnic minorities in psychology in the United States, in G. Bernal, J.E. Trimble, A.K. Burlew and F.T.L. Leong (eds) *Handbook of Racial & Ethnic Minority Psychology.* Thousand Oaks, CA: Sage.

Jones, J.M. (1983) The concept of race in social psychology: from colour to culture, in L. Wheeler and P. Shaver (eds) *Review of Personality and Social Psychology.* Beverly Hills, CA: Sage.

Kleinman, A.M. (1977) Depression, somatization and the 'new crosscultural psychiatry', *Social Sciences and Medicine*, 11: 3–10.

McLoyd, V.C. and Randolph, S.M. (1984) The conduct and publication of research on Afro-American children: a content analysis, *Human Development*, 27: 65–75.

Moodley, R. (2003) Double, triple and multiple jeopardy, in C. Lago and B. Smith (eds) *Anti-Oppressive Practice in Counselling.* London: Sage.

Moodley, R. (2007) (Re)placing multiculturalism in counseling and psychotherapy, *British Journal of Guidance & Counselling*, 35(1): 1–22.

Moodley, R. and Lubin, D. (2008) Developing your career to working with multicultural and diversity clients, in S. Palmer and R. Bor (eds) *The Practitioner's Handbook.* London: Sage.

Moodley, R. and Murphy, L. (2010) Multiple identities, multiple oppressions, in C. Lago and B. Smith (eds) *Anti-Discriminatory Practice in Counselling and Psychotherapy.* London: Sage.

Moodley, R. and Sutherland, P. (2010) Psychic retreats in other places: clients who seek healing with traditional healers and psychotherapists, *Counselling Psychology Quarterly*, 23(3): 267–82.

Moodley, R. and Vontress, C.E. (2006) Race and culture in counseling research, in C. Lago (ed.) *Race, Culture and Counselling: The Ongoing Challenge.* Buckingham: Open University Press.

Moodley, R. and West, W. (eds) (2005) *Integrating Traditional Healing Practices into Counseling and Psychotherapy.* Thousand Oaks, CA: Sage.

Netemeyer, R.G., Bearden, W.O. and Sharma, S. (2003) *Scaling Procedures: Issues and Applications.* Thousand Oaks, CA: Sage.

Okazaki, S. and Sue, S. (1995) Methodological issues in assessment research with ethnic minorities, *Psychological Assessment*, 7(3): 367–75.

Padilla, A.M. and Lindhoiwt, K.J. (1995) Quantitative educational research with ethnic minorities, in J.A. Banks and C.A. McGee-Banks (eds) *Handbook of Research on Multicultural Education.* New York: Macmillan.

Parham, T.A. (2001) Beyond intolerance: bridging the gap between imposition and acceptance, in J.P. Ponterotto, J.M. Casas, L.A. Suzuki and C.M. Alexander (eds.) *Handbook of Multicultural Counseling*, 2nd edn. Thousand Oaks, CA: Sage.

Ponterotto, J.G. (1988) Racial/ethnic minority research in the *Journal of Counseling Psychology*: a content analysis and methodological critique, *Journal of Counseling Psychology*, 35(4): 410–18.

Ponterotto, J.G., Costa, C I. and Werner-Lin, A. (2002) Research perspectives in cross-cultural counseling, in P.B. Pederson, J.G. Draguns, W.J. Lonner and J. E. Trimble (eds) *Counseling Across Cultures*, 5th edn. Thousand Oaks, CA: Sage.

Rogler, L.H. (1989). The meaning of culturally sensitive research in mental health, *American Journal of Psychiatry*, 146: 296–303.

Roth, A. and Fonagy, P. (eds) (1996) *What Works for Whom? A Critical Review of Psychotherapy Research*. New York: Guilford Press.

Sanchez-Hucles, J. and Jones, N. (2005) Breaking the silence around race in training, practice, and research, *The Counseling Psychologist*, 33: 547–58.

Spanierman, L.B. and Poteat, V.P. (2005) Moving beyond complacency to commitment: multicultural research in counseling psychology, *The Counseling Psychologist*, 33(4): 513–23.

Stanfield, J.H. (1993) Epistemological considerations, in J.H. Stanfield and R.M. Dennis (eds) *Race and Ethnicity in Research Methods*. Thousand Oaks, CA: Sage.

Sutherland, P. (in press) Traditional healing as a source of resistance, identity and healing among Grenadian women, *Canadian Women's Studies/les cahiers de la femme*, 29(1).

Sue, D.W. (2003) *Overcoming Our Racism: The Journey to Liberation*. San Francisco: Jossey-Bass.

Sue, D.W. and Sue, D. (1990) *Counseling the Culturally Different: Theory and Practice*. New York: Wiley.

Sue, D.W. and Sue, D. (2003) *Counseling the Culturally Diverse: Theory and Practice*, 4th edn. New York: Wiley.

Toukmanian, S.G. and Rennie, D.L. (eds) (1992) *Psychotherapy Process Research: Paradigmatic and Narrative Approach*. Thousand Oaks, CA: Sage.

Trimble, J. (1991) Ethnic specification, validation prospects and future of drug abuse research, *International Journal of the Addictions*, 25: 149–69.

Trimble, J. (1995) Toward an understanding of ethnicity and ethnic identification and their relationship with drug use research, in G. Botvin, S. Schinke and M. Orlandi (eds) *Drug Abuse Prevention with Multiethnic Youth*. Thousand Oaks, CA: Sage.

Trimble, J. (2007) Prolegomena for the connotation of construct use in the measurement of ethnic and racial identity, *Journal of Counseling Psychology*, 54(3): 247–58.

Utsey, S.O., Gernat, C.A. and Hammar, L. (2005) Examining white counselor trainees' reactions to racial issues in counseling and supervision dyads, *The Counseling Psychologist*, 33(4): 449–78.

Wells, E.M., Delgado-Romero, E.A. and Shelton, K.L. (2010) An analysis of race and ethnic categories in career research from 1990 to 2007, *Journal of Career Development*, 37(2): 503–18.

12 Culturally sensitive supervision

Judy Ryde

Introduction

Supervision always provides therapists with an opportunity to reflect on their work and it is therefore vital that it becomes a place to consider whether cultural issues are being attended to. This being the case, it is important that supervisors are always alert to the possibility that cultural difference may need to be understood, taken into account and responded to appropriately. The question 'Could there be cultural issues here?' is a good one for supervisors to have readily at the front of their minds. Without that, it is possible that cultural or racial issues can be reduced to the personal and pathological (Sue and Sue 1990: 12; Ryde 2000: 47). Factors such as not making eye contact can be put down to evidence of depression, for example, when cultural explanations could be nearer the mark (Ryde 2006: 154).

Race and culture in supervision

When considering cultural difference as a supervisor, or in any other setting, the issue of race is bound to arise too. However, race and culture, although related terms, are by no means synonymous. The word 'culture' is used to describe the societal milieu in which we live, where similar norms and assumptions are held by groups, usually unquestioningly (Trompenaars 1993: 21–2). These groups can be very large, like nations or regions, or small, like families or social groupings, organizations or professional groups. Most people live in several cultures at once.

In regard to race, we cannot say there is a 'black' or a 'white' culture as such but, as I point out in Chapter 8 of this book and elsewhere (Ryde 2009: 40), there is a white culture of sorts which dominates with its political, social and economic systems worldwide and is a factor within the 'field'[1] when thinking about race. Race itself refers to the way that 'white' people have categorized different groups according to inherited physical characteristics such as skin colour, facial features and hair colour, and then seem to see themselves as neutral in a racial

---

[1] I use the word here in a similar way to Kurt Lewin. Yontef (1993) describes this use of the word 'field' thus: 'The field is a whole in which the parts are in immediate relationship and responsive to each other and no part is uninfluenced by what goes on elsewhere in the field'.

context – almost 'unraced' (Aanerud 1997: 37; Bonnett 2000: 120; Ryde 2009: 19), as I describe in Chapter 8. Although race does not exist as a 'real' entity, it has a social meaning in which white people are more powerful. This means that we cannot simply dismiss the concept of race as it has a significant effect on people and their sense of identity.

When we think about culture as therapists and counsellors, race is one important factor, but it is not the only one. Everyone filters experience through the lens of their culture (indeed, Hofstede (1980) suggests that between 25 and 50 per cent of our attitudes are determined by our cultural origins), and consequently, when we work with others, it is important to realize that our own cultural lens may well be different from theirs. It behoves us, therefore, to know as much as we can about our own cultural beliefs, attitudes, biases and assumptions so that we do not automatically think of these attitudes as just 'correct' or 'normal'. For instance, if a client shakes your hand, how do you feel about that? In your own culture it may be something that only happens at a first meeting if the situation is quite formal. If a client always shakes your hand, how does your cultural attitude affect you? Do you recoil from this as over-formal or over-familiar or inappropriate? If you think 'this person is from a different culture and therefore shakes my hand', what do you feel about that? Do you feel that it is quite sweet or charming or annoying? You probably have a reaction to it which is not 'politically correct' and it can be important to catch that, rather than dismiss it, and see what it might mean for your relationship with the client or supervisee. As supervisor there is a double responsibility – to catch your own response, encourage your supervisee to catch theirs, and together reflect on the meaning it might have. When working with cultural difference it is important to start with your own cultural assumptions and not see them as the norm (Dyer 1997: 2)

Supervision as part of the intersubjective field

We must therefore always remember that supervision is part of the 'field' of the counselling and psychotherapy relationship. Cultural and racial issues may (or indeed, will inevitably) arise within the supervisory systemic context. They can originate directly from within the supervision relationship itself and subsequently impact the client–supervisee relationship and/or vice versa (Gilbert and Evans 2000). If aspects of cultural or racial difference originate in the supervision relationship, this will spring from the culture and experiences of the supervisee and supervisor and how that experience manifests in the intersubjective field they create together. Figure 12.1 shows how the fields of supervisee/supervisor and supervisee/client interrelate and form a whole system together. Race and culture can enter this system or field according to the experiences, attitudes, assumptions, emotional responses and mindsets that are brought there by any of the parties. Lago (2006: 161) has reflected on the complexity of the number of possible triangulated relationships in the supervisor/supervisee/client relationship, for example. In supervision it is necessary to develop a 'helicopter ability' (Hawkins and Shohet

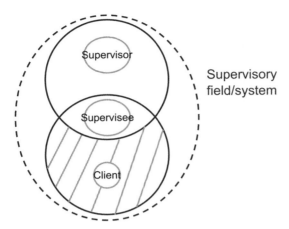

Figure 12.1   The intersubjective field of supervisor/supervisee/client

2006: 51) to discover these factors and reflect on the complex web of relationships which enter the field.

Power within the supervisory relationship

One of the factors that needs to be reflected on, and appropriately responded to, is how power is held within this field (Brown and Bourne 1996: 39; Shohet 1996; Lago 2006: 157). I have shown elsewhere (Ryde 2000: 41) that power within the therapeutic relationship can be thought about in three ways: role power; personal power; and cultural power. We could amend this list so that 'cultural power' reads 'cultural/racial power' as those who are white racially hold more power than those who are not (Dominelli 2006: 6; Ryde 2006: 131; Tuckwell 2006: 204), even where the culture may be the same or similar, such as where one of the parties is black British or African-American. In a situation where the supervisor is not white and/or comes from a culture with less power – mostly those who do not originate from what is often called the 'western' or 'developed' world – the other two aspects of power, which are the role and the personal power, will have some impact on the disadvantage of having less cultural/racial power. The role power is by necessity with the supervisor and she or he therefore needs to be able to reflect on how the power relationship impacts on the whole system, including that of the client. Although any of the three (client, therapist or supervisor) may become aware of these factors, it is the responsibility of the supervisor, in the first instance, to ensure that this is taken into account in the supervisory work.

Let us take some examples where the power lies in different places within the supervisor/supervisee/client system. As a white, western person I supervised a Middle Eastern supervisee who worked with clients from her own country. The supervisee had lived in Britain since she was a child and had clearly adopted, at least superficially, western attitudes and assumptions. She was often in conflict with her family because of the way she lived her life. Through exploration in supervision it eventually became clear to us that her adoption of counselling as a career was, at least in part, a way of trying to understand *herself* within a western context. It was important to her to make this understanding and she had found a way of doing so in a manner that was within a western frame of reference. The generally individualistic stance of counselling (Sue and Sue 1990: 35) meant that the assumptions normally found within her own culture were seen in a different light. Her desire to tread her own path without reference to her family was understood as legitimate within the counselling culture but was viewed as selfish by her family from their cultural perspective. This situation was at first unchallenged by me as I shared her new cultural values and expectations.

I began to understand that there was something more to explore here when she started to see clients who came from her country of origin. On the whole these clients had much more recently come to Britain and, among the issues that they brought to the counselling were the difficulties they had in meeting different cultural values and assumptions as well as a need to grieve for the loss of their home and community. I noticed that her counter-transferential response to these clients tended to be very impatient and bossy. Although many of them were much older than her, she became quite cross with them for being subservient to their husbands and sons and for not generally pushing themselves forward, an attitude to elders which would be unthinkable in her own culture. Her role as a counsellor seemed to be similar to that of 'doctor' in her clients' eyes and appeared to give them a way of tolerating such an attitude in a young woman. My noticing her counter-transference and the general lack of compassion for these particular clients led to an exploration which eventually allowed her to think about her own cultural situation and to reassess her attitude. She slowly began to appreciate her native culture and its values, and the dormant place within herself which longed to be held within it. This had a considerable effect on her work with these clients and her ability to empathize and think with them in a more complex way about the challenging nature of their having to live in exile.

From my position of cultural and role power and her position of comparative role power in relation to her clients, there was a difficulty with our cultural sensitivity which lasted until I was struck by the nature of my supervisee's counter-transference to her clients.

In another situation I brought my work with a black student supervisee to a black supervisor. This student was a potentially talented counsellor, creative and intuitive, who made good contact with clients. She was African and had been brought to Britain as a young child and so was well versed in British culture, although also living within an African culture at home. She often remarked that she could not bring her 'African side' to training or her 'counsellor side' to her home life. I found myself quite challenged by this assertion and made efforts to help her integrate the two. What I paid less attention to was the way she was falling more and more behind with payments for the training. This came to light in the supervision with the black supervisor who challenged my attitude which she found patronizing. She said that I should not be working with this student until she had fulfilled her obligation to pay for the training. Quite rightly she thought she was only getting away with this because she was black. My 'white guilt' (Ryde 2009: 76) had evidently been triggered here as I knew that as a general rule black people found it hard to pay for the training. However, this student was not more impoverished than other students and did eventually make it clear that she wanted to prioritize other areas of her life. She found it hard to say this, partly because of my strenuous efforts to encourage her to stay. Here I soft-pedalled on the legitimate power that I should take in my role to try to be culturally sensitive but actually let my supervisee down by not appropriately challenging her.

The working alliance when working across difference

If power relationships are to be well enough attended to, it is important, as in all supervisory relationships, to form a good working alliance. This is essential for a dialogic and enquiring stance to be maintained. Where there is a racial and/or cultural difference it may be particularly important to deepen the working alliance and therefore the trust between supervisor and supervisee. Most basically, whatever our race or culture, in order to develop a trusting relationship, we need to know, at the very least, that there is a genuine desire to understand. Showing that you have sensitivity to cultural difference will be one of the factors necessary for a good working alliance when working across races and cultures.

The better the working alliance the easier it is to reflect on any phenomenon that you see in your supervisee's client work or within the supervision itself. A good working alliance allows you to encourage this ability to reflect in your supervisee. The supervision session is primarily about reflecting together and, with a really good working alliance, you can develop an ability to be curious together about what you see arising between you in the spaces between any cultural or racial differences. As Joan Wilmot (2008) says, 'you can relish the ordinary and extraordinary all in one breath.'

Having said that, there are occasions when the supervisor has to be able to be authoritative, directive and sometimes prescriptive (Heron 1975), and a good working alliance will also allow for this without disrupting the supervision. A more authoritative stance may need to be taken with new counsellors and those who are still in training. For instance, when difference in culture has not been taught or thought about within the training, or the student has not understood it well, the supervisor might have to be more insistent about the supervisee considering cultural or racial implications apparent in the work. In this situation the supervision can legitimately fulfil a training function as well. We can never fully understand different cultures by 'mugging them up' because the field is very nuanced and complex and differences are subtle; small and very small cultural sub-groups exist within larger cultures. It is nevertheless possible to grasp some rough pointers about typical differences between larger cultures and these can be taught to supervisees as well as encouraging them to remain enquiring rather than basing interventions on assumptions about any particular culture. Part 2 of this book is helpful in this regard.

A more authoritative stance also needs to be taken when, in the supervisor's view, unethical or inappropriate work is being carried out. One white supervisee, for example, was working with a particularly vulnerable non-white client who barely had enough money and resources to survive. The supervisee became inappropriately drawn into this client's life and felt she must give her more and more material help in a way that was inappropriate within a counselling setting. Although she had the best of intentions, her counter-transferential behaviours, based on her own sense of deprivation, led her to overstep the mark. The supervisor had to be very prescriptive with this supervisee to help her draw appropriate boundaries and redirect her efforts to helping the client to find ways of meeting her own material needs, sometimes with the help of social workers.

Being directly prescriptive does not, however, preclude the need also to be enquiring and dialogic. In the case above it was quite hard to maintain this stance while supervisor and supervisee were in conflict. If a stance of acceptance underlies the work then anything which comes into its arena is material that can be reflected upon. If there is actually or apparently a lack of trust between the two, then this ability is curtailed. If we feel the outcome of our reflections will be a judgement on our integrity then it is hard to be open. While there is trust it is felt that the outcome of the dialogue between the supervisee and supervisor will be fruitful, even if painful.

'CLEAR' process in supervision

The best good practice, then, is to encourage a relationship in which open exploration, dialogue and non-defensive enquiry is the norm and this certainly holds good where culturally sensitive supervision is concerned. This attitude will then run through all types of supervisory interventions. It is tempting to think that addressing cultural difference is one, discrete, factor in supervision rather than something that runs through every aspect. Hawkins and Shohet (2006: 61) suggest a five-stage model for the process of supervision to which they give the acronym CLEAR: Contract, Listen, Explore, Action and Review. At each stage of this process, rather than just in the Explore stage, for example, it is important to bear in mind cultural issues.

Here are examples of each stage. The term *Contract* may have a different meaning to the parties within an intercultural setting. The authority of those 'in charge' has more weight in some cultures than others, for example. Some cultures have steeper hierarchies of power than others (Sue and Sue 1990: 147). It may be important to have an awareness of this and make sure that you, as supervisor, your supervisee and their client are clear about the meaning of authority within the contract. When *Listening* to clients it is important to listen with an ear for cultural difference as well as an understanding that how we listen might have a cultural meaning – a difference in the meaning of eye contact, for example (Ryde 2009:

154). In some cultures eye contact is considered rude, particularly with those in authority, while in others a lack of eye contact could mean that the person is not paying enough attention. The *Explore* stage is an obvious place for cultural issues to be teased out and talked through. In the *Action* phase it may be necessary to bear in mind the circumstances which the client returns to after the session and which may have cultural implications, including different kinds of pressures from family. The *Review* stage should also be sensitive to cultural issues.

Seven modes of supervision

Hawkins and Shohet (2006: 80) have also devised a model of supervision which looks at seven different foci. I have shown elsewhere (Ryde 2009) how each of these foci or modes can be approached from a transcultural point of view and thus demonstrate this assertion.

The focus of each is as follows:

- Mode One focuses on the phenomenon as it appears in the session with the client before any interpretation is put upon it. For instance, we might notice the client yawns a lot rather than say she or he is tired.
- Mode Two focuses on the supervisee's interventions in the session with the client.
- Mode Three focuses on the relationship between the supervisee and the client.
- Mode Four focuses on the responses or the counter-transference of the supervisee to the client.
- Mode Five focuses on the relationship between the supervisor and supervisee, including any parallel process between that which happens in the therapeutic relationship and is echoed in the session between the supervisor and supervisee.
- Mode Six focuses on the responses or counter-transference of the supervisor within the field of the supervision, both to the supervisee and the material presented.
- Mode Seven focuses on the wider environment in which the supervision takes place.

In each of the foci it is possible and desirable to consider how cultural difference is manifested and not just in Mode Seven where cultural difference more obviously belongs.

Mode One can be particularly important as it may be tempting for both supervisor and supervisee to rush into interpreting a client's behaviour before just attending to what happened in the session. In the example of the handshake above, it is important first of all just to *notice* that there has been a handshake and that the meaning of it is unknown. Not until that is properly noticed might the supervisor encourage the supervisee to look at what it means to them and only *then* to have some tentative thoughts about what it might mean for the client.

Lago (2006: 44) reaches similar conclusions and has other examples in his book, *Race, Culture and Counselling*.

In Mode Two, the supervisor will encourage each intervention to be culturally sensitive, not just interventions which are apparently about cultural difference. For example, in Chapter 8 I discuss my work with a client in which I empathized with her about a demanding aunt. In this situation I did not take into account the cultural bias of my intervention. In her own culture the demands are reasonable but I initially encouraged my client's apparent desire to draw limits on her aunt's demands. More nuanced interventions resulted when, through supervision, I began to understand that the family always comes first in her culture, a value my client shared.

When working in Mode Three we need to take into account the meaning that relating to a counsellor might have within a cultural context. For instance, in the work of the supervisee mentioned above who was irritated with clients who came from her own culture, the relationship was affected by the client's feeling that they should be subservient to someone in a quasi-'doctor' role.

Mode Four leads us to consider the types of responses to clients within the counter-transference which are affected by cultural difference. In the same situation mentioned above in Mode Three, the cultural field conditions led to a lack of empathy in the supervisee which might otherwise not have been there.

Mode Five often leads to a parallel process. In the same situation I found an irritation in myself for the supervisee's lack of empathy. This demonstrated a parallel with the irritation in the supervisee. In both situations we wanted the person we were working with to conform to our own cultural norms – I wanted the supervisee to take on counselling values and the supervisee wanted her clients to be more 'western' and individualistic.

Mode Six focuses on the (counter-transferential) reactions of the supervisor. In the case above it was noticing my irritation that led to uncovering the parallel process and the subsequent insights.

Mode Seven is a natural home for exploring difference in culture as this mode focuses on the social, political, organizational and cultural milieu in which the counselling occurs, including how institutional racism may affect the therapy. Any of the above foci might lead to a consideration in this mode and how the environment impinges on the work with the client. For instance, I supervise a group of counsellors and therapists who work with asylum-seekers and refugees. Some of these counsellors work in their own consulting rooms and some in health centres. The meaning of these two environments can have different impacts according to how the clients feel about being seen in a medical or less clinical setting. This can be different with the different cultural expectation of each client.

Group work

Much supervision occurs in groups and this is no less the case when working across difference in culture. Group work has many advantages, particularly because, with each group member, we have the resource of each particular contribution and ways of responding to each client which, of course, includes their cultural perspective. There is an obvious advantage when a group member understands the client's culture in a way that their counsellor does not. Puzzling matters can be explained or teased out. I had a client who talked about bringing her problems to the village elders when in her own country. A fellow group member had experienced this in her childhood in Guyana and could explain this form of helping to me, and the kinds of cultural expectations likely to be present for the client within the therapeutic relationship.

My own work as a supervisor is with two groups of therapists who work with asylum-seekers and refugees. I find that the depth of empathy that the counsellors and therapists can achieve with their clients is enhanced by the group supervision. Most of the clients have been in terrible extremis so that being able to stay with the depth of pain week after week is very hard. In addition, the clients' experiences in this country are also hard to bear – particularly when they are sent back to their home country into dangerous circumstances (see also Chapters 13 and 17). The sense of helplessness, anger and grief is felt very keenly by the therapists. Being with a group who also experience such horrors is particularly important in helping them to 'stay with' the pain even when nothing material can be done about it. Although I also experience these issues with my own clients, my job is a bit different from that of their peers in the group who can just stay with them in their pain, knowing what it is like. I also have to hold the whole group and make sure that all the therapists are held in mind and responded to well.

Conclusion

In conclusion, it is important as a supervisor always to bear in mind that cultural issues may be important to address. Rather than split these off by saying 'now let's think about cultural issues', they are threaded throughout the supervision. This includes all aspects in the process of each supervision session and with every focus – whether that be with the client, the supervisee's interventions, the supervisee's relationship with the client, their counter-transference, a parallel process between the session with the client and that had with the supervisor, the supervisor's counter-transference or the general environment in which the supervision happens.

Although it is important to have some knowledge of cultural differences, this is not a substitute for remaining dialogic, both in supervision and in the relationship with clients, so that clients are not reduced to supposed 'examples of their culture'. The complexity of the supervisor/supervisee/client triad within the intersubjective field that they create, needs to be acknowledged and teased out in this dialogue.

As with other aspects of psychotherapy and counselling, supervision can be key to ensuring good practice, particularly as it can bring theory and practice together. The supervisee is constantly going back into the work with the client which ensures that learning is always grounded in practice. The supervision provides a forum in which good practice can be explored in all its complexity while the work continues.

References

Aanerud, R. (1997) Fictions of whiteness: speaking the names of whiteness, in R. Frankenberg (ed.) *Displacing Whiteness*. Durham, NC: Duke University Press.

Bonnett, A. (2000) *White Identities: Historical and International Perspectives*. Harlow: Prentice Hall.

Brown, A. and Bourne, L. (1996) *The Social Work Supervisor*. London: Heinemann.

Dominelli, L. (2006) *Anti-Racist Social Work*. Basingstoke: Macmillan.

Dyer, R. (1997) *White*. London: Routledge.

Gilbert, M. and Evans, K. (2000) *Psychotherapy Supervision in Context: An Integrative Approach*. Maidenhead: Open University Press.

Hawkins, P. and Shohet, R. (2006) *Supervision in the Helping Professions*, 3rd edn. Maidenhead: Open University Press.

Heron, J. (1975) *Six Categories of Intervention Analysis*. Guildford: University of Surrey Human Potential Research Project.

Hofstede, G. (1980) *Cultures' Consequences: International Differences in Work-Related Values*. Beverly Hills, CA: Sage.

Lago, C. (ed.) (2006) *Race, Culture and Counselling*. Maidenhead: Open University Press.

Ryde, J. (2000) Supervising across difference, *International Journal of Psychotherapy*, 5(1): 37–48.

Ryde, J. (2006) Working with difference: the political context of pychotherapy with an intersubjective dialogue, in N. Totton (ed.) *The Politics of Psychotherapy*. Maidenhead: Open University Press.

Ryde, J. (2009) *Being White in the Helping Professions: Developing Effective Intercultural Awareness*. London: Jessica Kingsley.

Shohet, R. (1996) *Anti Discrimination and Oppression in Supervision*, CSTD Supervision Resource Book, *Working with Difference*. London: CSTD.

Sue, D.W. and Sue, D. (1990) *Counselling the Culturally Different*. New York: Wiley.

Trompenaars, F. (1993) *Riding the Waves of Culture*. London: Nicholas Brealy Publishing.

Tuckwell, G. (2006) Specific issues for white therapists, in C. Lago (ed.) *Race, Culture and Counselling*. Maidenhead: Open University Press.

Wilmot, J. (2008) The supervisory relationship: a lifelong calling, in R. Shohet (ed.) *Passionate Supervision*. London: Jessica Kingsley.

Yontef. G. (1993) *Awarness, Dialogue and Process*. New York: Gestalt Journal Press.

13 Psychotherapeutic work at Nafsiyat

Antony Sigalas

Introduction: the history of Nafsiyat

In 1983, after having identified the need for a new psychotherapy service for the culturally different population living in London, the late Jafar Kareem founded Nafsiyat, the Intercultural Therapy Centre, with the support of a group of professionals working in health and social services. His aim was to offer a culturally sensitive and a financially accessible service to adults, adolescents and children who felt that they could be excluded from any other psychotherapeutic treatment on the basis of their skin colour, their ethnic origin or their inability to communicate in English. His vision was to raise awareness of the importance of training and consultation concerning the efficacy of psychotherapeutic work with people from different cultural backgrounds, so that centres like Nafsiyat could gradually disappear and the identified barriers associated with black, Asian and minority ethnic (BAME) communities accessing mainstream mental health services would no longer exist. Twenty-eight years later, Nafsiyat, along with a great number of other culturally appropriate services, continues to feel the pressure of a long waiting list of people desperate to find help.

Born in Calcutta, Jafar Kareem studied cultural anthropology, psychology and physiology in India and qualified as a psychotherapist with the British Association of Psychotherapy in 1972. He was above all a humanist who was driven by his ability to empathize with the human struggle and suffering beyond any racial, religious or cultural difference – whether as a journalist and broadcaster in India and Pakistan back in the 1950s, emphasizing cross-cultural cohesion among Hindus, Muslims and Christians, or in the early 1960s as an organizer of the United Nations Community Development and Welfare Projects in Austria and Israel; or indeed later as a psychotherapist in the UK's NHS.

Intercultural therapy: our working definition and approach

Jafar Kareem's ideas on what intercultural therapy should be, his energy and passion for what he believed needed to be achieved, and his compassion for those in need, continue to inspire us today in our clinical work. Since the beginning,

Nafsiyat has followed the same definitional frame of reference underpinning its applied short-term psychotherapeutic approach, described by Kareem (1978) as:

> A form of dynamic psychotherapy that takes into account the whole being of the patient – not only the individual concepts and constructs as presented to the therapist, but also the patient's communal life experience in the world, both past and present. The very fact of being from another culture involves both conscious and unconscious assumptions, both in the patient and in the therapist. I believe that for the successful outcome of therapy it is essential to address these conscious and unconscious assumptions from the beginning.

At Nafsiyat, it is indeed the psychodynamic knowledge that we believe helps us as therapists to gain insight into how these assumptions:

- emerge in one's inner experience;
- impact on the client–therapist interaction as well as on the supervisory relationship; and
- how they could be approached psychotherapeutically.

Our approach however, in its technical sense, challenges us on a daily basis and encourages us to warm towards a more integrated, less rigid way of working in which new ideas and methods are considered, in order to strengthen the therapeutic potential. The emphasis on the issues of race and culture is reflected primarily in the way clients are encouraged to describe their realities as they perceive them, and to explore them within their own frames of reference, while being aware of the possibility that our Eurocentric psychotherapeutic realities could be imposed onto them inappropriately. Attention is paid to the fact that meanings are conveyed differently according to religious, familial and value-based influences that evolve continuously over one's life. In doing so, however, both the 'different' and the 'equivalent' across cultures are regarded as relevant to the process of understanding one's world. Experiences of racism, sexism, ageism, disability, class and immigration status, discrimination, homophobia, poverty, homelessness and social exclusion are considered as clinical themes that the clients are enabled to feel they can raise comfortably in the therapeutic environment. Understanding the significance of people's different levels of adjustment to the host culture, as experienced by the first, second and third generation clientele, and of their immigration status, has also been important in our process of achieving deeper levels of communication. Allowing clients the holding environment they need in order to develop trust in the therapeutic relationship has never been an easy task and our ascribed credentials as a non-statutory, long-established, non-stigmatizing, culturally sensitive service, appear to make that first step easier for those who seek our help.

The following strategies have all been generally found, in our experience, to reinforce therapeutic engagement: pre-therapy interventions; making and 'reminding' clients about arranged appointments; allowing advocates to be included in the initial appointments; offering clients the choice to receive psychotherapy in their own language without the use of interpreters; and the opportunity to express their preference as to what gender or race they would like their therapist to be.

Client demographics and therapist competences

At the Centre, the majority of our clients are between the ages of 19 and 45 and the female clients outnumber the male by a ratio of 3 to 1. Our referrals come from all the main boroughs of London, with GPs as the highest referrers, followed by self-referrals, mental health and social services and other third-sector organizations. Sixty-two different ethnicities, from African, American, Arabic, Asian, Caribbean, European and eastern cultures are included in our database, and our 15 therapists practise at the Centre in a number of different languages. Consultation and training have always been available since the early days of Nafsiyat, via seminars, conferences, diploma, postgraduate and MSc level courses. These have been both self-organized and created in conjunction with other bodies such as hospitals, therapy centres and academic institutions (e.g. St Bartholomew's Hospital Medical School, Islington Residential Social Workers Centre, University College London, the Tavistock Centre, Mind, Chase Farm Hospital, Asian Families, Westminster Pastoral Foundation, Birkbeck College and Cambridge University among others). Nafsiyat has also been offering a CPD (continuing professional development) programme for its registered professional members, and runs a number of individually funded projects for specific presenting diagnoses of certain minority groups, including refugees and victims of torture. In addition to previously conducted studies, the Centre recognizes the importance of continuing to undertake further research into its work, which we hope to be able to support with sufficient funds.

Clinical examples

Vicki is a 52-year-old single woman who was initially referred by her consultant psychiatrist after having been diagnosed with psychotic depression and suicidal ideation. Vicki presented a long history of trauma from early life, in addition to the more recent and very traumatic experience of witnessing the manslaughter of one of her siblings. While in the psychiatric unit of a local hospital, she appeared most of the time either withdrawn, or verbally abusive towards the staff, unwilling to cooperate with the professionals involved in her care who tried to communicate with her via different interpreters. Due to the language barrier, Vicki did not interact with anyone at the hospital, which intensified her feeling of isolation and her psychotic symptomatology of auditory hallucinations and persecutory anxiety. When she was referred to the Centre, her need to engage in a one-to-one, linguistically appropriate therapeutic relationship became evident within a short space of time, as she soon appeared to build up the trust she needed to be able to approach her emotional suffering with less fear, and more willingness to regain a healthier sense of self.

Claudette complained about low mood, insomnia, loss of appetite, lack of motivation and lack of confidence to do things after having suffered prolonged racial discrimination in her working environment. During her initial appointment at the Centre, this 42-year-old client presented very little background information and instead appeared rather anxious in her need to communicate her painful experience of having been treated unfairly and unjustly because her skin colour was not the 'right one'. Her emotional pain was overwhelming, and her efforts to substantiate her experiences with evidential information made her feel resentful of the thought that she felt compelled to do so, in fear of having to deal with the prospect of yet another failed attempt to have her reality acknowledged and respected as such. A single previous experience of therapy was described negatively, due to her white therapist being perceived as defensively unable to empathize. Claudette sounded concerned about taking the Centre's declared cultural sensitivity for granted on the one hand, and on the other surprised, as she would not have expected to experience the healing effect of the therapeutic interaction with a white therapist.

Abdul, aged 28, was initially unable to talk about his past or his current situation, as he could not understand how 'talking about it' could help him feel better. A pre-therapy intervention of using metaphors, examples of other similar experiences, and efforts to de-stigmatize the clinical process with a jargon-free empathic communicative engagement allowed the client to start revealing his anguish and his difficulty sleeping, due to the flashbacks of his imprisonment and torture. The uncertainty of his future, reinforced by the prolonged wait and the possibility of having his asylum application rejected by the Home Office, exacerbated the already severe level of his anxiety. Abdul associated this fear of being deported with the fear of his captivity, whereby hearing the footsteps of his persecutors approaching his prison cell at night, for yet another tormenting form of abuse, felt as excruciating as his current state of being. His inability to commit to the therapeutic process by failing to attend his weekly appointments in any consecutive order was approached patiently and sensitively by acknowledging primarily the client's inability to feel safe outside his sheltered accommodation; and on a secondary level, by his need to maintain this sense of control over a small part of his life, which most of the time was insufferable and only at times began gradually to get 'a little bit better'.

Farah has over the years been diagnosed with personality disorder, depression and dissociative disorder and has been treated with antidepressants and brief interventions by mental health professionals, for what Farah and her family described as a state of 'jinn possession'. At the Centre, this 58-year-old mother, while escorted by a family member, attributed her 'sufferings' to both her difficult history and to the spirit, which appeared to have taken control of her recent life. A number of spiritual healers who tried to exorcise the spirit were described at best as 'unhelpful' and at worst 'traumatically abusive'. Within the clinical time, empathic reflections on the client's painful history induced intense states of jinn possession, during which Farah was left emotionally drained and physically exhausted. Both family members seeking help in this instance seemed to appreciate the culturally sensitive understanding of the presenting experience in comparison to the mainstream professional dismissive approach, determined by psychiatric diagnostic categorization. The prospect of the psychotherapeutic process being imposed onto the client at a time when the confrontation with her worst fears might have felt equally abusive and consequently unbearable by her, was explored further with the family members who were included in the possible alternatives of therapeutic intervention.

The Kara family was referred by the local community mental health team, who raised concerns about the dynamics of two generations of family members being affected by cultural and religious conflicts in a destructive way. Both parents, in their late sixties, shared the belief that the future well-being of their two British-born children was doomed, as they appeared disrespectful, disobedient and uncommunicative with the rest of the family. Mr and Mrs Kara were desperate to help their 22-year-old daughter to realize, with the help of a therapist, that her decision to marry someone from a different cultural and religious background would have a disastrous effect on her and her family's life. They were also concerned about their 19-year-old son, whose lifestyle they feared would bring shame to the family and their cultural community. The Centre provided the space for all the members involved, within their individual expectations, to explore gradually how their different inter- and intra-psyche experiences had been affecting their interactive patterns, in order to gain, within a context of new adjustments, some insight into how to restore the balance in the family system.

Conclusion

The above cases are indicative of the work that is carried out at the Centre for a growing population that changes rapidly, and whose needs other services may fail to meet owing to their limitations such as inadequate training, or funding/policy restrictions, among others. However, limitations cannot take us from the reality of having to deliver effective therapeutic outcomes, which are quite often achieved because of innovative ways of work that need adequate funds to develop evaluation systems in order to sustain their credibility. Within a climate of evidence-based commissioning, we cannot indeed fail to ignore that the aim to be credible in the eyes of those that fund us should result from our empirical efforts to be primarily credible in the eyes of all our clients, so that we can continue to respond effectively to the needs of our culturally diverse communities.

Reference

Kareem, J. (1978) Conflicting concepts of mental health in a multicultural society, *Psychiatria Clinica*, 11: 90–5.

Further reading

Alayarian, A. (ed.) (2007) *Resilience, Suffering and Creativity*. London: Karnac.

Eleftheriadou, Z. (1994) *Transcultural Counselling*. London: Central Book Publishing.

Kareem, J. and Littlewood, R. (1992) *Intercultural Therapy: Themes, Interpretations and Practice*. Oxford: Blackwell.

Krause, I.-B. (2002) *Culture and System in Family Therapy*. London: Karnac.

Lago, C. (ed.) (2006) *Race, Culture and Counselling*. Maidenhead: Open University Press.

Littlewood, R. and Lipsedge, M. (1982) *Aliens and Alienists: Ethnic Minorities and Psychiatry*. London: Penguin.

Mckenzie-Mavinga, I. (2009) *Black Issues in the Therapeutic Process*. London: Palgrave Macmillan.

Palmer, S. and Laungani, P. (eds) (1999) *Counselling in a Multicultural Society*. London: Sage.

Papadopoulos, R. (ed.) (2002) *Therapeutic Care for Refugees: No Place Like Home*. London: Karnac.

Pedersen, P.B., Draguns, J.G., Lonner, W.J. and Trimble, J.E. (eds) (1981) *Counseling Across Cultures*. Honolulu: University of Hawaii Press.

Sigalas, A. (2000) The client's reality in therapy: perceiving the culturally different, unpublished MA thesis, University of East London.

Sue, D.W. and Sue, D. (1981) *Counseling the Culturally Different: Theory and Practice*. New York: Wiley.

14 A relational understanding of working interculturally with survivors of torture

Tony Wright

Introduction

The Medical Foundation for the Care of Victims of Torture has several centres working exclusively to support survivors of torture, including a diverse and substantial counselling provision.[1] The interplay of cultures between counsellor, client and interpreter, when present, represents the heart of the matter when addressing trans-/multi-, cross-cultural issues. I present here my own relational understanding of this interplay of cultures, represented as intercultural work situated within several complex, interwoven, complementing and competing discourses, which I illustrate with some example case material and specific discourse links and resources.

Intercultural working and the counselling discourse

The torture discourse is contextual and is related to a social, cultural and political context. The counselling discourse in the West has predominantly avoided this wider discursiveness despite strong political leaning in many of its influential founders and writers (see Totton 2000). Unacceptable limitations to understanding the counselling and torture discourse occur if considered only through a single western therapeutic approach (see Elsass 1997). Burchell (2007) and Boyles (2006) indicate the ethical and justice issues involved. Agger (2008), Drees (1989), Gonsalves *et al.* (1993), Papadopoulos (2002), Regel and Berliner (2007) and Schauer *et al.* (2005) are representative of various approaches within the counselling discourse.

I have diagrammatically represented my relational understanding of counselling interculturally in Table 14.1.

---

[1]Full information, contact and referral details can be obtained at: www.torturecare.org.uk.

Table 14.1 A relational understanding of counselling interculturally

Counsellor		Client
Retains awareness of own culture, its biases, particular understandings, expressions and ways of relating.		Typologically needs: • to feel safe in the therapeutic space, including communicated sensitivity;
Remains open to the cultural dimension of the client's frame of reference in all its complexity and expression with a willingness to suspend any cultural assessment and judgement that diminishes encountering the client and relating fully and immediately.		• time to be able to trust, expand personal narratives and share therapeutically particular experiences; • to be related to as a person and not within a torture narrative or psychopathology; • a sense of the counsellor's understanding of *self* culturally and experientially;
Relates in a phenomenologically open and client-focused manner, actively engaging with the client and their narrative.	Person to person relating and encountering	• to know the counsellor's capacity to hear difficult and intense experiences and maintain a therapeutic relationship;
Actively listens to the culturally informed way in which the client speaks, responds, conceptualizes, represents and symbolizes psycho-emotionally.		• clarity concerning personal power and politics and human rights issues as experienced within the counselling relationship, including their own cultural and political frame of reference and torture experiences;
Identifies the typological elements and themes contained in encountering the client as accurately represented by their self-expression and narratives.		• help to make sense as much as is possible of the complex interrelationship of multiple traumas, torture reactions and possible personal development from this;
Seeks to enhance intercultural counselling ability and capacity for specific clients through recognizing points of contact with the wider discourses represented by the client's experiences and experiencing.	Including interpreter when present	• clear and accurate information and understanding of the counselling being offered; • assistance to understand other discourses, medical, health, asylum-seeking, cultural; • appropriate engagement with their asylum or refugee needs.

Intercultural work with a client

Mr One, referred by a consultant psychiatrist, came to an assessment session with an interpreter present. When asked about his experiences leading to his claiming asylum in the UK he gave the following typological, anonymized response.

> I was arrested for being a gay man and beaten, so badly beaten, it took me three months to be able to walk again, I am still suffering from that beating, so much pain. I escaped only because my uncle helped me. They were going to hang me, the town mayor was away on business and had to sign my death warrant. I escaped before he came back. It took me 14 months to get to the UK; I don't know how I survived the journey. I have been here for eight years and I am homeless. I live in a bin to keep safe, my own people attack me because someone let them know about me being gay and the charges against me back home.

Typically brief and yet very revealing, Mr One's narrative, together with his manner of expressing himself, presents a number of typological elements and themes that enabled me to engage with wider aspects of several discourses: torture (including pain); trauma (including life threat); asylum (including homelessness); human rights (including sexual identity); and medical (including treatment). Mr One presented as frightened, anxious, solely focused and driven on by his asylum case, struggling with his own torture and trauma reactions (physically, emotionally and mentally), despairing and at times angry.

Identifying these typological aspects through Mr One's assessment, including identifying his country of origin, language, tribe, family, religious and social background, I was able to focus on the limits of my own understanding of the complex cultural background and individual cultural frame of reference of Mr One. I was also aware of being greatly influenced in my attitudes towards Mr One's country of origin through the regular media news reports of war and other forms of violence taking place, and of having to actively 'screen' this influence out.

I began counselling with Mr One and worked with him to tackle the more immediate issues first: his destitution and health needs. I enabled Mr One to gain for himself fresh representations from a solicitor and access to a GP, with an acceptable interpreter in attendance. This gave Mr One relative safety and initially eased his anxiety, and so he began to expand his initial brief narrative. He typically moved between 'here and now' issues and the experiences that had led to his being in the UK – arrest, torture, fleeing, asylum application, homophobic violence, homelessness and destitution. Mr One's self-expression was often jumbled if not chaotic.

Linking to Mr One's culture

A number of intercultural aspects in Mr One's counselling emerged. I needed more specific information about his cultural background, including: homosexuality and Sharia law; matters of property and inheritance; revenge for perceived injustices from within the extended family; tribal conflicts and positioning; and the prevalence of warlords and their influence on Mr One's home rural area. One place to start searching for this kind of information is the Home Office: (www.homeoffice.gov.uk/rds/country_reports.html#countries). I also used the briefing and debriefing elements of working with an interpreter from the same country to advantage.

Further intercultural aspects of working with Mr One could be identified, for example: spiritual; loss of soul and sense of own humanity; the preference of death despite surviving; revenge as holding onto hope; working with magnified scenes of humiliation and shame.

Using my own culture

I also identified the need to be able to offer, from my own acculturated learning, clear information and understanding about Mr One's trauma and torture experiences and reactions, and his experiences of mental health treatment in the UK. This meant identifying how best to say things via the interpreter. Mr One is from a country where mental health issues are not recognized, so I needed to become familiar with how he might ordinarily talk about these. Linguistically this meant attending to Mr One's expression, idiom, emphasis, specific words, sentence construction, ability to conceptualize, use of images and metaphors, pace, tone, range and breadth of language, and adapting my own to create a mutuality in understanding each other. This also required the interpreter to be briefed.

I was particularly keen to enable Mr One to find ways to manage his severe and at times extreme anxiety about being returned to his country of origin. I knew for myself that I needed to understand more clearly how the multiple traumas experienced by Mr One were interacting with each other. Real and external events could trigger this anxiety. Consider, for instance, Mr One walking to his solicitor's office one day and recognizing one of his torturers coming the other way. Similarly, Mr One was thrown into suicidal despair when he could not bear to face the fact that there was simply nothing more that he or anyone else could do about his asylum case. He was being forced to wait for a decision by a systemic set of parameters, which he temporarily lost the ability to cope with. Mr One had a detailed and carefully planned suicide, involving his making a protest about his treatment as an asylum-seeker by pouring petrol over himself and setting himself on fire. Mr One's planned suicidal protest linked his mental health, human rights and justice issues.

Additionally, in consequence of not having the right to work, Mr One was left with many hours alone, leaving him to dwell on his experiences that still had him suffering severely. In this time-laden isolation the (galactic) constellations of traumatic experience become constellated into trauma and torture reactions.

Torture discourse

Mr One's arrest and torture discourse was relatively uncomplicated. It is worth noting that he suffered due to the particular legal interpretation of his sexual identity that prevails in his country of origin. Mr One's attempts to authenticate his identity are replete with life and death experiences.

Other clients' experiences of torture involve more sophisticated physical, sexual and psychological techniques (see Peel 2004). Torture discourse awareness and consequent enhanced counsellor intercultural ability can be gained from relevant studies and research texts that emphasize the centrality of this discourse. Good examples are: Athey (2007); Başoğlu (1992); Danner (2004); Einolf (2007); Hannah (2006); Rejali (2007); and Schulz (2007). Specifically related to pain is Dostrovsky, *et al.* (2003).

Trauma discourse

Attempting to understand Mr One's experience of trauma included talking about: his torture; walking through a minefield (to escape his country of origin) and seeing others blown up; strapping himself beneath the Eurostar train to gain entry to the UK; and his many losses. Multiple trauma in survivors of torture is to be expected and often the traumas can continue once in the UK if the family a person has left behind are in turn made to suffer. Mr One was abandoned by his wife (who also abandoned their two children), whose whereabouts was still unknown.

There are competing and complementary elements to this discourse, for example: a triple trauma model (Baker 1992); psychotherapy for the massively traumatized (Kinzie 2001); understanding and recovering from trauma (Herman 1992); trauma and psychological torture (Ojeda 2008); loss of home and adversity-activated development (Papadopoulos 2007); treatment and traumatic attachment (Solomon and Siegel 2003); and assessing psychologically traumatized clients for post-traumatic stress disorder (Wilson and Keane 2004).

Asylum discourse

The life situation of all asylum-seekers is that they are governed under a system that is experienced as traumatic and unjust (see Chapter 17). Refugees will also have their experiences of going through the process of application and waiting for a Home Office decision. To understand the asylum system is to understand a subculture created out of the UK government's approach to asylum-seekers. Mr One's initial counselling required an appreciation of how linked his anxiety and despair were to his position within the asylum system. Useful information on this can be gained by accessing www.ukba.homeoffice.gov.uk/asylum/process and www.refugeecouncil.org.uk.

Human rights discourse

The political and legal discourse of seeking asylum involves awareness of human rights issues, including the UN conventions, charters and protocols. This is a complex and technical area and one which links to a client's self-empowerment and hope. The human rights discourse is prevalent among asylum-seekers and survivors of torture. Relevant texts and sources of information (including the Convention Against Torture and other Cruel, Inhuman or Degrading Treatment or Punishment) can be found at: www.un.org/en/ and www.amnesty.org.uk, as well as in Beitz (2009), Ishay (2007) and Mahoney (2007).

Medical discourse

As a result of his torture Mr One has lost a kidney, suffered severe headaches, neck ache, permanent pain in his lower back and blackouts. The medical discourse, while specialist, can shed much light on a client's experience. Clients may, for example, have no language for a diagnosis, or lack the knowledge of specific physiology, or initially the ability to conceptualize medically and accurately in a western manner. Gaining knowledge of the client's previous experiences of ill health and medical or healing practices, prior to coming to the UK, can help significantly to avoid assumptions and build a shared language and understanding of their current medical treatment. This is potentially a means to assist clients in reducing anxiety states which occur through lack of knowledge and understanding. The counsellor may also be useful in informing medical staff about any aspects of treatment that may prove difficult or problematic due to the possibility of the torture experiences being replicated. Recommended texts in this respect include Ashman *et al.* (2006), Bolderson and Simpson (2004), Gross (2004), Harvey *et al.* (1998) and Mind (2009).

Counsellor self-care and supervision needs

The full height, length, breadth and depth of relating interculturally have been only partially detailed in this brief chapter. The counsellor taking up this difficult, challenging and rewarding client work is encouraged to think carefully about their own self-care and supervision needs. Counsellor review of these is recommended to take into account the possible impact of secondary or vicarious traumatization or even compassion fatigue, which are well noted in this field (see McKenzie *et al.* 2007).

Conclusion

The counselling requirements of torture survivors provide the counsellor with significant challenges and self-enrichment. Torture survivors contribute much from their own personality, culture and experience. The intercultural approach I have outlined here is based on an understanding of mutuality. The counsellor has much of their own personality, culture and experience available as a means through which to fashion the unique counselling relationship each client requires. Counselling survivors of torture is a personal encounter replete with the intensity of what the client has physically, psychologically and emotionally suffered at the hands of other human beings.

References

Agger, I. (2008) Justice as a healing factor: psycho-legal counselling for torture survivors in an Indian context, *Peace and Conflict*, 14: 315–33.

Ashman, T.A., Gordon, W.A., Cantor, J.B. and Hibbard, M.R. (2006) Neuro-behavioural consequences of traumatic brain injury, *The Mount Sinai Journal of Medicine*, 73(7): 999–1005.

Athey, S. (2007) Rethinking torture's dark chamber, *Peace Review: A Journal of Social Justice*, 20: 13–21.

Baker, R. (1992) Psychological consequences for tortured refugees seeking asylum and refugee status in Europe, in M. Başoğlu (ed.) *Torture and its Consequences, Current Treatment Approaches*. Cambridge: Cambridge University Press.

Başoğlu, M. (ed.) (1992) *Torture and its Consequences, Current Treatment Approaches*. Cambridge: Cambridge University Press.

Beitz, C.R. (2009) *The Idea of Human Rights*. Oxford: Oxford University Press.

Bolderson, H. and Simpson, K. (2004) *Mental Health Services in Kosovo*. London: Medical Foundation.

Boyles, J. (2006) Not just naming the injustice – counselling asylum seekers and refugees, in G. Proctor *et al.* (eds) *Politicizing the Person-Centred Approach: An Agenda for Social Change*. Ross-on-Wye: PCCS Books.

Burchell, S. (2007) Counselling asylum seekers and refugees, BACP G8 information sheet. Rugby: BACP.

Danner, M. (2004) *Torture and Truth, America, Abu Ghraib, and the War on Terror*. London: Granta.

Dostrovsky, J.O., Carr, D.B. and Koltzenberg, M. (eds) (2003) Proceedings of the 10th World Congress on Pain, *Progress in Pain Research and Management*, 24.

Drees, A. (1989) Guidelines for a short-term therapy of a torture depression, *Journal of Traumatic Stress*, 2(4).

Einolf, C.J. (2007) The fall and rise of torture: a comparative and historical analysis, *Sociological Theory*, 25(2): 101–21.

Elsass, P. (1997) *Treating Victims of Torture and Violence*. New York: New York University Press.

Gonsalves, C.J. *et al.* (1993) The theory of torture and the treatment of its survivors: an intervention model, *Journal of Traumatic Stress*, 6(3).

Gross, M.L. (2004) Doctors in the decent society: torture, ill-treatment and civic duty, *Bioethics*, 18(2): 181–203.

Hannah, M. (2006) Torture and the ticking bomb: the war on terrorism as a geographical imagination of power/knowledge, *Annals of the Association of American Geographers*, 96(3): 622–40.

Harvey, A.G., Bryant, R.A. and Dang, T. (1998) Autobiographical memory in acute stress disorder, *Journal of Consulting and Clinical Psychology*, 66(3): 500–6.

Herman, J.L. (1992) *Trauma and Recovery*. New York: Basic Books.

Ishay, M.R. (2007) *The Human Rights Reader*. London: Routledge.

Kinzie, J.D. (2001) Psychotherapy for massively traumatized refugees: the therapist variable, *American Journal of Psychotherapy*, 55(4): 475–90.

Mahoney, J. (2007) *The Challenge of Human Rights, Origin, Development, and Significance*. Oxford: Blackwell.

McKenzie Deighton, R., Gurris, N. and Traue, H. (2007) Factors affecting burnout and compassion fatigue in psychotherapists treating torture survivors: is the therapist's attitude to working through trauma relevant? *Journal of Traumatic Stress*, 20(1): 63–75.

Mind (2009) *Mental Health Provision for Refugees and Asylum-Seekers in England and Wales*. London: Mind.

Ojeda, A.E. (2008) *The Trauma of Psychological Torture*. London: Praeger.

Papadopoulos, R.K. (ed.) (2002) *Therapeutic Care for Refugees: No Place Like Home*. London: Karnac.

Papadopoulos, R.K. (2007) Refugees, trauma and adversity-activated development, *European Journal of Psychotherapy and Counselling*, 9(3): 301–12.

Peel, M. (2004) *Rape as a Method of Torture*. London: Medical Foundation.

Regel, S. and Berliner, P. (2007) Current perspectives on assessment and therapy with survivors of torture: the use of a cognitive behavioural approach, *European Journal of Psychotherapy and Counselling*, 9(3): 289–99.

Rejali, D. (2007) *Torture and Democracy*. Princeton, NJ: Princeton University Press.

Schauer, M., Neuner, F. and Elbert, T. (2005) *Narrative Exposure Therapy*. Cambridge, MA: Hogrefe.

Schulz, W.F. (ed.) (2007) *The Phenomenon of Torture: Readings and Commentary*. Philadelphia, PA: University of Pennsylvania Press.

Solomon, M.F. and Siegel, D.J. (eds) (2003) *Healing Trauma, Attachment, Mind, Body and Brain*. London: Norton.

Totton, N. (2000) *Psychotherapy and Politics*. London: Sage.

Wilson, J.P. and Keane, T.M. (eds) (2004) *Assessing Psychological Trauma and PTSD*, 2nd edn. London: Guilford Press.

Part 2

Heritage and identity formation: transition and identity transformation

15 Introduction to Part 2: addressing the issues of description, ascription, projection and British heritage

Colin Lago

... when we take the time to explore other communities, other movements, as more than just a casual tourist, new worlds and new depths open up. The facile stereotypes are recognised more readily for what they are and the full beauty of diversity has the chance to emerge.

(Levitt 2008: 227)

Of course it is important as therapists to develop an awareness of how race, gender, sexuality, or ability levels might impact upon one's experience, and we can develop these understandings through reading and by immersing ourselves in the struggles of oppressed people. However, in the therapy room, we should let clients lead us to understand their social locations and how various forces have come to shape their lived experiences in unique ways. This is not to assume that clients have access to knowledge about how all the discourses and forces that have shaped their being. Rather this analysis prepares us to come with an openness to take part in a journey of discovering how unique individuals make sense of their social realities and being in the world!

(Diamond and Gillis 2006: 227)

Having lived for six years in Africa and three in Singapore, I knew how to be an alien. Keep your head down and stay current; save all documents and receipts; take nothing for granted ... 'Nothing personal' is the alien's motto, because the alien has no security and no discernible future ... 'You Yanks', people sometimes said to me when they heard my accent, as though I needed to be reminded. I was an alien. But an alien is reminding himself of that every moment in the foreign country. The alien has to practise cunning to disguise this twitchy state of mind; but insecurity stretches the nerves, heightens the attention and makes the alien remember ... for an alien, life in a foreign country, never completely comprehensible, is always eventful.

(Theroux 2011: 26–31)

When we describe another person, what aspects do we include and exclude in our description? What is it that determines our selection of data to describe them? How do we know when our descriptions are fuelled by our projections of the 'other'? If describing ourselves, do we use the same categories as we use when describing others, or different ones? These questions underpin the complex tensions surrounding this second part of the book.

This chapter addresses, among other things, the tension between two opposing views within the field of cross-cultural training. That is, from one perspective, to even attempt to describe a group of people, a culture, is a foolhardy activity in that, however complex and detailed the description, it cannot ever do complete justice to the lived complexity of that group and the persons within it; and such descriptions inevitably reflect, to some extent, the values and cultural heritage of the 'describer'. However, from a different perspective, there are those who find such descriptions assist them in deepening their understanding of a particular group and their way of life; such information contributes to a useful source of knowledge for professionals working with clients originating from differing cultural origins. In short, there is a dire need by some therapists for such information (some clients report considerable resentment at being/feeling used as a source of such knowledge), but it must be combined with a maturity of view that comprehends the limits of such descriptions and a willingness to enter into each individual client's psychological and experiential world.

The intention of the following chapters is to attempt to offer insight into the effects of different heritages upon people now living in a new host society (e.g. people whose own or family origins are from elsewhere and who now live in the UK or another 'western' country). Many of the following chapters make multiple references to the challenges and differences of living in collectivistic societies and making the transition to western/UK society, which is highly individualistic (Hofstede 1980). Indeed, Hofstede's four dimensions of cultural difference (individualism–collectivism, masculinity–femininity, power–distance and uncertainty–avoidance) provide a template against which the cultural patterns revealed in these chapters can be conceptualized.

About the chapters

The chapters that follow were envisaged originally in the context of (a) particular groups who originate from many countries and cultures (e.g. international students and asylum-seekers) and (b) consideration of the significant parts of the world from which people have migrated: from Africa, the Americas, the Indian subcontinent, the Far East, Europe and so on. Inevitably, choices had to be made as to which cultural origins were selected for inclusion, and these were based, in substantial part, on a consideration of the significant geographical/regional/national areas from which significant parts of the black and minority ethnic (BME) communities in the UK have originated.

The first two chapters (16 and 17) are dedicated to broad collectives of disparate persons of many origins, who may be considered within the rubric of either

Table 15.1 Numbers of 'foreign born' individuals living in the UK as at 2001

Country of origin	Population	Relevant chapter in Part 2
Australia	107,871	19
Bangladesh	154,362	28
Germany	266,136	21
India	467,634	29
Ireland	553,901	23
Jamaica	146,401	20
Kenya	129,633	18
Pakistan	321,167	27
South Africa	141,405	18
USA	158,434	25

Source: derived from the 2001 National Census

'international students' or 'asylum-seekers'. While courting the danger of over-generalizing the circumstances of both groups, I venture to suggest that the very causes by which they are here might be described either as 'pull' factors (that is, international students will have predominantly chosen to live and study in the UK or another country) or as 'push' factors, where the majority of asylum-seekers have been driven, by circumstances, from their homes of origin. Interestingly, Alison Barty (Chapter 16) and Renate Motschnig and Ladislav Nykl (Chapter 22) note that the motivation to move, be it externally or internally driven, is likely to have a significant (and different) effect upon the transitional process to a new culture. Both groups (international students and asylum-seekers) nevertheless experience considerable transitional stresses and strains, and many require psychotherapeutic assistance at some point.

Table 15.1 shows the population of those people originating from countries other than the UK, defined as 'foreign born'.

One of the challenges in compiling this part of the book was to acknowledge and pay homage to particular areas of cultural heritage while knowing that not all cultures and countries could be featured. A further problem was the recognition of the rather crude reductionist names for complete swathes of countries and territories. As one colleague, Golnar Bayat, wrote to me in the early stages of developing this book:

> Colin, you may be interested in hearing of a reservation I have concerning the use of the term 'Middle Eastern', a phrase I never heard until I came to live in the UK. The term has always felt like one which has been imposed on a group of 'us' from a colonial phrasebook. A group of 'us' who stretch from Lebanon to Israel, to Turkey, to all of the rest? The use of this category in this context is highly problematic for me since I believe the cultural and historical diversity subsumed by the term raises serious doubts about the

analytical efficacy of the phrase. I am sure that you have considered all objections like mine but feel it may still be useful if I communicate my thoughts!

Another complex example of this is in Chapter 18, dedicated to those of an African heritage. As Divine Charura, the writer, explains:

> Africa is a continent consisting of 53 countries of which 34 are considered the least developed countries in the world. Currently it has an estimated population of 922 million (as of 2009). The most populous African country is Nigeria with over 148 million, followed by Egypt (79 million) and Ethiopia (78 million)...There are many languages, dialects and variations spoken by people of African Heritage...As with African languages, there are also hundreds of traditional African religions.

Divine was therefore faced with the very considerable task of striving to locate generalized themes linking cultural patterns, family life, belief systems and so on across this vast continent. As editor, I do take responsibility for this apparent 'glossing over' of so much detail, of inviting authors to consider such extensive regions that cannot possibly be given the detailed cultural and historical accounts they deserve. I apologise unreservedly to readers sensitive to the many societies missed and can only offer, in my defence, the realization that I had to work within the necessary limits of the book length (practical) and the overall aims of the book – this is not an anthropological textbook, but rather a contribution to aid transcultural therapists in conducting their work in a sensitive and informed manner.

In a similar vein requiring a broad-brush approach, Delroy Hall (Chapter 20) has written on the subject of an African Caribbean heritage, Andrea Uphoff (Chapter 21) on being a European in Europe, Jin Wu (Chapter 30) on Chinese heritage and Tiane Corso Graziottin (Chapter 26) on South American heritage.

Contained by slightly more defined borders, Renate Motschnig and Ladislav Nykl have focused on their own experiences of transition between the Czech Republic and Austria, (Chapter 22), Farkhondeh Farsimadan on her Iranian heritage (Chapter 24) and Yuko Nippoda on Japanese heritage (Chapter 31).

A specific note on 'mixed race'

The British Crime Survey conducted in 2002/3 revealed that 'adults from a 'mixed race' heritage were more likely than those from other ethnic groups to be victims of crime in England and Wales. Almost half (46 per cent) of adults of mixed race had been the victim of a crime in the previous 12 months. This compared with 30 per cent of Asians, black adults and those from the 'Chinese or other' groups who experienced similar levels of crime to white people. Sadly, these figures reveal a further complexity and challenge to life for those whose origins are 'mixed race' and for which we have not been able to include a chapter in this current text.

The effects of transitions

Change of any kind is one of the monumental stress factors of our time.

(Eaker 1994)

Despite my early years of being steeped in Anglophilia, Britain was, and still is, essentially alien.

(Tan 2000)

As noted above, this second part of the book is dedicated to an understanding of those from many different heritages. Alison Barty, in the next chapter dedicated to an exploration of the challenges of being an international student, quite rightly expands upon the emotional and psychological complexity that can be triggered by transitions to new environments. This may be as (apparently) undramatic as moving from one location to another within the same country. For example, Shirley Fisher (1989) conducted a substantial research project on just this theme when she explored the impact of homesickness on UK students who moved away from their home environments to a new location for their studies. The results were quite startling: 60 per cent of her research sample reported the experience of homesickness, with 5–10 per cent reporting it as prolonged and distressing (in excess of one year). Other studies examined by Fisher revealed that homesickness was associated with lowered health, lowered concentration capacity, raised inefficiency, raised depression levels, absentmindedness and greater swings in mood than had previously been experienced in the home environment.

Moving between cultures and countries, then, may have an extreme impact upon people's lives, as both the terms 'culture shock' and 'uprooting disorder' imply (see the next chapter for a greater exposition of these specific models). One workshop participant shared with me, many years ago, how useful these theoretical models had been to her in understanding the immense difficulties and mental ill health (requiring both medication and hospitalization) she had experienced during her first decade in the UK, and even then, some 18 years into residency in Britain she acknowledged that her own stage of development, as theorized by these models, was still only at the fourth level of Adler's (1975) five-stage model. More recently, both Fevronia Christodoulidi (2010) and Mary Heffernan (2011) have written on their experiences, as persons and therapists with cultural origins outside the UK, who have trained and now practise within the UK as counsellors.

In overall terms then, the impact of such transitions calls upon each person's capacity for resilience, for withstanding long-term difficulties, chronic self-doubt, sustained non-understanding of cultural codes of behaviour and language in the new resident population, a lack of identity 're-enforcers', strained relations with home nationals and so on. Additionally, these effects may also have a transgenerational impact, leading, at worst, to the experience of 'received transgenerational hatred' and 'transgenerational haunting', terms discussed more fully by Sutherland and Moodley (2010).

Lastly, in addition to the impact of transition upon those who have moved cultures, there is also the challenge to those within resident, dominant majority cultures to move from a position of 'ethnocentrism' to one of 'ethnorelativism' (Bennett 1993).

On being British

> ... Britain, as much as anywhere, is a laboratory of change – a place joined to the continent, then separated by rising seas; a place peripheral to world civilisation then central to it; a place of thinly scattered population and now one of the most densely populated parts of the globe. A place where some of its tribal languages have stuttered to extinction and another has spread across the globe. A place created by immigrants which excels at xenophobia; which has one of the richest histories in the world but still suffers from amnesia.
>
> *(Miles 2006: 12)*

> In England, then, being Canadian was like being cross-eyed, only less interesting: most people would gamely pretend not to notice, or throw you a look of pity and then swiftly escape to talk to someone else.
>
> *(Atwood 1993)*

Having invited so many colleagues in the following chapters to share aspects of their cultural heritages, it seemed not only inappropriate but completely unfair of me not to also venture into this territory by defining, however briefly and un-satisfactorily, the effects of a British heritage. It is only too easy for the resident, the power holder, the member of the dominant majority, to dedicate much as-cription to the 'outsider', the 'other' and pay scant attention to an analysis of their own cultural origins (see Chapter 8 and Lago and Haugh 2006). This general tendency is further corroborated by Harbrinder Dhillon-Stevens' doctoral research (2004) which revealed that therapists from the majority group in society tend not to explore, in their training therapy, the nature of their identity in direct con-trast to those from BME communities who invariably consider this dimension of their being.

At this point in writing I really became struck by the sheer audacity of the task I had invited others to engage in within the following chapters. What is it to be British? Just what range of evidence or artefacts or historical factors do I proceed to include? And, by implication, how much then might be missed from my descriptions? The rising anxiety created by the sense of impossibility of this task was somewhat ameliorated by the knowledge of the volume of recent publications dedicated to describing aspects of British heritage. For example, see Miles (2006), Hutchinson (1999), Golby (1986), Tan (2000) and Jacobs and Worcester (1990). Further, within the overall inclusivity of the UK there also seems to have been both a crisis of identity and subsequent interest in the nature of Englishness in recent decades. This is exemplified in texts by Fox (2004), Bragg (2006), O'Briain (2010), Paxman (1998), Scruton (2000), Aslet (1997) and Miall (1993).

Interestingly, the UK has always been a land mass populated by different incomers who have conquered or immigrated, settled, intermarried, imported and contributed their unique skills and languages, belief systems and so on. These various influences have historically included the Picts, Celts, Angles, Jutes, Vikings, Romans, French and Dutch. Over recent centuries more substantial patterns of migration have occurred from all parts of the world, a factor supported by modern developments in the capacity to trace DNA blood lines to their geographical origins.

Frequently, when conducting training within transcultural counselling, I have invited course participants to consider the question: 'Who am I, culturally speaking?' This whole text is predicated upon, among other factors, the belief that having a deep sense of one's own origins and influences will facilitate the therapist's capacity to engage more empathically with clients of different origins. In one sense this is a sociocultural extension of the therapy dictum 'therapist, know thyself'. Returning to the above training question facilitates this writer's capacity to dare to commit descriptive material to print here in the knowledge that, whatever is written is only partial, that it originates out of the complex blend of my background, experience, training and reading, and that I can only ever realistically 'catch' particular elements of a British heritage (perhaps more accurately an English heritage) that might be quite at odds with those of many other writers and indeed others of British origin whose cultural shapers (e.g. those of Scottish and Welsh origin) have been distinctly different from mine. Nevertheless, I hope that, somewhat like facets on a diamond surface, these factors not only may contribute to a snapshot of 'Britishness' but may be combined with other elements and resource materials for the whole 'diamond' to emerge.

Romance, decency, radicalism and the impact of TV!

The following material is thus centred in identified artefacts, behaviours, figures and events that, within my mind, certainly, have become metaphors upon which the notion of (British) cultural identity is rooted. One tendency that I note within myself when considering 'Britishness' is that of the romantic resonance evoked by imagined scenes such as depicted in George Orwell's essay 'The lion and the unicorn: socialism and the English genius', extolling the national characteristics of Englishness as 'long shadows on county [cricket] grounds, warm beer, invincible green suburbs, dog lovers and pools fillers and old maids bicycling to Holy Communion through the morning mist!' (Interestingly, the former prime minister John Major cited these very lines in his infamous anti-European Union speech in 1993.)

In direct contrast I am also influenced by the more politically radical reflections of Billy Bragg who argues that if fairness is the central value of 'Britishness', then it is the so-called dissenters who demanded it and fought for it who constitute the central core of 'Britishness' (Bragg 2006.) This statement reflects a long history of those significant figures from many walks of life that have stood up for a sense of social justice within society, despite the manifest social divisions created by a deeply historically embedded class and judicial system and grossly uneven wealth distribution. Exemplars of this tradition include the Society of Friends (the Quakers), Elizabeth Fry, the trade unions, Charles Dickens, the Society for the Abolition of the Slave Trade, Friedrich Engels, Emmeline Pankhurst, Mary Carpenter, Thomas Fowell Buxton, William Beveridge and many, many more.

John Pilger, a contemporary radical, notes a cultural tension that I believe is resonant of British culture and which he exemplifies in his reference to BBC broadcasting standards in his book *Heroes* (1986), where he writes, 'The 1960's jargon for an assumed authority of the BBC was the consensus view which was served and buttressed by "objectivity, impartiality and balance". These, of course, are words resonant with "fair play, decency and moderation". They are sacred words in the lexicon of broadcasting . . . however, they are words which do not mean what they say'. Suffice to say there are many metaphors within English associated with the notions of 'fair play', 'balance', 'respect' and other values redolent of what is considered to be decent behaviour towards others.

Though only briefly touched upon here, I am fascinated by the cultural effects of the media. For example, what is it to be part of a dominant majority that celebrates such TV programmes as *Big Brother* and *The Apprentice*? What do the sheer number of TV programmes about homes, gardens, travel and cooking tell us about ourselves? And what about those programmes dedicated to buying property, and then even buying properties abroad? Perhaps we are still stuck in the older metaphors of 'our home being our castle' and 'the nice place to live is in the country'? Apparently, well over 275,000 Brits have homes (or second homes) abroad. As one Swiss psychotherapist said to me, 'Why do so many of you want to leave . . . what is it that is pushing you out?' An interesting question!

On naming British 'cultural' behaviours

In 2006 Lucy Mangan wrote an article with the title 'What it means to be British' in response to the UK government's initiatives to incorporate tests of 'Britishness' into the legal process of seeking British nationality. She suggested a list of the following British cultural traits that she identified as distinctive: snobbery, insularity, anti-intellectualism, self-deprecation, humour, repression, politeness, nostalgia, pessimism and slobbery. Some two years prior to this article, Kate Fox ventured a somewhat similar list under the title of 'Defining Englishness' (2004: 400–14). She listed the following characteristics and conceptualized these within a diagram at the centre of which lies 'social dis-ease'. This quality then connects to three clusters of:

1 (Reflexes): humour, moderation and hypocrisy.
2 (Outlooks): empiricism, 'Eyorishness' and class-consciousness.
3 (Values): fair play, courtesy and modesty.

Fox thus constructed a basic system for understanding English behaviour divided into three clusters, each comprising three distinct elements, all linked together via the quality of 'social dis-ease'. Needless to say, the impact of class, power, wealth, accent and position are all reflected in the above characteristics.

On faith and religion

Religion, perhaps inevitably, has had, over the centuries, a considerable impact upon the British state, upon governance and upon the country's populace. Perhaps the most dramatic incident involving religion and state was the cleavage from the Roman Catholic Church during the Reformation in the sixteenth century. This was effected by Thomas Cromwell in anti-papal legislation in 1529, the main consequence of which was the acknowledgement of the sovereign as the head of the English Church. This move facilitated, among other things, Henry VIII's divorce of Catherine of Aragon, the execution of Anne Boleyn and the dissolution of the monasteries (Hutchinson 1999: 751). Hutchinson has noted that

> it was the sheer length of Elizabeth's reign which allowed the Reformation
> to triumph in Britain, so that by the 1580s the majority of its people
> had been so thoroughly re-educated in the new faith that they genuinely
> identified with it ... the Church of England reflected Elizabeth's wish for
> compromise, yoking Protestant doctrine to a Catholic structure of bishops,
> cathedrals and festivals. Many Protestants remained deeply unhappy with
> it. The Church of Scotland, formed in revolution, made a more radical
> departure to a Presbyterian structure and a complete abolition of the old
> festivals and vestments.

In the ensuing centuries there were developments within religious forms that included the Quakers, Methodists, Baptists, Plymouth Brethren, Pentecostalists, Congregationalists, Unitarians, and so on. Although this is but a snapshot of the role of faith, religion and the populace within the UK, the emergence of secularism was already being noted by Horace Mann in the *Report of the Religious Census* in 1851 (Golby 1986: 40): 'The most important fact which this investigation as to attendance [at churches] brings before us, is, unquestionably, the alarming number of non-attendants'. In addition the report expressed considerable concern that church attendance was lowest among the working classes. Mann continues: 'there is a sect, originated recently, adherents to a system called "Secularism", the principal tenet being that, as the fact of future life is ... susceptible to some degree of doubt, while the fact and necessities of a present life are matters of direct sensation, it is therefore prudent to attend exclusively to the concerns of that existence which is certain and immediate ...'

It is fascinating to note that the counselling and psychotherapy profession was strongly influenced by secular views from the 1960s, views which currently appear to be shifting to embrace wider spiritual influences. Certainly, for transcultural therapists to be effective in their task, they will require an appropriate respect for, knowledge of and understanding of the role that religion and faith have to play in their clients' lives.

Language and material wealth

> *He's as poor as a church mouse.*
>
> *(Old saying)*

> *Language re-arranges the furniture of the mind.*
>
> *(Hall 1990)*

Space prevents me from expanding greatly on both these themes (material wealth and language) that are deeply significant aspects of British cultural life. The recent use of the phrase 'material wealth', by a client, reminded me of the enormous range of phrases and sayings used within the British context, some having universal understanding across the nation and others being quite particular to certain regions, with others still being seen as curious or oblique in their meanings. If I, as a therapist, do not understand a phrase or saying that originates from another part of the UK, think how much harder it is, for example, if you are a speaker of English as a second language. Suffice to say that many of these expressions have long histories, their original meanings sometimes being buried in history. As a personal reflection linked to my own appreciation of 'British' heritage, I continue to be profoundly amazed by the sheer amount of such phrases that have emanated from the writings of Shakespeare. Indeed, Bragg (2003: 144) claims that Shakespeare had a vocabulary of at least 21,000 different words and suggests that, by contrast, the average educated person now only has a working vocabulary of less than half this amount!

One website describes English as:

> a West Germanic language which is the dominant language in the United Kingdom, the United States, many Commonwealth nations including Australia, Canada, New Zealand and other former British colonies. It is the second most spoken language in the world. It is estimated that there are 380 million native speakers and 300 million who use English as a second language and a further 100 million use it as a foreign language. It is the language of science, aviation, computing, diplomacy, and tourism. It is listed as the official or co-official language of over 45 countries and is spoken extensively in other countries where it has no official status.
>
> (www.englishlanguageguide.com/english/facts/history)

In one step, this sheer spread and influence of the language is both a blessing and a curse to monolingual English-speaking therapists within transcultural settings. The blessing is obvious – we can be understood by many people – but the curse of having this advantage in some ways makes us both lazy in acquiring other languages and certainly deprives us of nuances of meaning and perception conveyed by other languages.

In discussing this subject of British heritage with a friend who has a great interest in history, he referred to the 'grinding poverty' that has afflicted many generations of the British population going back through the centuries. The deleterious effects of both agrarian, rural life and then the industrial revolution upon life expectancy and ill health for the 'working' classes were devastating. These effects continue to impact to this day within Britain and are evidenced in an excellent book by Wilkinson and Pickett (2009) which provides overwhelming evidence that the more unequal a society, the greater will be its social malaise. Countries with the greatest income inequalities (e.g. the UK, Portugal and the USA), where the top 20 per cent have over seven times that of the bottom 20 per cent, have higher levels of addiction, higher homicide levels and prison populations, lower levels of trust, higher levels of obesity, higher levels of teenage pregnancy and higher levels of mental illness. For example, 25 per cent of Britons experience mental health problems in any one year compared with fewer than 10 per cent in Japan, Germany, Sweden and Italy where there is much less differentiation between incomes. Wilson and Pickett refer to this differential as the 'social gradient'. This all too brief reference to the role and consequences of wealth and poverty in the UK (and other countries) yet again points us to the importance of the development of our collective and individual potential as competent transcultural therapists.

A final note on therapist profiles in the British setting

I am most grateful to colleagues at the British Association for Counselling and Psychotherapy (BACP) (2011) (currently the largest professional membership organization within the UK for therapists, with 34,579 members) for the following profiles of the membership in terms of ethnicity, age, gender, ability and theoretical orientation. In addition, I also quote from an article by Hope Massiah citing the diversity and equality statistics of the United Kingdom Council for Psychotherapy (UKCP) (2010). The UKCP figures are based on 4,051 respondents. In some circumstances where the data between the two organizations are recorded slightly differently, I have attempted to converge the two sets of statistics. Any errors, therefore, in the following figures, are all mine. Also, not all percentage statistics quoted below add up to 100 per cent, as both organizations record a small number of members for whom they have no record.

Gender

BACP membership is 84 per cent female while the UKCP figures reveal a slightly lower figure of 77 per cent. Certainly this is a profession that attracts and reflects high female intake and interest. Hope Massiah notes that, by contrast, the percentage of women in the general population indicates that for the 31–55 age category, 51 per cent are female and this rises to 56 per cent for those over 65.

Ethnicity

Both organizations are predominantly white, with BACP having 84 per cent of its membership as white and UKCP 96.5 per cent. Massiah notes that white people comprise 88 per cent of the UK population. In the remaining categories under

Table 15.2 UKCP and BACP ethnicity statistics

	UKCP (%)	BACP (%)
Asian	0.8	2
Black	2.7	2.5
Mixed race	0	(BACP includes this in the next statistic)
Other	0.1	3.1

ethnicity, for the purpose of simplicity of presentation, I have condensed the other seven collected by BACP into the four categories employed by UKCP (see Table 15.2).

Age profile

The age profiles of both professional organizations follow a remarkably similar distribution where the percentage of membership for both is exactly the same at 63 per cent for members aged between 40 and 59! Younger people (from 20 to 39) represent only 6.4 per cent of UKCPs membership, while BACP figures reveal a higher figure of 16 per cent. The proportion of UKCP's membership over 60 years of age is 30 per cent while that of BACP is 21 per cent.

Disability

The article by Massiah (2010) records 5 per cent as disabled and 94.1 per cent as not disabled within the UKCP membership. BACP has a more detailed registering system that records those with visual and hearing impairments, those who are physically disabled and either in or not in receipt of benefits and a further 'other' category. In total, 85 per cent of BACP membership records as able-bodied and the remaining categories (defined in the previous sentence) total to approximately 8 per cent.

Sexuality and theoretical models

UKCP also collects figures on sexuality: 3.5 per cent are recorded as bisexual, 7 per cent as lesbian and gay, 7 per cent offered no response and the remaining membership is recorded as heterosexual at 82.5 per cent.

BACP, interestingly, records figures based upon the theoretical models that members are trained in which offer the following profile: Gestalt 5 per cent, humanistic 25 per cent, integrative 35 per cent, person-centred 46 per cent, psychodynamic 26 per cent, cognitive-behavioural 18 per cent and other models 9 per cent. (Please note that these figures do not add up to 100 per cent; rather they reflect the broad range of initial and supplementary training that colleagues in the profession have followed during their careers.)

Conclusion

This chapter, in introducing the second part of the book, has attempted to address various elements connected to the issues of heritage and how this impacts upon self and the other. In line with another attributed British cultural phenomenon, the compromise (e.g. the continued existence of the monarchy alongside a parliamentary democracy), the opening paragraphs addressed the tension between the values and dangers of describing others. In striving to maintain a creative tension between these apparent opposites, the chapter proceeded to introduce the manner through which the heritage chapters have been selected and noted that, however comprehensive they may be, there is always so much more to know and understand. I then attempted to offer a brief account of some aspects of British culture in an overall commitment to the notion, 'therapist, know thy (cultural and ethnic) self'.

References

Adler, P.S. (1975) The transitional experience: an alternative view of culture shock, *Journal of Humanistic Psychology*, 15(4): 13–23.

Aslet, C. (1997) *Anyone for England? A Search for British Identity*. London: Little-Brown.

Atwood, M. (1993) *A Virago Keepsake*. London: Virago.

Bennett, M.J. (1993) Towards a developmental model of intercultural sensitivity, in R. Michael Paige (ed.) *Education for the Intercultural Experience*. Yarmouth, ME: Intercultural Press.

Bragg, M. (2003) *The Adventure of English: The Biography of a Language*. London: Hodder & Stoughton.

Bragg, B. (2006) *The Progressive Patriot: A Search for Belonging*. London: Transworld/Random House.

British Association for Counselling and Psychotherapy (BACP) (2011) Membership breakdown, February, personal communication.

Christodoulidi, F. (2010) The therapist's experience in a 'foreign country': a qualitative inquiry into the effect of mobility for counsellors and psychotherapists, unpublished doctoral dissertation, University of Manchester.

Dhillon-Stevens, H. (2004) Healing inside and out: an examination of dialogic encounters in the area of anti-oppressive practice in counselling and psychotherapy, unpublished doctoral dissertation, Middlesex University.

Diamond, S.L. and Gillis, J.R. (2006) Approaching multiple diversity: addressing the intersections of class, gender, sexual orientation and different abilities, in C. Lago (ed.) *Race, Culture and Counselling: The Ongoing Challenge*. Maidenhead. Open University Press.

Eaker, L. (1994) Quoted in C. Lago and G. Shipton (1994) *Personal Tutoring in Action: A Handbook for Staff Working with and Supporting Students*. Sheffield: Sheffield University Counselling Service.

Fisher, S. (1989) *Homesickness, Cognition and Health*. London: Lawrence Earlbaum Associates.

Fox, K. (2004) *Watching the English: The Hidden Rules of English Behaviour*. London: Hodder & Stoughton.

Golby, J.M. (1986) *Culture and Society in Britain 1850–1890*. Oxford: Oxford University Press.

Hall, E.T. (1990) *Understanding Cultural Differences*. Yarmouth, ME: Intercultural Press.

Hefferenan, M. (2011) Home is where the couch is, *Therapy Today*, 22(1): 23–5.

Hofstede, G. (1980) *Culture's Consequences: International Differences in Work-Related Values*. Beverly Hills, CA: Sage.

Hutchinson. (1999) *The Encyclopedia of Britain: An A–Z Guide to its People, Places, History and Culture*. London: Helicon.

Jacobs, E. and Worcester, R. (1990) *We British*. London: Weidenfeld & Nicolson.

Lago, C. and Haugh, S. (2006) White counsellor racial identity: the unacknowledged, unknown, unaware aspect of self in relationship, in M. Cooper, B. Malcolm, G. Proctor and P. Sanders (eds) *Politicizing the Person-Centred Approach: An Agenda for Social Change*. Ross-on-Wye: PCCS Books.

Levitt, B. (2008) *Reflections on Human Potential: Bridging the Person-Centred Approach and Positive Psychology*. Ross-on-Wye: PCCS Books.

Mangan, L. (2006) What it means to be British, *Guardian*, 16 May.

Massiah, H. (2010) Diversity and equality statistics: what they reveal and what they conceal, *The Psychotherapist*, 46: 42–4.

Miall, A. (1993) *Xenophobe's Guide to the English*. London: Oval Books.

Miles, D. (2006) *The Tribes of Britain*. London: Phoenix/Orion.

O'Briain, D. (2010) *Tickling the English*. London: Penguin.

Orwell, G. (1998) The lion and the unicorn: socialism and the English genius, in P. Davison (ed.) *The Complete Works of George Orwell*. London: Secker & Warburg.

Paxman, J. (1998) *The English: A Portrait of a People*. London: Michael Joseph.

Pilger, J. (1986) *Heroes*. London: Jonathan Cape.

Scruton, R. (2000) *England: An Elegy*. London: Chatto & Windus.

Sutherland, P. and Moodley, R. (2010) Spirituality and traditional healing, in R. Moodley and R. Walcott (eds) *Counseling Across and Beyond Cultures: Exploring the Work of Clemmont E. Vontress in Clinical Practice*. Toronto: University of Toronto Press.

Tan, T. (2000) *Culture Shock: A Guide to Customs and Etiquette in Britain*. Singapore: Times Media.

Theroux, P. (2011) This was England, *Observer Magazine*, 13 February.

Wilkinson, R. and Pickett, K. (2009) *The Spirit Level: Why More Equal Societies Almost Always Do Better*. London: Penguin.

16 International students: who are they?

Alison Barty

Introduction

International students are an increasingly significant part of the UK student population. The term 'international student' already presents a problem. It has become a convenient 'shorthand' of UK education providers (universities, colleges, language schools) to describe students who come to the UK for the purpose of study. When the term is unpacked it covers an almost infinite range of individuals from every possible ethnic, cultural, religious, social, political, historical and language background, perhaps shared with the host, perhaps very different – and different from each other. The term can be used to describe a Chinese undergraduate with no prior history of education in English, a mid-career African student taking a PhD or an EU teenager on a short language course.

Some 'international students' may have much in common with any local student at the same developmental stage (Ward *et al.* 2001); others will have significant commonalities with other black and minority ethnic (BME) students, while possessing distinct experiences and histories. It is a complex matrix indeed, and one to which the term 'international student' will always struggle to do justice.

Diversity in population

For counselling and psychotherapy practitioners working with this client group, the diversity is, of course, relevant. The expectations of a student seeking therapy from an environment where psychotherapy in the 'western' sense is well established will be different from those of a student where this model is largely unfamiliar (much of the world outside North and South America, Australasia and western Europe). Even within these latter populations, expectations will vary. The ways in which counselling and psychotherapy are delivered and by whom will, of course, not necessarily be the same as those experienced by international students in their countries of origin. If the expectation is that counselling/psychotherapy will be provided by a psychologist or psychiatrist, then finding a system (in the UK, for example) where that is not a given may influence uptake and confidence (Barty 2006).

Transition/uprooting

Well I've been here six years now and I don't feel at home still.

(UKCISA 2007)

'Culture shock', a term first used by Oberg in 1960 to describe the process of adaptation to new cultures, has been rejected by some as simplistic and clichéd (Ward 2004). Lago (2006: 392) states that concepts of culture shock or 'uprooting disorder' (Zwingmann and Gunn 1983: 14) are 'not at all deeply understood or appreciated in terms of the demands and pressures they place upon those who suffer this process. At worst, culture shock can cause breakdown and long term illness'. However conceptualized, a common experience for a significant proportion of 'international students' is that caused by the transition or 'uprooting' from their 'home' environment, which may have been recent or some time in the past.

For some, the transition will have been essentially one of choice, voluntarily undertaken for positive reasons – frequently described as 'pull' factors such as personal development or perceived social, career or professional status. For others, the transition may have come about more as a result of 'push' factors. These can include lack of higher education facilities or options nearer home, economic factors, internal mechanisms in the home country which discriminate, parental pressure, ambition or family tradition, or, as Madison (2005) observes, simply not 'fitting into' the culture of origin. While some international students may be 'de facto' refugees, for most the experience is significantly different from that of refugees, who are overwhelmingly likely to be 'pushed' with little if any choice in the matter. It is important to be aware that different students will be at different points on this 'push–pull' continuum.

Research conducted by Allen and Higgins (1994: 11) analysed the motivations of study abroad for international students. Key 'pull' factors identified in the study included:

- 'opportunity to travel/experience different cultures' (68 per cent);
- 'receive a better education' (59 per cent);
- 'better job prospects in their home country' (43 per cent);
- 'difficult to get into university/college in own country' (40 per cent).

Theoretical representations of the transition process include the U or W curve (Gullahorn and Gullahorn 1963), a developmental model (Bennett and Bennett 2004), psychological uprooting (Zwingmann and Gunn 1983) and a form of bereavement (Anderson 1994), while a Buddhist model (Lago 2004) identifies three stages: endings (with characteristics similar to Adler's (1975) disintegration stage); a transitional state; and finally new beginnings. However portrayed, there is an emotional and psychological process which occurs and which challenges the student following their move to the new host environment. The process is never linear: there will be ups and downs, reverses and recycling.

Loneliness and homesickness

Loneliness and homesickness can be an inherent part of dislocation, as students experience shifts of place, language and status where familiar sources of support are no longer accessible (Maundeni 1999; Sawir *et al.* 2007). Also absent are established 'landmarks', whether physical or social, which act as 'identity re-enforcers' (Lago 2004). Even though the early stages of transition are likely to be a time when psychological, social and cultural adjustments are most acute (Ward *et al.* 2001), cultural isolation and social loneliness can persist over time, seriously impacting well-being.

Students will be helped by having realistic expectations, linguistic confidence, and previous cross-cultural experience, while contact with the host culture (too often lacking) provides positive human connection and builds a stronger sense of belonging (Madison 2005). When 'integration' is difficult, separation (immersion in the culture of origin) becomes an alternative, and can afford some psychological protection (Berry 2004). Seeking strong same-national groupings may serve, or indeed save, a struggling student.

Yet, while transition puts some students at risk, a sense of perspective is important: this is an educative and formative process (Anderson 1994) which most students navigate without serious consequence (Ward *et al.* 2001)

Traditions of help-seeking and help-giving

Students may find the distinction between a psychotherapist, psychiatrist, psychologist or counsellor confusing (Okorocha 1994; Barty 2006), though the unfamiliarity of counselling/psychotherapy can be overplayed, with international students patronized or stereotyped as being less able to use counselling or psychotherapy. I would argue, as do Lago and Thompson (1996), that all societies have, and always have had, traditions of help-seeking and help-giving – whether family, communal, spiritual or medical (including traditional practices). Similarly, counselling values are not so distant from other traditional belief systems (Cowley 2005). So our practices are not so special or modern but take their place among these traditions.

Western counsellors and psychotherapists, with their own theoretical cultural frames, may undervalue or even be hostile to other helping traditions. Such traditions may include informal methods such as family and friends (Weiss 1973; Bradley 2000; Fleet 2009), 'locals' (Ward *et al.* 2001), elders or authority figures (Okorocha 1994), religious or spiritual leaders, or prayer (Sawir *et al.* 2007; Pakaslahti 2009). A secure attachment to God appears to mitigate against loneliness and depression (Sawir *et al.* 2007), though I have counselled students who project a harsh 'inner judge' onto God, feeling unable to be good enough.

The use international students make of university or college counselling services is under-researched. However, annual statistics from student counselling services suggest that, while usage varies, these services are used by international students from all over the world. Fleet (2009), in a study comparing African and UK postgraduate students, found that both groups sought family support but would also recommend counselling. While the African students put family and friends before 'outsiders' and the UK students valued more highly the perceived neutrality of the professional helper, it can be misleading always to assume that international students will use informal networks, or that these will be sufficient. These networks will not prevent loneliness (Weiss 1973) or other psychological vulnerability.

Language and 'language'

> When I'm here I dream in English because I don't only think in English, I feel in English as well. Every message and image is in English and I do dream in English. When I go back to Greece, the first week or so I still dream in English and when I start dreaming in Greek again I kind of feel maybe I've landed now in the new territory, so the dream is an indicator about what happens in that switch in me between the languages and the cultures in me.
>
> *(UKCISA 2007)*

All therapies are conducted in a language of some kind – verbal, embodied, music, art, play. Within any international student population, the degree to which language between therapist and client is shared will vary. For example the dyad may consist of:

1   *English first-language-speaking therapist and English first-language-speaking client.* Here there is an apparently high level of shared language familiarity, but pitfalls lie in the *apparent* familiarity. Behind the initial assumptions may lie significant differences in vocabulary and register (politeness, respect, directness, indirectness), which can be subtly or overtly disorienting for both parties.

2   *English second- or third-language-speaking therapist and English first-language-speaking client.* Given that more and more colleges and universities will have therapists, as they do academics, from different language backgrounds, who is the most or least at home here? How does the power dynamic work, as language can be power?

3   *English first-language-speaking therapist and English second- or third- (etc.) language-speaking client.* Here the dynamics of power are more obvious. The client is expected to speak about personal and perhaps early life experiences in a language different from that in which the experience was lived. Some clients find this an advantage, providing some distance from the initial 'disturbance'. For a deeper connection with the early experience, if this is sought, it may be relevant for the client to speak in their 'mother' tongue (the expression 'mother tongue' itself is of course significant). What is it like for the therapist to sit with the client and listen, yet

not understand the words? Very often, if able to attune, it is possible for the therapist to hear, absorb and connect with the emotion of the communication, perhaps even to connect more deeply when not distracted by, interpreted by, or even reduced to spoken words.

4   *English second- or third-language client with English second- or third-language therapist.* This dyad introduces yet another interesting dynamic: how to find a 'shared' language. The common experience of linguistic shift may enhance the therapeutic alliance. However, as with a therapist and client who share English as a first language, there may be unexpected pitfalls or assumptions confounded. Assumptions or identifications may be more likely where the language is literally shared – and there may be surprising challenges. A Japanese therapist, trained in English, working with a Japanese-speaking client for the first time, realized that though her 'first' language was indeed Japanese, her 'therapeutic' first language was *English*. English was the language in which she thought therapeutically and theoretically: she had suddenly to develop a way of thinking and working in Japanese (this specific scenario has recently been the subject of a doctoral study by Christodoulidi 2010).

Whatever the dyad, the question of language is usefully addressed early on and its potential and ongoing impact considered by both parties.

Language is a powerful vehicle for the expression of self and for contact with others. For international students, there is an expectation that they will be proficient in the English language, and, in the academic setting, articulacy carries high value. While for many, English is their second, third or one of many more languages, students may feel profoundly deskilled when having to operate alongside first-language speakers (even though many of these will speak *no* other languages!). They can feel a loss of 'self' in the loss of fluency and range. In the counselling setting too, students may feel reduced in their ability to express themselves (Okorocha 1994), with the potential for shame. Yet there can be a sense, sometimes liberating, of having a different 'self' in a different language.

Much has been written on the complexity of non-verbal language (e.g. Hall 1959) and its significance, whether deliberate or unconscious – and such expression provides yet another rich dimension of communication capable of aiding or complicating understanding. Using metaphor can enhance communication, accessing visual or auditory cues/clues – and can confuse if metaphors and analogies are not shared or are too culturally specific. Counsellors of international students would be wise to use metaphor judiciously and ensure they understand the metaphors used by their clients. There are many stories of misunderstandings that have only come to the counsellor's awareness some time after the student has left.

Ward *et al.* (2001) stress the importance of language to successful adaptation while for Weiss (1973) linguistic loneliness may exacerbate social loneliness, with language differences, sometimes quite subtle, leading to a sense of exclusion.

Mental health issues

A potent combination of uncertainty and anxiety can be evoked in counsellors through experiencing and perceiving a sense of 'cultural distance' between themselves and the client, and this anxiety is likely to be further heightened if they also perceive there to be issues of mental (distress and) ill health as well. Those working with international students, therapeutically or otherwise, can be derailed in such circumstances, suddenly feeling deskilled and unsure of the most appropriate intervention. For instance, though serious mental illness is not culture-specific, its presentation may be, with potential for confusion (Brislin 2006).

Anecdotal evidence suggests that in all cultures mental ill health carries a stigma. In most societal contexts it is rarely spoken of openly or comfortably, with the result that ignorance and prejudice persist. One possible consequence is that a family where a young person has mental health instability may see an option to 'export' the problem, if they can afford to do so, by enabling the young person to study abroad. This may bring a dual advantage: removing the risk of stigma by distancing the young person, and gaining the kudos, or added value, of a son or daughter studying overseas. A variation of this theme may be the student who believes that by moving abroad to study they will leave their mental health problems behind and be able to start afresh. Sadly, both attempts to solve a problem of mental health vulnerability can result in more extreme problems, as the person finds themselves distanced, not from the problem, but from the familiar and the known. As Stanley and Manthorpe (2002) observe, pre-existing mental health difficulties can be compounded by cultural differences.

Other related factors affecting the mental health of international students, including those who have shown no previous vulnerability, may be a sense of loss of control (Stanley and Manthorpe 2002), excessive expectations, the need for achievement (Ward *et al.* 2001), or not knowing the 'rules'. The absence of familiar networks may significantly reduce resilience to stressors.

Quick, effective and sensitive intervention is important to avoid the risk of a student deteriorating further and jeopardizing their studies, perhaps even their personal safety. As the case below illustrates, even seemingly minor difficulties can lead to sudden destabilization.

Case example

An international student from West Africa arrived with his family, as a scholarship student. Bureaucratic difficulties meant he was unable to open a bank account and consequently was unable to access the funds needed to support himself and his family. An apparent stalemate developed between him and the bank: within days his physical and mental health deteriorated markedly. He became reclusive, almost mute, and unable to focus on his studies or interact with others. His wife became alarmed for his safety. Only when a member of staff took it upon themselves to intervene directly with the bank was the problem resolved and he gradually began to recover.

In extreme cases, the best outcome may be a repatriation of the student, with an option of return if their resources can be rebuilt sufficiently.

Counselling interventions: the challenge to counsellors

Counselling/therapy offered to international students, from whatever background, takes place in the context of the institution. The learning process has inherent elements of assessment and competition. It carries the polarities of pass and fail. The pressures apply equally to local students, but the impact of failure, the potential loss of 'face' (Ting-Toomey 2004) may have particular cultural and social significance for an international student, and unless understood may jeopardize the effectiveness of any intervention.

Are specific interventions favoured or contraindicated when working with international students? It is suggested here that the counsellor needs to have sharply attuned antennae to notice the effectiveness, or ineffectiveness, of any intervention used. There may be less common ground than assumed to support an intervention that might otherwise appear to be appropriate. It is likely to be more fruitful for a counsellor to start from a stance of not knowing: not in the sense of expecting the client to teach the counsellor what they don't know, but more from a 'researcher' perspective (Fleet 2009).

Numerous factors may prevent international students accessing counselling: concern about confidentiality, a taboo on discussing private concerns to someone outside immediate family, perceived lack of relevance and perceived pressures of time. These may be shared with local students but felt more acutely where confidence in cultural understanding may be missing. Pelletier (2003), in a review of unpublished literature, highlights the lack of any critical appraisal of the effectiveness of western counselling as a 'framework of understanding' when considered from the perspective of a 'non-western' client.

Equally, there has been no substantial study of developmental issues among this client group. A counsellor/therapist trained in the West is likely to have absorbed a developmental model based on western assumptions about family, child-rearing and the need for independence over dependence, perhaps unconsciously assuming these to be universals. Culturally aware counselling requires a move from an ethnocentric to a more 'ethno-relative' therapeutic perspective (Bennett and Bennett 2004).

The challenge for a counsellor/psychotherapist, however experienced, may be to set aside familiar 'frameworks of understanding' (Bennett and Bennett 2004), holding that stance of 'not knowing' in order to find a mutually understood formulation, or at least a place where they and their client can acknowledge their differences. Thomas (2009) describes how, unless a genuine working alliance is established in this way, with the culturally different client feeling accepted and any differences recognized, the client may present a protective 'proxy' self to the therapist which, if not understood, will reduce the possibility of effective work.

More case examples

Student X, from China, presented in the first weeks of a foundation course. It was his first experience of the UK and his first experience of leaving China. In China the student had always been high-achieving, supported by his parents, who were heavily invested in his success. He was feeling totally disoriented. He described himself as feeling 'very sad, like a stone in his heart'. He was unwilling to tell his parents or they would worry. He had experienced several initial setbacks: his mobile phone had been taken, his first marks had disappointed him and he had developed a skin rash that was causing him anxiety. His sleep was disturbed and he had lost his appetite, compounded by finding a lot of the food available unpalatable. He was worried that what he perceived as a succession of 'bad luck' would follow him through the year.

Much of the time the counsellor felt they were doing little more than 'sitting with' the student and using interventions that felt some-times like a low-key conversation more than a 'therapeutic' exploration. The counsellor focused on more concrete aspects of the situation than usual, such as how investigation of the theft had been handled, devel-oping contacts with academic staff and other students and discussing the student's routine self-care. Cultural dimensions were also explored: what would happen in China in these circumstances? What did 'bad luck' mean? They explored the idea (more western?) that the theft had been 'bad' and had left him feeling 'bad' with consequent feelings of distrust of the host, white community, being seen as uncaring and dismissive.

Though at times coming to the counselling room was the only time the student left his room, gradually he engaged more with some of his fellow students and developed greater confidence in speaking to his teachers. Though the year was not the experience the student anticipated, he was able to complete the course and progress to an undergraduate degree. In the process of ending, he said to the counsellor, 'Now I know why they have people like you.'

Student Y was a female student from Pakistan, studying for a masters. She shared a flat with her younger brother who was in the second year of an undergraduate degree. Their older brother and sister were married and living in Pakistan. Her brother had recently disclosed to her that he was gay. She reported that this information had placed her in an extremely difficult situation. She was close to her brother and felt responsible for him while he was in the UK. She knew that her parents would find his homosexuality wholly unacceptable and that they would expect her to tell them, which might result in his being taken back to Pakistan, away from 'harmful influences'. She felt equally unable to talk to her older siblings, who in her view were very traditional in their outlook. Personally she felt caught between her affection for her brother, her reluctance to intervene in his life and her own highly ambivalent feelings about the information he had given her.

Specific therapeutic issues arising from this last scenario include:

1   The interaction between potentially incompatible values – here, different cultural attitudes to homosexuality. (It is important to acknowledge that prejudice against homosexuality/homophobic attitudes exist in all cultures and religions and plenty of 'western' students feel the need to hide their sexual orientation from family and friends.
2   Family responsibility.
3   Parental authority.
4   Hierarchical sibling relationships.
5   Isolation.

Possible considerations for counsellors include:

1   Assumptions about what might need to happen or what stance Y should take.
2   Awareness of own 'western' assumptions about autonomy, independence and the priority of the individual.
3   Own attitudes to same-sex relationships.

Possible therapist interventions might include:

1   Discussing what might happen if she and her brother were in Pakistan (what would be easier and what more difficult).
2   Exploring and comparing contrasting perspectives:
    • Whose problem was it? Counsellor accepting that in one frame it was a family concern, involving possible consequences for all the family.
    • Who might be implicated if the son's sexual orientation became public? Her own marriage prospects? Her older brother's position as a head teacher?
    • Aspects of religious teaching. How God would judge her in these circumstances; the counsellor perhaps not knowing, if not Muslim, while appreciating that within Islam, different interpretations exist, as they do within other faiths.

Possible outcomes are:

1   Information about a support organization for young gay Muslims.
2   Y talking with brother but also with another older Muslim female student with whom she had become friendly.
3   Using her prayers to support herself.
4   Becoming more able to sit with her dilemma and step back from feeling she has to choose between her brother and her parents.

An assumption that an international student will prefer a more directive or practical approach may be as limiting as a therapist assuming that their preferred orientation will work for every client. Creativity and flexibility in approach may enable the counsellor to arrive at a stronger working alliance, even if this means moving out of their therapeutic comfort zone.

International students of whatever country of origin have lost familiar sources of support and guidance; they have also lost a level of cultural competence and confidence. This can undermine, indeed deconstruct, their sense of identity. They may need a psychological 'holding', a 'container', and most of all from their counsellor (Christodoulidi and Lago 2010), requiring a process supporting 'reconstruction' as opposed to the 'deconstruction' involved in some therapeutic interventions. A student may need, above all, a 'transitional space', somewhere to exist, to be; where they can experience themselves reflected in the counsellor's eyes, ears, words and full presence.

Outside the traditional consulting room, group programmes with a psychosocial/educative approach have shown evidence of success in increasing students' confidence and esteem (Martin and Harrell 2004) and can be particularly tailored to the challenges of the academic environment (Mak *et al.* 1998; Barty and Raven 2003).

Training implications

There are counsellors in most universities, colleges and in many schools. Many educational institutions seek to receive and recruit international students, yet there is limited specific training on counselling an international student population. Training programmes have developed for other staff working with international students, notably for specialist 'international student advisers' as well as more generic training for university staff in general. Training on cultural awareness has expanded too, including masters degree programmes with an intercultural focus. While of broad relevance, such programmes are not focused on the therapeutic setting. It is a significant gap.

Even within the student counselling profession, significant documents which have been produced, such as *Degrees of Disturbance* (Rana *et al.* 1999), *Counselling Students* (Rana 2000), the RAPSS report into student suicide (Stanley *et al.* 2007) and the Royal College of Psychiatrists report *The Mental Health of Students in Higher Education* (2003) contain little or no reference to international students.

Counsellors who inevitably work with international students express concern about the demands made by such students and question how to provide a relevant service. In looking mainly to their own profession for guidance and education, they may ignore some of the expertise on their doorstep, in the form of international student advisers and English language teaching staff, where there may be cultural knowledge on which to draw.

Similarly, in the choice of supervisor, how many university counsellors look for a supervisor with any expertise or understanding of international students? Even if they did, these supervisors are likely to be hard to find.

Conclusion

International students, in their diversity, are both like and unlike other students – culturally different and with cultural overlaps. The culturally informed counsellor of any international student will aim to step skilfully and sensitively without losing sight of either 'in between' similarities or differences.

References

Adler, P. (1975) The transitional experience: an alternative view of culture shock, *Journal of Humanistic Psychology*, 15(4): 13–23.

Allen, A. and Higgins, T. (1994) *Higher Education: The International Student Experience*. London: HMSO.

Anderson, L. (1994) A new look at an old construct: cross-cultural adaptation, *International Journal of Intercultural Relations*, 8(3): 293–328.

Barty, A. (with Young Minds) (2006) *Higher Education Institutions and International Students' Mental Health*. London: Young Minds.

Barty, A. and Raven, S. (2003) Reaching out to the international students, *AUCC Journal*, winter.

Bennett, J.M. and Bennett, M.J. (2004) Developing intercultural sensitivity: an integrative approach to global and domestic diversity, in D. Landis, J.M. Bennett and M.J. Bennett (eds) *Handbook of Intercultural Training*, 3rd edn. Thousand Oaks, CA: Sage.

Berry, J.W. (2004) Fundamental psychological processes in intercultural relations, in D. Landis, J.M. Bennett and M.J. Bennett (eds) *Handbook of Intercultural Training*, 3rd edn. Thousand Oaks, CA: Sage.

Bradley, G. (2000) Responding effectively to the mental health needs of international students, *Higher Education*, 32: 417–33.

Brislin, R. (2006) *Understanding Culture's Influence on Behavior*, 2nd edn. Orlando, FL: Harcourt College Publishers.

Christodoulidi, F. (2010) The therapist's experience in a 'foreign country': a qualitative inquiry into the effect of mobility for counsellors and psychotherapists, unpublished PhD thesis, University of Manchester.

Christodoulidi, F. and Lago, C. (2010) Tortoise and turtles: Pittu Laugani, cultural transitions and the therapeutic relationship, in R. Moodley, A. Rai and W. Alladin (eds) *Building Bridges Between East–West Psychology and Counselling: Exploring the Work of Pittu Laugani in Clinical Practice*. New Delhi: Sage.

Cowley, J. (2005) Developing student counselling in Sri Lanka, *AUCC Journal*, autumn.

Fleet, E. (2009) Counselling and culture: a comparison of attitudes to depression among African and western post-graduate students, unpublished paper.

Gullahorn J.T. and Gullahorn J.E. (1963) An extension of the U-curve hypothesis, *Journal of Social Issues* 19: 33–47.

Hall, E.T. (1959) *The Secret Language*. New York: Doubleday.

Lago, C. (2004) Welcoming the visitor long after the welcome is over, *AUCC Journal* Winter: 41–4.

Lago, C. (2006) Pittu Laugani in conversation with William West: personal reflections, (some) considered thoughts and emotional impacts, *British Journal of Guidance and Counselling*, 34(3): 392.

Lago, C. and Thompson, J. (1996) *Race, Culture and Counselling*. Buckingham: Open University Press.

Madison, G. (2005) Existential migration, PhD thesis, Regents College, London.

Mak, A.S., Westwood, M.J., Barker, M.C. and Ishiyama, F.I. (1998) Developing sociocultural competencies for success among international students: the ExcelL programme, *Journal of International Education*, 9(1): 33–8.

Martin, J. and Harrell, T. (2004) Intercultural reentry of students and professionals, in D. Landis, J.M. Bennett and M.J. Bennett (eds) *Handbook of Intercultural Training*, 3rd edn. Thusand Oaks, CA: Sage.

Maudeni, T. (1999) Females and adjustment to study abroad, *Gender and Education*, 2(1): 27–42.

Okorocha, E. (1994) Barriers to effective counselling of overseas students: implications for cross-cultural counselling, Society for Research in Higher Education conference paper.

Pakaslahti, A. (2009) Health seeking behavior for psychiatric disorders in North India, in M. Incayawar, R. Winrob and L. Bouchard (eds) *Psychiatrists and Traditional Healers*. London: Wiley.

Pelletier, C. (2003) Project report, in D. Leonard, C. Pelletier and L. Morley, *The Experiences of International Students in UK Higher Education: A Review of Unpublished Research*, www.ukcisa.org.uk/files/docs/ioereport.doc, accessed 19 November 2009.

Rana, R. (2000) *Counselling Students: A Psychodynamic Perspective*. Basingstoke: Palgrave Macmillan.

Rana, R., Smith, E. and Walkling, J. (1999) *Degrees of Disturbance: The New Agenda*, A report of the Heads of University Counselling Services. Rugby: BACP.

Royal College of Psychiatrists (2003) *The Mental Health of Students in Higher Education*. London: RCP.

Sawir, E. *et al.* (2007) Loneliness and international students: an Australian study, *Journal of Intercultural Education*, 12(2): 148–80.

Stanley, N. and Manthorpe, J. (2002) *Students' Mental Health Needs: Problems and Responses*. London: Jessical Kingsley.

Stanley, N. *et al.* (2007) *Response and Prevention in Student Suicide: The RAPSS Study*. Preston: University of Central Lancashire.

Thomas, L. (2009) Finding oneself in the crowd, *AUCC Journal*, September: 12–14.

Ting-Toomey, S. (2004) Translating conflict face-negotiation theory into practice, in D. Landis, J.M. Bennett and M.J. Bennett (eds) *Handbook of Intercultural Training*, 3rd edn. Thousand Oaks, CA: Sage.

UKCISA (2007) *Bridging Our Worlds*. London: UKCISA.

Ward, C. (2004) Psychological theories of cultural contact and their implications for intercultural training and interventions, in D. Landis, J.M. Bennett and M.J. Bennett (eds) *Handbook of Intercultural Training*, 3rd edn. Thousand Oaks, CA: Sage.

Ward, C., Bochner, S. and Furnham, A. (2001) *The Psychology of Culture Shock*. London: Routledge.

Weiss, R. (1973) *Loneliness: The Experience of Emotional and Social Isolation*. Cambridge, MA: MIT Press.

Zwingmann, C.A.A. and Gunn, A.D.G. (1983) *Uprooting and Health: Psycho-social Problems of Students from Abroad*. Geneva: WHO.

17 On being an asylum-seeker

Sheila Mudadi-Billings and Patricia Eschoe

Introduction

The experiences of asylum-seekers prior to, on arrival, or during their stay in the host country (in this instance the UK), are often overlooked, trivialized, are of diminutive interest, or receive little consideration by the host populace. Nevertheless, services exist throughout the UK that have been specifically set up for meeting the needs of asylum-seekers. Statutory services usually consist of a mix of professional staff, including general practitioners (GPs), nurses, therapists (including complementary therapies), physiotherapists and administration staff. The voluntary sector also plays a vital role in providing much needed support, filling gaps that the statutory sector may overlook or deem not a priority. In geographical areas where these provisions are neither considered a priority nor financially viable, or where resources are limited, integration with standard services (i.e. GP surgeries) is expected as a likely course for asylum-seeking individuals. In our experience, attempts are occasionally made to employ an ethnic mix of professional workers within specialized asylum-seeker services. However, such attempts are often short-lived for numerous reasons, some of which include loss of funding, cross-cultural discord/misunderstandings and covert discrimination. However, it can be said that most of these services are set up by well-meaning individuals of western origin operating through western lenses which overlook the knowledge, skills and awareness of both black minority ethnic (BME) staff members and the needs of services users for which the organization was formed. Rifkind (2007: 14) asserts that

> Western thinking suggests superiority of its civilisation, which allows us to impose our agenda on others ... Western diplomacy involves a set of assumptions about how people will react and what they want – but this shows little understanding of war torn countries that have been involved in endless conflict ... embedded in Western diplomacy are fine ideals about what we consider to be reasonable behaviour. Our language is around conditionality.

Inclusion is currently high on the agenda of recent government protocols. Some services have been equipped with the monetary means of increasing access to psychological therapies ('Increased Access to Psychological Therapies': IAPT) regardless of all the strands of diversity. With reference to asylum-seekers, the task of inclusion may not be as simple as that for the indigenous population. Therefore, there are legal implications upon agencies offering access to psychological therapies for asylum-seekers. For this particular group there are several imperative issues to consider, which will be highlighted and expanded in this chapter by giving the reader an insight into the world of an asylum-seeker so that practices are better informed.

Who are asylum-seekers?

> *Remembering that most of our clients will be operating from the 'We-self' culture and not the 'I-self', a person from a collective culture does not leave home psychologically; rather, the collective identity remains a big part of their identity, so they may continue to have powerful family scripts and projections replaying throughout their lifespan.*
>
> *(Kapinda 2008)*

Asylum-seekers usually flee their country of origin in the pursuit of safety from political regimes that deny and abuse their human rights. Asylum-seekers flee not only for political or financial reasons but also because of issues such as domestic and sexual violence. These reasons are not readily recognized or accepted by government bodies placed in decision-making positions governing the issue of asylum status. This may make it difficult for this group to secure refugee status (an individual who has been granted a 'type' of 'leave to remain'). Not all individuals fleeing their country of origin arrive as asylum-seekers − some may have been granted refugee status prior to arrival.

Some asylum-seekers travel to nearby countries while others go further afield, taking arduous journeys of high risk. Some, sadly, do not survive the flight to exile (Samura 2004). Those who travel further afield may experience additional traumas adding to pre-existing levels of distress because they may have to enter a number of countries before reaching their intended place of refuge (e.g. an asylum-seeker fleeing Rwanda may have gone through Burundi, the Democratic Republic of Congo and Zambia before finally arriving in the UK). On each section of the journey they may experience varying degrees of regional exploitation, including financial, practical, physical and mental. The journey can span a numbers of weeks to years.

Asylum-seekers may have expectations of the host country stemming from various sources, including information from the media, information sent back to the indigenous country by other people who have sought asylum and are 'presumed' settled in the host country, and from colonial history (especially in those countries that have experienced colonization/colonialism). The term 'presumed' is used here because the information reported back may be distorted for various reasons pertaining to the reporting individual.

Pre-asylum experiences

Prior to fleeing their countries of origin, asylum-seekers may have had a meaningful existence. This existence would/may include some of the following aspects or more.

- An ancestral heritage.
- Spiritual/faith beliefs.
- Most significant elder.
- Own status within family and community.
- Social and political stance/networks.

This list is by no means exhaustive, nor is it in a hierarchical order.

Ancestral heritage

Some asylum-seekers may hold symbolic reverence for their ancestral heritage. This could appear in many forms and may include ritualistic practices such as calling on their ancestors for guidance – connecting through channels such as water, earth and fire or objects of significance. Their existence may be experienced as incomplete without their ancestral heritage being acknowledged (see Chapter 18).

Spiritual/faith beliefs

Spirituality/faith seems to be a key factor regardless of country of origin. This could be considered as the core or essence of an individual's existence. Some asylum-seekers may lean towards specific religious practices which may differ from those of the host country. This may not even be around religion but in connection with certain beliefs that are culturally based.

Most significant elder

Significant elders hold positions of power within a collective family and community. Elders are seen as possessing wisdom and knowledge and are called upon by others for guidance and decision-making. This could mean that family and community members do not have to make major decisions.

Status within family and community

Status is experienced by everyone within a family and/or community. This is stratified differently in different cultural settings. For example, birthright: the first born may automatically be placed at the top of the 'pecking order'. This positioning may be practised as a non-verbalized given or otherwise made explicit through language. Other factors such as gender, education and so forth are also of significant importance in hierarchical positioning in some cultures.

Social/political stance and networks

Very often, asylum-seeking individuals come from large social networks which involve living in the same household with many others (extended family), communal cooking and eating, sleeping and socializing as a central part of their daily existence. Individuals may hold the same or contrasting/opposing political views that may or may not be apparent or shared.

Asylum experiences

In recent years negative attention has been focused on asylum-seekers in the UK (Eschoe 2006). Their first taste of seeking asylum often comes through being detained in a holding centre in the UK. Such centres have been described by some asylum-seekers as 'being held in a concentration camp' in which they felt criminalized. It has been reported by some detainees that atrocities such as women being approached by male workers demanding sex in exchange for preferential treatment have occurred. The poor standards of treatment and discrimination within these centres have been evidenced by undercover documentaries (e.g. BBC1 2005). Their initial experience may parallel parts of their pre-asylum experience and create suspicions both of the host country and those who work within its systems.

One of the authors of this chapter witnessed the segregation enforced on some asylum-seekers once they were living in the new society. While she was waiting in a post office, a long queue of people was seen waiting to be served in a separately organized area outside the usual queuing section. Some of those individuals were recognized as clients, and it was left in little doubt to other customers that these were people waiting to sign for their monetary allowance. Such experiences create an environment for asylum-seekers where they feel alienated, devalued and targeted, and reinforce discrimination. Some have described this experience as 'feeling like beggars', which contributes further to feelings of embarrassment and shame.

Age is another contributory factor to the experience of asylum-seekers that can leave people who are deemed to be adults on arrival feeling less supported and unwanted. Unaccompanied minors are seen to be better supported within the asylum system and can be helped to have a sense of security, safety and settlement. However, when such individuals reach the age that they are classified as adults they are expected to manage their lives and claim asylum independently. This can lead to re-experiencing a sense of abandonment, rejection and create a psychological setback or relapse for the young person. Regardless of age, individuals who flee with family members and manage to arrive together in the host country may feel more secure, less isolated and to a degree socially supported (safety in numbers). However, when family members are separated during flight, increased distress is apparent. These individuals have an overwhelming sense of loss because they are unsure if their family reached a point of safety in the host country after separation.

Once in the host country, an asylum-seeker experiences further traumas in variable degrees, as well as hostility, while going through the asylum system of application for 'leave to remain'. For some, this process can unfortunately take up to 10 years or more, resulting in a sense of overwhelming helplessness and hopelessness for the individual. As we all know, hope can fade with time, and everyday life may become bleak.

In 2005, a new asylum model was introduced by the British government (Home Office 2005), stipulating that all asylum-seeking processes would, supposedly, be dealt with within 10 to 12 weeks from the beginning of an application to completion. Unfortunately this administrative change has proved problematic for some. For instance, an individual arriving in this country without the ability to speak English, who then lodges a claim, and is subsequently granted 'leave to remain' within a short space of time will not have had the opportunity to become either linguistically fluent or acculturated to the new host culture. During the short period that their case is being processed they are given material/financial support which includes housing etc. As soon as a decision is made, which could be either positive or negative, their support is withdrawn within two to three weeks and they are then expected to fend for themselves. Those that get a negative response find themselves destitute (this acute predicament is experienced by a large percentage of the asylum-seeker community). The so called 'lucky' ones may find themselves homeless (because they are then expected to apply for housing with their local council or private renting), or with a home that is totally bare and consequently uninhabitable because the National Asylum Support Service (NASS) repossesses all essential items. An individual known to one of the authors reported having this same experience which resulted in her sleeping on the floor, without amenities to cater for her needs (i.e. launder clothes or cook food). She was expected to manage like an indigenous member of the community without the knowledge base, contacts and 'know-how', let alone any source of income.

Legacy cases

In addition, there are documents specifying that old asylum claims, so-called 'legacy cases' would be put on the 'back burner' and be dealt with within a certain time frame. (Interested readers may wish to access further information from the Home Office website as such information changes regularly: www.homeoffice.gov.uk.) These individuals who are classified as 'legacy' cases could have been pursuing their failed asylum claim for between 5 and 10 years. It is known that most individuals in this group are destitute, having to rely on friends and voluntary organizations that provide support in terms of free accommodation and money for survival. Others in this category are supported by the Home Office under a scheme called Section 4. However, certain criteria have to be met to be eligible for this very limited support and it comes with conditions attached (further information can be accessed on the Home Office website). Under this nightmare of a life, Section 4 financial support is given by means of a token book/card of vouchers received weekly. These vouchers can only be used in a limited number of supermarkets and include an even more limited number of shops that provide specific cultural foods as well as personal grooming products (e.g. hair oils). Another condition of Section 4 is that the asylum-seeker can be removed from the country whenever the Home Office decides. Hence there is a requirement to report and sign in at the nearest police station (or designated Home Office building). Unfortunate individuals have to report weekly and the fortunate ones monthly, depending on their circumstances. Asylum-seekers describe this as having a negatively devastating impact on their overall well-being, causing symptoms such as increased anxiety and fear because of the possibility of being detained when reporting to the police to sign in. As Imberti (2008: 8) has noted: 'So many [asylum seekers, refugees and immigrants], particularly those whose immigration status is ambiguous or undocumented, suffer a chronic state of hyper vigilance, alertness to danger and possible catastrophe that can be powerfully debilitating.'

Those that are detained include families with young children as well as single adults. Detention means that deportation to the country of origin is imminent and may be unavoidable. Some individuals have stayed in detention for some time, ranging between days and three months or more; again this includes children of all ages. Unfortunately, deportation is not always successful. There are circumstances where some individuals have gone as far as reaching their destination of origin only to be rejected by their country and then returned to the host country to resume their impoverished life of destitution or under Section 4.

The criteria continue to change for failed applicants on Section 4. They include limited access to free education, no permission to seek employment, limited access to medical care and cataclysmic environmental conditions. Individuals in this category may fall into different groups, of which the following two have been identified:

- A group that has been able to 'park' their asylum difficulties and restrictions and manage to secure some normality which may include working illegally and getting on with everyday life, such as marrying and having a family etc. This group seem to be able to maintain reasonable mental and physical health and to integrate into the indigenous community, or join a community that comprises members from their country of origin.
- A group that seem to suffer enormously from gradually deteriorating psychological and physical health as they are not able to make the adjustments of the former group. Individuals in this group have anecdotally described this existence without any kind of freedom as 'torturous'. These individuals then require medical and psychotherapeutic interventions which have major financial implications to different services, including the NHS. Their self-confidence, self-esteem and identity are chronically eroded, leaving them feeling dehumanized. One individual in this group said: 'Nobody cares for me, my life is like a cancer with roots destroying me every minute; surrounded by darkness, hopelessness and helplessness.' Practitioners involved with these individuals on a regular basis frequently hear such feelings expressed, as this set of life circumstances depicts the lives of most destitute asylum-seekers.

Implications of being an asylum-seeker

There are inevitable 'life' ramifications of being an asylum-seeker These may manifest in the following (and of course many other) areas.

Medical

New asylum-seekers are entitled to receive the same medical attention as those belonging to the indigenous population. However, this may be complicated by prejudices held by individual workers who may believe that asylum-seekers should not be allowed this right and as a result can deliver a poorer service. In such cases genuine physical presentations that might be a medical problem can remain undetected or inaccurately assumed to be psychological. Jude Boyles (2006) asserts: 'What struck me was how this group of people were most in need of health and welfare resources and did not have access to either, including to the statutory mental health counselling service ...'

Educational

Asylum-seekers often report that after being housed they are initially led to believe that they have full and free rights to access all educational institutions (i.e. play groups, nurseries, primary and higher education, including university). This belief may be gleaned from various sources (e.g. family and friends that are already settled in the host country) or through misunderstandings of the limitations of what is actually being offered and available. In reality, education is limited and is only available free of charge to a certain level. Without some kind of refugee status, individuals can gain qualifications to A level standards only to find that progression to university is barred without independent financial means. There are cases where individuals without refugee status may be financially supported through higher education by members of their family who remain in their country of origin. It is important to note here that this 'luxury' only occurs in the minority of cases. However, in most cases assumptions or misinformation lead to expectations which are then shattered.

Sociocultural

It has already been noted in the section on the pre-asylum experience that most asylum-seekers have a lifestyle that has some form of structure that may have been in existence for centuries. Not only is this lifestyle structured but it is also readily recognized, accepted and gives stability, security and a sense of belonging and cohesion to individuals within that community. Within this existence it is understood that everybody holds core beliefs that are determined by a range of factors such as religion, race, culture, parenting and community. Kareem and Littlewood (2000) identify these as 'personal values'. The loss of this 'original fabric' of values can be considered as central to the majority of difficulties experienced by asylum-seekers as they have frequently experienced gross disruption, displacement and torture. The lived experience in their new host, almost alien, country is now devoid of previous kinship ties and a communitarian existence that had originally been built around respect of self, neighbour, elder and political leaders. This earlier existence can be, and has been, illustrated beautifully in the African way of life known as *Ubuntu*. *Ubuntu* is a well-known concept that is practised in most parts of southern Africa. Bishop Tutu (1999) explains *Ubuntu* as: 'The essence of being human. *Ubuntu* speaks particularly about the fact that you can't exist as a human being in isolation. It speaks about our interconnectedness. You can't be human all by yourself, and when you have this quality – *Ubuntu* – you are known for your generosity.'

The dissonance experienced in the new host culture often leads to feelings of isolation, impotence, loss of sense of community and, worse still, an inability to participate meaningfully with others. Intrusion into value structures and beliefs causes long-term psychological and physical effects and impacts on the asylum-seeker's sense of identity. For example, many asylum-seekers hold rigid religious beliefs about sex outside marriage and the non-existence of rape within marriage. If a woman has experienced rape, this intrusion could pose difficulties because of the victim's fear of judgement if she reveals this – both from the indigenous population that hold the same faith, but also from others who are from the same country of origin. This is one potentially hidden trauma (and there may be many others) that is carried by the asylum-seeker and remains, regardless of where they are placed.

Some assessment considerations

The complexities involved when attempting to form a therapeutic working alliance with asylum-seekers must not be underestimated. Nijad (2003) suggests that the therapist's first job is to assess the client and asserts that: 'The complex aspects of communication involving culture, symbolic gestures, attitudes and world view assist the therapist in examining the service user and in recognising and understanding the key signs.' Assessment can often span several sessions. It is important to note that in the first or second assessment, one is not guaranteed to capture all that may be important to the client, or that may be necessary to aid collaborative understanding of presenting issues to assist the therapist towards appropriate and effective therapeutic interventions. To forward this aim, thoroughness of assessment, appropriate pacing of dialogue exchange between the interpreter (if present), therapist and client, allowing the client to work at their own pace, and being empathic and non-judgemental are some of the essentials.

Figure 17.1 is an attempt at guiding readers towards capturing several essential components of the psychotherapy/counselling assessment with asylum-seeker clients. The model essentially outlines the process of assessment which can cover a number of highlighted areas. It is important to note that the beliefs of

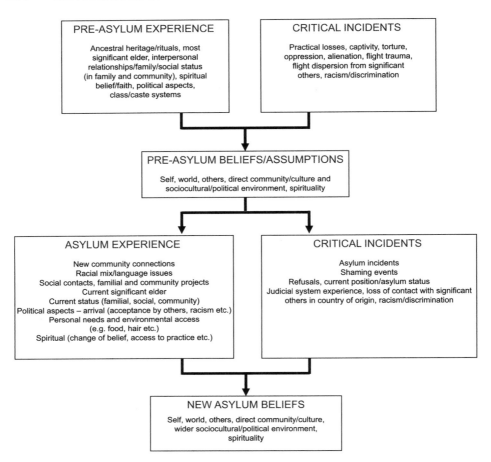

Figure 17.1 Assessment model for psychotherapy assessment of asylum-seekers

asylum-seekers are not always positive or negative but are often mixed, due to the complex nature of their position.

Therapeutic considerations

The asylum-seeker's experiences, pre-flight, have great significance for the processes of psychological therapy. There are several issues to be considered when working with such individuals, beginning with the point of referral. How the referrer explains therapy to the individual is of paramount importance, especially if this is the first time that this person has been introduced to the concept of talking therapy in the 'western context'. Additionally, therapy/counselling is not for everybody, and referrers need to keep this in mind. Morrison (1995) proposes that all clients have their own agendas when attending therapy which may conflict with the goals of the psychotherapy assessment. Three areas are to be considered here: (1) if the referrer promotes therapy as a solution to all their problems then this may give false hope and may also 'set up' the therapeutic process to fail; (2) if therapy is 'undersold' as merely 'seeing someone to talk to', then the individual may not consider this worthwhile because they may believe that talking is not beneficial, especially if practical problems are deemed paramount; (3) on the other hand, if therapy is promoted in a balanced and objective manner, this enables the individual to understand that there are limitations to what can be achieved and also that even where practical needs cannot be met, anxieties, distress and worry can be relieved through talking and understanding. An attempt made by the referrer to introduce and explain therapy thoroughly assists the individual who is being referred to make an appropriate and informed decision about the uptake of therapy. Therapists need to be mindful that due to their pre-asylum-seeking existence some individuals may not have the capacity to decide for themselves.

Further aspects to consider are restrictions on the choice of therapist based on professional experience, geographical variations and agency provision. Asylum-seekers and their referrers may experience a limited choice of practitioners who are sufficiently experienced in working with this client group. For example, finding a practitioner experienced in working with interpreters (which is a necessity if the client's command of English is limited), having an understanding of the impact of pre-asylum losses and an understanding of the adjustment difficulties within an alien environment, can be very difficult.

This lack of choice is further extended and complicated by linguistic barriers. For example, on arrival in the UK such individuals may speak no English at all; others may speak some English; while others will be fluent. When a person's distress is heightened, even when there is fluency in the host language, there is often a tendency to favour the mother tongue or mix the host language with that of their mother tongue. Clients themselves have said that it is much easier to express their emotions and feelings in their mother tongue rather than a second or third language. Because of this, it is important that the possibility of using an interpreter is introduced as an option. Additionally, if the offer of an interpreter is declined by the individual accessing therapy and their communication in the host language is restricted, then the level of skill and concentration required from the therapist is magnified.

It is becoming increasingly apparent that asylum-seekers who have been in the UK for a number of years are beginning to voice their refusal to work with certain interpreters. This is may be for a number of reasons. First, interpreters and asylum-seeker clients may live in the same area in the new host country and belong to the same community group, church congregation or in other ways have potential association or linkage to each other. As a result, trust in the interpreter not to divulge personal circumstances outside the counselling process has to be high. If the requested interpreter is not available, many clients prefer to struggle through their sessions without interpreter support.

Second, over years of contact with different interpreters, some clients develop a strong bond of trust with one particular interpreter. After some time in the host country they will have acquired a fairly good command of English and are able to 'work out' who is new in the job and lacks sufficient experience, who they believe to be 'untrustworthy' and what the interpreter's motivation may be (e.g. is the interpreter there for financial reasons or do they have the best interest of the client at heart?). As Nijad (2003: 79) states: 'The right interpreter on the other hand can facilitate communication, point out cultural factors, clarify important and ambiguous points and overall make it possible for two people from different worlds to communicate the true meaning of the words'.

These considerations are not exhaustive, but hopefully demonstrate the level of experience that is required, both of the interpreter and therapist, when working therapeutically with asylum-seekers.

Modality/orientation

Some practitioners may believe that, within the context of working with asylum-seeker clients, their particular orientation may hold precedence over another. This could imply that a single psychotherapy approach will suffice. However, being a 'theoretical purist' practitioner may not be sufficient to meet the needs of the asylum-seeker client, as 'one hat certainly does not fit all'. It has already been mentioned that asylum-seekers often come from a 'we' culture. Consequently, implementing orientations that concentrate purely on the individual could be detrimental rather than supportive or helpful to these individuals. It may be useful therefore to explore other ways of working that are more suited to the individual asylum-seeker client, than to impose what 'feels right' or what we think is right for that individual. Total collaboration with the client is desirable, asking the question, 'What do you need from us in order to help you?' Facilitating clients towards empowerment is the goal. It is also about adapting our approaches in order to relate and form meaningful relationships with our asylum-seeker clients.

The basis of an alternative approach has already been mentioned above: the *Ubuntu* concept. *Ubuntu* is considered to have various aspects to it, including as a religious concept, a philosophy, a psychological orientation and even a political concept. What is helpful to remember is that it is considered 'a way of life' in many parts of Africa. It is said that South Africa is founded on the principles of *Ubuntu*. Bishop Tutu (1999) further defines *Ubuntu* as follows:

> A person with *Ubuntu* is open and available to others, affirming of others, does not feel threatened that others are able and good, for he or she has a proper self-assurance that comes from knowing that he or she belongs in a greater whole and is diminished when others are humiliated or diminished, when others are tortured or oppressed.

Conclusion

Debate will continue regarding the credibility and genuineness of asylum-seekers, as well as the appropriateness of western psychotherapeutic approaches to their presenting problems. It is important that therapists examine their own beliefs and biases towards this group and that this group is included in therapeutic decisions. (This will require being willing to refer on if your psychotherapy/counselling approach is not experienced as helpful by the client.) Therapists must resist the temptation to assume that language difficulties and cultural difference amount to simplicity and reduced intellect, as well as possible doubts that human beings could survive the reported atrocities. As shown here, many have survived intense difficulties and demonstrated much courage.

In the current climate where social inclusion is seemingly on the political agenda, the *Ubuntu* concept (although only one idea among many), encapsulates the humanness fundamental for all therapists to adopt in their endeavour to include asylum-seeker clients (regardless of therapeutic orientation). As is evident throughout this chapter these individuals have varying experiences pre-, mid- and post-asylum-seeking. It is hypothesized that as global economic struggles increase and persist, asylum-seeker groups could experience increased difficulties through discrimination by their indigenous populations. Historically, we live in a blame culture where difficulties are projected towards visibly/racially different individuals. Therapists are not expected to be perfect. Nevertheless, there is a strong argument for increased self-awareness, self-challenge, acquisition of knowledge and adaptability when working with asylum-seekers.

References

BBC 1 (2005) *Detention Undercover, the Real Story*, see www.wsws.org.

Boyles, J. (2006) Not just naming the injustice: counselling asylum seekers and refugees, in G. Proctor, M. Cooper, P. Sanders and B. Malcolm (eds) *Politicizing the Person-Centred Approach: An Agenda for Social Change*. Ross-on-Wye: PCCS Books.

Eschoe, P. (2006) An in-depth study of existing literature which examines the triad relationship when working alongside an interpreter with asylum seekers and refugee survivors of torture in the cognitive behavioural psychotherapy assessment, MSc dissertation, University of Derby.

Home Office (2005) *Controlling Our Borders: Making Migration Work for Britain. Five Year Strategy for Asylum and Immigration*, www.archive2.official-documents. co.uk/document/cm64/6472/6472.pdf.

Imberti, P. (2008) The immigrant's odyssey, *Therapy Today*, 19(6).

Kapinda, M. (2008) Adapting to difference: the hairdryer theory, *Therapy Today*, 19(6).

Kareem, J. and Littlewood, R. (2000) *Intercultural Therapy*, 2nd edn. Oxford: Blackwell Science.

Morrison, J. (1995) The first Interview, revised for DSM-IV, in P. Eschoe (2006) An in-depth study of existing literature which examines the triad relationship when working alongside an interpreter with asylum seekers and refugee survivors of torture in the cognitive behavioural psychotherapy assessment, MSc dissertation, University of Derby.

Nijad, F. (2003) A day in the life of an interpreter, in R. Tribe and H. Ravel (eds) *Working with Interpreters in Mental Health*. London: Brunner-Routledge.

Rifkind, G. (2007) Western diplomacy and psychology, *Therapy Today*, 18(9).

Samura, S. (2004) *Living with Refugees (Surviving Sudan)*, Channel 4 *Dispatches*, 9 December.

Tutu, D. (1999) *No future without forgiveness*. New York: Doubleday.

18 The effects of an African heritage

Divine Charura

Introduction

This chapter explores the general historic, cultural, religious and other influences of an African heritage and considers how these influences might impact a therapeutic relationship conducted in another country where the cultural style is different. I present some of the components of African heritage, including some cultural values, beliefs and common practices in the life cycle of those people and discuss some methods of working with those from an African heritage. To conclude, I propose 10 points to consider when working with such clients. I feel honoured to write this chapter because I am passionate about transcultural counselling/psychotherapy and anti-discriminatory practice.

What does African heritage mean?

In my work as a psychotherapist and having travelled to different parts of Africa and the world, I am aware of the richness of the diversity and culture of people who have an African heritage. I acknowledge that it is impossible for me to give complex, detailed descriptions of the peoples of Africa, the cultures or the effects of their African heritage on their lives. Nevertheless, I encourage you to explore the influences and impact of an African heritage in a therapeutic relationship further for yourself.

Although the majority of native African people are black, there are many other ethnic groups born in Africa who also have an African heritage. These include Indian Africans, white Africans, Chinese Africans, African Arabs, Portuguese Africans and many other mixed heritage groups. In this chapter, therefore, I use 'African heritage' to refer to all these peoples.

African demographics

Africa is a continent consisting of 53 countries of which 34 are considered the least developed in the world. Currently it has an estimated population of 922 million (as of 2009). The most populous African country is Nigeria with over 148 million people, followed by Egypt (79 million) and Ethiopia (78 million) (WHO 2009).

Diversity of languages

There are many languages, dialects and variations of these spoken by people of African heritage. Some of these languages are also spoken around the world. Examples include French (Congo, Cameroon, etc.) Portuguese (Mozambique, Angola, etc.) and Arabic (Algeria, Morocco, etc.). Some of these languages carry the history of past colonialism, which is often a reminder of previous oppression, prejudice and dilution of original heritage through the colonization process. It is through these languages that heritage, traditional philosophies, religions, cultural beliefs and knowledge are transmitted among the people. Language therefore is a critically important element in the construction and affirmation of identity and heritage.

Diversity of religions and spirituality

There are also hundreds of traditional African religions. Within the African milieu, religion and spiritual beliefs are a fundamental part of life and existence. This chapter cannot possibly cover all the religious practices and beliefs of Africa but will explore some common links and themes. Fundamentally, from an African perspective, religions constitute practices, teachings, rituals and beliefs that are linked to cultural practices and ways of life (Mbiti 1999). Many African religious and spiritual practices have been orally transmitted from generation to generation, while others have been scripturally transmitted (Karenga 2002; Walker 2007).

In order to understand the concept of African religions and beliefs it is important to say that, pre-colonization, the peoples of Africa had many religions, termed 'primal-indigenous religions' (Thomas 2004; Cox 2007). Due to the close link between beliefs and values, there are individuals of African heritage who hold a combination of traditional religious and non-traditional religious beliefs. Some, however, are not religious or hold to only 'non-African primal indigenous religions' such as Christianity and Islam (Mbiti 1999).

Primal indigenous religions

These religions can be grouped into four categories linking them to specific linguistic phylum: Afro-Asiatic, Nilo-Saharan, Niger-Congo and Khoi-San (Cox 2007). Walker (2006) highlights the supposed evolution of religious ideas as being: animism (believing in many spirits); polytheism (believing in many gods); henotheism (believing that there is one supreme god out of many); and monotheism (believing in one god). Using monotheism as an example, god or the supreme being is given different names in different languages and tribes, including *Mwari* (Zimbabwe), *Unkulunkulu* (South Africa), *Mulungu* (Malawi), *Yahweh* (Congo), *Olurum Chenekeh* (Nigeria) and, in Islam, Allah. Furthermore, some cultures and clans deify and worship nature, such as the sun, the moon, rivers etc. Deity gender also differs among cultures in Africa (Lugira 2004). In some parts of West Africa, for example, some believe that God is androgynous (having both male and female attributes) and is called *Nana-Buluku*.

An important aspect of such beliefs is the diverse religious offices that individuals of African heritage can hold. These include priests and traditional healers who practise non-western medicine and are believed to have abilities to deal with spiritual, physical and mental illnesses or crises. These offices also include rainmakers, who have meteorological powers to manipulate the environment, magicians, witches, shamans and sorcerers (Lugira 2004; Cox 2007). The role of individuals holding these offices is that of leadership in specific practices and rituals. Common names for traditional healers are *Sangoma* (South Africa), *N'anga* (Zimbabwe) and *Onisegun Ibile* (Nigeria). Although there is a diversity of these beliefs and religions, the generalized effects of such systems are that an individual's understanding of life experiences is partly and sometimes profoundly informed by their religious roots.

Places of worship, holy places and religious activities

Many individuals of African heritage will have places of worship which they attend on specific times, days or months for prayers, sacrificial ceremonies, specific practices and rituals (Walker 2007). These places of worship include churches, mosques and synagogues. Traditionally, however, there are other places of worship, including human-made alters, shrines, tombs and sacred spaces located within nature, such as trees, rocks, hills, rivers, lakes, caves and mountains (Mbiti 1991).

Mythology and association with African heritage

Mythology plays a big part in tribal and community living in most parts of Africa. Often, African mythologies are specific, detailed stories that offer explanations and existential philosophies about creation, human life, death and existence after life. Mythologies frequently elaborate stories through symbols and metaphors (Walker 2006). Although there are differences in African mythologies, their main objectives are similar: to communicate and offer explanations about African existence and at times discourage immorality (Scheub 2000; Belcher 2005).

Altered states and possession

Altered states and possessed ways of being are another aspect of spirituality that individuals with an African heritage understand and can often refer to in times of crisis. This capacity is believed to exist as either a positive or a negative force. Positive beliefs about possession are that any individual or spiritual medium can achieve an altered state or be possessed to give a specific message to the people or perform traditional healing rites (Karenga 2002). Altered states are induced by drumming, dancing, chanting specific mantras, saying specific prayers, eating/drinking or smoking specific psychoactive substances. Following this initial stage, the possessed goes into a trance-like state and then delivers the message from the 'spirit'/ancestors or performs healing rites. Positively possessed people are often referred to as being 'anointed' by a higher deity or spirit.

Negative beliefs about possession are often associated with illness, misfortune and mysterious experiences in life. It is common practice that for restoration of 'normality', families can take a 'troubled' individual to a healer or priest to have the 'evil spirit' cast out, particularly in cases of serious mental or physical illness or distress (Manji 2003). Closely linked to this are beliefs about interactions between the natural and the supernatural, often affirming beliefs in and experiences of voodoo, magic, witchcraft and sorcery. There are widespread beliefs and evidence among many African societies that an individual can be bewitched or have an evil spell – *voodoo* or *juju* – cast on them. This frequently results in serious physical and mental illness or misfortune. In these practices, animals, particularly nocturnal animals, can be used to transmit a spell. These include bats, owls, snakes, hyenas or other mythical beings (Kapferer 2002; Manji 2003). It is also possible in specific witchcraft and sorcery practices to use natural elements and to control them to harm another – e.g. the wind, lightning and hailstorms. In witchcraft it is believed that ghosts and humans, particularly the individuals doing the bewitching, can also be seen, particularly at night, visiting the individual being bewitched.

Perceptions and views of self

The concept of self is one that has been widely argued in postmodern psychology. Among those of African heritage, this perception of self is often related to their connection with their tribe or heritage and gives them their sense of identity. In my experience, individuals will often have a collective sense of 'we' in relation to their own clan or extended family. Ramose (1999) suggests that individuals from collective communities often perceive themselves only in relation to other members of their group or tribe. He stated that there is a perception of social glue which he noted from a common traditional African aphorism which, in Zulu, is *unmuntu ngumuntu ngabantu*, often translated as 'a person is a person through other persons'. This concept of identity and relatedness through others is known as *Ubuntu*. Louw (2006) postulates that *Ubuntu* is a central self and societal concept among those of African heritage. The concept of *Ubuntu* appears to be embedded not only in the self and one's identity but in the ways in which an individual lives his or her life. *Ubuntu* is recognized in Zimbabwe, where it is termed *unhu*. In Rwanda and Burundi it translates as 'humanity and human generosity' and in Uganda and Tanzania it is termed *Obuntu*, which refers to the consideration of others within the community through generosity and participation. Louw (2006) remarks that *Ubuntu* therefore means 'humanity', 'humaneness' and 'humanness'.

Ramose (1999) points out that according to traditional African heritage, within the *Ubuntu* concept, 'becoming a person through others' involves living through various community prescribed stages and having involvement in certain ceremonies and rituals. Prior to this, a person is regarded as an 'it' and is therefore not yet a person, or has no identity in themselves. Ramose further argues that as a result of this concept, not all humans are persons, as personhood is *acquired*. I suggest that among those of African heritage there is a sense that personhood is *bestowed* upon an individual by others. Individuals, however, can also be 'de-personified' to become 'it' if they do not live up to the expectations of the required cultural group norms.

Life cycles in African heritage

Ramose (1999) postulates that the concept of *Ubuntu* is also central to the life cycle which is traditionally embedded within clan/tribal beliefs and values. It consists of 'life pre-birth', birth, growing up, adult life, marriage, old age, death and afterlife. Within the life cycle, many practices are informed by African heritage, including use of traditional medicine and consultation with traditional spiritual leaders. Ritual practices are closely linked to the life cycle. One example is circumcision; another is genital modification, such as elongating genitalia in both women and men. These procedures are not meaningless exercises: through circumcision and other rituals, the individual's blood is spilled onto the soil, a symbol of sacrifice which binds the initiated person to his or her own people (Mbiti 1999; Ramose 1999).

Traditional marriage and family life constitute significant aspects of African heritage. There are traditional guidelines, including mentoring on how to be the best lover, wife or husband. In some tribes polygamous marriages are often acceptable. An important part of marriage is the payment of the 'bridal price' (*dauri/lobola*) to the bride's family. This signifies a strong bond/union of the two families and thanksgiving to the bride's family. Depending on how wealth is valued, there are wide variations of what is paid as the 'bridal price' and in what form. The price may be paid in money, domestic animals (e.g. cows) or special clothes for the bride's family. After marriage, the emphasis is on procreation and raising a family, in which African traditions, values and heritage are passed on. As a result of this emphasis on procreation, many African societies are homophobic and discriminatory towards those who choose not to have children.

Different constructions of gender identity and role expectations are central to African heritage. Gender inequalities between men and women are common in most African societies. Hierarchies and gender-role stereotypes are engrained in both men and women from a young age and maintenance of these stereotypes is a possible explanation for gender inequality.

Mentoring

Mentoring is a major part of life and interaction between the old and the young. In most tribes there are traditional apprenticeship systems where the mature adults, generally viewed as wiser, mentor the young in different aspects of life. This includes activities of daily living, life philosophies, religious beliefs and societal norms. Beliefs, skills and knowledge are passed on from generation to generation through oral teaching (Mbiti 1999). Some (1998) points out that mentoring seeks to invite and develop the *genius within a young person*. He postulates that through this process the young person is enabled to reach their full potential and share their talents with the community, which in turn benefits others. Some further highlights the importance of seeing the genius in young people and assisting them by providing the right conditions when mentoring. He argues that failure to see or assist young people to bring forth this genius kills the genius along with the person carrying it: 'To see the genius in the young person is to give it the fertile ground required for it to burst forth and blossom, for it is not enough to be brought into this world loaded with such a beauty. The community responsible for the death of a genius is like an assassin' (pp. 102–3). In African heritage I believe therefore that mentorship is a central process to the life cycle of both the individual and the community.

Death and afterlife

An important stage in the life cycle centres around death, dying and the afterlife. Issues around death and dying are explored through metaphors and discussion of traditional wills and burial wishes. Most people of African heritage place great importance on the burial of the dead. Often, burials are in particular places which have meaning to them – i.e. their home country, or next to their ancestors, or within family homesteads. Burning or cremation of the dead body is often considered disrespectful.

Burial rituals, mourning the dead and bereavement vary widely. Often mourning the deceased involves families/tribes coming together, staying with the bereaved family and performing specific rituals. These gatherings can last from days to weeks depending on the specific cultural beliefs. Although beliefs and practices surrounding death among those of African heritage are varied, there appears to be a consensus that life after death is part of the life cycle. As a result, there are specific practices which continue weeks and years after burial in remembrance of the deceased. One example is an arranged marriage of the deceased's wife/husband and adoption of the individual's children by close family.

Other practices include yearly rituals to remember the dead, worshipping ancestors and requesting them to look after those still living. Others believe however that the deceased continue living in another realm or that they can/will return in another bodily/spiritual form and influence the living. These beliefs form the basis of possession, ancestral worship, beliefs in ghosts, communication with the dead and beliefs in the afterlife. Such beliefs signify that life cycles are infinite.

However, these practices are changing and some individuals have embraced other beliefs which have different outlooks. This is evident in most non-African traditional religions such as Christianity, Islam, Hinduism, etc. Nevertheless, I suggest that it is very important for therapists to be aware of these encompassing concepts in the life cycle of those with African heritage.

Understanding and learning more about the client in therapy

I believe that it is important to be aware of the collective sense of self when working with individuals or families of African heritage. In some of my work I have often heard clients saying, 'In Africa *we* do things *this* way...' Often the plural notion carries a specific meaning of identity, perception of self and a sense of belonging. Lago and Smith (2003) suggest that an awareness of cultural patterns helps the client to feel more accepted. Reading/learning more about clients' cultures, beliefs and values can also enable the therapist to gain more understanding (Sue and Sue 1990; Patterson 2000). In cases where I have been unsure or unaware of what the client is talking about, I have found that seeking to understand them better enables the client to say more. For example, I might say to a client, 'I don't know much about your culture or beliefs, but I would really like to know more.' I therefore suggest that an openness to explore the effects of the client's heritage on their experiences frees the client in therapy.

The therapeutic relationship with individuals of African heritage

Fernando (1995) highlights that, traditionally, 'therapy' is given by a professional to people identified as requiring such treatment. Therapy however is not universally accepted as the absolute remedy in all cultural and social settings (Littlewood 1992). The concept of talking to a therapist who is a stranger can often be a challenging one. Most individuals of African heritage will be aware of their own specific ways of dealing with problems and most of these will include talking to their *own* elders (i.e. aunts/uncles, spiritual leaders, shamans or group members) who are often culturally seen as wiser.

For others, another way of making sense of life and dealing with problems or crises is through spirituality, religious practices and rituals. For an individual who has lived with a traditional way of being, the concept of therapy can often be challenging. The therapist therefore has to be tentative and aware of the client's perception of therapy (Charura 2009). Ibrahim (1991) suggests that in the relationship with clients the ability to convey empathy in a culturally consistent and meaningful way is the most important factor in engaging with a client. It is therefore important at this point to affirm the importance and maintenance of the therapeutic relationship as highlighted by other authors (e.g. Patterson 2000; Lago and Smith 2003; Haugh and Paul 2009). Through the *Ubuntu* philosophy, an individual only becomes a person through their relationship with others. Therefore, not only is the therapeutic relationship important but so are other relationships in enabling an individual to have an identity as a *person*.

An important tool in the therapeutic relationship, available to both therapist and client is, language. Many authors argue that language is the main instrument available within the therapeutic relationship (Depestele 2006). For some clients, English might be a foreign language and hence they might not feel confident exploring their experiences and emotions in that language. In cases where an interpreter is used, specialist training is needed for both therapist and client. In my experience, when working with interpreters/translators, special attentiveness should be paid to the sophistication of interpretation of metaphors or somatic language that clients use. For example, a client might say something that is interpreted directly as 'My head feels hot.' In fact what the client really means is that they feel *confused*. When working with clients of African heritage an understanding of the importance of somatic language rather than literal translations is paramount in comprehending what the client is really saying. Many authors have extensively written on the importance and complexity of the therapeutic alliance between therapist, client and interpreter (e.g. Marshall *et al* 1998; Mudakiri 2003; Tribe and Raval 2003).

Differentiation of experiences among individuals with African heritage

In African beliefs there are different ways of understanding and explaining mental illness. Often there is openness to an exploration and acceptance of paranormal phenomena such as issues of possession or special powers in those presenting with signs of mental distress. This differs from western psychiatric systems in which symptoms often inform the basis of a diagnosis. I am, however, also aware that there are individuals who legally and ethically need psychiatric treatment and I accept the place for this medical model. I agree however with Fernando (1995) that at all times the validity of the concept of experiences which can be interpreted as mental illness being reduced to purely medical issues should be questioned.

I therefore advocate that it is important, through the therapeutic relationship when working with individuals of African heritage, to explore their thoughts and feelings and alternative ways of understanding their experience. For example, while I was working with a client with a diagnosis of schizophrenia, we explored her experience of hearing very distressing voices. An example of a key question that enabled her to view her world differently was, 'If you were back home, how would your elders explain what is happening to you?' Although the client was not in her home country this enabled us to explore her experiences within *her* world view, including the effects of her African heritage.

A question I often ask myself is: how can I differentiate between a belief or experience that would be considered normal within the client's particular heritage, and one that would denote that the individual is experiencing mental ill health? This usually enables me, via the therapeutic relationship and through supervision, to work within the therapeutic process more openly. The effects of an African heritage are often *embedded*, even in experiences of mental illness, despite alternative western diagnoses.

Effects of an African heritage when living in a foreign country: a discourse in self-identity

The complexity of holding one's own values whatever one's original heritage, yet living within an alien society, can often have an impact on mental health. My experience, as an international student, many years ago, new to a western system, brought with it both positive and extremely challenging situations. Learning new values about what is acceptable and what is not, the perspectives of issues of gender, power and culture, issues of sexuality, disability, prejudice and ways of life were all areas in which my experiences of self started to change. As a result of similar experiences many clients who present for therapy in an alien country are going through a similar 'identity shift'.

Conclusion

Supervision that encompasses difference and diversity is essential. Through supervision and when working with clients, I maintain an openness to explore the clients' experiences, including possibilities of unscientifically explicable phenomena and the interrelatedness of human and spiritual networks. These experiences include traditional rituals such as voodoo and witchcraft, and any other frames of reference that the client might bring. I also have an awareness of the *Ubuntu* or 'we' concept and the impact of family roles on individuals' value systems.

An important issue I am aware of when working with individuals of African heritage is that of power within their own people. While the concept of *Ubuntu* highlights fundamental values such as respect, humanity, group participation and generosity, there is the potential danger of being ostracized, isolated and rejected if an individual does not show conformity or loyalty to the group and its cultural values. In such a case, individuals can question their identity and the resulting isolation and rejection often lead to psychological maladjustment. I am therefore open to exploring the impact of extra therapeutic variables in terms of the client's heritage with regard to power and their interrelatedness with their tribe or family.

In my experience, clients can often share or speak in metaphors in the therapeutic relationship. Smale and Perry (2003) state that stories/metaphors fulfil a useful purpose and can be used as agents for change in therapeutic work, particularly when a client may find it easier to confront a painful experience through the externalized metaphor of the story. In my work I am aware of the importance of stories, myths and metaphors for those of African heritage and hence am open to exploring these with clients.

When working with individuals of African heritage, I propose the following 10 principles, and would advocate the reader also examine the 19 key points proposed by Lago and Smith (2003), which highlight key issues in therapeutic practice, including anti-oppressive practice and a commitment to reflective practice.

1   Acceptance that their world view is influenced by African heritage and is culturally specific to their experiences.

2   The therapist should maintain an openness to explore the client's inter-personal relationships in the we/*Ubuntu* paradigm, and the functioning and development of the client's self-concept within a collective culture.

3   Openness to explanations and concepts of mental and physical ill health which can be different from western medical and psychiatric diagnostic systems.

4   Awareness of the client's perceptions of the power of his/her tribal group and the possible consequences of lack of conformity to their 'we' values.

5   Openness to processing the interrelatedness of human and spiritual networks, particularly in exploring and understanding the crises, ill health and life experiences which lead clients to therapy.

6   Having an openness to explore life space/cycles that are infinite and unlimited, often relating to possibilities pre-birth, through-life and after-life experiences and/or beliefs.

7   Exploration of experiences through symbolic, metaphoric expression and meaning.

8   Openness to accepting possibilities of unscientifically explicable phenomena as relevant when clients bring them to therapy as part of their cultural/heritage world view or experience (e.g. issues of voodoo/possession).

9   Awareness of the complexities and evolving nature of heritage.

10   Willingness to learn from clients despite perceived therapist's own knowledge of client's heritage.

I am aware that African heritage is not one transparent, demarcated whole but a constellation of many individuals, societies and cultures; however, in this chapter important overlaps have been identified. At all times it is vital for practitioners to acknowledge the complexity and evolving nature of individuals of an African heritage through space and time.

References

Belcher, S. (2005) *African Myths of Origin*. London: Penguin.

Charura, D. (2009) An exploratory study of clients' (refugees and asylum seekers) perceptions of client-centred counselling/psychotherapy before and after therapy, MA dissertation, University of Leeds.

Cox, J.L. (2007) *From Primitive to Indigenous: The Academic Study of Indigenous Religions*. Bodmin: MPG Books.

Depestele, F. (2006) Linguistic characteristics of the different spaces of experiential Psychotherapy, *PCEP*, 5(1).

Fernando, S. (ed.) (1995) *Mental Health in Multi-ethnic Society: A Multi-disciplinary Handbook*. London: Routledge.

Haugh, S. and Paul, S. (eds) (2009) *The Therapeutic Relationship: Perspectives and Themes*. Ross-on-Wye: PCCS Books.

Ibrahim, F.A. (1991) Contribution of cultural worldview to generic counseling and development, *Journal of Counseling and Development*, 70: 13–19.

Kapferer, B. (2002) *Beyond Rationalism: Rethinking Magic, Witchcraft and Sorcery*. New York: Berghahn Books.

Karenga, M. (2002) *Introduction to Black Studies*, 3rd edn. Los Angeles: University of Sankore.

Lago, C. and Smith, B. (2003) *Anti-Discriminatory Counselling Practice*. London: Sage.

Littlewood, R. (1992) Towards an intercultural therapy, in J. Kareem and R. Littlewood (eds) *Intercultural Therapy*. Oxford: Blackwell Scientific.

Louw, D.J. (2006) *Ubuntu and the Challenges of Multiculturalism in Post-Apartheid South Africa*. Sovenga: University of the North, Department of Philosophy.

Lugira, A.M. (2004) *African Religion*. New York: Facts on File.

Manji, A. (2003) *Magic Faith and Healing: Mysteries of Africa*. Pittsburgh, PA: Sterling House.

Marshall, P.A., Koenig, B.A., Grifhorst, P. and Van Ewijk, M. (1998) Ethical issues in immigrant health care and clinical research, in S. Loue (ed.) *Handbook of Immigrant Health*. New York: Plenum Press.

Mbiti, J.S. (1991) *Introduction to African Religion*, 2nd edn. London. Heinemann Educational.

Mbiti, J.S. (1999) *African Religions and Philosophy*. London. Heinemann Educational.

Mudakiri, M.M. (2003) Working with interpreters in adult mental health, in R. Tribe and H. Raval (eds) *Working with Interpreters in Mental Health*. London: Routledge.

Patterson, C.H. (2000) *Understanding Psychotherapy: Fifty Years of Client Centred Theory and Practice*. Ross-on-Wye: PCCS Books.

Ramose, M.B. (1999) *African Philosophy Through Ubuntu*. Harare: Mond Books

Scheub, H. (2000) *A Dictionary of African Mythology: The Storyteller as Mythmaker*. New York: Oxford University Press.

Some, M.P. (1998) *The Healing Wisdom of Africa :Finding Life Purpose Through Nature, Ritual and Community*. New York: Jeremy P. Thatcher.

Tribe, R. and Raval, H. (eds) (2003) *Working with Interpreters in Mental Health*. London: Brunner Routledge.

Smale, R. and Perry, J. (2003) Narrative as therapy, *Person centred Practice*, 11(1).

Sue, D.W. and Sue, D. (1990) *Counselling the Culturally Different*. New York: Wiley.

Thomas, D.E. (2004) *African Traditional Religion and Philosophy: An Introduction*. New York: McFarland.

Walker R. (2006) *When We ruled*. London: Every Generation Media.

Walker, R. (2007) *Ancient and Traditional African Religions*. Leeds: Author.

World Health Organization (2009) Demographics statistics for African countries, http://www.who.int/research/en, accessed 28 December 2009.

19 The effects of an Australian heritage: counselling in a land down under

Fiona Hall and Bernie Neville

Introduction

Mark Twain is supposed to have described Australia as 'an entire continent peopled by the lower orders' (Pilger 1989: 239). This may no longer be entirely accurate, but it still figures prominently in the Australian narrative. Australians, or at least many of them, differ from some superficially similar peoples in seeing such a description as a source of pride rather than shame. Indeed, in the narrative which underpins notions of a distinctive Australian culture, membership of the 'higher orders' does not give any boasting rights. There's much more satisfaction to be had in claiming descent from a convict or two. It is often alleged that Australians have an inferiority complex. This should not be surprising. 'Descent' from the 'lower orders' fits nicely with the universal experience of Australian school children of finding that their country is 'down under' at the bottom of a globe where everything important happens in the top half.

The authors of this chapter come from contrasting backgrounds to comment on the culture within which counselling takes place in Australia. One of us (FH) is a counsellor who came to Australia seven years ago from the UK:

> I remember the culture shock when I first arrived – new experiences such as the dawn birdsong that could sound like a Greek chorus, kangaroos munching on next door's lawn, new phrases to decipher, 'she'll be right' and 'no worries'. Now I have my own home in Canberra, and a therapy room – a 12-sided wooden hut called a yurt – which I have to persuade the mouse-sized spiders to leave before my first client arrives each day. I arrived with a climbing (or rather 'falling') injury and a sports specialist therapist worked at getting the soft tissue injury better. She asked me to take on a referral and this started my practice in Australia. So initially I counselled a number of sports professionals and people they referred. This beginning has been a backdrop to my understanding of my other experiences.

The other author (BN) is a university academic who has been involved in the education and training of client-centred counsellors and student-centred teachers for several decades. He writes:

Most of my professional life has been spent in Melbourne but I have also worked in Adelaide and Sydney. I am fairly blasé about the presence of mouse-sized spiders and venomous snakes. Culture, especially the culture of organizations and other groups, has been a major focus of my research. This has enabled me to make the outlandish generalizations found in the following pages.

Culture and cultural understandings

Talking about culture and distinguishing between cultures used to be the exclusive province of anthropologists. However, in recent decades a wider range of social scientists have got into the act, and even psychologists and psychotherapists are now likely to see cultural understanding and 'cultural competence' as desirable attributes in their professions.

In his *Atlas of World Cultures* (revised edition 1981), American anthropologist George P. Murdock listed 1,200 cultures distinguished by 100 variables. In collaboration with Douglas White he developed the 'Standard Cross-Cultural Sample', selecting 186 cultures and coding 2,000 separate variables by which they can be distinguished from one another (Murdock and White 1969). The codings Murdock and White developed have provided a widely accepted framework for comparative studies of culture.

Knowing that there are 2,000 variables which might distinguish the values and habitual behaviour of a British or North American counsellor from those of an Australian client might seem a good place to start. However, it's not that straightforward.

Australian culture: early non-Aboriginal beginnings

When Murdock and White selected their sample of 186 cultures they were seeking cultures which were independent of each other. Consequently they had to leave dominant European and Asian cultures and their derivatives out of their list and focus on pre-industrial societies. They certainly had no reason to be interested in contemporary Australian culture. It did not evolve in isolation and there is little about it that is independent. Indeed, Claudio Veliz refers to Australia as 'an island off the coast of Sussex' (in Carroll 2006). The British colony was founded in the late eighteenth century as an extension of the penal system. English officers gave the orders, English soldiers carried the guns, English tradesmen and farmers established and made the colony viable, and the convicts – Irish rebels and members of the English 'lower orders' – provided the slave labour. However, the politicians who thought that they were establishing a cone of Englishness in the Antipodes would have soon been disappointed. From the beginning there was a clash of values – between the officer class and the rest, between English and Irish; between those who regarded the indigenous inhabitants as 'noble savages' to be treated with respect and those who were unwilling to concede them human status; between the 'sterling' colonists who looked back to England as home and the insolent 'currency' lads and lasses who were born in the colony and were content to stay there and thumb their noses at the English.

John Pilger (1989: 75) suggests that it is not possible to understand present-day Australian society without appreciating the convict heritage:

> It is such a potent part of our psyche that its appanage is passed to new-comers who are not from Anglo-Celtic backgrounds. It touches the way we are with each other, our language and humour; where else but in Australia is the vocabulary of irony, even perversity, such everyday currency?

In noting the dissimilarity between Australian and American cultural assumptions, Pilger makes the point that 'unlike the first white Americans, who imagined themselves on a mission from God, the first white Australians *knew* they were Godforsaken'. Unlike the USA, Australia has no 'creation myth' of great and wise founding fathers, and no 'civil religion', in which it could 'cast itself as God's chosen people, selected for its virtue and set a divine mission' (Carroll 2006: 28).

Oppression and racism

We should add that if culture is shaped by a heritage of subjection to oppression and enslavement – which applies not only to the original settlers but to a good proportion of the 'huddled masses' who have arrived more recently – it also inherits a culture founded on the oppression and slaughter of the indigenous inhabitants. The very problematic notion of 'race' has from the beginning defined who gets categorized as outsiders, though Australians may reasonably claim to be one of the least racist countries in the world. About 40 per cent of Australians acknowledge some prejudice against particular ethnic groups, yet public expressions of prejudice are rare and discrimination on the grounds of ethnicity is illegal.

Throughout the nineteenth century, waves of immigrants from Europe and Asia, fleeing war and starvation or seeking gold, added to the mix of racial tolerance, radical politics and xenophobia in Australia. These tensions have played themselves out, passionately, though rarely violently, over the past 200 years. The English–Irish (Protestant–Catholic) conflict seems to have largely exhausted itself by now, though 'beating the Poms' is still a good enough reason for spending five days on a game of cricket. Australians don't refer to England or Ireland as 'home' any more. At federation in 1901 Australia was ahead of most of the world in socially progressive policies, such as universal suffrage, secret ballot, universal education, pensions and workers' rights, and Australians still think of themselves as energetically egalitarian. Yet the management structures in Australian organizations tend to be unrelentingly hierarchical and the gap between the very rich and the very poor is now enormous. The unlamented 'White Australia Policy' was abandoned decades ago and in the seventies politicians from both left and right publicly embraced the notion of a multicultural society, yet Australians still succumb to xenophobic fear campaigns. (It used to be the 'yellow peril'. Currently it's the 'boat people'.) It is nearly half a century since Aboriginal Australians were belatedly given full citizenship, yet they remain one of the most disadvantaged groups in the world. Australia projects an image of wide-open spaces, isolated beaches and untouched rainforests, inhabited by beer-drinking 'Crocodile Dundees' and a handful of surfers and sunburnt men in wide-brimmed hats. Yet it is one of the most urbanized countries on the planet.

Contemporary cultural issues

Australian politicians, especially those on the right, are fond of upholding 'Australian values' and declaring certain behaviours 'unAustralian'. They love to refer to the 'Australian Way' which is apparently superior to most other ways. When John Howard was prime minister this seemed to involve militarism and a lot of flag-waving. More broadly, our leaders seem to think that we must be continually reminded of these apparently unique Australian values. There is even an official list published by the Department of Immigration and Citizenship (2007: 4):

> To maintain a stable, peaceful and prosperous community, Australians of all backgrounds are expected to uphold the shared principles and values that underpin Australian society. These values provide the basis for Australia's free and democratic society. They include:
>
> * respect for the equal worth, dignity and freedom of the individual;
> * freedom of speech;
> * freedom of religion and secular government;
> * freedom of association;
> * support for parliamentary democracy and the rule of law;
> * equality under the law;
> * equality of men and women;
> * equality of opportunity;
> * peacefulness;
> * a spirit of egalitarianism that embraces tolerance, mutual respect and compassion for those in need.

Australians may be happy to identify with such values, but many of them still treat Aboriginal Australians with contempt and they keep electing politicians who fail to apply these values in their treatment of asylum-seekers. One way our initiative and resourcefulness seem to be expressed is in waiting until some innovation or reform (in education or health, for instance) has been tested and failed in North America or Europe before adopting it as a uniquely Australian response to a uniquely Australian problem.

The Australian population is diverse. That is not an unusual situation in the twenty-first century, but Australia has been ethnically and culturally diverse for longer than most. It may also claim to be more diverse and more successful in achieving a multicultural society than most. There is a constant stream of immigrants. In the most recent census figures (2006) we find that 22 per cent of

Australia's permanent residents were born overseas, and that more than half of these were born in non-English-speaking countries. There are over 400 languages, including indigenous languages, spoken in Australia, and 16 per cent of Australians don't speak English at home. (It's noteworthy that 30 per cent of the latter were born in Australia.) Nevertheless there is a dominant mainstream Australian culture which has sufficient pull over the various minority cultures to force people whose origins are from outside the UK, Ireland and New Zealand to become bicultural if they wish to participate in the life of the larger community.

The rhetoric of multiculturalism waxes and wanes as governments change. It has generally been more in favour among politicians on the left than among those on the right, but there have been notable exceptions. It must be admitted that the influence of some minority cultures does not go much further than affecting the eating habits of 'skippies' or giving them the opportunity to have exotic friends. Mainstream culture may have got a lot of its genes from the Old Country, but the Australian Way is decidedly not the British Way, as British migrants soon find out. There is clearly more to the difference than an accent and the presence of such dialectical idiosyncrasies as 'fair go', 'goodonya', 'she bright' and 'owzitgoinmateorrite?'

External points of reference

We often look to outsiders to tell us who we are. We smirk a bit when foreigners say nice things about us, when, for instance, Howard Jacobson describes how he 'fell in love with the cleverness of Australians, with their sense of humour, their affability, their sentimentality and their recklessness' (in May 2011); when Bill Bryson (2001) reports that Australians are 'cheerful, extroverted, and unfailingly obliging' with an 'effortlessly dry, direct way of viewing the world'; or when the *Guardian* reported, in respect of the 2000 Olympics, that 'The mixture of efficiency, friendliness and boundless enthusiasm is uniquely Australian' (in Carroll 2006: 21).

It must be a real joy for therapists to interact with such clients.

On the other hand, some local commentators have been so 'unAustralian' as to suggest that Australian neighbourliness, egalitarianism and 'fair go' serve as camouflage for aggressiveness and a penchant for social engineering designed to eliminate those who don't belong (Rutherford 2000; Darby 2008). They even suggest that

> Even the image of ourselves which Crocodile Dundee personifies, that of the outrageous, yet skeptical 'larrikin' who rejects all convention and authority, is mostly wrong. True, generations of us were encouraged to distrust, even despise, the police: a bequest of our convict past, it was said. But we made only anti-authoritarian noises behind authority's back and, in the end, we did as we were told.
>
> (Pilger 1989: 75)

Theorized cultural differences

Therapists who want to look further than novelists, journalists and travel writers in their desire to understand the Australian psyche might find some assistance from the anthropologists and sociologists who have taken on the task of distinguishing cultures from each other in the past couple of decades. Geert Hofstede (1984, 1997) has classified cultures along a number of dimensions, and found that Australian culture could be best labelled 'low power distance', 'weak uncertainty avoidance', 'masculine', 'individualist' and 'short-term oriented'. Trompenaars and Hampden-Turner (1998) have categorized Australians as universalist (treat everybody the same) as opposed to particularist (friendship has special obligations); individualist as opposed to communitarian, feeling-neutral rather than emotional. They tend to separate personal and professional roles, attribute status on the basis of accomplishment rather than on the basis of birth, focus on the present, are more concerned with getting the job done than with nurturing relationships, and prefer to do what suits them rather than try to meet the expectations of others. In a classification of national cultures designed (like Hofstede's and Trompenaar's) to sensitize business people to the hazards of intercultural communication, Richard Lewis (2000) distinguishes between three kinds of culture: *multi-active* cultures, *reactive* cultures and *linear-active* cultures. People in *multi-active* cultures (Brazil, sub-Saharan Africa, Saudi Arabia, Italy) are inclined to show their feelings, do several things at once, talk a lot and have a flexible view of truth; people in *reactive* cultures (Vietnam, Japan, China, Indonesia) are inclined to hide their feelings, hate to lose face, are polite and indirect and avoid confrontation. Australians belong to the third group – *linear-active cultures*. People in *linear-active* cultures (Germany, USA, England, Switzerland) like to do things step by step, are job-oriented, depend on the facts and put truth before diplomacy.

With due allowance for the selectivity of the samples on which these categorizations are based, we might warn counsellors based in Europe or North America to expect Australian clients to be unsubtle in their communication, not very respectful of authority or social status, task-oriented, preferring to do one thing at a time, not inclined to waste too much energy on relationships, inclined to keep their personal and professional roles separate, more concerned with the present than either the past or the future, ready to take risks, and not inclined to let feelings or relationships get in the way of business. This information would be more useful if it were not for the fact that Australia belongs to a cluster of countries whose 'corporate inhabitants' responded to the surveys in almost exactly same way. The other countries in the cluster are Great Britain, USA, Canada, New Zealand and Ireland. No surprises there.

A significant dimension which does not figure in these categorizations is religiosity. Church attendance in Australia is very low, yet 60 per cent of Australians report to census-takers that they are Christians. About 25 per cent report no religious allegiance. Meanwhile, the fastest growing religion in Australia (though still less than 2 per cent) is Hinduism. We might note David Tacey's (2000) observation that whereas in the past Australians were publicly religious and privately secular, now they are more likely to be secular, even anti-church, in public and spiritual in private. My (BN) experience of teaching for some years in an alternative institution which offers programmes in holistic counselling and transpersonal art therapy has given me evidence enough that there is a demographic which has had enough of living by the social norms of a consumer society. Both the students I have taught or supervised and the clients who come to them are looking for a better reason for living than the joy of owning a plasma TV or a two-door refrigerator. They understand the word 'spirituality' in many different ways, but it is the word they inevitably use.

Australian cultural differences, home and abroad

Australians visiting the USA are amused or bemused by the religiosity of the natives, their fondness for flying flags and their tendency to shoot each other. They return from London with stories about soccer hooligans, a class-ridden society and the rudeness they encountered from officials at Heathrow. They find their New Zealand neighbours a little odd, especially in their amusing accent, their obsession with rugby and their totally irrational paranoia about Australia. There are always good yarns about their experiences in Ireland, largely relating to the impossibility of communicating simple ideas to the natives. They tell jokes about Americans, New Zealanders, the Irish and the British, but Canadians don't seem to evoke a similarly amusing cultural stereotype. There may be some fellow feeling derived from the shared experience of being bullied by the USA.

There are also differences within Australia, between north and south, east and west, urban and rural. A colleague who works as a consultant to major corporations underlines some common stereotypes in comparing the response he gets around the continent when he introduces himself at a workshop and explains what he intends to do. He asserts that the first question he is asked in Melbourne is, 'What's your ideological framework?' In Sydney it is, 'Is there any money in this?' In Brisbane they suggest finishing early and going to the beach. In Darwin he's invited to go to the pub. In Perth he is told that, 'We did this stuff ten years ago and we did it better.' In Adelaide he is asked what school he went to. In Hobart they don't know what he's talking about.

The Indian cultural philosopher Ashis Nandy (2002: 157–209) suggests that every value position we take has a polar opposite and the tendency to turn into it. The first century and a half of Australian identity saw a gradual move towards democratization. However, in recent decades there has been an increasing assault on democratic ideals. The egalitarian rhetoric is still current, but political practice has moved us towards increasing centralization and control. Australians like to see themselves as egalitarian, democratic and anti-authoritarian, yet this perception is often contradicted by their behaviour. Visitors to Australia comment on the Australian obsession with sport and our expectation that sportsmen and women in international competition will achieve excellence on our behalf. However, no matter how high their achievements they need to be self-deprecatory when they talk about themselves. Arrogance (even when associated with excellence) is not readily tolerated, either in athletes, artists or politicians. People who think too highly of themselves tend to be cut down pretty promptly. Many Australian cricket-fanciers like to see the national team beaten (very occasionally) by Bangladesh or Zimbabwe. (However, it should be noted that the same tolerance does not generally extend to being beaten by the English.) Prime ministers who display arrogance tend to be quickly voted out of office.

We see the same tension between value polarities in the Australian attitude towards war. The late conservative government devoted some energy to militarizing Australian culture, with some success – if bigger crowds at the annual Anzac Day march are anything to go by. Yet they couldn't persuade the general population that invading Iraq and Afghanistan was a good idea, and couldn't persuade them to join the armed forces. In the popular mind the Australian war hero from World War I is Simpson (the man with the donkey) and the hero of World War II is Weary Dunlop (the PoW doctor on the Burma railway). The popular image of the 'digger' incorporates notions of mateship, modesty and resilience, not success in killing people. The national Anzac Day commemoration is commemoration of a defeat by a people we had no argument with (the Turks) in a war which really wasn't our business.

Mental health issues

In a culture defined by its prosperity and its inhabitants' tendency to identify with a national stereotype which labels them relaxed, friendly, laid back and tolerant, it is not surprising that counsellors find that most people who seek their services are depressed or anxious.

The Australian Bureau of Statistics, in its most recent survey of mental health and well-being (2007), reports that:

- One out of every five Australians (and one out of every four Australians under the age of 25) will experience some form of mental illness each year.
- Nearly 1 in 10 Australians will experience some type of anxiety disorder each year.
- Around 1 million adults (in a population of 20 million) and 100,000 young people live with depression.
- At least one-third of young people have had an episode of mental illness by the age of 25.
- Thirteen per cent of young people (16–23) have a substance abuse disorder.
- Sixty-five per cent of all people with a common mental illness (depression/anxiety etc.) do not receive any treatment.

Counselling in Australia

The Australian Bureau of Statistics bases its assessment of mental disorders on the definitions and criteria of the World Health Organization's international classification of diseases. There is no challenge to the classification of depression or anxiety as a 'disease' at the official level, and very little challenge at any other level. A farmer whose livelihood has been destroyed by flood or drought, or a young woman who finds that she is going blind might well seek counselling. If they seek it from a psychologist they will most likely be told that they are suffering from a disease call 'clinical depression' and prescribed the medication required to fix the condition.

As a counsellor in Britain, I (FH) was accustomed to dealing with depressed and anxious young people, and made certain assumptions about my role in this. However, I found myself struggling to understand the world of counselling in Australia. Soon after my arrival I heard a very eminent counsellor talk in a matter of fact way about a new client. She had responded to his talk about depression by telling him to consult his doctor for an assessment and medication before starting counselling. Feeling as if I had strayed into the wrong party I tried to step back and take a wider look at the field.

In my practice in England I saw myself offering a service that was an alternative to the medical approach to distress. I was fortunate that I could spend an hour a week, week after week, listening. I felt fortunate that I was able to offer clients the luxury of time. Who paid for this time? In many cases, NHS funds were earmarked for counselling and managed by the referring general practices.

It was by no means a perfect system, but professionally I felt that counselling occupied a space alongside other caring professionals: doctors, psychologists, social workers, each having distinct roles which would of course occasionally overlap. So what challenged me most about my Australian colleague's deference to the medical is just that, the deference to the medical diagnosis. I had worked under the assumption that what I offered was an *alternative* – respectful of the other, but different. Alongside this was the assumption that the client had come to me because I am not medical and do not follow that paradigm. I believe medical practitioners and counsellors can learn a lot from each other, and in good relationship we can identify the overlaps and limits to our practice. Our differences are the most creative ingredient in working well together. Most important to me was my relationship with the client. If a person sought my services as a counsellor, what mattered was whether we could work together in a way that was useful to them. My respect for the agency of the person seeking counselling is the essential difference between me and someone trained to treat.

So when my new Australian client Jane looked for help, she typed 'depression Australia' into Google. The first two hits told her that depression is an illness, treated by first consulting her doctor. Her doctor offered her antidepressants and suggested a psychologist she could consult. Jane received cognitive behavioural therapy (CBT) from her psychologist and was able to function well, and achieve. Then she was severely bullied at work by her superiors. Her methods of coping, her sense of growth, both failed her. She came to see me. I had no relationship, no status, no communication, in the rest of her care. She simply came to me as a last resort. I was to find that this would be the norm in my practice.

From Jane I soon also learned that there is a distinctively Australian way of being unhappy. Jane too went through a period of cultural adjustment. She offered the technical language used between her and her previous therapist. I responded to her deep pain and her resilience and creativity. I responded as much as I was able to the whole Jane. Slowly we both experienced her self-acceptance coming to the fore – that by being more fully herself she gained access to wisdom in facing criticism and judgement. I saw in her a pattern I was to experience in many of my clients in Australia: a shift from doing to being and a shift from keeping the rules to playing their own game.

My experience of my clients was that they initially expected something like coaching from me: a description of the problem, an insight from me about what could be done 'better' and a new mantra for being a better student, worker, lover and so on. What I gained from this experience was a fresh look at personhood in the context of person-centred therapy. These people came to me because they wanted to improve their performance. The insights they gained from the relationship became new mantras. I understand why Australia does so well in sports; I saw an embracing – more – a living of the rules, almost at any cost. Around this time, the Olympic swimmer Ian Thorpe retired unexpectedly: 'It's like swimming lap after lap staring at a black line – then all of a sudden you look up at the world around you,' he has said. 'I started looking at myself, not just physically, but also as a person. I haven't balanced out my life as well as what I should have' (*ABC News Online*, 21 November 2006).

As a therapist I (FH) see people in my counselling room who have achieved much, but hold themselves up against the measure of a 'better team member' – they work too hard, try too hard and don't know that those 'how to achieve better/ more' maxims no longer apply to them. I introduce them to acceptance of themselves, now and how they are. That they are their own experts, they have within them what they need to grow. When this individualism melds back into a team the results can be spectacular. I think of the leader of a difficult community project. The combination of his new self-acceptance and his teamwork leadership style is a heady mix. His achievements have risen exponentially. More important, he is happier.

So, seven years on, I am more of an Australian. I have learned about the value of being a team player by enjoying all that can be achieved by a group of people facing the same way. I have also seen clearly how the individual can be sacrificed to this greater good, to achieving, not complaining, being a 'mate' at any cost. There is much distinctive Australian suffering, and counsellors can and should help, working alongside the others, doctors, psychologists, social workers, all those who care. As trained facilitators of growth and healing, we should be working more closely, more in a team, with our colleagues in caring. Until that happens, I don't think I will ever be able to say, 'She'll be right.'

References

Australian Bureau of Statistics (2007) *Survey of Mental Health and Wellbeing*, www.abs.gov.au.

Bryson, B. (2001) *In a Sunburnt Country*. New York: Broadway Books.

Carroll, J. (2006) The blessed country, in P. Beilharz and R. Manne (eds) *Reflected Light*. Melbourne: Black Inc.

Darby, P. (2008) An Ashis Nandy travelling kit for Down Under, in V. D'Cruz, B. Neville, D. Goonawardene and P. Darby (eds) *As Others See Us*. Melbourne: Australian Scholarly Publishing.

Department of Immigration and Citizenship (2007) *Life in Australia*, www.immi .gov.au/living-in-Australia.

Hofstede, G. (1984) *Culture's Consequences: International Differences in Work-Related Values*. London: Sage.

Hofstede, G. (1997) *Cultures and Organizations: Software of the Mind*. New York: McGraw-Hill.

Lewis, R. (2000) *When Cultures Collide: Managing Successfully Across Cultures*. Naperville, IL: Nicholas Brealey.

Murdock, G.P. and White, D.R. (1969) Standard Cross-Cultural Sample, *Ethnology*, 9: 329–69.

Nandy, A. (2002) *Time Warps: Silent and Evasive Pasts in Indian Politics and Religion*. London: Hurst & Co.

Pilger, J. (1989) *A Secret Country*. London: Jonathan Cape.

Rutherford, J. (2000) *The Gauche Intruder: Freud, Lacan and the White Australian Fantasy*. Carlton, VIC: Melbourne University Press.

Tacey, D. (2000) *Re-Enchantment: The New Australian Spirituality*. Sydney: Harper-Collins.

Trompenaars, F. and Hampden-Turner, C. (1998) *Riding the Waves of Culture: Understanding Diversity in Global Business*. New York: McGraw-Hill.

20 The effects of an African Caribbean heritage: living as a problem

Delroy Hall

Introduction

The phrase, 'what you see is what you get' is not always true. In this chapter I briefly sketch some of the darker, untold and unacknowledged aspects of African Caribbean life. I will use the term 'African Caribbean' throughout chapter to chart a specific group of people. In writing this chapter, I run the risk of being classed as the stereotypical angry black man. However, I have committed thought to paper; therefore, I will leave the reader to make the decision. Angry or not, this is a view of an African Caribbean man in terms of how he understands the effects of an African Caribbean heritage accompanied with living as a problem within British society.

Heritage and its various meanings

What is heritage and who decides what comprises a heritage or heritages? Heritage is a simple word with a multiplicity of meanings. Heritage refers to something which is handed down from a previous generation and, as argued by Peter Howard (2003: 147–8), it is those things people want to save, collect or conserve – heritage is recognized, designated and self-conscious by definition. Emphasizing its importance, Helaine Silverman and D. Fairchild Ruggles (2007) argue that heritage should be ranked equal to human rights because the very concept of heritage demands that individual and group identities be respected and protected. Furthermore, they stress that heritage insists on the recognition of a person's or community's essential worth. This synopsis elucidates the fact that heritage relates to human existence and significance. The inclusion of human significance is a major development from previous concerns about monuments, historic sites and buildings. For this chapter I use Brian J. Graham and Peter Howard's (2008) definition where they recognize the complex linkage between heritage and identity. Using a constructionist position they conceptualize heritage as referring to the ways in which selective past material artefacts, natural landscapes, mythologies, memories and traditions become cultural, political and economic resources for the present.

Needless to say, what is of social worth to a specific group of people cannot be always understood by outsiders of the cultural group. Furthermore, there is danger when one cultural heritage considers itself superior to others. With this in mind, describing an African Caribbean heritage is complicated.

African Caribbean heritage

As African Caribbeans living in British society, there is a contextual similarity to the time W.E.B. Du Bois wrote *The Souls of Black Folks* (Du Bois 2008). He was asked, 'How does it feel to be a problem?' This labelling was not an incidental moment in the life of African Americans in early twentieth-century America, but is the daily experience of most African diaspora people. One never acclimatizes to this way of life but learns to live painfully with it; however, an anecdotal account illustrating a counter-narrative might be of use here.

In May 2010 I was privileged to present a paper at the Caribbean Studies Association in Barbados. After a few days of being in Barbados I had an unusual experience. Being arrested by this occurrence I spent some time reflecting on what was happening. Eventually, it became evident why I sensed this unfamiliar freedom. First, I was with my own black people where I was one with the dominant population, and second, I felt connected to the land even though my parents are not from Barbados. I have never felt such psychological liberation in England, the land of my birth. This anecdotal experience, while not the focus for analysis, serves to highlight the plight of many African Caribbean people living in Britain.

It must be emphasized that 'an' African Caribbean, or 'the' African Caribbean heritage does not exist. The Caribbean is not a homogenous group of islands or a people group. Each has areas of particularity and its own peculiarity. One of the common features comprising African Caribbean heritage is the legacy of the institution of enslavement. Slavery permeated the whole of the Caribbean, but the island exhibiting the most symptoms of enslavement is Jamaica (Fletchmen-Smith 2008). The violent past began in 1492 when Christopher Columbus happened to 'bump' into the West Indies (Grant 2007). While being highly praised for his expeditions, the history on Columbus often omits the elimination of the Arawak Indians, the natives of Jamaica (The Gleaner 1995). With various nations fighting for control of Jamaica and other Caribbean islands, coupled with the institution of enslavement and the overlap of colonialism, Jamaica, in particular, has experienced various forms of violence over the past 500 years; hence, it seems logical that behaviour concomitant with a history of conflict, violence, subjugation, exploitation and extreme suffering is normal. Thus, the protracted process of dehumanization affected the enslaved on the plantations and subsequent generations right until this present day (Akbar 1996). The enslaved Africans were originally 'drafted' in to work the plantations and were ultimately laid off due to the abolition of slavery, not so much due to Wilberforce but more due to the fight for liberation led by Baptist deacon Sam Sharpe (Dick 2009). The abolition of slavery rendered the enslaved redundant without a welfare package.

African Caribbean heritage: the make-up of myths and stories is generally exoticized through the lens of excellent cuisine and music, in particular reggae, calypso, the steel pans, dance, fashion and literature; but the underbelly of African Caribbean life is demonized, marginalized and counts for nothing. The question is, given its horrific history, is it possible for a heritage to exist?

The existence of African Caribbean heritage

Heritage, whether good or bad, is heritage. The possibility of a heritage is similar to the question posed by African American historian John Henrick Clarke when, as a boy, he told his school teacher he wanted to learn about black people's history. He was told in no uncertain terms that black people did not have a history or a culture (Clarke 1998) – a belief still held by many today (Garvey 1986). What must be vehemently argued is that if there are people existing today, which manifestly there are, then a heritage must be present that has passed through subsequent generations. If heritage is the transmission of the essentials of life vital for ontological existence, it goes without saying that there is an African Caribbean heritage. The addition of conflict, violence and dehumanization is a part of that heritage. The unwelcome addition of mistreatment has become a part of an unconscious baggage which has attached itself like a limpet to Caribbean life and culture. The effects of an African Caribbean heritage take up the rest of this chapter.

The effects of an African Caribbean heritage

It is not possible to exoticize the totality of Caribbean life. The problem with 'exoticization', which is the charm of the unfamiliar to the eyes of the European (Rousseau and Porter 1990), is that it fails to take seriously the brutal Caribbean past and renders holistic care virtually impossible. Is there a need for clinicians to have an awareness of the effects of the African Caribbean legacy on its descendants today?

Having an awareness of the history is insufficient. Colin Lago, commenting from a counselling context, asserts that many counselling approaches focus on the present, but it must be recognized that a relevant understanding of history is necessary to understand current events (Lago and Thompson 1996). While there is a phenomenon called 'empathy' it is virtually impossible for people of the host population to comprehend the depth of pain, trauma and suffering of people living in a civilization that was not created for them (Clarke 1998). As an outsider of an ethnic group, one can have an idea of oppression, but not the experience. The Caribbean proverb, 'he who feels it knows it' is apt here. Race awareness training comes a poor second in attempting to help non-black people understand the dynamics of race and the experience of being black.

The effects of an African Caribbean heritage on its people have been detrimental and the effects are still not fully known. A negative psychological effect of a

Caribbean heritage is one of self-loathing. Self-hatred is a destructive byproduct of hundreds of years of enslavement where the black body was simultaneously an instrument of torture and a receptacle of European projection.

Leaving aside for a moment the physical brutality of enslavement, colonialism also has to be considered as another form of dehumanization. Just as enslavement was appropriating black bodies as objects of property for the production of sugar (Patterson 1969) so colonialism was the commandeering the property and minds of African Caribbean people. The capturing of African Caribbeans took place under the guise of British rule, thus continuing a veiling of the black self from itself. An anecdote may suffice here. In a recent conversation with an African Caribbean woman in her mid-eighties, who migrated to England in the early 1960s, she commented, 'We were born in Jamaica, but we never knew Jamaica.'[1] During the 'Windrush' epoch, migrants arrived in Britain with a strong desire to embrace English values (Banton 1953). England, known as the 'Mother Country' in the Caribbean, was the Promised Land and African Caribbean people were schooled that they would be welcomed, embraced and accepted as children of the Empire. In the main this never happened. The rejection of African Caribbean migrants and subsequent labelling of them as a societal problem is a well-documented fact (Beckford 1998). Gus John makes it clear that the rejection highlighted fissures and weakness within British society (John 1976). In highlighting the fracture in British society, Kenneth Leech (2006) alluded to the fact that the British government had had a real opportunity to educate the nation on race relations but sadly had caused greater exclusion and the demonization of race with the development and implementation of the 1968 Race Act.

Another effect of an African Caribbean heritage is historical amnesia. Many African Caribbeans living in Britain do not know who they are. There is little sense, or indeed no sense or knowledge, of an African or Caribbean history. Many African Caribbean people have accepted the exoticization of their islands without any considering their past. A stark analogy of African Caribbeans not knowing who they are is similar to adopted children who were never told of their adoption. One day, during adulthood and searching through old papers in the attic they discover to their dismay they were adopted. Other people knew important, personal and intimate details about their existence, but not them. Some African Caribbean people sense that something is not right but opt to ignore their existential rumblings as their current life is comfortable, so why rock the boat? Why pursue painful revelations? For some, the uncovering of the past is just too painful, so best leave it alone. The fact remains that most African Caribbean people can only trace back as far as their grandparents at best. If mass historical amnesia exists, what are the psychological, emotional and existential consequences for people who cannot lay claim to their own unique history? Marcus Garvey's comment is worthy of reflection. He writes, 'a people who do not know their history is like a tree without roots'. Garvey's philosophical analogy contains much truth. His statement indirectly suggests another dimension. If an observer ignores or denies the existence

---

[1] Conversation with my mother-in-law, a migrant of the Windrush epoch – 26 August 2010.

of the roots of the other, the plant ceases to exist. Grant (2007: 158) uses similar language in supporting Garvey's comments by saying, 'If you don't know where you are going any road will do, and if you don't know your culture any culture will do'. This failure of historical memory leads to another danger.

Failure to examine, understand or consider the culture, collective history of enslavement, colonialism and trauma of African Caribbean people often leads to inappropriate and ineffective treatment in the restoration and rehabilitation of African Caribbeans who suffer from an array of mental illnesses. There is the danger in only considering the here and now. Of course, it is possible to talk of awareness of the difference of the other, but in reality what effect does 'an awareness' play in affecting or influencing the methods of diagnosis, which are Eurocentric constructs and consequently make assumptions about their universality and applicability? An example is warranted here in illustrating the partial inadequacy of Eurocentric concepts. Some years ago I was in conversation with Emmanuel Lartey, a Ghanaian, who at the time was a senior lecturer in pastoral theology at the University of Birmingham, UK. As we spoke about mental illness and the impact of culture, he said that someone from Africa is at a huge disadvantage being in Britain in terms of cultural understanding, 'because what is understood as normal behaviour in Uganda is perceived as abnormal behaviour in the UK'. He illustrated his point by saying that it is normal for a young person in Africa in their twenties to remain at home, but in the UK such behaviour is generally misinterpreted as the individual having attachment issues.[2]

In treating African Caribbeans the diagnostic process must include, whether implicitly or explicitly, an understanding of the African Caribbean person's collective history, even if the patient/client does not subscribe to or know anything about their cultural history. It is unfortunate, but the fact remains that in the twenty-first century with all the 'mod cons' we have at our disposal to make life comfortable we are still plagued with derogatory ideology about race (Grant 2007). Highlighting the detriment of negatively describing non-white people, Cornel West (2002) comments on 'the notion that black people being human beings is a relatively new discovery in the modern West'. The dehumanizing views of race and the difficulty in its articulation are juxtaposed with the apparent ease of people being able to talk about homosexuality. Homosexuality, by and large, other than protests from certain sections of society, is a generally accepted part of British life. Failure to adhere or accept the 'in vogue' ideology can lead to people being ostracized, disciplined or even dismissed from their employment. Yet the ease and readiness observed in discussing such issues are not mirrored in the discourse on race. One can talk of gay rights in an open way, but if one talks about race, comments such as 'they have a chip on their shoulder' or that the issues of race are now 'sorted' are expressed. However, the real difficulty is not so much the discourse on race, but rather the visible 'uncomfortableness' of talking about blackness. The muting of one's voice or opinion is not a new strategy. On the conscious and unconscious muting of

---

[2]This is still generally the case, but at the time of writing there is an international recession which is causing many young people to remain at home until the economic climate changes.

the black voice, Anthony Reddie (2006) comments that a black person is rendered voiceless when their experiences, history and ongoing reality are ignored, disparaged or ridiculed. Thus, the strategies of silencing and rendering one powerless are not methods of physical violence, but violence in the form of mind games while continuing the propagation of white hegemony. Grant cogently argues that psychological techniques are used more readily than the machinery of violence in an attempt to pacify the Afrikans. By the term Afrikan with a 'k', Grant means people of African descent engaged with the struggle against oppression. The negation of African Caribbean life further compounds feelings of disempowerment and marginalization leading to other detrimental effects of a turbulent history, as the following point demonstrates.

One of the most damaging features of an African Caribbean heritage is the breakdown of African Caribbean families in the UK. Further evidence of family breakdown in the Caribbean is highlighted with the high incidence of Caribbean children born into single-parent families. The instability of many African Caribbean families in the diaspora is not an easily unravelled problem, if indeed it can ever be unravelled. If the current trend of breakdown continues, the future for African Caribbean families in the UK looks bleak. Much of the evidence is supported by Robin Mann's research (2009). Mann's work is interesting, but there still exists a failure to examine the historical context of how African families were disrupted during enslavement, the consequences of which the community is still grappling with today. The breakdown of African Caribbean families on another level signifies major problems in relationship-building; however, this was not always the case.

Olaudah Equiano (2003) comments on how marriage and family life were highly honoured dimensions of African life. But African life became fractured during enslavement. Anthony Pinn (2003) describes in graphic detail how the structure of African families was destroyed on the auction block during slavery. Pinn asserts, 'it did not take much imagination to recognise the traumatic experience the auction block entailed – separation from family, intrusive inspections and travels to new regions of the country and unfamiliar environments'. Thus, African family life became a distorted configuration of the life that had sustained African civilizations for centuries. On the plantations, African family life was heavily scrutinized by the slave masters and was only encouraged as a means of providing extra labour for economic purposes. Emotional, psychological, spiritual and relational links were severed, thus adding to and extending a life of suffering.

Black suffering: an existential crucifixion

The African Caribbean heritage of brutality, the decimation of black life for the benefits of European profit, and the denial of one's humanity are a crucifixion of the black self. This crucifixion began with the capture of Africans for the transatlantic slave trade, continued during colonialism and arguably still exists in modern life. Existential crucifixion, a death of the self, has travelled with people of African Caribbean descent as an unwelcome parasitic enemy for centuries. Other marginalized groups also suffer, but there is a particular reference to people of African Caribbean and African American descent due to a particular historic episode in the formation of the Americas.

The 'Middle Passage', the horrific transhipment of human cargo across the Atlantic from Africa to the Americas was one of the worst protracted episodes of human misery and mistreatment ever recorded. It is estimated that approximately 12 million Africans were inhumanely shipped across the Atlantic on slave ships that were constructed deliberately to carry as many slaves as possible (Gomez 2005). The consequence of so-called 'tight packing' was major health problems. It seems impossible to imagine the depth of human despair, misery and suffering experienced on the slave ships, but Michael Gomez (2005: 79) attempts to capture the magnitude of human tragedy when he writes that 'the stench of the ships was so overpowering that it could be scented for miles and the slave deck so covered with blood and mucus it resembled a slaughter house'. With such an impact on the existence and health of the enslaved, it mattered not if they died en route because they were considered as chattels, not human beings. Whatever was lost at sea would be compensated by the insurance company as loss of property. The three-month journey from Africa to the Americas traumatized the human cargo so significantly that many who survived the journey arrived in the Americas insane (Gomez 2005: 78). Anne Bailey (2007), in attempting to describe the Middle Passage, employs the term 'terror', indicating that terror is designed to harm its objects physically and psychologically.

As a result of the horrors of the Middle Passage, dislocation from their home-land and displacement to another country, the enslaved Africans experienced an existential crucifixion. Hall (2009) admits that this concept is difficult to define but suggests that existential crucifixion includes the moment when the enslaved were forced to denounce their name, culture, religion and, ultimately, their iden-tity. This act of dehumanization was an attempt to annihilate the self, distort the *imago Dei*, and to reinforce the idea that black people could never be human be-ings because they do not look like white folk. Furthermore, dehumanization was an ideological means of crucifying Africans while keeping them alive as disposable units of labour. Existential crucifixion further describes the destruction of life, pre-venting the possibility of enslaved Africans and African Caribbeans ever reaching their potential.

Given the lingering torture of African peoples in the Americas for over 350 years, one cannot fully estimate the damaging legacy that the descendants of such ex-perience faced. Anne Bailey (2007: 143) makes special reference to children and offers a vital insight when she asserts:

> from what we know from the field of psychology about the importance of the formative years in shaping the future adult, again, we may only imagine the trauma of witnessing the constancy of death, dying, and vi-olence without the palliative of traditional customs passed on by family and loved ones. Again, where the physical and psychological horrors co-incided, this must have dealt additional blows to African customs, values and psyche.

Reflecting on this human tragedy or 'Black Holocaust', as conceptualized by Joe Feagin (2000), the question is asked, how have they survived? Na'im Akbar (2001) asserts that the most important aspect is recognition that our continued survival in spite of these conditions is a phenomenon of greater significance than the conditions that continually threaten black life.

Resilience in the face of elimination: an effect of an African Caribbean heritage

Despite the continual onslaught on black life there are two indomitable dimensions of African Caribbean heritage that have stood the ravages of dehumanization: first, the inner strength, life force or resilience of the African, and second, a belief in the creator. The belief in the creator and its enduring legacy for people of African descent will be examined later; however, for now the concept of resilience is considered.

What is resilience? On the surface it is the ability to endure difficult times or the ability to withstand pressure; however, there is an additional component to the concept of resilience. John W. Reich defines it as an outcome of successful adaptation to adversity (Reich *et al.* 2010). But for Reich resilience goes beyond coping. He suggests that two important questions must be asked. The first is about recovery: how well do people bounce back and recover? Second, what capacity exists for moving forward after recovery? There are some difficulties with Reich's understanding of recovery. For example, what or who defines the notion of recovery? Reich asserts, 'in traumatic episodes, people are able to decide what matters to them' (Reich *et al.* 2010: 5). Within African cosmology, resilience is understood as a life force, an energy that defines existence (Parham 2002). Drawing on the laws concerning the conservation of energy, Parham uses an African understanding of the human spirit which he posits as an integral dimension of spirit found in all things living. He continues that what may be really manifested in each person is a recreation of an 'old soul' whose spirit is destined to confront the challenges, pitfalls and opportunities of this lifetime (p. 40).

Enslavement did much to crush the lives of African human beings, but what made endurance possible was the possibility of the resilience of the African spirit that has the ability to withstand anything that confronts it. In the western mind the spirit can be conceived of as an ephemeral entity, but Parham (2002: 40) is quick to point out that the concept of spirit is not some religious vision or mystical 'hocus pocus'. It is, in fact, the life force or energy that is fundamental to every living thing that exists in the universe.

The emphasis on the spirit being the life force found in all things links to the notion of one creator who is the father of all and whose spirit, or essence, lives in all animate and inanimate objects. The cosmological belief of a creator leads us into discussion of how religion, as a life-giving force, was used by African Caribbean people as a means of survival, recovery and advancement.

For people of African descent a belief in the creator is not an appendage, but is an inseparable dimension of humanity. A belief in the creator does not necessarily mean an adherence to religious or church affiliation, but rather that the consciousness of God permeates African Caribbean life and daily existence. John Mbiti (1992) refers to Africans as carriers of religion and in comparison African Caribbeans are no different. In reflecting on the 'religiousness' of African Caribbean people, Clifford Hill (1958) comments that when the migrants arrived in Britain, 95 per cent were regular churchgoers when back in the Caribbean.

The African Caribbeans' religiosity came into play when they were rejected. Their response was to retreat to a place where their faith sustained them. The religiousness of African Caribbeans is a West African cultural retention and had already been an indispensable mainstay for their ancestors on the plantations. Leonard Barrett (1975) makes it clear that slavery was fought not only physically but spiritually. The arrival of European missionaries and subsequent conversion to Christianity of many of the enslaved, created a fusion of African traditional religion and Christianity (Stewart 2005). This religious mix is not without controversy as it is commonly accepted that the Christian Church was complicit in the development and maintenance of slavery. Belief in God, that had enabled their ancestors to fight enslavement, both physically and spiritually, once again became a source of strength for African Caribbean people in Britain. John Mbiti (1992) demonstrates that religion permeated every dimension of African life, and modern scholarship corroborates his argument about the inseparability of religion and life (Gehman 2002). Thus Africans were religious before the arrival of Christianity, and while there is good ground to comment that Christianity was used to enslave people it is also true that Christianity was used as a tool for the liberation of the enslaved. Religion, therefore, was and still is a pivotal dimension of African Caribbean life in Britain and it is not likely that they will be jettisoning that dimension of their existence any time soon.

Conclusion

The effect of an African Caribbean heritage has yet to be fully explored. But from this chapter it is obvious that an understanding of Caribbean history and its effects must be acknowledged and taken seriously in the development of new psychological methods of treatment and care. To take such matters sincerely will mean a re-examination of many Eurocentric theories of human psychology and an acknowledgement and acceptance that such constructs are not universally applicable. We have been here before; one wonders how courageous western clinicians will be in critiquing their tools of diagnosis because this will invariably mean that white hegemonic practices must be placed under the spotlight where the implicit reins of power, white privilege, dominance, assumed universality and control must be relinquished or at least loosened. Again, one wonders about the bravery needed to examine the effectiveness of Anglo-American theories, current diagnostic tools and methods of analysis. To administer appropriate care is a two-element process involving appropriate diagnosis based on an understanding of the legacy of an African Caribbean heritage and a critical analysis of whiteness.

References

Akbar, N. (1996) *Breaking the Chains of Psychological Slavery*. Tallahassee, FL: Mind Productions & Associates Inc.

Akbar, N. (2007) *Visions for Black Men*. Tallahassee, FL: Mind Productions & Associates, Inc.

Bailey, A. (2007) *African Voices of the Atlantic Slave Trade: Beyond the Silence and Shame*. Kingston: Ian Randle Publishers.

Banton, M. (1953) Recent migration from West Africa and the West Indies to the United Kingdom, *Population Studies*, 7(1).

Barrett, L. (1975) *Soul Force: African Heritage in Afro-American Religion*. New York: Anchor Press/Doubleday.

Beckford, R. (1998) *Jesus is Dread: Black Theology and Black Culture in Britain*. London: Darton, Longman & Todd.

Clarke, H.J. (1998) *A Great and Mighty Walk* (DVD), African Images.

Dick, D. (2009) *The Cross and the Machete: Native Baptists of Jamaica – Identity, Ministry and Legacy*. Kingston: Ian Randle Publishers.

Du Bois, W.E.B. (2008) *The Souls of Black Folks*. Rockville, MD: Arc Manor Publications.

Equiano, O. (2003) *Olaudah Equiano: The Interesting Narratives and Other Writings*. London: Penguin.

Feagin, J. (2000) *Racist America: Roots, Current Realities, and Future Reparation*. New York: Routledge.

Fletchman-Smith, B. (2000) *Mental Slavery: Psychoanalytical Studies of Caribbean People*. London: Karnac Books.

Garvey, M. (1986) *The Philosophy and Opinions of Marcus Garvey or African for the Africans* (Pt. 2), in *The Philosophy and Opinions of Marcus Garvey*. Dover, MA: The Majority Press.

Gehman, R.J. (2005) *African Traditional Religion in Biblical Perspective*. Nairobi: East Africa Educational Publishers.

Graham, B.J. and Howard, P. (2008) Heritage and identity, in B.J. Graham and P. Howard (eds) *The Ashgate Research Companion to Heritage and Identity*. Farnham: Ashgate.

Grant, P.I. (2007) *Blue Skies for Afrikans: Life and Death Choices for Afrikan Liberation*. Nottingham: Navig8or Press.

Gomez, M. (2009) *Reversing the Sail of the African Diaspora: New Approaches to African History*. New York: Cambridge University Press.

Hall, D. (2009) The Middle Passage as existential crucifixion, *Black Theology: An International Journal*, 7(1): 45–63.

Hill, C. (1958) *Black and White in Harmony: The Drama of West Indians in the Big City from a London Minister's Notebook*. London: Hodder & Stoughton.

Howard. P. (2003) *Heritage: Management, Interpretation, Identity*. New York: Continuum.

John, G. (1976) *The New Black Presence in Britain: A Christian Scrutiny*. London: Community and Race Relations Unit of the British Council of Churches.

Lago, C. and Thompson, J. (1996) *Race, Culture and Counselling*. Buckingham: Open University Press.

Leech, K. (2006) *Soul in the city: urban ministry and theology*, the Samuel Ferguson Lecture, University of Manchester, 19 October.

Mann, R. (2009) *Evolving Family Structures, Roles and Relationships in Light of Ethnic and Social Change*. Oxford: Oxford University Press.

Mbiti, J. (1992) *Introduction to African Religion*. Nairobi: East Africa Educational Publishers.

Parham, T.A. (2002) Understanding personality and how to measure it, in A. Thomas (ed.) *Counselling Persons of African Descent: Raising the Bar of Practitioner Competence*. London: Sage.

Patterson, O. (1969) *The Sociology of Slavery: An Analysis of the Origins, Development and Structure of Negro Slave Society in Jamaica*. Vancouver: Fairleigh Dickinson University Press.

Pinn, A. (2003) *Terror and Triumph: The Nature of Black Religion*. Minneapolis, MN: Augsburg Fortress.

Reddie, A. (2006) *Dramatising Theologies: A Participative Approach to Black God-Talk*. London: Equinox.

Reich, J., Zautra, A., Hall, S.J. and Murray, K.E. (2010) Resilience: a new definition of health for people and communities, in J.W. Reich, A. Zautra and J.S. Hall (eds) *Handbook of Adult Resilience*. New York: Guilford Press.

Rousseau, G.S. and Porter, R. (1990) *Exoticism in the Enlightenment*. Manchester: Manchester University Press.

Silverman, H. and Fairchild Ruggles, D. (2007) Cultural heritage and human rights, in H. Silverman and D. Fairchild Ruggles (eds) *Cultural Heritage and Human Rights*. New York: Springer Science & Business.

Stewart, D. (2005) *Three Eyes for the Journey: African Dimensions of the Jamaican Religious Experience*. Oxford: Oxford University Press.

The Gleaner (1995) *Geography and History of Jamaica*. Kingston: The Gleaner Company.

West, C. (2002) *Prophesy Deliverance: An Afro-American Revolutionary Christianity*. Louisville, KY: Westminster John Knox Press.

21 The effects of a European heritage: between two chairs

Andrea Uphoff

> *The willingness to understand and the wish to be understood go together and constitute the two sides of a single hermeneutic coin.*
>
> (Mall 2000)

Introduction

Before I launch into this chapter, the reader needs to know something of the personal background against which it is written. I left England as a teenager with my family to live in Ethiopia for two years. Being young, I was very open to the experience of observing and interacting with a different culture for the first time, albeit from a privileged ex-pat existence. On leaving Ethiopia, I moved to Germany where I have been domiciled for the past 38 years. For the last 18 years I have studied and worked as a psychotherapist in Germany and England, moving between the two countries on a regular basis. My clientele hails from diverse origins across Europe, the Caribbean, as well as parts of the Near East, Africa and Asia.

What I believe has drawn numerous clients to work with me over the years is an experience that we share of being '*zwischen zwei Stühlen*', or 'between two chairs', as a German would describe this unsettled position. It is an experience of straddling two (if not more) countries and cultures and never truly being entirely at home in any. In this experience, length of time spent in either culture seems not to be the most potent factor, but the experience itself and the tension it creates constitute a backdrop against which all sorts of issues are amplified. Mobility is a key factor in globalization and is actively promoted within the European Union. It is reasonable to assume that a diverse European client group will increase significantly in the coming years and that therapists will need to equip themselves to work with this diversity from within the context of their own culture.

Invisible diversity

Let me begin by sharing an experience with you. Walking along the Thames recently I was caught up in a large class of school children exiting The Globe.

The Globe, a replica of Shakespeare's sixteenth-century theatre, is dedicated to the performance of Shakespeare's plays, recreating the atmosphere and history of Elizabethan England – a significant period of that country's history and of its conquest over others. What struck me at that moment was the fact that the school children, with the exception of two white faces, were black or Asian – in the first instance a *visible* incongruence with the English historical setting from which they had emerged. This visible diversity said nothing about the way in which the children might have described themselves in terms of their ethnicity or origins. Nor did it say anything about how English/British[1] they considered themselves or, in the case of not having been born in the UK, how integrated or not they may have felt. Whatever the case, it was a reasonable assumption that because of an immediately noticeable difference, there might also be other things about these young people that could be culturally diverse.

Continuing with my walk, I passed many people speaking many languages other than English. However, had I not been within hearing distance of their conversation I may, or may not, have been able to say whether they hailed from a different culture. Their diversity was *invisible*. While many would concede that there may be considerable difficulties for those with an Asian, Caribbean or African heritage to integrate into the UK, because of visibility of difference from the white majority, those of (white) European origin can also experience lack of tolerance and understanding. Books on intercultural counselling most often focus on the former and ignore the latter. Here, we have the crux of this chapter – we may look the same but it would be wrong to assume that we *are* the same or even similar. I believe that invisible difference may indeed be the cause of a disruptive or distressing experience. I am aware that this is disputable and that one could argue that visible difference is a far more potent factor in, for example, discrimination. I am also aware that London is a microcosm of diversity that cannot be representative of the rest of the UK. At the same time, London offers a unique place to hear, as I do in my work, many nationalities speak from their perspective of living in the UK for extended periods of time.

It is with this and my own experiences in mind that I intend to address and illustrate issues which may arise for the 'invisibly diverse', the effects of which are often underestimated. I also consider those moments when fundamental differences are transcended and endeavour to offer some insight into the potent factors of those moments.

The rationale underpinning this chapter

Culture, in my view, is always in flux – tradition and customs are open to influence, changes and adaptations occurring over time. For the purpose of this chapter I

---

[1] I use the terms English/British and Britain/UK interchangeably in order to avoid lengthy explanations and in the awareness that Scotland, N. Ireland and Wales are culturally diverse in their own right.

define culture as the sum of social norms – customs and customary behaviour derived experientially from within the culture of origin; conformed implicit and explicit learning of the appropriateness or inappropriateness of certain values, beliefs and attitudes. In short, the way people live. I also maintain that many of these 'conventions' are not in the conscious domain and are unlikely to become apparent unless violated, remarked upon by another, or until an individual comes to reside in a different culture. There, differences will likely express themselves in attitudes towards time, work, education, personal space, emotions, humour and tactility,[2] just to name a few. These are explicated graphically in the 'Iceberg conception of culture' diagram in Lago 2006 (p. 58).

To accommodate my examples of the effects of a European heritage on persons now living in a new host society I draw on anyone hailing from those countries currently included in any context which is titled European. My rationale for this is simple: Europe has (and has had) many faces. Over the centuries, borders have shifted many times (and continue to shift) to include or exclude neighbouring countries. Any view of Europe is apt to be a description of a collection of countries which may differ depending on historical context, political treaties, shared cultural roots, common languages, economics and/or an author's nationality and perspective rather than pure geography, so to which part of Europe each country belongs is a matter of perspective and sometimes debate. Also, I allow for variance of culture within individual countries.

As anybody who reads or writes about culture and diversity knows, the topic is extensive in breadth and depth and I cannot attempt to cover all aspects of what must remain an experience unique to each individual. However, Carl Rogers (1995) found that what is most personal to an individual is often that which is pertinent to many. So, by drawing on some of the themes that have influenced my and my clients' experiences of integrating one European heritage into another country within Europe as defined, I expect to find resonance in a wider audience and raise awareness on areas of identity, language, personality and professionalism for those practising psychological therapies.

Identity and location

One might argue that psychotherapy has western European origins and that its application within Europe is essentially unproblematic. However, this is a simplistic view that does not do justice to either group or individual experience. While the experience of living elsewhere can be broadening in outlook and give the individual a sense of confidence in the world at large, resulting in a healthy 'heterocultural personality' (Taft 1981: 94), it may instead cause a huge sense of insecurity, impermanence and disempowerment in both personal and professional domains where questions of identity become crucial.

---

[2]For more on the issue of tactility and culture see Uphoff-Chmielnik (1999).

Identity is an important part of what is understood as the self. Erikson (1968: 22), son of a Danish father and German-Jewish mother, regarded identity as intrinsically psychosocial: 'We deal with a process "located" in the core of the individual and yet also in the core of his communal culture'. Proschansky *et al.* (1983: 60) tell us that identity is at least in part geographical: 'Through personal attachment to geographically locatable places, a person acquires a sense of belonging and purpose which give meaning to his or her life'. Whether the choice to live in a different country and culture is voluntary or not, it interrupts our sense of continuity, narrative and sense of agency. The loss of familiar ties, values and conventions when confronted with new social attachment patterns can cause a sense of dislocation, possibly isolation, or even alienation.

The welcome and acceptance that one experiences in the host country will play its part in a person's ability to relocate their identity. This may be influenced by the positive or negative stereotypes and prevalent zeitgeist. In the UK, for example, Italians enjoy a positive stereotype based on holiday experiences – sunshine, good food, friendliness, a melodic language – which makes their presence, in these days, easy to welcome. In Germany during the fifties and sixties there was considerable resistance to what was seen at the time as an influx of 'loud' Italian people. I myself benefited from the anglophilia of many Germans when I came to live here in the seventies. This was expressed in a fondness of English culture and its eccentricities and, by default, with warmth towards me. In contrast, someone currently arriving from Poland in the UK or Germany may find themselves confronted with anything ranging from polite neutrality to hostility and an expectation that they will take up a menial job. At the same time they may also find political attempts to integrate those of a migration background in the public arena through specially contrived events, for example, a season of Polish cinema, as recently shown in London, or a German initiative to integrate Muslims from a seemingly 'parallel' society. Germans arriving to live for a period in the UK may find themselves confronted with the negative historical legacy of National Socialism, attitudes which are still openly expressed in the UK today. Specific current events may also bring unconscious cultural attitudes to the fore, as has the current financial crisis. A stereotype has emerged in the German and British media of the Greeks as chaotic spendthrifts. The stereotype propagated in response is that of the prudent Germans, resentful at having to share their money (yet again) out of recompense and solidarity. Individual characteristics and behaviours tend to enforce or deconstruct existing clichés when we interact with other cultures.

The immigrant also brings their expectations of the host country – their own perceived stereotypes and sometimes illusions of what life will be like, what will be possible personally and professionally. The power of Britain's colonial past and the dominance of English as the lingua franca manifest themselves in negative attitudes expressed by those in the host community. On many occasions I have heard people complain of British arrogance towards those of foreign origin. They speak of intolerance when immigrants do not speak English in the same tempo and same range of expression or when cultural differences between understandings of a situation occur – when they do not do things as the British do. Unfortunately, some British people are apt to interpret accents as harsh or the tone of interaction as demanding, bad-tempered or insolent. Such para-linguistic phenomena can be the source of further misunderstandings and reinforcement of negative attitudes – see, for example, the work of Gumperz *et al.* (1981) which was later screened in a programme by the BBC entitled *Crosstalk* in 1991. But what is the outcome of acquiring a new language?

Lost in translation

Christodoulidi (2010: 106) considers that 'bilingualism may be the strongest factor that affects a migrant's life', and I would agree. To live in and between two languages can be tricky when one can no longer depend on the seamless connection established between objects and words as in the mother tongue. Loss or partial loss of the use of the mother tongue and inadequate skill in the host language is disempowering and can become a 'dis-ability', leaving one possibly unable to participate fully in professional or social life. Even those who are fluent sometimes just stop talking because there is too much effort involved in translating or explaining, and so there is a lapse into silence. One client described it as a battle: 'You battle with the language, you battle with the culture because you don't understand what is going on and then you have to battle with the fucking colonial attitude as well!'

The psychotherapist will need to understand that their client may be fluent in the host language but lose their skill under the stresses of the therapeutic process (as one client put it, 'Some days the foreign language just doesn't function!'), just as they may lose a certain proficiency in their own tongue through lack of opportunity to use it.[3] Does the person constantly translate one language to the other before they speak – slowing them down? Or is there no vocabulary available for a particular topic? A temporary 'lapse' may also occur where a word is available but only in the language not currently being spoken!

Furnham and Bochner (1986) point to the pitfalls of believing that because the psychotherapist and client are speaking the same language, they will necessarily understand one another. No language learned beyond childhood is so viscerally felt and so connected to experiencing as the mother tongue. The words of a second language, even when spoken fluently, do not do justice to experience and we should not mistake the words spoken as being synonymous with the experience. For example, the word 'anger', a symbol for the emotion in the mother tongue, may stir a felt phenomenology in the body while the new word symbolizing anger

---

[3]This phenomenon may also affect the next generation and deprive children of a true 'mother tongue' as well as affect their ability to form a cohesive identity. This can happen when the parents' native language is 'contaminated' through years of living elsewhere or when a choice is made to rear the child in the host country's language as an aid to integration. For example, a client with one Turkish and one Italian parent who grew up in Germany and was only allowed to speak German at home had considerable difficulty reconciling her language to her physical appearance and was thereby unable to recognize herself or her location in the world.

in the second language may be used cognitively to describe the experience without the anger being felt experientially. So when a client is able to speak of their hatred for their father in their second language during therapy, but is inhibited from doing so in their mother tongue, it gives pointers to the meaning and enormity of feeling encompassed in what is, for them, unspeakable.

Our language is embedded in our cultural history but we are seldom aware of cultural context as a central stakeholder in our language, imperceptibly moulding our thought processes and attitudes. Edward T. Hall refers to the subtle way 'in which language arranges the furniture of the mind' (1990: viii). Meanings and patterns of speech originate from within culture, and therapists owe it to their clients to be conscious of their own cultural imprint. For example, in western Europe when talking business we tend to do so directly and in linear ways, using logic to build sentences, one on top of the other, taking us from A to B. Many other European cultures appear to 'meander' extensively in order to get to the point, and talk about anything other than the issue at hand, because other things are important to be 'aired' first, like the well-being of family, local occurrences, events, etc. In English culture this meandering is 'small talk', not 'business speak', and is likely to take place over the garden fence or at the bus stop, probably focused on the weather. For an apt and humorous description of this and other English cultural behaviours I highly recommend Kate Fox's *Watching the English* (2004).

Misunderstandings arising out of failed communication are often about what is considered polite (a counselling student from Mongolia tells me that interrupting a person is welcomed in her culture as a joining-in and enthusiasm for the person and topic). We are, generally speaking, blissfully unaware of the uniqueness of our own embedded culture and idiosyncrasies. An experience of clashing time cultures occurred during a period of time spent on Madeira. Portuguese friends, intent on making us welcome, issued an invitation to spend time with them. However, my partner's attempts to elicit a day or time for the arrangement were unsuccessful, much to his frustration. Unwittingly he kept on insisting, the friends resisting. Here the two cultural attitudes clashed: linear time versus Latin time, which is so much more relaxed (as seen from our own cultural viewpoint). This, Hall (1990) refers to as the *cultural unconscious*. It follows that we do not truly know or understand our own culture until we have lived in a different country. My partner eventually let go of pinning our friends down and the visit took place enjoyably a few days later.

Consequences of migration

> *Two souls alas! are dwelling in my breast.*
>
> (Goethe's Faust)

The idea of the globetrotting polyglot may be an enticing one but is not without far-reaching effects. After living for a time in another culture people describe their experience as never again feeling entirely comfortable and at home within the culture of origin, so in a sense they become permanently displaced. Eva Hoffman (2003) sees this dislocation as 'an upheaval in the deep material of the self'. Seldom have I felt so much resonance with words as with these. As I watch my clients question their identity I continue to wrestle with my own; hear echoes, some distant and some not so distant, of my own struggles. I hear them focusing on different parts of themselves that come into focus in either one country or the other, hear them saying that they are not the same person in Italy, Greece or wherever, and so who are they? For my English originally extrovert self, the German acculturation experience has interposed and generated an introvert – a useful but less gregarious twin, neither parts of self ever completely at home with the other[4] – never quite melding into a comfortable or coherent hybrid. And so, when one client describes it as never being able to 'fill' his 'true' personality using the English language I have a more than approximate understanding of what he means.

Choices about where one wants or needs to be located can become tortuous. One might suppose that this experience gets easier to live with as the years go by, but I have found that this is not the case for most clients. Day-to-day living becomes easier to handle as the necessary cultural skills are acquired, but yearnings for a time absented from the home culture sometimes become more acute as time passes. With the passing of family and friends, some find that although the yearning to go back is strong, they are changed and they often cannot settle when they return, experiencing the negative aspects of their own culture. For others there is in fact nothing/no one to go back to and there can be a sense of isolation and loneliness never to be filled. In my experience many shuttle backwards and forwards between the two, inhabiting permanently migrant lives, literally straddling both, never able to decide where to be. Some decide to live in one culture and work in another, creating a 'patchwork' life. Both these 'solutions' sap energy and create stress, with only temporary satisfactions, but are bona fide attempts to address and reconcile the experience of fragmentation, the incoherence, the feeling of always leaving a part of oneself somewhere else that may accompany the client, sometimes for the rest of his or her life.

There are also communal political consequences to migration which develop over time. In the 1960s it was not unusual to find white, native-born Britons protesting against what was seen as the influx of immigrant blacks and Asians, particularly Muslims. In the most recent UK election, early Pakistani immigrants were prepared to vote for the Conservative Party because of their manifesto promising to cap immigration (*International Herald Tribune*, 6 May 2010). This was targeting the mostly eastern European Polish population in the UK even though, since the expansion of the European Union and its labour laws, Britain has to guarantee free movement among member nations. Those who have settled in the UK find themselves identifying with their chosen culture and have adopted a latent cultural attitude towards immigrants. Admittedly this attitude is aimed towards a population and not necessarily individuals but I would argue that it is indeed the first step

---

[4]Contributors to de Courtrivon's (2003) book *Lives in Translation*, offer numerous descriptive examples of this phenomenon.

towards an insidious colouring of attitudes as a whole and that, as history shows, it has a propensity to develop into much more destructive behaviours. Protest against the increase of other populations is something as old as history itself. As far back as the sixteenth century Queen Elisabeth I is documented as saying that something needed to be done to limit the increase of 'black-a-moors', the term at the time for black people in England (Fryer 1984: 10). A therapist will need to be aware of attitudes developing in these directions and the effect they may have on the individual.

Yet another dilemma is posed when the 'home' culture is transported into another country, creating ghettos and parallel societies. Particularly those of second and third generations find themselves shuttling between cultures on a daily basis, as is the case for many young Turkish people in Germany. This has caused some serious problems such as alienation from parents who do not engage in acculturating to the new society and which is sometimes 'solved' through complete severing of family ties as the young person breaks with tradition or, at worst, through so-called 'crimes of dishonour'.

Others carry a legacy of war within their cultural history. A Greek client speaks of the personal effects of his father's imprisonment during the civil war (1946–9) and the politically polarized climate in which he grew up. He also describes the outbreak of violence during the recent financial crisis in terms of a cultural throwback of distrust of authority. His subsequent distrust of British authority is a topic subtly influencing his whole life in England.

Professional identity

Qualifications brought to the UK from other European countries are not an automatic approbation to practise in the UK, and vice versa. The attempt to create European standards across the board is not yet successful in many areas and there are inadequacies inherent in any attempt to create that equality. This book will undoubtedly be read by a large number of counsellors/psychotherapists, a profession which is currently in the process of statutory regulation in the UK. Concurrently, standards are being developed in Europe to create a platform for practitioner mobility and professional recognition across the continent. Nobody yet knows how equivalence standardization will be achieved. Will the standards set for UK qualification and professional status be compatible with those required by organizations such as the European Association of Psychotherapy and the European Association for Counselling? Will the years of training, personal and financial investment pay off or will practitioners find themselves unable to use the qualifications and titles they have accomplished?

Professions are a considerable component of an overall feeling of identity, and when the right to practise is withdrawn, the consequences can be dire personally and financially. Questions of how the self is experienced become crucial but are inevitable in this kind of scenario and feelings of self-esteem can be seriously undermined. Even if the question of equivalency is clarified, practitioners still face the inevitable cultural differences manifested as a central feature of their clinical actions.

Transcending the divide

When discussing these matters many years ago with Colin Lago, he said, 'Sometimes when I work with a person from a vastly different culture we get off the ground immediately, whilst someone stemming from my own culture, well, we never get off the starting blocks.' I have since had the same experience – so, what is it that gets us off the starting blocks? At which point is cultural heritage transcended?

In recent years there has been such great emphasis on understanding difference – in fact making it a central focus of therapy (see Moodley 1999) – that I propose that we miss opportunities to find common ground. On the contrary, stand-alone knowledge of cultural difference may indeed highlight a separateness which undermines our shared humanity and the potential for relationship. Portera (2010), on the other hand, gives an insight into how we might err into drawing general and false conclusions about cultural influence. He describes a research study designed to understand the factors in second-generation immigrant Italian youths becoming disaffected and behaviourally disturbed while living in Germany. He warns that the detrimental elements contributing to their 'pathology' rested clearly in the factors of their economic and social environments and not solely in their cultural background – his a word of caution lest we all too quickly name culture as the culprit when things are difficult for our clients. At the same time the danger of becoming undiscerning, throwing us all into the 'human' basket without enough attention to our diversity, makes a balanced consideration of all influencing elements essential.

The Indian philosopher Ram Adhar Mall (2000) tells us that intercultural dialogue can only take place from a position of rapprochement and understanding. Without the neuroscientific proof we have today, Rogers discovered empirically that change happens in a climate of empathic understanding in which the importance of subjectivity is the focus, not only in one-to-one relationships (1951) but also in groups (1970). Empathy and awareness stem from culture as does our capacity to be with another in relationship; a network of connections forged in our brains through experience in relationship (Grawe 2004); an experience in which mutable brain structure changes and new experience is stored. Can we cultivate an understanding with the other party, despite difference, through the power of the relationship? Are we willing to be changed?

Recently I had an experience in Germany of training a group of Muslim women and men of a number of European and African origins in counselling skills – people who have had arranged marriages or love matches, were illiterate or academics, who grew up in Germany or were recently arrived, some from war zones. We could not have been more invisibly diverse and the whole exercise could have become redundant. We were all speaking a second language and initially I couldn't see how, or even if, we might connect. As we all stood under some tension in the situation, even those of us who speak good German lost some of their fluency. However, there was goodwill on both sides and we were willing to take time to explain things to each other which we did not understand. We strove to find connections through our experiences as migrants. We spoke about customs and behaviour, modes of dress and their meanings, age difference, body language, and explored our various worlds. The more I spoke about Rogers and the person-centred approach the more they began using the prophets of Islam to find similarities as illustrations, and were not the first to discover these. Mhairi Macmillan, when comparing the writings of Carl Rogers and the Andalusian Sufi mystic Ibn al'Arab, notes, 'I have come to see them not so much as "parallels" but as "signposts pointing in the same direction"' (1999: 47). Location of our common philosophies and values changed the quality of our relationship enough to transcend our cultural divisions and I can truly say that I have never felt more accepted in any group.

I have had great fortune in working with my clients who hail from many countries within and beyond Europe and my person-centred orientation has served me well – its credo of acceptance, empathy and congruence extended to include the culture of my client without using my own as a measure against which it is compared. For me, this means that each culture is equal in all senses to my own and that I engage with my clients with a sense of curiosity and willingness to learn not just about them, but also about their culture. This demands my person-centred discipline balanced with some flexibility and on occasion idiosyncratic empathy (Bozarth 1998). A day comes to mind when an Italian client was trying to describe the importance of *Festa della Donna* (International Women's Day) in her home village. An important part of the festival is gifting mimosa flowers to other women. It was a sunny day and she had discovered a mimosa tree in an old churchyard in a back street of south London. Her longing to be doing something with this day was palpable and when she asked whether I would go with her to the churchyard, it was important to do so and we gave each other mimosa blooms.

In these times of globalization, multicultural reality is with us and learning about *all* our cultural differences and similarities is simply not practicable. What I have found to be an invaluable asset in my work is a good working knowledge of current affairs – demonstrations, earthquakes, military threats, war zones, epidemics – any of these may be affecting the way my client feels. A passable knowledge of history and politics might put behaviour and attitudes in context. This, plus letting go of any sense of competition or superiority of culture and engaging in Rogers' strategy of being in the other's world, as if it were my own, allows a deeper understanding of the many facets inherent in belief systems and critical situations.

Let me give you an example. Having lived in Germany for so many years and carrying my husband's name, I am sometimes mistaken as a German when in Britain. Just as I am consciously white, I am conscious of being acculturated into Germany, including its history, and similarly as I rely on my perceptions to know when I ought to raise my whiteness with a black client, I may also raise the fact of my German life and family. This I did when a young Israeli woman started therapy with me a few years ago. She dismissed the matter as unimportant at the time.

However, my flexibility and ability to remain true to the person-centred approach were severely tested when the aid flotilla in Gaza was subject to an attack by Israel. The mixed Muslim group I was working with on the day were shocked and disgusted at the action taken, with propensity to expression of anti-Israeli sentiments. In this situation, but without needing to mention it, I drew on my knowledge of the complexities of the Arab–Israeli conflict and the roles both Britain and Germany have historically played. I found that just having the knowledge was a huge aid to understanding and it enabled me to respond to the distress before me without condemning or condoning the attack. The very next day I was working with the young Israeli woman who had just decided to leave London and move back to Israel. One of the most enduring difficulties in making her decision was Israeli politics on a national and familial level. This became the most intimate of sessions in which the client reassessed her decision to leave London. She let me know at the end when we embraced that, 'I could not have done this with anyone but you.' In a review of our work together before she left, she let me know how important it had become after all to know about my German connections and how facilitative that had been in creating the space for her to deeply explore and dwell with even the negative cultural legacies.

In both cases a flexible prism was needed to view things from that particular perspective, an understanding how the situation looks and feels from a specific angle without agreement or judgement. But this is not a solely cognitive process; rather it entails what the researcher Todres (2007) calls reading the (con)text of a human situation: 'we relate ourselves to its mood – and can thus understand with our hearts'.

Hope for the future

When one engages in this type of work it is inevitable that yearnings for global peace make themselves felt; yearnings that become painful when I look at the bigger picture of what is happening in the world today and know my own failings as a human being. Rogers made considerable contributions to peace processes,[5] among others in South America, South Africa and Ireland, knowing that before we can live together peacefully we must communicate and understand each other's perspectives and experience. Along with many others I strive to offer Rogers' conditions for a constructive relationship towards individuals and smaller groups within my work, in the ambitious hope that the relationships we build on mutual respect and understanding will expand from the personal to the universal, allowing a future of true interdependence.

---

[5] For a comprehensive history of Rogers' peace work see Kirschenbaum (2007).

Conclusion

This chapter has striven to amplify the issues that may come to light in the 'invisible' realms of inter-European psychotherapy and to give an indication of the kind of awareness and flexibility that is required to engage in this work. While residence within another culture can be a source of richness and development, it can equally be a source of anxiety and distress. Culture and identity are dynamic processes and both are subject to change, with new experiences and relationships. Coming together with diverse cultures can be challenging and transforming for client and psychotherapist alike, giving us pause to reflect on our values, norms and behaviours. In short, we shouldn't assume that because appearances are the same that we are the same. Mobility across countries comes at a price, and can be psychologically tough; however, there are ways to connect and transcend that diversity if we are willing and flexible enough to find them.

References

Bozarth, J. (1998) *Person Centred Therapy: A Revolutionary Paradigm*. Llangarron: PCCS Books.

de Courtivron, I. (ed.) (2003) *Lives in Translation: Bilingual Writers on Identity and Creativity*. New York: Palgrave Macmillan.

Christodoulidi, F. (2010) The therapist's experience in a 'foreign country': a qualitative inquiry into the effect of mobility for counsellors and psychotherapists, PhD dissertation, University of Manchester.

Erikson, E.H. (1968) *Identity: Youth and Crisis*. London: Faber & Faber.

Fox, K. (2004) *Watching the English: The Hidden Rules of English Behaviour*. London: Hodder & Stoughton.

Fryer, P. (1984) *Staying Power: The History of Black People in Britain*. London: Pluto.

Furnham, A. and Bochner, S. (1986) *Culture Shock: Psychological Reactions to Unfamiliar Environments*. London: Methuen.

Grawe, K. (2004) *Neuropsychotherapie*. Göttingen: Hogrefe.

Gumperz, J.J., Jupp, T.C. and Roberts, C. (1981) *'Cross-Talk' – The Wider Perspective*. Southall: Industrial Language Training Laborotory.

Hall, E.T. (1990) *The Silent Language*. New York: Anchor Books.

Hoffman, E. (2003) 'P.S.', in I. de Courtivron (ed.) *Lives in Translation: Bilingual Writers on Identity and Creativity*. New York: Palgrave Macmillan, p. 3.

Kirschenbaum, H. (2007) *The Life and Work of Carl Rogers*. Ross-on-Wye: PCCS Books.

Lago, C. (2006) *Race, Culture and Counselling: The Ongoing Challenge*. Maidenhead: Open University Press.

Macmillan, M. (1999) In you there is a universe: counselling as a manifestation of the breath of the merciful, in I. Fairhurst (ed.) *Women Writing in the Person-Centred Approach*. Ross-on-Wye: PCCS Books.

Mall, R. A. (2000) Polylog. Forum für interkulturelle Philosophie 1, http://them .polylog.org/1/fmr-de.htm, accessed 30 December 2010.

Moodley, R. (1999) Psychotherapy with ethnic minorities: a critical review, *International Journal of Psychology and Psychotherapy*, 17: 109–25.

Portera, A. (2010) Personzentrierte interkulturelle Beratung und Therapie, *Gesprächspychotherapie und Personzentrierte Beratung*, 2.

Proschansky, H.M., Abbe, K.F. and Kaminoff, R.D. (1983) Place identity: physical world socialization of the self, *Journal of Environmental Psychology*, 3: 57–83.

Rogers, C.R. (1951/1965) *Client-Centered Therapy*. London: Constable.

Rogers, C.R. (1970) *Carl Rogers on Encounter Groups*. New York: Harper & Row.

Rogers, C.R. (1995) *A Way of Being*. New York: Houghton Mifflin.

Taft, R. (1981) The role and personality of the mediator, in S. Bochner (ed.) *The Mediating Person: Bridges Between Cultures*. Cambridge, MA: Schenkman.

Todres, L. (2007) *Embodied Enquiry*. Basingstoke: Palgrave Macmillan

Uphoff-Chmielnik, A. (1999) An exploration into touch in search of a rationale for its use within and as an adjunct to psychotherapy, with an emphasis on a person-centred model, or Beware – Here There Be Tiggers! Unpublished MA dissertation, City University, London.

22   The effects of an Eastern European heritage

Renate Motschnig and Ladislav Nykl

Introduction

Revealing some of the effects an Eastern European heritage is likely to have on people coming from Eastern Europe poses numerous challenges that we need to take into account. Firstly, the term 'Eastern Europe' is interpreted differently in different contexts – sometimes subsuming central and northern European states, at other times excluding them and including only countries such as Belarus, Estonia, Latvia, Lithuania, Moldova and Ukraine. In this chapter, although we favour the inclusive view of the European Union, when we write about Eastern European heritage we think of the former communist states, in particular Poland, former East Germany, the Czech Republic, Slovakia and Hungary. But even making this selection, there's the difficulty that states like Poland and Hungary have very different histories, languages, cultures and religions such that describing their heritage under one label would not match any of them. This insight and the fact that we're not experts in cultural studies made us decide to focus on one particular instance of a Central or Eastern European state that we know best from our own roots: the Czech Republic. However, even focusing on one single state, it seems impossible to deal with all its ethnic groups, such as Slovak, Polish, German, Roma (Gypsy) and Ukrainian in one chapter. So being aware of the injustice we make to them and also to the other eastern neighbours, in the following we concentrate on the Czech majority (Moravians and Bohemian Czechs). Although statistics differ (Smekal *et al.* 2003), the ethnic composition of the Czech Republic is about 94 per cent Czech and 6 per cent ethnic minorities.

Even if focusing on the Czech majority, we are facing another challenge when wanting to describe the effects of Czech heritage: we are Czech ourselves. While this puts us in a position to have authentic experiences of moving to a more western state, in our case Austria, we sense we can't be objective. As much as we were excited when being asked to write this chapter, we both felt that it would be hard or even impossible to distance ourselves from our current social position in life and our own, often strong, experiences resulting from leaving our Czech homeland. So the question arose: taking into account all these challenges, what would be most appropriate to communicate in order to help psychotherapists better understand clients with an Eastern European heritage? Step by step, our path towards resolution became the following. The next section will describe a personally coloured selection of historical events, legends and values that are intended to throw some light on what the ancestors of contemporary Czech people were going through. In the next section we allow ourselves to be simply us, fully subjectively exploring our own experiences in having left our homes and each of us having started a new phase of our life in a more western state. Motivated by Carl Rogers' insight, 'What is most personal is most general' (1961: 26), we hope readers will gain some understanding of what it can mean to people to move to a more western culture. We also describe how we perceive Eastern European, particularly Czech, people in encounter groups and therapy sessions. Following our subjective perceptions, we reflect on the Czechs from the point of view of Hofstede's studies on cultural dimensions (see www.geert-hofstede.com/hofstede/dimensions) and from the point of view of the 'World Value Survey' (Inglehart and Welzel 2005). If the insight that therapists gain from this chapter does not distract them from listening to the immediate meaning of a given client's expression but rather helps them to understand their contexts more comprehensively, we will have fulfilled our purpose.

A personally coloured glimpse of history, legends and values

Settlement

Around 500 BC Celtic tribes settled in those parts of Europe that are now the Czech and Slovak Republics. About 1,000 years later, Slavic tribes pushed out Germanic tribes who had pushed out the Celtic tribes. The Slavic peoples were the first farmers in these lands.

Legends

Ladislav recollects that when he reads Czech legends he feels that they must have something to do with him. His preferred legend is about Bruncvik, who went to sea on a ship. It ran ashore on a dry island and he couldn't leave the island for several years, since the magic forces of this island always pulled the ship back. His last servant realized that every year a giant bird came to the island and looked for prey. So he packed his lord into the skin of a horse and the bird took it and flew back to the mainland such that Bruncvik found himself in the bird's nest. On an adventurous trip thereafter he met a lion who was fighting against a dragon. He helped the lion and, almost exhausted to death, he and the lion survived. Bruncvik feared the lion but the lion stayed faithfully with him for ever. To honour his faith, the lion was put on the Czech coat of arms where he remains to this day.

A brief historic overview

In the ninth century the missionaries and scholars Cyril and Methodius arrived from Macedonia. Due to their efforts the Slavic peoples were among the very few at that time who could worship God in their own language, today called Old Slavic. The Slavic peoples often had to fight against the Germanic peoples but there were also battles for power within their own group. For instance, Prince Václav (903–35) a humane man, was assassinated because of his relatives' hunger for power. Later he was declared a saint of Bohemia and his statue can still be found on the main square ('*Václavák*') in Prague. In 1031 Bohemia and Moravia permanently joined together as the Czech Crown Lands.

The middle of the thirteenth century saw the reign of King Přemysl Ottokar II, also called the King of Iron and Gold. He expanded the area of the Czech kingdom into today's Austria and Slovenia but finally was defeated by Rudolf von Habsburg. During the reign of Charles IV in the middle of the fourteenth century, Prague grew into one of the most important cities in Europe. Charles University was founded in 1348 and construction of Charles Bridge was begun.

The priest and also rector of Charles University, Jan Hus (1369–1415) became highly important in Czech history. Hus preached against extreme wealth, corruption and hierarchical tendencies (e.g. that nobles are better than common people). His martyrdom sparked a religious as much as a nationalistic rebellion centred in Bohemia. On 6 July 1415, Hus was burned at the stake in Constance (in today's Switzerland). His enormous influence sparked the Husite Wars (1419–39) under commander Jan Žižka. Interestingly, the Husite era was an age of great nationalism and of broad universal education: everyone, every peasant, could read and write. No other nation at that time was so well educated! An important educator in Czech and European history, and a renowned reformer of education, was the theologian Jan Amos Komenský (1592–1670).

In the battle of Bila Hora (White Mountain, 1620) the Czechs lost to the Imperial Austrian Army and Catholic mercenaries who then forced most of the Czech nobility and educated classes to leave their country. Twenty-seven Czech noblemen were assassinated. This critical event in Czech history started a 300-year long Habsburg reign in which the German heritage dominated the Czech Crown Lands.

It was only at the end of the nineteenth century that a huge wave of resistance developed that affected the whole country. The Czech people built their national theatre (begun in 1868) from the donations of the ordinary people from all towns and villages. The omnipresent aspiration and drive to liberation and assertion became apparent, as exemplified by the fact that after a fire destroyed large parts of the theatre, further donations were collected to ensure that construction work could be completed in 1883. The reputation of Czech culture was fortified by this event.

The dissolution of the monarchy in 1918 after World War I meant the liberation and foundation of a Czech state in union with Slovakia. The first Czech president, Tomáš Garrigue Masaryk (1850–1937), was a highly respected and influential European politician. Famous composers of that time were, for example, Bedřich Smetana and Antonín Dvořák, a most famous painter was Mikuláš Aleš. Karel Čapek's stories are considered classics of Czech literature.

After Masaryk's death the Munich Agreement ceded a large area of Bohemia and Moravia, the Sudetenland, to Nazi Germany which then also took over the remaining Czech lands. After the head of these lands had been assassinated, the Nazis exterminated two villages. In 1945 Czechoslovakia was liberated by the Russians from the east and the Americans from the west. Most people of German background were expelled to Germany. In 1948 the Czechoslovak Communist Party seized government power. The Warsaw Pact armies invaded the country to end the 'Prague Spring' resistance movement and increase Soviet pressure. Up to 800,000 people left Czechoslovakia. After 31 years, the Velvet Revolution startled the world: the communist government resigned and dissident playwright Václav Havel was appointed president. Due to too many differences and a wish for more freedom, in 1993 the federated republic peacefully separated into the Czech Republic and the Slovak Republic.

Values

What effects did this long struggle have on the people? Would the Czechs have survived at all without their stubbornness? What did the fears later in World War II leave behind?

As a very young child, Ladislav witnessed some of the struggles. He recollects: 'When I was three years old, the village Ležáky in the neighborhood of my town was extinguished by German soldiers. What fears my mother must have had because my father knew quite a bit about the *Partyzans*!'

And what effect did the communist era have on the psychic condition of the people? For several more years there was much fear. This was caused by extensive imprisonment, fines, local spying and threats. People's resistance became apparent in the hidden criticism of the political system, the envy and the dreams. However, the creative and entrepreneurial power of the populace remained and continues to blossom in the new world that is promising, although not void of, problems. We have the impression that education tends to have a particularly high value for Czech people, and seems to be deeply ingrained. As Renate's mother used to say: 'They can take away everything from you, but they can't take away what you have in your head.'

Coming to a more western state: a personal perspective

Ladislav

It might be interesting to complement the above historical data with my personal perceptions and feelings upon having entered western ground, although inevitably this tends to be very particular and subjective. It is not easy, of course, to leave one's family and everything behind. However, for me the opportunity to go to Austria for one year arose and I felt that I wanted to go. This step was courageous since I didn't feel I wanted to go back. I didn't even dare to think that if I didn't manage to get married in Austria, thus securing a right to remain there, I wouldn't see my children, mother, grandmother and sister any more – for ever. After having stayed in Austria for one year, I dared to travel back to get a 'renewed permission' visa to leave the country for 10 months. While there, I saw my children and my relatives. However, when I returned to Austria I had nightmares for several months. I was in a daze, waiting and waiting for the next 'permission' that had been promised but never arrived. I felt like I was pinned down by circumstances beyond my control. Eight years then elapsed, a time in which I had to understand that I might never see my family ever again. I also feared that something might happen to me that would harm my family.

Despite desiring it, I also didn't feel as good in Austria as one might imagine. In the first years I was anxious — I no longer formally had a homeland. Life was very hard. I had to learn the language, had to pass the exam allowing me to study at the university and, of course, I needed to work. Once, as a driver, I delivered a package to the Vienna University of Economy. I immediately knew that I wanted to study there. I never really felt like a foreigner, although I knew that without support it would be almost impossible to completely achieve a sense of complete settlement in the new society. I knew acquisition of the new language was important so I deliberately interrupted my contacts with Czech people to ensure continuous practice in German. Subsequently I achieved academic success. This process consumed lots of time and for some years I didn't progress in my job, but now I think it was worth it. The final years of my studies were hard to finance but, term after term, I was happy to make progress. At the end I had money only for one or two more months but then I found a job and everything was rescued. Apparently, my unconscious motto was, and still is: 'Don't give up'.

The feeling during the first years was like being a caged bird. It required too much effort to really integrate myself and establish new relationships – and I wasn't used to this. However, time allowed me to collect and learn from various experiences in several jobs and also to experience and know myself more – and this was what I continued doing during my studies, in groups, and during my training as a counsellor and psychotherapist. It was a path of stepping out of my personal naivety and inexperience, out of the darkness of the political and economic system of the communist East. One of the milestones of my experience was my study. Not only that I had to relearn how to learn, at the university I also entered other worlds and got to know people who were much more tolerant and free in their relationships to each other than I had known before.

After the Velvet Revolution, when the way back was open again, I encountered a hard but equally wonderful task: the encounter with my children who, in the meantime, had grown to adulthood. Fear and uncertainty resided in me – how would they receive me? – and at the same time I felt the desire for encounter and a new relationship.

When asked what it means for me to have two 'homes' I believe that in Austria I feel at home and more free, but when I travel to the Czech Republic I say: 'I drive home'. I love both countries and people, here and there. In the Czech Republic I feel more warmth and I have my children there, my friends from school and from my second study (of psychology), but in my new home country I'm now *really* at home.

Renate

Let me share my story in order to allow readers to understand the context accompanying my experience of having moved from the Czech Republic to a more western state – Austria. More precisely, rather than 'having moved' I should say 'having *been* moved', since, to me, this is a big difference. Making the move from one home-base to another, culturally and linguistically different, one, even if it is quite close, means a major change. Whether this change is self-chosen or in some way imposed by parents, partners or regimes is a key issue in particular in the initial period and may even be decisive in whether the new home-base is predominantly accepted or rejected. In other words, self-determination or determination from some external force tends to have an enormous influence on how a person feels in their new environment.

I was born in the Czech Republic (former Czechoslovakia) and went there to kindergarten. I spoke only Czech in my first six years. At the age of 6 (in 1966), right before entering school, my mother moved to Vienna, Austria. She took me with her and we joined her father who had stayed there since before World War II. I attended a private Czech bilingual elementary school, then transferred to an Austrian grammar school, graduated from the University of Technology in Vienna and currently hold a professorship at that same university.

My husband, Herbert, doesn't speak Czech, but being of both Austrian and Slovenian origin, hearing a Slavic language isn't anything unusual for him. Our two sons were raised bilingually (German and Czech). They attended the same Czech bilingual elementary school as I did, even if taking them there meant crossing half the city.

After having lived in Vienna for about a year my mother asked me whether I wanted to go back. I replied: 'Yes, I'd *immediately* go back. But in any case, I want to stay *with you*, so I'll stay in the place where you'll be staying.' So I stayed in Vienna, but travelled back home quite often. From age 8 onward, I used to travel to Ostrava on my own, even though I needed to take the night train to get there.

Interestingly, the higher living standard in Austria was not an incentive for me to prefer the West. It was the social environment that encouraged me to travel to Ostrava. My cousins were closer friends than my schoolmates from the Austrian grammar school who, in my perception, seemed not really to engage, either in learning or in real friendships. School life at secondary level felt quite shallow, with fewer highs and lows than in primary (bilingual) education. Visits to the Czech Republic gave me, and still give me, energy, and I also like to return to Vienna, where my current 'centre of being' is located.

Although, logically and most evidently, I should be happy to have more opportunities in my life and career due to having been brought to the West, I view this as just one side of the coin. I see and feel this side more strongly now that I can 'give back' something to the people I had left and can see all my experiences mainly as broadening my perspective. Still, the aspect of also having lost something is, slightly but perceivably, present in me. Part of it is that I lost much continuity and contact with several members of my family. Another part that I have often puzzled about has to do with language. I feel that my chronologically first language is not the one in which I can express myself most fully. At times I am frustrated by not finding the fullest expression in the language that I resonate with most deeply. I enjoy using every opportunity to improve my Czech but also my English, since it opens up bridges to the world, to other cultures that can be experienced and explored.

Having two 'homes' makes me feel like belonging to each of the cultures to a large degree, but equally to neither of them completely. For example, I perceive that in formal meetings I may say something that causes puzzlement or I don't find jokes really amusing. However, I believe that I can connect faster and better to persons coming from various different cultures. This may be due to my 'mixed' culture but I think that it also has another reason: my personal choice of an approach to life and relationships that is based on Carl Rogers' person-centred approach (PCA). I owe to it much of my understanding and positive valuing of experience that I perceive as deeply enriching and energizing. It is my third 'home', so to speak, the home of my conscious choice that transcends cultural heritages. I am deeply thankful to Rogers for this most significant, cross-cultural heritage, expressed in a language to which I feel I can connect profoundly.

A most enriching experience was when Ladislav invited me to co-facilitate a small group with his Czech students in 2003, and this is described in the next section.

The authors' experiences with people with Eastern and Central European origins in groups and psychotherapy

Some of the students of Ladislav's self-experience-based class on person-centred counselling at the Masaryk University wanted their encounter group (Rogers 1970) to continue. So I (LN) offered to facilitate it if they organized it. About 15 people met at a small hut in the countryside for an extended weekend. Students shared a lot about their experiences as working students in Britain and the USA, about their families and the mostly authoritarian school system with often little place for the person to develop in their own way. This experience offered us an intensive immersion into our roots and showed Renate that it had not just been rosy things that she had missed when she left. She still felt a deep contact and, given the new political situation in Europe, was happy to realize that it was her decision in which state she would spend her future.

This experience, like several others, strengthened Renate's devotion to the PCA as an approach to transcend cultures (Lago and MacMillan 1999). Let us illustrate this with a quote from a Bosnian encounter group participant who had to overcome hard challenges upon coming to Austria: 'Most of all I liked to get to know colleagues from different countries. I loved hearing your experiences, opinions, struggles, and to understand you!' Interestingly, most students, national and international, tend to feel enriched by a person-centred way of being in groups, as they acknowledge in their responses and numerous written reactions.

My experiences (LN) with people from Eastern European countries are as diverse as with people from other origins. The young generation hears about the practices of the era behind the Iron Curtain as more than just stories. The older people are sometimes quite bitter and anchored in a self-pity and a one-sided view. I need to mention that often it was not easy for me to encounter clients who voiced their hatred against the old regime since I felt their devaluing attitude was directed against everybody. This attitude, ironically, is more frequently expressed by those who were never really involved in the former political system.

Whenever I perceived some differences, they lay in the vitality, the liveliness and in the way children were raised – in a sense mirroring the relationship be-tween children and parents. In some people I perceived a high level of liveliness and at the same time a lot of stubbornness, inner inflexibility and an urge for solutions as well as an inclination to friendship and conversation. I find that in accepting such persons in therapy a few interviews suffice to open up the doors to change.

Reflecting on Czech culture from the perspective of cultural dimensions and world values

In the following we refer to two studies on intercultural differences: Hofstede's cultural dimensions (Hofstede and Hofstede 2005) and the World Value Survey (Inglehard and Welzel 2005). While the former is based on data stemming pri-marily from a business context, the World Value Survey was designed to provide a comprehensive account of all major areas of human concern, from religion to politics to economic and social life.

Hofstede found that four cultural dimensions, namely power distance, uncer-tainty avoidance, individualism and masculinity, throw light on essential cultural differences between nations.[1] The *power distance index* (PDI) represents inequality. It is the extent to which the less powerful members of organizations and institu-tions (including the family) accept and expect that power is distributed unequally – According to Hofstede's estimates, the PDI is higher in the Czech Republic than in the UK and Austria. We believe that the long communist regime during which the Communist Party ruled the nation significantly contributed to the perceivably higher inequality between people. The Communists had power over almost any-thing; a 'wrong' word or action in the 1950s could mean that you were imprisoned, lost your job, etc. Not belonging to the Party made it hard to be admitted for stud-ies, and people had no choice but to depend on the regime. This contributed to people expecting to be told what they should do, and of course what they should *not* do. We consider that, even now, teachers as well as parents tend to be more

---

[1]Hofstede collected data in 50 states before 2001. From that time on the studies have been complemented. Since survey data for the Czech Republic do not exist, the discussion in this section is based on estimated values derived from Hofstede's web page: www.geert-hofstede.com/hofstede/dimensions.

authoritarian in their attitudes. Not surprisingly, the response of those with less power was to be critical and also not to expect to be supported to find their own, creative paths. No wonder Ladislav has described his feeling when returning to Austria as 'I feel more free'.

The *uncertainty avoidance index* (UAI) deals with a society's tolerance for uncertainty and ambiguity. It indicates to what extent a culture programmes its members to feel either uncomfortable or comfortable in unstructured situations which are novel, unknown, surprising and uncommon. Uncertainty-avoiding cultures try to minimize the possibility of such situations via strict laws, rules and safety measures. On the philosophical and religious level they tend to search for and believe in absolute truth, being more emotional, and motivated by inner nervous energy. Contrarily, uncertainty-accepting cultures tend to be more tolerant of different opinions and try to have as few rules as possible. On the philosophical and religious level they allow many currents to flow side by side, being more contemplative and not so demonstrative emotionally.

The UAI is higher in the Czech Republic than in the UK and Austria, as is evident from the history of the Czech nation. Czech people had to fight, had to be better, superior, in order to overcome suppression and even to survive. This may have led to higher motivation for education in order to find the truth, dominate in knowledge and (re)gain power. Parents and teachers are more 'motivated' to show their youngsters the right way, so as to protect them from getting lost and to guide them by exhorting and correcting them more frequently and insistently than the more tolerant western parents tend to do.

Undoubtedly, the communist regime with its planned economy, strict laws and regulations replacing trust, explains the higher UAI index of the Czech nation. The Czech, in our perception, are more anxious to move on, more direct and less patient than western nations. Perhaps it should also be said that the stricter the rules, the more 'satisfaction' may be felt in succeeding to circumvent these artificial constructs thus being more self-directed and less oppressed. Renate believes that Ladislav's personal perception derives from his therapeutic experience, and his description of the Czech as having a tendency to 'more vitality as well as stubbornness and criticality' is very apposite.

Interestingly, before the opening of the borders, the Czech tended to describe 'westerners' as people for whom 'baked turtles fly into their mouths', meaning they didn't need to work hard and got results for free. However, once Czech people were free to travel to the West they realized that prosperity doesn't come for free but requires hard work coupled with the ability to take responsibility, initiative and risk.

Individualism (IDV) versus collectivism describes the degree to which individuals are integrated into groups. In individualist societies everyone is expected to look after him or herself and his or her immediate family, whereas in collectivist nations people are integrated into strong, cohesive 'in-group's. Individualism is estimated to be lower in the Czech Republic than in the UK and we believe that individualism is somewhat higher in Austria than in the Czech Republic. This becomes apparent, for example, in the labels that Austrians and Eastern European people use to call the other: for the Polish, Austrian are 'chestnuts' – closed in their shell and stinking when you want to get inside. Complementarily, some Austrians refer to people from south-eastern Europe as *Tschuschn*, negatively noting their origins from poorer countries. Also, if a Czech person speaks German with a specific accent, they are called *boehmakeln* with a deprecative tone, a 'bohemian'.

We are convinced about the essential importance of 'cultural mediators', i.e. people who open up the way for others into their society. Coming from elsewhere you lose or break up your original 'collectives' and need to find and become part of new ones in order to satisfy your relational needs, regardless of their particular strength. For this to work, the knowledge of the language matters crucially – it is the linguistic mediator to the new culture. Interestingly, the Czech, as a small nation, have realized this importance and not only value knowledge of languages particularly highly but also tend to be highly motivated towards language-learning. At the same time, retaining your own language is also important in order to stay connected with your 'native collectives', something that we perceive as enriching, energizing and supportive of one's sense of identity.

In the our view, interpersonal distance and courteousness (or politeness) are more highly valued in Austria, though Austrians may be judged to be overly formal by outsiders, while Czech people seem to be more straightforward and direct, though sometimes this may be perceived as more rude!

Masculinity (MAS) versus its opposite, femininity, refers to the distribution of roles between the genders. MAS is lower in the Czech Republic than in the UK and Austria. We believe that this goes back to the communist regime in which everybody had the duty to work, regardless of being male or female. In fact, Renate feels a smaller gap between male and female in the work context in the Czech Republic, feeling 'more inside the mainstream, less special, more accepted as an equal partner'.

The World Value Survey

The World Value Survey by Inglehart and Welzel (2005) covers 90 societies in all major regions worldwide from 1981 to 2007. The Czech nation is situated in the upper right square, meaning that secular/rational values precede traditional and religious ones, and self-expression is valued more strongly than survival. In the dimension of traditional versus secular/rational values the Czech figure more on the rational side than both the UK and Austria. Again, the influence of the communist regime on the Czech is visible in this dimension. On the dimension of survival versus self-expression both the UK and Austria are recognized as more self-expressive than the Czech Republic. Hence, considering the worldwide trend towards rational values and self-expression (Inglehart and Welzel 2005), the Czech nation can be seen as follows: it is still further away from self-expression than the UK and Austria; however, regarding valuing secular/rational values it is ahead of the UK and Austria. All this confirms what we believe: 'It is desirable to significantly learn from each other'.

Conclusion

In this chapter we have shared our subjective feelings, meanings and observations on coming from the Czech Republic to a more western state, Austria. Although we included some experiences with people from neighbouring Eastern European states we are aware that this is an inadequate way to describe Eastern European heritage. However, at the same time it seemed the most appropriate way to write this short chapter. This is because we believe that the kind of complex, 'fuzzy knowledge' that reveals something *from* rather than just *about* cultural heritage comes more from within than from outside. For readers who want to learn more about the Czech and Slovak nations we refer to an insightful English book called *The Little Czech and the Great Czech Nation* (Holý 1996).

We honestly hope that our writing doesn't distract you from your immediate, genuine experience with the other person. We appreciate your interest in our heritage and personal stories and hope they bring something to you that will facilitate your understanding of people who might share some of the background and values that we have tried to capture. On a more implicit level, the style we were free to choose and the words we used might well communicate something about our Czech roots, our growing up in a German-speaking country, and our having discovered the PCA as a most desirable way of (transcultural) being. The writing of this chapter was a most valuable and touching experience for which we sincerely thank the editor! As parts or members of our nation we feel respected by your attention to our roots. If you want to drop us a line we'd be happy to learn about the ways this article may have influenced your being with Eastern European people. Contact us at: renate.motschnig@univie.ac.at and nykl.psychotherapie@aon.at.

References

Hofstede, G. and Hofstede G.J. (2005) *Cultures and Organizations: Software of the Mind*, 2nd edn. Maidenhead: McGraw-Hill.

Holý, L. (1996) *The Little Czech and the Great Czech Nation: National Identity and the Post-Communist Social Transformation*. Cambridge: Cambridge University Press.

Inglehart, R. and Welzel, C. (2005) *Modernization, Cultural Change and Democracy*. New York: Cambridge University Press.

Lago, C. and MacMillan, M. (eds) (1999) *Experiences in Relatedness: Groupwork and the Person-Centred Approach*. Ross-on-Wye: PCCS Books.

Rogers, C.R. (1961) *On Becoming a Person: A Psychotherapist's View of Psychotherapy*. London: Constable.

Rogers, C.R. (1970) *Carl Rogers on Encounter Groups*. New York: Harper & Row.

Smekal, V., Gray, H. and Lewis, C.A. (eds) (2003) *Together We Will Learn – Ethnic Minorities and Education*. Brno: Barrister & Principal.

23 The effects of an Irish heritage

Seamus Nash

Irishmen . . . respect no laws at all . . . though this may be socially deplorable it is humanly admirable, and makes life much more tolerable, and charitable, and easy-going and entertaining.

(O'Faolain 1956)

Introduction

This chapter considers the effects of an Irish upbringing and the impact my heritage has had on me as a person-centred psychotherapist. Following in the footsteps of Carl Rogers I write in a personal manner, as this chapter gives a personal account of the effects of my heritage. With this in mind I am reminded that 'it is in the meeting of people who are strangers that friendship begins', to paraphrase an old Irish proverb.

I am 'Irish'. My 'Irishness' is unique to me. It is not my intention to imply that 'Irishness' is uniform for all persons who describe their cultural heritage as such. I am simply reporting my own phenomenological experiencing of how my upbringing has shaped and impacted on my views of what my Irish heritage is, which in turn has influenced me as a person and as a clinician. My reflections may thus be 'shared' by others, added to and qualified, and if a common ground is achieved, that, it strikes me, is a satisfactory and encouraging position. Following on from my consideration of different aspects of my cultural heritage I have included additional sections devoted to amplifying the effects these have had upon me.

Autobiography

I was born on 18 April 1966 in Derry, in the north of Ireland at a time when there was a growing civil rights movement. I grew up in a Roman Catholic family. It is commonplace now to talk of two 'traditions' within northern Irish society — the Roman Catholic and the Protestant tradition. Often within the British media, Catholics are referred to as 'nationalists' or 'republicans' and are regarded as sympathetic to the creation of an all-Irish state. Catholics see themselves as Irish. The Protestant tradition is referred to as 'unionist' or 'loyalist', favouring the continued union with Britain. Protestants see themselves as British. These views are reflected in the name of my home town: Derry or Londonderry. This simplistic view of the conflict and history is extremely reductionist and does not take into account 'actual realities'.

Darby (1995) and Fitzduff and O'Hagan (2009) both outline the history of this period in a concise manner. Darby notes that the civil rights movement had considerable successes by the end of 1970, yet the local administration, unable to manage the civil disturbances, deployed British troops in August 1969. The Provisional Irish Republican Army (PIRA), which had largely been dormant, came to prominence as a result of a lack of impartiality of the British government and British army coupled with the growing realization among many Catholic shades of opinion that the situation faced by the minority was not improving.

The single most prominent event to swell the ranks of the PIRA was that known as 'Bloody Sunday' which happened on 30 January 1972. The Saville Inquiry, which concluded in June 2010, has found that those who were killed on that day were 'not guilty' and hopefully this will pave the way for further peace and reconciliation. It is not an exaggeration to write that this atrocity remains vital in the minds of the Catholic/nationalist community *and* it may be fair to state that the impact of Bloody Sunday has left a significant scar on *all* within the communities of the north of Ireland.

I am the eldest of six – my identical twin brother died a few hours after our birth. I have two brothers and two sisters. My father was a dock worker, incapacitated by an accident, and my mother looked after my family until she took a job as a house-person for a dentist. My mother still works. She and my father have always attended Mass daily and we were 'brought up' as practising Roman Catholics. My father's political opinion I would describe as 'socialist': he was actively involved in the Northern Ireland civil rights movement and was an active community welfare worker. I feel I inherit their keen sense of fair play, justice and service which is my own 'moral compass'. I have been exposed to politics since my birth and have lived through bombs, bullets, death and chaos, as have a lot of my family and friends. A mural on a wall early in the seventies at home read: 'Is there a life before death?' and I have pondered that many times – as I have come from a community that was incredibly poor, oppressed and terrorized.

It was always impressed upon me and my friends that education was the 'way out': education is valued and great emphasis is placed upon learning and literacy. I was educated in both a Catholic primary and secondary school and later left home to join a Roman Catholic religious community, as a monk, through which I completed my initial stages of university education. I left the Church to pursue a career in social work, counselling and psychotherapy. Currently I am a doctoral student researching person-centred psychotherapy.

Irishness

I am from the ancient kingdom or 'province' of 'Ulster' or *Uladh*, in Gaelic. There are four 'provinces' in Ireland: Ulster, Munster, Leinster and Connaught, each with their own traditions, variations on Gaelic (Irish language), sports and customs. Ireland is divided into two regions by government: the six county states of 'Northern Ireland' which is governed by Westminster and the 26-county 'Republic of Ireland' governed by the Irish *Dail*, based in Dublin. I am, indeed, an Ulsterman, and I share with my Protestant neighbours the proud history of Ulster, their love of a wider 'Gaelic' culture, sense of reverence for spiritual matters and loyalty to family and culture.

Traditionally, the government of the Irish Republic or 'Eire' recognized the full 32 counties and had articles of the Irish Constitution claiming sovereignty; however, these articles were ceded when the Good Friday Agreement was accepted in 1998. I grew up feeling and thinking I was 'Irish', and that my Protestant neighbours were British. In reality I was classified officially as a 'British subject'. I felt the 'Free State', as we referred to the Irish Republic, did not want 'us'. I shared a common opinion that somehow we in the 'north' were less 'Irish' than the 'Irish' in the south. I now reside in West Yorkshire and Irish people in Britain constitute the biggest ethnic minority community.

Irish culture

Culture, language, music, art and literature are often described as the 'backbone' of a culture (Sue and Sue 1990; Lago and Thompson 1996). Kerr (1996: 1) writes that 'language, history and typography, these are probably our defining characteristics, we are a parochial people and we believe we are different'. Kerr believes these aspects actually enable the communities in the north of Ireland to 'talk' to each other.

I was exposed to Gaelic language, music and literature from an early age. Gaelic
Irish culture prides itself on being informal, attempting to provide a sense of easiness, generosity, reciprocity and informality; people are addressed by their first names, strangers are welcomed, food and drink are shared, and these 'levelling mechanisms' are commonplace. There may well be an anarchic quality to Irish culture with its fierce informality, yet I have often felt that, upon reflection, I see and experience within my culture a valuing of not taking anything at face value, of irony, scepticism regarding social hierarchies and of any person taking themselves or life 'too seriously'.

I was exposed to Gaelic language, music and literature from an early age. Gaelic is a Celtic language (Indo-European) and part of the Goidelic branch of insular Celtic. Although I am not fluent in Irish Gaelic, I can understand, read and converse to a satisfactory level. There is a growing recognition within the communities in the north of Ireland of 'Ulster Scots', a dialect that sections of the Protestant community employ. (Ulster Scots is a variant of Scots, the language used by Robert Burns in many of his poems. It is Germanic in origin and different from Scottish Gaelic.) I am pleased that Gaelic, in whatever form, is being spoken as it is an ancient language that is now shared in each of the 'traditions' in the north of Ireland and may be seen as a common cause for celebration, creativity and dialogue. In recent years a divergence has occurred, again, with both communities feeling the strain of power-sharing resulting from the new political system now established in the north.

Effects

Fennell (1986: 396) writes that:

> the national image, in its full development, showed Ireland as an ancient, virtuously rural, self-sufficient nation, democratic and republican in its politics, comprising (in all but political fact) all the inhabitants of the island, and scattered widely beyond seas and oceans; an anti-imperialist and neutral nation, with a long history of freedom struggle; Gaelic essentially, and engaged in reviving its Gaelic language, while in the interim speaking English, Catholic... but proudly including Protestants and Jews.

I am, however, the product of my specific history, specific values and behaviour patterns formed living within an Irish culture which has allowed me to expand and redefine my own unique Irish identity and to purge myself of the sequaelae of orthodox Catholicism. Not an easy task.

British media representation

Great damage has been done by the British media over the years with regard to both traditions within the north of Ireland. Many of my English friends had no idea of what was taking place a few hundred miles from their own homes, across the water, in the north. Yet to reduce the past conflict and the current situation to religious or identity concerns only was and is simplistic and misleading. To label the conflict in the north of Ireland as 'The Troubles' many felt was reductionist and irresponsible, playing into fears and prejudices. This was construed by many within my own community as British propaganda and many also felt the *British* media were primarily interested in cultivating and reporting stories that portrayed the PIRA or our community's cause as sectarian and separatist, which was inaccurate. I encourage readers, if interested, to peruse the CAIN website at the University of Ulster (http://cain.ulst.ac.uk). I grew up knowing that the SAS, more often than 'ordinary' soldiers, were patrolling my estate, that my community was systematically discriminated against and that both my parents had taken part in civil rights marches at Burntollet and Magilligan Strand, had been on Craigavon Bridge when the Royal Ulster Constabulary attacked an early march there and indeed had been present at the 'Battle of the Bogside' and 'Bloody Sunday'.

Effects

The picture that has been painted of my community externally, and more so internally, has been a major issue for me growing up in the north of Ireland. I have lived with a sense of not being wanted by either Eire or Britain, I have grown up in a society that was torn asunder, labelled as 'extreme' in its religious and political views, and portrayed as inflexible, discriminatory and extreme or even backward by the British media (Curtis 1984). However, despite the horror and propaganda of these political and media attributes and dynamics I take very human and spiritual values from my Irish heritage. I now outline the various aspects of that heritage and how they have impinged and formed/informed the person I have become.

Family and community

Irish culture is built around the family: both nuclear and extended. From an early age I was taught to respect authority – that meant my mother, father and significant others. Children are welcomed, perceived as a 'blessing' and completely 'doted' on. Older people are viewed as wise and knowledgeable and have many things to offer. Respect is paramount – for people, animals, nature and self. Neighbours, friends and the wider community are important. I grew up in a city estate feeling that everyone 'knew' my business, and therefore if I 'dobbed off' (didn't attend school) someone would indeed report back to my parents (I never did). Cultural distinctions are recognized between urban and rural areas: a common term for a 'countryman' when I was young was *culchie*. Travellers were also looked upon with suspicion then, though this is difficult to generalize because travellers are a recognized minority in their own right and my tradition often sought to give sanctuary to them.

Humour, literacy and verbal acuity are valued, social boundaries are more drawn invisibly, and there are few rules to govern social interaction – only respect. Sarcasm and wit are used when a person strays into antisocial behaviour, which is not tolerated.

Effects

I am a confluence of my parents, my community and my peers. Peter Schmid (1993) resonates with me and thus captures and reflects these aspects of my heritage accurately in his concept of the 'fundamental We'. I am brought forth as an individual by a union from hence I spring: 'none of us came to us from the outside; everyone was born within and into this We' (Schmid 1993: 110). Schmid explains that this 'We' includes our history and culture: 'it is not an undifferentiated mass, nor is it an accumulation of "Me's"; it includes commonality *and* difference, valuing both equally. Only a common esteem for diversity constitutes and accepts a "We" (p. 111). Although there was no formal 'rite of passage' the closest I came to any such rite was my Confirmation service which marked my passage into secondary school.

Community was about 'blood relationship' or *Gemeinschaft* as Tonnies (1967) described it. The family enshrines the ultimate solidifying principle and the three pillars of blood, place/land and mind are essential to this espousal of community. Custom, folk-ways and religion are integral to community, as the reader will see.

Gaelic

The Gaelic language reflects the Irish tension between the individual and the communal. For instance, *ta uchrais orm* means literally 'there is hunger upon me'. A thing is not 'possessed' by a person or a community – ownership is a material as well as a spiritual issue, reminding us that even in deeply human matters a power other than oneself may be in operation. In learning the Gaelic language at school I was opened up to a new understanding of what it meant to live in a community. I met the spiritual, which was fascinating and peaceful, and pointed to the deeply human dimension of living as an individual within a community, and of the community living within the individual. This mirrors work that has been produced and developed by Peter Schmid within the person-centred and experiential tradition.

Resistance

There is a long history of modern Irish uprisings/revolutions, notably those of 1798, then 1803, 1848, 1867 and 1916. Leaders of these rebellions were both Catholic and Protestant. Eire was finally created after the War of Independence of 1919–22 which established the IRA – the Irish Republican Army – as a formidable guerrilla force which succeeded in forcing the British government of the time to the negotiating table. The Irish Civil War was a response to the treaty that led to the creation of the northern Irish 'statelet' and partition of Ireland.

The 'spirit of freedom' as Bobby Sands has written, is indelibly marked in the Irish psyche and character, as is a deep desire for unity and peace.

Effects

A close friend of mine invited another friend and myself to a fireworks party. We had all grown up together and my friend had just moved to a new house. This was around 1990. We all gathered for the party and the fireworks began. The two of us who had been invited had never been to a 'proper' fireworks party, had neither seen nor heard fireworks being ignited. They sounded like bullets. My friend and I dived to the ground while all the other guests remained standing. It was embarrassing yet from that incident my friend and I realized that as we had grown up during a war, we did not have a 'normal' childhood experience. Army searches, covert attacks by the PIRA, British army soldiers often on high alert, scared and nervous, always looking at us through the telescopic sight on their guns, abuse, bomb explosions, curfews. This was my childhood. To this day I hate being searched, asked my name or having to answer security questions at airports. My heritage and upbringing in a time of war have had lasting effects.

Folklore

Readers may be familiar with the 'leprechaun': 'fairy folk' (*sidhe* in Gaelic) and the banshee (*bean sidhe* – fairy woman). O'Hogain (1991) has collected these myths and legends in great detail. These are part of my cultural upbringing and Irish heritage. Folklore and the telling of stories are integral to the Irish/Celtic imagination. The great Ulster Cycle – The Cattle Raid of Cooley (*Tain Bo Cuailgne*), Cuchulainn, The Red Branch, Fionn MacCumhaill and the Fianna are central to my heritage. These tales often mirror the struggle which happens in life – to remain committed and free, to face challenges – and they contain great wisdom. My folklore heritage inspired me to face challenges with self-assurance and self-belief. A Celtic warrior never died face down and always remained standing (see the bronze statute of Cuchulainn in the GPO in Dublin). This fired my imagination and search for integrity.

Literature and the arts

Ireland has produced four Nobel laureates in literature. Through school I was exposed to the works of Joyce, Lady Gregory, Wilde, Swift, Bram Stoker (*Dracula*), Shaw, O'Casey and W.B. Yeats. My personal favourites are Samuel Beckett, Brendan Behan and Flann O'Brien, and another County Derry poet, Seamus Heaney. Beckett, particularly, has written one of my favourite pieces in his book *Watt* (1953), entitled 'the poor oul earth':

> if I could begin it all over again knowing what I know now – the result would be the same, and if I could begin it all over again a third time, knowing what I would know then, the result would be the same, and if I could begin it all over a thousand times, knowing each time a little more than the time before, the result would still be the same!

This illustrates the philosophical bent of the Irish personality perfectly.

Effects

This piece, for me, brings into play the existential philosophical roots of my Irish heritage and conveys with ironic sadness and honesty a certain contempt for just 'being'. Irish culture, as with the Irish mind, is, to quote John O'Donohue (1997), 'ontologically friendly': life is accepted, unbroken, equal, not taken as single disjointed events but rather as a flowing, free-form gestalt.

Religion and sprituality

I grew up and inherited much from a Roman Catholic Christian religious background. My Irish heritage is part Catholic and part folk/Celtic and this is central to my core personal, philosophical, political and spiritual beliefs. Irish Celtic Catholicism is heavily influenced by its Celtic-druidic past (Bradley 1993; O'Donohue 1997).

Effects

I have been rediscovering my Celtic spiritual roots and have been reading avidly for the last two years around this area. John O'Donohue has been a major catalyst for me. In *Anam Cara: Spiritual Wisdom from the Celtic World* (1997) I have found solace and grace. O'Donohue writes that the Celtic mind was neither discursive nor systematic, the Celts 'lyrically' speculated about the unity of life and experience (p. 15). Importantly, the Celtic mind was 'not burdened by dualism, it did not separate what belonged together' – mind, humanity, nature, divinity, underworld, were all united. All is/was lived at once: temporal and eternal, human and divine, this world–other world. The Celtic mind was a rich texture of otherness, 'ambivalence, symbolism and imagination'. Contradiction and living with opposites and uncertainty with a sense of hope are vital effects of the spiritual aspects of my cultural heritage which I embrace wholeheartedly.

I resonate deeply with these sentiments and apply them in my way of being, seeking to embody them. Bradley (1993: 1–30) writes also of the rich spiritual legacy left by the Celts – for example, environmental friendliness; embracing nature; celebrating the goodness of people and creation, primitive innocence and directness; the circular knot of life and eternity; a strong sense of the supernatural; a sense of the tribal; the importance of the feminine; the sacredness of places – groves, wells, rivers; the importance of art and music; wanderlust; love of autonomy and freedom. In the symbol of the Celtic knot which interweaves the old and the new, I am reminded that you and I are intertwined, interdependent and independent, fully acknowledging the possibilities of human life.

My experience of anti-Irish racism

I am sad to report that I have suffered bouts of anti-Irish racism while living in England. I was arrested and abused verbally in West Ham and held under the Prevention of Terrorism Act. Later, the PIRA exploded incendiary devices in Leeds in 1992–3 and I clearly remember going to the general post office – when I spoke, some customers heard my accent and racially abused me. This also happened when getting a taxi back home with my then partner who was shocked and extremely apologetic. The shock for me was that I was abused by an Asian taxi driver and then some of the other people in the taxi queue!

Curtis (1984) traces the roots of anti-Irish racism and some of the popular words that racism uses to perpetuate the myth that Irish people are violent, drunken or stupid. The word 'Paddy' is often used in Yorkshire, for example, to denote a temper tantrum that a child has. This is directly rooted in the ingrained opinion that Irish people are violent, aggressive and cannot be reasoned with. The phrases 'Paddy-wagon', 'Paddy-whack' and having a 'Paddy' also allude to this. When Irish immigrants flooded into England in the seventeenth, eighteenth and nineteenth centuries they could not speak English, only Gaelic. Hence the 'thick Paddy' moniker that became attributed to Irish people. Sadly, Irish people could not understand English or the social conventions as immigrants at that time. 'No, Irish, no blacks, no dogs' was a common sign greeting the hopeful tenant. Curtis explains that anti-Irish racism often led to increased alcohol consumption among the immigrant Irish to numb the pain of separation from their loved ones and homeland and hence the need for the police to break up drunken disorder ('Paddy-wagon'). Having a 'paddy' was literally resorting to violence to get one's own way by force.

I also marvel when people, often attempting to be friendly, tell me 'Irish' jokes. I know a fair amount of them myself – yet I do wonder if those that tell me Irish jokes do the same to other black and ethnic minority persons!

My heritage and practice of person-centred and experiential psychotherapy

O'Donohue (1997) introduced the notion of the Celtic social construct *Anam Cara*. This was a real and enduring form of relating and relationship in early Irish/Celtic societies – the *anam cara* was a trusted person with whom a person could entrust their innermost 'secrets'. I operationalize my own psychotherapeutic practice based on this construct – that I provide an environment and space within which the person can reveal themselves and their own intimate secrets to me, without fear of judgement. My heritage thus affects my practice in the following ways:

- Its Influence on my personality, world view and values: equality, justice, integrity, respect, tolerance.
- The image of the person – as a relational and as a substantive being. As having inherent dignity, to respect the person's own self-actualizing process and to respect their own life experiences, culture and faith.
- The concept of a 'fundamental We' (Schmid): we spring from the union of our parents, community, family. Likewise for others: 'I am someone elses's Other'. We are all interconnected. For a full exploration see Nash (2006).
- I learn from the client because person-centred and experiential psychotherapy focuses on, affirms, validates and witnesses the clients 'experiencing'. My task is to build a human and emancipatory relationship, working collectively with the client as a 'person'.
- My own conditions of worth: to stand 'up' for my beliefs, faith, culture and also 'for' others' rights: to use what I have received to aid and serve others.

I grew up in a war. A very real war in which I saw human beings destroyed, maimed, hurt. My father once said the war had 'knocked on every door in the north'. I have great empathy for those in war-torn areas, for those fleeing from war and intolerance. I have witnessed what Walter (2009) labels the 'sequestration' of death within this war – dying in the north of Ireland converting death from a human experience into anonymity as a result of the 'authorities' placing an emphasis on *murder* when someone loyal to them was killed (e.g. a police officer was 'murdered'). On a positive note, communities dealt with death in full view, acknowledging the loss, supporting the grieving and engaging in the healing and reconstructing process. My experiences of poverty are similar – grinding and hard. I did sense 'hope' though, and this was communicated by my family and Others' sense of 'faith': things will work out, there are Others 'worse off', and I witnessed great compassion, humility and thankfulness.

Working psychotherapeutically with people of Irish decent

Sue and Sue (1990: 150–8) define the 'cultural implications' of therapy. Therapy with any client from black and ethnic minorities must seek to promote the client's racial/cultural/religious identity and pride, promote the client's internal locus of evaluation and control and understand the client's world view.

The client of Irish heritage will have an awareness of the therapeutic relationship conventions and etiquette – appointment, times, the nature of the relationship context – and will have a firm awareness of how they will have culturally dealt with and characterized their 'problems'. Each person will have, however, their own perceptions of therapy and how they evaluate themselves in relation to their problem-solving. The main barrier of language will be overcome as English will usually be the mediated language unless the Irish person wishes to converse in Gaelic. As an Irish psychotherapist I can claim an 'insider's view' and thus have privileged access and understandings of context and history. Yet I cannot generalize from the individual client to a 'population'.

The following is not an exhaustive list of 'dos and don'ts' but an invitation to be mindful when working with a person of Irish heritage:

- Acknowledgement of anti-Irish racism for both traditions (Catholic and Protestant), the world view of Irish clients and the complexities of both traditions.
- Mental health: Irish people have a high incidence of mental health problems, with suicide rates high among 16–25-year-old men. Women suffer from high rates of depression and hospitalization.
- A new Prevention of Terrorism Act moves towards a focus on terror activities among the immigrant community. This may well lead to suspicion of those of Irish descent and withdrawal of contact by this population.
- Importance of self-concept and family links: garner the client's story and view of self.

- Importance of locus of power: remind yourself of the client's experience of oppression and powerlessness and their views about rules and regulations.
- Importance of spirituality and folklore traditions: therapist respect of these aspects.
- Importance of the supernatural: openness of therapist to the client's experience.
- Therapist held as a person of respect and influence: working in an interrelated and interdependent manner.
- Openness and respect for contradiction and uncertainty.
- Therapist valuing the client's humour.
- Therapist being open to the client's warmth and natural curiosity.

O'Donohue writes that we forget that there is no such thing as empty space. In working with those of Irish heritage and in honour of my heritage and all the effects it has had on me, may we remember this: all space is full of presence, of those of us meeting in the 'now' and those who are in the 'eternal' now: the eternal and the transient world are forever woven in and through each other – *fighte fuaighte*.

Go gcoinne Dia thu

Acknowledgements

I wish to acknowledge the love and care of my mother, Lily, and father, Michael. This has been an emotional piece to write and many people came to 'visit' me. I wish to acknowledge some of them here: Sheila Lewis, RIP, my Uncle John, Aunt Carmel, RIP, Fr Declan Boland and Fr Patsy Arkinson, Paddy Deery, RIP, John Sweeney, RIP, my friends Declan Quigley, Paul Nelis, Liam Mc Laughlin, Paul Doherty and Paul Crumley. In honour of those who died on Bloody Sunday (*Beidh said Linn go deo*) their families who showed tremendous courage and faith to hold out for justice. And last but not least Lisa: *mo anam chara, agus mo chroi*.

Travesties finally arrested, innocence vindicated and promises kept.

References

Beckett, S. (1953) *Watt*. Paris: Olympia Press.
Bradley, I. (1993) *The Celtic Way*. London: Darton, Longman & Todd.
Curtis, L. (1984) *Nothing but the Same Old Story: The Roots of Anti-Irish Racism*. London: GLC.
Darby, J. (1995) Conflict in Northern Ireland: a background essay, in S. Dunn (ed.) *Facets of the Conflict in Northern Ireland*. Basingstoke: Macmillan.
Fennell, D. (1986) Creating a New Irish identity, *Studies: An Irish Quarterly Review*, 75(300): 392–400.

Fitzduff, M. and O'Hagan, L. (2009) *The Northern Ireland Troubles*. An INCORE paper, http://cain.ulst.ac.uk.

Kerr, A. (ed.) (1996) *Perceptions: Cultures in Conflict*. Derry: Guildhall Press.

Lago, C. and Thompson, J. (1996) *Race, Culture and Counselling*. Buckingham: Open University Press.

Nash, S. (2006) Is there a political imperative inherent within the person-centred approach? in G. Proctor, M. Cooper, P. Sanders and B. Malcolm (eds) *Politicising the Person-Centred Approach: An Agenda for Social Change*. Ross-on-Wye: PCCS Books.

O'Donohue, J. (1997) *Anam Cara: Spiritual Wisdom from the Celtic World*. London: Bantam Press:

O'Faolain, S. (1956) *The Irish*. London: Pelican Books.

O'Hogain, D. (1991) *Myth, Legend and Romance: An Encyclopaedia of the Irish Folk Tradition*. New York: Prentice Hall.

Schmid, P. (1993) The characteristics of a person-centred approach to therapy and counselling: criteria for coherence and identity, *Person-Centred and Experiential Psychotherapies*, 2(2): 104–20.

Sue, D. and Sue, D. (1990) *Counselling the Culturally Different: Theory and Practice*. New York: Wiley.

Tonnies, F. (1967) *Community and Society*. East Lansing, MI: Michigan State University Press.

Walter, T. (2009) Jade's dying body: the ultimate reality show, *Sociological Research Online*, 14(5): 1.

24 The effects of a Middle Eastern (Iranian) heritage

Farkhondeh Farsimadan

Introduction

This chapter attempts to demonstrate why it is important for a therapist to learn about the 'other's' culture, experiences and perceptions. Therapists' ability to listen cross-culturally and to have an awareness and understanding of sociocultural factors affecting a client's presentation, interpretations and expression of their presenting problems can be the beginning of the healing process in therapy. Conversely, therapists' failure to understand their client's frame of reference may lead to distortions and/or premature termination.

Although it would be impossible to give a thorough description and an in-depth view/account of Iranian culture and heritage, some basic Iranian cultural characteristics that influence Iranian individuals are described here. Prior knowledge of such characteristics enables western therapists to gain a deeper insight into and a greater understanding of an Iranian client's 'inner world' and frame of reference.

Origins and demography

Iran or Persia (used interchangeably, with the latter being used in historical and cultural contexts and the former in political contexts) is one of the oldest continuous major civilizations of the world alongside India, Egypt and China. The term 'Iran' is a cognate of *Aryan* and means 'Land of the Aryans' (Gill 2007). Iranians are descendants of Indo-European Aryan tribes (Medes and Persians) and arrived on the Iranian plateau at the end of the second millennium BC.

Cyrus the Great, a Persian king, united the Medes and Persians and established the first Persian Empire (Achaemenid: 559–330 BC). After Cyrus, his son Cambyses stretched his father's conquest to Egypt, and after Cambyses, Darius I was declared king and ruled between 522 and 486 BC. Under Cyrus the Great and Darius the Great, the Persian Empire became the most powerful and the largest in human history at the time, circa 500 BC (Shepherd 1923; Hooker 1996). Its borders stretched from the Mediterranean and Black Seas in the west (including Iraq and Turkey) to the Middle East and North Africa (Syria and Egypt), and to the south in

Asia (Afghanistan and the Indus and Oxus rivers). In 334 BC Alexander the Great conquered Iran and throughout history other invaders followed, including Arabs, Mongols and Turks, each influencing Persian culture.

Iran is located in south-western Asia, has an area of 1,648,195 square kilometres (636,372 square miles) and a population of over 70 million. Iran shares its northern border with Armenia, Azerbaijan, Turkmenistan and Uzbekistan; its western border with Turkey and Iraq; its eastern border with Afghanistan and Pakistan, and in the south is bordered by the Persian Gulf and the Gulf of Oman.

Iran is a diverse country comprising various ethnic backgrounds, languages and religions brought together by the Persian culture. The main ethnic group in Iran are Persians who are descendants of Aryan tribes. The other ethnic groups include Azeris, Gilakis and Mazandaranis, Kurds, Lurs, Baluchis, Arabs, Turkmens, Turkic tribal groups (e.g. Qashqai) and non-Persian, non-Turkic groups such as Armenians and Assyrians.

The official language of the country is *Farsi*, or Persian, which is spoken by the majority of the population. Other languages in use are Turkic (spoken by Azeris, Turkmen and the Qashqais), Kurdish, Luri, Arabic and Baluchi.

Religion and spirituality

Indo-European Aryans established Zoroastrianism as the main religion of ancient Iran. Iranians were of the Zoroastrian faith and converted to Islam following the Muslim conquest in the seventh century. Islam is the official state religion with 89 per cent of the population belonging to the 'Twelver' Shi'ite branch of Islam, 9 per cent affiliating to the Sunni branch of Islam and the remaining 2 per cent belonging to non-Muslim religious minority groups including Christians, Zoroastrians, Jews and Baha'i.

The Quran, the holy book of Islam, guides Muslims to five basic obligations that are known as the 'Five Pillars of Islam'. In order to live a good and responsible life, every Muslim must practise all five obligations. These are: 1) *Shahadah*, which is believing in and reciting the words, 'There is no God except Allah, and Mohammad is the messenger of Allah'; 2) *Salat*, which is praying five times a day; 3) *Zakat*, which is paying a fixed amount of your income to charity on a yearly basis; 4) *Sawm*, or fasting, during the month of Ramadan; 5) *Hajj*, or a pilgrimage to Mecca once in your life, if you can afford it.

Worldwide, Twelver Shi'ites are the second largest sect within Islam. The majority of Muslims worldwide are Sunni, except in Iran, Iraq and parts of India, where Shi'ism is more prevalent. The Shi'ite sect of Islam was established following the death of the Prophet Mohammad in AD 632 over a dispute for religious leadership. The Shi'ites believe that Mohammed appointed his son-in-law and cousin, Imam Ali (a divinely guided leader) as his successor and the rightful heir to the caliphate (leadership of the religion) in his farewell pilgrimage. The Sunnis, however, dispute this and regard Imam Ali as the *fourth* caliph following on from Abu Bakr, Umar and Uthman.

Shi'ites believe that the caliphate should pass down to descendants of the Prophet Mohammad, *Ahlul-Bayt* or 'people of the house'; hence, Ali and his 11 descendants were regarded as religious leaders in the seventh, eighth and ninth centuries. Shi'ites believe that the twelfth Imam, Mahdi, did not die but is concealed and one day will return to earth to establish peace.

Shi'ism is a highly emotional and mystical form of Islam and focuses on the life of the 12 Imams, 11 of whom were martyred (e.g. assassinated, poisoned or beheaded) for their causes. In Iran there are public holidays to mourn for the martyred Imams. To weep and mourn for them is considered highly commendable and reminds Shi'ites of the pain and horrors that the martyrs went through.

Pilgrimage to the shrines of the Imams is very important to Iranians. The most important shrines in Iran are those to the Eighth Imam in Mashhad and his sister in Qom. Daily visits to lesser shrines known as *imamzadehs* honour descendants of the Imams in virtually all towns and villages and are a part of Iranians' daily ritual and spiritual practice. They believe that the Imams and their relatives have power to plead with God on their behalf.

Iran is a very religious country and religious life is largely influenced by Shi'ite customs and rituals which people use as a means of coping with physical and emotional problems and stress, as well as for emotional support and spiritual fulfilment.

Characteristics of the Iranian national heritage

Iranians are an ethnically heterogeneous group and given the regional and ethnic diversity any collective profile has a very limited applicability (Banuazizi 1977). Nevertheless, some of the personal and national characteristics reported here have also been reported by many Iranian and non-Iranian researchers.

Iranians historically have been in contact with various cultures and races and throughout history have demonstrated a tolerance towards the 'difference' between themselves and their invaders' race and cultures, from the Greeks with Alexander the Great in the fourth century, to Arab invaders in the seventh century, and on to the Mongols and Genghis Khan in the thirteenth century. Nevertheless, in spite of numerous foreign invasions and internal turmoil, Iranians have managed to retain their uniqueness and their own cultural identity as well as managing to absorb other cultural influences (Jalali 1982).

It would seem that living with uncertainty due to rapidly changing political circumstances throughout history has led to the formation and maintenance of distrust and cynicism among Iranians (Zonis 1976). Mistrust manifests itself in their generalized interpersonal relationships, whereas trusting relationships exist mainly with family members and lifelong friends (Jalali 1982).

Honour and face-saving (*aaberoo*) are important aspects of Iranians' social and interpersonal relationships. The way one conducts oneself in social situations, the way one talks, dresses, eats and drinks, one's mannerisms and with whom one associates are all very important. Embarrassment can be brought to the entire family by an individual's breach of manners. As a result, Iranian social gatherings can be very draining and distressing, as you may be under constant scrutiny, in particular if you are single and female. Children, especially girls, must be polite, respect the authority of older family members (grandparents, aunts/uncles, great aunts/uncles, etc.) and refrain from disgracing the family. For instance, it is unusual for Iranian girls of first generation parents to work as waiters or in bars or clubs where alcoholic drinks are served, or to smoke or drink in the presence of parents and family.

Iranians are generous and hospitable people and *taarof* (to offer) governs the rules of hospitality in the culture. *Taarof* is a cultural obligation for the host, who must put the guest's comfort before their own − for example, by offering the guest their best food even if this means going hungry themselves. The term encompasses a wide range of social behaviours, including the tradition that if the host is offering you food, it is not considered polite to accept in the first instance even if you are starving. You need to wait for the host to offer the food several times before you accept. The host is obliged to offer several times and the guest is obliged to refuse, and this can go on for a while. Thus, as far as *taarof* is concerned, the word 'no' or telling a 'lie' takes a whole different meaning in Iranian culture.

Entertaining others is an important part of Iranian culture and life. Close family members and friends often arrive unannounced and stay until they please. The host's task is to amuse and make the guests comfortable without rushing them away until they choose to leave. Punctuality and time-keeping are concepts which are only loosely adhered to by Iranians.

Iranians refrain from criticizing or embarrassing each other in public, therefore truthfulness may be avoided if it is hurtful (Arasteh 1964). Nevertheless, disagreements tend to be expressed through humour, sarcasm and wit as these are socially acceptable ways of communicating the expression of resentment and releasing tension and aggression, as opposed to the use of outright criticism and argument to settle disagreements and disputes (Jalali 1982).

Iranians put a great deal of effort into their relationships with friends and family and expect a great deal in return. Friendship ties are only second to family ties and the granting of favours is a common norm among Iranian friends, with an expectation of reciprocal treatment in the future.

Iranians tend to be warm, demonstrative people. Expression of emotion is very common between the same sexes but less socially acceptable between a man and a woman in a traditional Iranian family. Expression of emotion between brothers and sisters, fathers and daughters, and mothers and sons is common but tends to be limited to kissing the parent or the elder's forehead or hand.

The family system and interpersonal relationships

The traditional Iranian family unit is patriarchal and the father, as the head of the family, is at the centre of Iranians' social, economic, emotional and spiritual life and in return expects respect and obedience (Jalali 1982). The father has authority over his wife and children whereas the mother's authority is subtle and indirect and often mediates between father and children by softening the father's attitude while encouraging her children to respect his authority when conflict arises (Nyrop 1978). Iranian children are raised to be reliant on their parents and to remain as such throughout their lives. The father often pays for his children's education and the children are expected to live with their families while they are studying and beyond. In return, it is the responsibility of the children to look after their elderly parents.

The traditional Iranian family is based on male supremacy (Behnam 1985). There is a double standard of morality – one set of social mores governs the male and another governs the female, even in modern Iranian society (Touba 1978). Traditionally, Iranian girls are taught to speak and laugh rarely, to be innocent, beautiful and obedient and be good wives and mothers, while Iranian boys are taught to work hard, achieve status, command and protect (Sedghi 1976; Tohidi 1984, 1993). The inequality between genders and the rigidity of sex roles may be attributed partly to the influence of Islam on Iranian culture (Tohidi 1984; Ghaffarian 1987).

First generation Iranian mothers are not usually career oriented and devote their lives to their children and husbands, making huge sacrifices in so doing. In return they have high expectations of their family. Iranian mothers play a crucial role in regulating a family's emotions and emotional affairs. They are affectionate towards their children and, in particular, they have strong bonds with their sons. Preferential treatment of sons by parents is often the cause of conflicts in Iranian families, with sons having more rights and freedom outside the home and daughters often being controlled and dominated by their parents. This is often the cause of great tension between first and second generation Iranian immigrant families.

'Dating', as westerners understand it, is non-existent in Iran (Zonis 1979) and marriage is still almost exclusively the major route to sexual experience (Shapurian and Hojat 1985). Young Iranians living in the West are, on the one hand, confronted by messages from their peers and the mass media presenting the social norms of western culture, which encourage social dating and premarital relationships, and on the other, are restricted within their parents' traditional culture. Thus, they live in the traditional culture of their parents at home while being exposed to a strongly contrasting culture in their social environment. Therefore, their world is neither purely traditional nor purely modern but rather a complex combination of both, which can often be a cause of tension and distress (Hanassab and Tidwell 1993).

Acculturation and acculturative stress in Iranian immigrants

Over 3 million Iranians have emigrated to other countries during the past three decades, making them one of the largest new immigrant groups from the Middle East (Bozorgmehr 2001; Sahami-Martin 2009). The first wave of Iranian immigrants *chose* to leave their homeland from the 1950s to the late 1970s, and were mainly middle- or upper-middle-class students, affluent businessmen or skilled professionals. The second wave began immediately before and after the Islamic Revolution (1978–80). Those in this group of Iranian immigrants were very similar to those in the first wave with the exception of a proportion having links with the overthrown royal family in the context of their occupations, roles, responsibilities and associations with the previous government. This latter group were *forced* to flee their homeland in fear of their lives; some left their extended families and possessions behind, lost their status and power and chose a life in exile. These were mainly middle-aged politicians, businessmen and their families. This group of first generation Iranian immigrants tend to maintain the main aspects of their traditional culture and hence may be resistant to some features of the host culture, including western values and social norms and women's role in western society, leading to a host of intergenerational conflicts in the family.

The third wave took refuge in the western world during the eight-year war with Iraq (1980–8) in order to avoid the war and for economic reasons. They are often young, middle- or lower-middle-class single men or young married men who have often left their wives and children behind (they hope temporarily) in the pursuit of a better life in the 'promised land'. Although they do not conform to a typical refugee profile, they do tend to experience psychological problems arising from separation from their families and uncertainty, leading to alienation, depression and anxiety problems.

Jalali (1982) identifies three modes of adaptation for Iranian immigrants: denigrating the old culture, denying the new culture and 'bi-culturation'. Internal intergenerational conflicts among Iranian families as a result of some family members adhering to one mode of adaptation and others following another is a significant source of acculturative stress.

Culturally related stress or acculturative stress is one of the main challenges to adaptation among Iranian immigrants. The hardship of separation from close-knit family and the loss of ties to an extended family and social network places a great deal of strain on many young Iranian immigrants. In addition, the challenge of integrating new ways of thinking, being and behaving into their traditional culture is considerable. Many Iranian immigrants are torn between a yearning to be included and to fit in with the host culture and feelings of guilt for rejecting the norms of their traditional culture. Such 'values-derived' tensions can potentially lead to internal conflict and in turn to emotional and psychological problems. For older Iranian immigrants, the experience of loss of status and position, fear of financial instability and destitution (and consequent reliance on state benefits) together with feelings of alienation, emotional and physical isolation and culture shock are among the major stressors.

Research on the acculturation of Iranian immigrants suggests that Iranian men tend to acculturate into the host culture at a faster rate than Iranian women, are less stressed in comparison with Iranian women and yet tend to keep more traditional views regarding the role of women in society in comparison to Iranian women, who hold more modern views (e.g. freedom and equality of the sexes).

For both sexes, acculturation is shown to be positively related to better mental health (Ghaffarian 1987, 1998). Therefore, for both sexes, there appears to be a discrepancy between values held and behaviours that could potentially lead to interpersonal conflict in Iranian immigrant families.

In a traditionally oriented Iranian society, females are expected to be passive, submissive and obedient and males are trained to command, protect and achieve status (Tohidi 1993). Thus, Iranian men have been more accustomed to freedom, independence and self-determination, whereas Iranian women have traditionally lacked or been deprived of such privileges. A move to the western world may have put Iranian women in a new situation where they are exposed to a more modern and liberal society. This may explain the reason for Iranian women's slower rate of acculturation and why they tend to be more stressed in comparison to Iranian men. Nevertheless, migration has been the source of autonomy for some Iranian women, providing them with opportunities to escape the patriarchal control of their families, gain more independent and personal freedom and become less economically dependent on their families (Bauer 1991; Tohidi, 1993).

Research on Iranian families' adaptation to the host culture indicates that Iranian women are adopting more flexible attitudes regarding premarital relationships, marriage and the family, while Iranian men hold more traditional views and attitudes (Ghaffarian 1987; Hannasaab and Tidewell 1996). The gender differences in the adoption of western values may have contributed to the rise of family conflicts, relationship breakdown and divorce among Iranian couples in the USA.

Nevertheless, despite their liberal attitudes, Iranian women immigrants have neither abandoned their own, nor accepted all aspects of the host culture. Many Iranian women in the USA criticize the individualism of American women, believing that more sacrifice and dedication from women preserves a marriage, in particular when there are children involved (Mahdi 2001).

Research on acculturation of Iranian immigrants suggests a negative relationship between age at immigration and level of acculturation (Mahdi 1997; Ghaffarian 1998; Emami *et al.* 2001). Older Iranian immigrants have been found to be resistant to acculturation, struggle with language, feel isolated and remain highly dependent on their children (Lipson and Meleis 1982).

Since the 1979 Islamic Revolution and the rise of Islamic fundamentalism, Iranian immigrants have had to overcome stereotypes and negative attitudes about their country and religion during the process of integration (Mahdi 1997). Actual and perceived hostility and discrimination appear to have made the process of acculturation even more stressful for Iranian immigrants by evoking feelings of alienation among this ethnic group (Sahami-Martin 2009).

Conceptualization of mental illness and help-seeking behaviour

Western medically trained doctors and clinicians are primarily schooled in and draw from the biomedical model, the dominant western model of health and illness, to arrive at a biomedical diagnosis. The biomedical model mainly focuses on the biological explanation of the cause of physical and mental illness and thus tends to ignore or overlook a range of sociocultural influences and factors, including the individual's culture, concepts of health and illness, body, mind, spirit and emotions, cultural meaning and expression of emotional difficulties and psychological stress.

It is important for western-trained therapists to be familiar with Iranian clients' conceptualization and expression of emotional problems in order to understand their frames of reference, to connect with them and to refrain from erroneous interpretations and misdiagnosis.

The terms *nakhoshi* (unwell) and *narahati* (depressed, anxious, worried), from the Persian language, can be used interchangeably by Iranians to describe a wide range of physical and emotional problems, including being not at ease, troubled, bothered, upset, low in mood and generally unwell. Problems may arise for a western therapist when an Iranian client complains that they are *nakhosh* or *narahat*, as this could mean they may have physical *or* emotional problems. Although, *narahati* and *nakhoshi* are undifferentiated terms, *ghamgini* (sadness, sorrow) is more specific and is often associated with a range of deeply felt negative emotions to do with grief and loss.

Iranian immigrants describe health in terms of two permeable categories: physical (*jesmi*) and spiritual/mental (*ruhi*). Iranians refer to 'physical' to mean one's body (*jesm*) and spiritual (*ruhi*) to mean one's mind, emotions, spirit or soul. Thus, when an Iranian immigrant complains that their problem is *ruhi*, they refer to a problem in their state of mind or spirit (Sahami-Martin 2009).

For Iranians, *ghalb* or *del* (heart) is the centre of emotion. Therefore, spiritual (*ruhi*) health is experienced in the heart and chest, rather than the head or brain as often described in the western conceptualization of 'mental health' (Sahami-Martin 2009). Idioms such as *ghalbam* or *delam gerefteh* (distress of heart) relate to sadness and emotional problems that may manifest through somatization and anxiety symptoms including heart fluttering, palpitations, pounding or aches and pains, dizziness and headaches. Among Iranians, somatization is more culturally acceptable than revealing personal and/or family emotional problems to a stranger, which signifies weakness and vulnerability. Thus, when Iranian immigrants see a western therapist they are more likely to complain about physical problems rather than deep emotional and psychological difficulties which may be blocked.

For western therapists who may not be familiar with Iranian culture and its conceptualization of mental health and cultural expression of emotional problems, potential misinterpretations and misunderstandings, leading to misdiagnoses and failures in establishing a therapeutic relationship, may be expected. What the western therapist may perceive as a psychological problem may be viewed as medical by Iranians. While major mental illnesses are highly stigmatized in the culture, minor psychological or emotional problems are somatized, as this removes the pressure and the blame from the individual and the family. Iranian clients are more likely to resist treatment when diagnostic labels are used – therefore, resistance in the form of non-compliance/concordance should be expected in these instances.

Talking therapy is not common among Iranians. They prefer to seek help from their family, relatives or friends as they have a close network of support and they prefer to 'keep it in the family'. They seek help from a psychiatrist or doctor only when everything else fails and even then they expect medication to help them rather then talk therapy. In addition, Iranians can become impatient with their treatment if speedy recovery or symptom reduction is not achieved. With major and serious ailments, they go from doctor to doctor to hear what they want to hear. Jalali (1982) uses the term 'doctor shoppers' to refer to Iranians' help-seeking attitudes.

Therapy and therapeutic considerations

As noted above, talking therapy is not common in Iranian culture. Therefore, the following considerations and strategies are effective and recommended when working with Iranian clients.

- Iranians appreciate and respond well to a directive therapeutic approach and problem-solving strategies as opposed to passive, non-directive, analytical exploratory approaches. The therapist should be perceived as an expert in the field who has the authority to treat, advise, teach and problem-solve.
- They need to hear that their therapist has the expertise, competence and credentials to help them with their problems. It is very important to know whether they have dealt with such problems before and how successful this was. Therefore, it is helpful if the therapist provides information regarding his or her qualifications and credentials early on in therapy in order to establish a rapport and therapeutic alliance.
- Many Iranians may not see any connection between their personal and emotional problems and their physical pain or somatization. They often refrain from talking about their social situation. While taking a medical history it is helpful to ask about any difficulties adjusting to the new country and culture (Pliskin 1992).
- When discussing diagnosis or, in particular, when bad news is to be conveyed to Iranian clients, care should be taken to avoid making them *narahat*. This means that the clinician needs to tone down their honesty and make sure that a family member is present for support (Pliskin 1992).
- Iranians are generally compassionate and demonstrative and respond well to attentive, warm, empathic and non-judgemental attitudes. For older Iranian immigrants, loss of status and position and culture shock, and for young Iranian immigrants the hardship of separation from family and loss of support and guidance, have created a yearning for warmth, empathy and compassion. Thus, provision of a safe space for these groups of Iranian immigrants to explore their concerns is immensely therapeutic.
- Iranians are generally not direct people. They tend to 'beat about the bush'. Thus, the therapist should be patient in order to bring focus to the sessions

and facilitate exploration. In particular, Iranians are not forthcoming in providing personal information, including sexual problems.

- When working with Iranian clients, possible gender and age matching may be considered. Consistent with the traditional culture, Iranians rely on same-gender friends and relatives for reassurance, guidance and advice. Iranian men have difficulties disclosing painful issues to a female therapist and the same applies to Iranian women with male therapists. Age is synonymous with respect, experience, expertise and knowledge among Iranians. In particular, with older Iranian immigrants, age matching should be considered for better therapeutic processes and outcome. Research indicates that ethnic matching in multiethnic areas tends to benefit the therapeutic process and outcome, at least when minority clients express a preference (Farsimadan *et al.* 2007) (see also Chapter 6 in this volume).

- When working with Iranians, western therapists should adopt a more flexible approach and be mindful of practical issues and boundaries of the therapeutic relationship. Iranians' concepts of time, appointment booking, space in the therapeutic relationship, ending and termination, and confidentiality need therapists' special attention. Iranians may be early or late, turn up without appointments and cancel appointments due to family obligations (e.g. guests may have turned up at the doorstep unannounced). Reassuring Iranian clients of the confidentiality surrounding the therapy needs to be reiterated by the therapist.

- When treating Iranians with major mental illnesses, therapists need to sensitively utilize psycho-education to increase their clients' awareness of the disorder, its symptoms, aetiology, treatment and prognosis in order to increase their engagement and concordance and reduce the stigma. Sharing a psychological formulation of the problem and provision of a normalization rationale tends to remove the blame/responsibility from them and their families and strengthen the therapeutic alliance.

- When working with Iranians with limited command of English, the use of interpreters is strongly advised due to the culture's conceptualization of mental illness and expression of emotional difficulties and psychological stress. Thus, allowing time so that the Iranian client can describe his or her problem in their own words either directly or through an interpreter is recommended. In addition, when booking interpreters, be mindful that Farsi spoken by Afghani interpreters may be of a different dialect which may be not familiar to all Iranians.

Conclusion

When working with Iranians the therapist should be mindful that it is 'collectivism' and not 'individualism' that governs and is of value to the Iranian client. Therefore, individuals' family structure, dynamic and relationships may regularly surface in therapy and need to be worked on. In addition, Iranians appreciate a more directive therapeutic approach with problem-solving strategies as opposed to non-directive, analytical exploratory approaches. Furthermore, they generally respond well to non-specific therapeutic factors, including empathy, warmth and compassion.

When working with Iranian clients the use of interpreters as and when required and utilizing psychological interventions such as psycho-education and normalization are effective in dealing with the stigma of mental illness and improving engagement in therapy.

References

Arasteh, A.R. (1964) *Man and Society in Iran*. Leiden: E.J. Brill.

Banuazizi, A. (1977) Iranian 'national character': a critique of some western perspectives, in L. C. Brown and N. Itkowitz (eds) *Psychological Dimensions of Near Eastern Studies*. Princeton, NJ: Darwin Press.

Bauer, J. (1991) A long way home: Islam in the adaptation of Iranian women refugees in Turkey and West Germany, in A. Fathi (ed.) *Iranian Refugees and Exiles since Khomeini*. Costa Mesa, CA: Mazda.

Behnam, V.N. (1985) Change and the Iranian family, *Current Anthropology*, 26(5): 558–62.

Bozorgmehr, M. (2001) No solidarity: Iranians in the U.S., *The Iranian*, www.iranian .com/today.html.

Emami, A., Benner, P. and Ekman, S. (2001) A sociocultrual health model for late-in-life immigrants, *Journal of Transcultural Nursing*, 12: 15–24.

Farsimadan, F., Draghi-Lorenz, R. and Ellis, J. (2007) Process and outcome of therapy in ethnically similar and dissimilar therapeutic dyads, *Psychotherapeutic Research*, 17(5): 567–75.

Ghaffarian, S. (1987) The acculturation of Iranians in the United States, *Journal of Social Psychology*, 127: 565–71.

Ghaffarian, S. (1998) The acculturation of Iranian immigrants in the United States and the implications for mental health, *Journal of Social Psychology*, 138: 645–75.

Gill, N.S. (2007) Iran: the ancient name of Iran, http://ancienthistory.about.com/ od/persianempiremaps/qt/Iran.htm.

Hanassab, S. and Tidwell, R. (1989) Cross-cultural perspectives on dating relationships of young Iranian women: a pilot study, *Counselling Psychology Quarterly*, 2: 113–21.

Hanassab, S. and Tidwell, R. (1996) Sex roles and sexual attitudes of young Iranian women, *Social Behaviour and Personality*, 24(2): 185–94.

Hooker, R. (1996) Mesopotamia: the Persians, www.wsu.edu:8080/~dee/MESO/ PERSIANS.html.

Jalali, B. (1982) Iranian families, in M. McGoldrick, J. Giordano and J.H. Pearce (eds) *Ethnicity and Family Therapy*. New York: Guilford Press.

Mahdi, A.A. (1997) The second generation Iranians: questions and concerns, *The Iranian*, www.iranian.com/today.html.

Mahdi A.A. (2001) Perception of gender roles among female Iranian immigrants in the United States, in S. Ansari and V. Martin (eds) *Women, Religion and Culture in Iran*. London: Curzon Press.

Nyrop, R.F. (1978) *Iran: A Country Study*. Washington, DC: American University Press.

Pliskin, K.L. (1992) Dysphoria and somatisation in Iranian culture, *Western Journal of Medicine*, 157: 295–300.

Sahami-Martin, S. (2009) Illness of the mind or illness of the spirit? Mental health-related conceptualization and practices of older Iranian immigrants, *Health Social Work*, 34: 117–26.

Sedghi, H. (1976) Women in Iran, in L.E. Iglitzin and R. Ross (eds) *Studies in Comparative Politics*. Santa Barbara, CA: Clio Books.

Shapurian, R. and Hojat, M. (1985) Sexual and premarital attitudes of Iranian college students, *Psychological Reports*, 58: 67–74.

Shepherd, W.R. (1923) *The Historical Atlas*. New York: Henry Holt & Co.

Tohidi, N. (1984) Sex differences in achievement/career motivation of Iranian boys and girls, *Sex Roles*, 11: 467–84.

Tohidi, N. (1993) Iranian women and gender relations in Los Angeles, in R. Kelley, J. Friedlander and A. Colby (eds) *Irangeles: Iranians in Los Angeles*. Berkeley, CA: University of California Press.

Touba, J.R. (1978) Marriage and the family in Iran, in M.S. Das and P.D. Bardis (eds) *The Family in Asia*. New Dehli: Vikas Publishing House.

Zonis, M. (1976) *The Political Elite of Iran*. Princeton, NJ: Princeton University Press.

Zonis, M. (1979) Social, cultural, and religious factors affecting Iranian students, in G.R. Athen (ed.) *Students from the Arab World and Iran*. Washington, DC: National Association for Foreign Students Affairs.

25 The effects of a North American heritage

Susan McGinnis

Introduction

An American living anywhere else in the world is not a 'typical' American. Americans, on the whole, are insular. This is due in part to the fact that North America is such a huge geographical area but, more importantly, it is a result of a frame of mind which is nurtured from the earliest age and anchored in the belief that America is the biggest, the best and the greatest place on earth. I can remember being a small child in primary school and starting every day with my classmates reciting, 'I pledge allegiance to the flag of the United States of America'. This attachment to a flag now seems obsessive and peculiar but if you go to America you will see the 'Stars and Stripes' everywhere. The flag represents power and nationalism and Americans revere it with a fervour that America itself would consider in any other country to be dangerous fundamentalism.

This is just one of the marvellous paradoxes that characterize the country of my birth. It is the land of the free and the home of the brave, founded by religious outcasts who were seeking asylum from political persecution and based on the principle of separation of church and state, yet I will never forget watching men in military uniforms march into a church carrying guns during an Independence Day celebration in North Carolina. America is one of the richest countries in the world yet the conditions of those living in poverty in its cities and rural areas rival those of the developing world. Its passionate anti-abortionists hold the lives of children paramount, yet America is one of only two countries in the world not to adopt the UN Convention on the Rights of the Child – the other is Somalia. America's constitution is grounded in the ideals of liberty and justice for all, but its wealth is forged on the wholesale genocide and ethnic cleansing of the indigenous peoples and the importation and enslavement of another race. Perhaps this is an example of the old British chestnut that Americans don't understand irony.

A new perspective

Compared to other Americans I have met who live in Britain, I am an anomaly. I have not been homesick for a moment, I cannot think of anything that is better about America and I am not in any way proud of my birth heritage. This eye-opening perspective is one of two significant ways that coming to Britain 26 years ago changed my life; the first is about values, and the second is about discovering what 'home' means and how you know it where and when you find it. Both are about belonging.

I should say at this point that I had no feelings one way or the other about America or being American until I left. My reasons for leaving were related to work, not politics or principles. However, the more I travelled in Europe and saw America as others see it, I began to understand how what Americans view as patriotism is experienced by others as arrogance and how a blind belief in the American way as the right and true way is an insult to those who value their own beliefs as strongly.

I suppose that my pervading feeling about being American since I left has been one of shame. I felt embarrassed standing behind an American couple in a queue at the ticket counter of a London Underground station while they treated the ticket seller like a flunky at a theme park who was not making their day fun. I felt ashamed as the first person with an American passport at the immigration desk at Heathrow the morning after America bombed Libya, when the non-white clerk glowered at me and said 'How did *you* sleep last night?' I found out later that the bombing had been timed to coincide with the six o'clock news so that Americans could watch Colonel Quaddafi's son being killed while they enjoyed their steak and potatoes. I cannot think of any way to describe my shame at coming from the country that elected George W. Bush – twice – and thought that Guantanamo Bay was a good thing, or the place where a man was acquitted after shooting and killing two teenagers in an apartment swimming pool because they refused to give his son's ball back. Surely this is not what Thomas Jefferson and the founding revolutionaries had in mind when they set out the Declaration of Independence, the Constitution and the Bill of Rights. My shame is so great that I take pride in the fact that I have never spoken by whining through my nose and am always pleased to be mistaken for Canadian. It is important to me to maintain the stance that I am not one of 'them'.

As has been the case with much in my life, I came to the UK on what appeared to be impulse but was in fact the culmination of a subtle process of which I was not fully aware at the time. To me, and to everyone else, it looked as if I suddenly packed up my instruments and a few clothes (I was a professional classical musician), took myself to JFK Airport, sat there until my name was called from a standby list, boarded a plane and, seven hours later, stepped out into a world where I didn't know how to use the money and was nearly run over the first time I crossed a road. Yet what stands out the most for me, and I will never forget it, was not the sense of difference but the immediate euphoria of a feeling of coming home, of finally being where I belonged. Initially this came from something intangible but, as I spent more time in my new home, it showed in more concrete ways: people read books and newspapers, and thought and talked about ideas. I always felt like a freak in America because I did these things so in some sense my difference was more pronounced in my own country than it was once I left. I was raised by a father who loves history and, in leaving a country where anything from the eighteenth century is 'old' and 'history' started with the arrival of white people, travelling initially to places like Greece and Rome nourished a hunger I did not know I had. When I stand in Canterbury Cathedral at the coffin effigy of the first Archbishop (poignantly small), or sit in twelfth-century Glasgow Cathedral or walk a few miles down my road to the well where William Wallace was betrayed in the fourteenth century I feel a great sense of peace. I am part of the flow of humanity. I belong to something larger and older than myself that will be here long after me.

Laughter and tears

There have been moments of comedy along the way, especially in those early days when everything British was new to me, including the language. Discovering that I had lost a great deal of weight from excitement and the alien food on offer (this from possibly the only American on the planet who has never eaten a McDonald's hamburger) I went in search of something to hold up my sagging waistband. I had already been into several men's clothing shops when one gentleman kindly took pity on me and suggested that I might be looking for braces to hold up my trousers rather than suspenders to hold up my pants. When I came to Scotland 18 years ago, language again became an issue. It was months before I could understand completely what was being said to me and, while looking back now I can recall several situations which were funny, I did feel somewhat lost and isolated even while being swept up in the magic of arriving somewhere that felt even more like home. I learned the language of my new country through sitting in my counsellor's chair in a GP surgery in a former shipbuilding community on the River Clyde. To my musician's ear that language is lyrical and expressive, and full of humour. From my clients – most of them lonely and elderly – I discovered what it means to 'chap the door', 'clap the cat' and 'get the messages' (knock on the door, pet the cat and pick up the shopping). This linguistic adventure was a rich vein of contact for both my clients and me. Now my friends from my days in London tell me that I have a Scottish accent and I am content with that since I feel part of this place.

As much as I am grateful every day to be here where I look out at 'my' hills, I occasionally feel too what might be described as cultural phantom limb pain. This was most evident in my response to watching two planes crash into the twin towers of the World Trade Center on September 11, 2001. Even now it is hard to communicate the particular grief I felt that separated me from everyone around me and only felt shared when I spoke to a friend from America who has lived in Amsterdam for 20 years. The same blinkered, brash, simplistic, black-and-white positivism that normally encapsulates everything I dislike about America was lost that day and watching it happen was like a punch which took me by surprise.

I have found it difficult, too, to find the same close relationships with women friends that I had in America and blundered painfully in my early days here in Britain by inviting women I liked on acquaintance to get to know me better only to be met with a reserve that left me feeling gauche and rebuffed. This is not to say that British women do not form deep friendships or that American women are automatically best friends just by virtue of being female, but that it took me a while to understand the dynamics of relationship here. I have very close women friends in this country, and those friendships still feel different from those that I have with my women friends in America.

On this theme but in a larger context, another phenomenon of living half one's life in one country and half in another is the feeling at some level of not being fully known at all in either place. In my adopted country I lack the continuity of family and of the sort of friends who have known you since you had funny hair and glasses in primary school. I spend Christmas on my own since I find it even lonelier to be the visitor in another family's celebrations, regardless of how much I love them. Parallel to this is having the experience that my own family no longer know me. This is expressed eloquently in Christmas and birthday presents that are clearly chosen with care and affection but seem to be for someone whose tastes and interests are miles from my own. The people who share my real, daily existence do not know my history and my family and cultural roots; those with whom I share those deep and abiding connections of family and history do not have a clue about what I like to wear and what I like to read.

Stereotypes, prejudice and a dangerous fascination

Less welcome aspects of being known are the assumptions that people may make about me based on my country of birth. I am American so I must be loud, garrulous, can-do, patriotic, gun-toting and, of course, lacking any appreciation of irony. As most of these types of beliefs are unspoken, I can never know what people are really thinking, and that in itself could be socially crippling. To be honest, I rarely think about it. However, just as there are times when my American accent comes in handy (I can get away with making a fuss over something and all they will think is, 'Awful American woman!'), there have also been occasions when I have wondered whether it also invites prejudice. I applied for a counselling post once where I was the only one of the interviewees who had all the skills – including an expertise with the client group – in the job description. Almost immediately on entering the interview room and introducing myself I sensed the atmosphere change and felt a wave of disapproval. It goes without saying that they gave the post to someone who was not even a qualified counsellor. I can think of two other posts I applied for where I felt a similar negativity in the air at interview stage once I spoke and my nationality was revealed. Perhaps I simply did not fit their ideal candidate criteria. Still, the unpleasant whiff of what amounts to racism has occasionally been in the air.

Stereotypes exist about all groups of people and, just as silly as the Americans' belief that the English are classy and wear tweed or that Scotland is all about the tartan and whisky, are some of the more amusing British stereotypes of Americans, America and the American way of life, most of which arise from watching movies. My favourites are: 'America is warm' (Florida and California are warm, everything in between is very much in between); service in shops and restaurants is better (it isn't – they are just being extra nice when they hear a British accent); just about everything is better (Americans have this same view about everything British). Here in Scotland I am repeatedly asked in bewildered tones why I would want to live *here* when I could live there. I have discovered that this question most often appears to be based on the assumption that 'America' equals 'Florida' and Disney World. One boy in a school for children with social, emotional and behavioural needs where I was working asked me, on hearing my accent, 'Do you know Madonna?'

At the less benign end of the spectrum of Britain's enchantment with things American is the British penchant for embracing wholeheartedly ideas and trends as soon as they have failed or have proven themselves to be harmful in America, such as the learning community model in education or huge shopping malls that destroy local economies. When I first came to the UK it was rare to see anyone obese; now obesity is an epidemic that is destined to have far-reaching repercussions thanks to the proliferation of franchise food and the adoption of American eating habits. Even more ominous is the increase in gun crime. Britain felt so safe to me when I arrived here in 1984. No longer. I am sad to see those things that I thought I had left behind following me here. Perhaps most dangerous of all was the 'special relationship' and the consequences of Tony Blair's willingness to follow unquestioningly America's misguided and cynical hidden agenda in invading Iraq.

The outsider from within

As a psychotherapist, another entrenched misconception I encounter is the belief that all Americans have a therapist and, Woody Allen-like, are deeply interested in their own feelings. Any number of variations on this can have an impact on the therapeutic relationship. There have been clients who, on meeting me for the first time and discovering my birth nation, have apologized for not being as emotionally literate as I might be used to, coming from America where everyone has a therapist (which of course they do not). Alternatively, I find myself wondering whether I am seen as a cartoon character or a cliché and risk being dismissed as fluffy and superficial due to the combination of my nationality and my choice of profession. And there am I, sitting face to face with the fabled British stiff upper lip or, rather, the Scottish one which is somewhat different from the English one.

Being a therapist in a country not my own also affords me the unique perspective of an outsider from within. Britain is an island of just 94,525 square miles that dominated most of the world for centuries. It is the nation that until not so long ago sent its 8-year-old sons off to boys' schools, often cold and brutal places, with the blind faith that it was good for them. Its people survived the Blitz with dry humour and dogged determination and went in dinghies to Dunkirk. The British have a magnificent ability to do extraordinary things and a talent for making the extraordinary appear ordinary. It's a matter of national pride not to make a fuss. Britain is a country that finds virtue in 'just getting on with it'.

With this sort of history I can see how tragedy on the merely personal level could seem trivial. Yet this cultural ethos can cause great individual conflict; how does someone who is unable to 'just get on with it' manage without feeling that they are letting themselves and everyone else down? I have worked with many who were certain that they should have been able to get over the loss of a parent, child or partner within a matter of weeks when, in fact, they were still struggling with their grief a year later. By that time not only do they have their loss to contend with but also their guilt and shame over not having coped in the way they think they should have done.

These feelings are exacerbated by all of those around them who say things like, 'Don't cry, love, s/he wouldn't have wanted you to be so upset' or – as happened to one of my clients who was pregnant when her mother died – 'You mustn't get upset, you'll hurt the baby'. As a result, people who are suffering deeply find it impossible to talk about their distress since it will only be met with discomfort or dismissal, most often in the guise of love; we don't want those we love to feel upset.

I have listened to people trying to articulate how hopeless and pointless it feels to be alive who then say, 'Of course, I would never do anything silly'. Exasperated mothers on the street say to their crying children, 'Oh, stop being silly!' when the child is clearly hurt or frightened or angry. 'Don't be silly, everything will be fine' is considered a loving reassurance. People who arrive for a first counselling session will sit down and blurt out, 'I know this is silly but . . .' and then tell a story that is full of genuine and intense feeling. While I am appalled and embarrassed by the American impulse to make a big deal out of every situation, I am equally affected by my experience of people here in Britain who feel that they must dismiss their most profound and human acts and emotions as 'silly'.

I recall at the time of Princess Diana's death reading an article called 'Crybaby Britain' that dripped with contempt for the public outpouring of grief and what the author described as a 'creeping plague of emotionalism' that threatened to destroy the fabric of the country. Almost 15 years later I think that I sense a shift in the national attitude while the fabric remains miraculously intact. While we have not degenerated to the exhibitionism of Oprah, there seems to be a more comfortable relationship with being human, such as David and Samantha Cameron and Gordon and Sarah Brown sharing with dignity their feelings on the deaths of their respective children, for instance. Sobbing X Factor contestants swearing that singing/winning/doing it for their mums means the world to them, however, remind me of the slippery slope that admiration for all things American represents. Even worse, it seems to me to be in some degree the flipside of the stiff upper lip coin, equally emotionally incongruent.

I suppose that, in some sense, I work with difference every day although I am not by nature someone who looks for it or cares a great deal about it. One of the comforts of being a person-centred therapist is the freedom I have to get things wrong; I have great faith in my client's capacity to teach me what I need to know about them. Indeed, it is taking the stance of not knowing that enables my commitment to invest all parts of myself in any moment I am with a client – and hopefully my client's perception of that intent – that allows us, together, to understand his or her experience, including experience of difference and even how that difference enters into our relationship. There is a danger in letting a focus on difference hijack the relationship. In taking care to value difference there is a risk of losing the richness of what is *not* different and what we long for, which is connectedness and sameness at relational depth. Is that better facilitated by a therapist's interest in understanding cultural difference?

As a client here in Britain I had the luxury of speaking fundamentally the same language as my counsellor, though I feel that good therapeutic relationships which reach relational depth transcend the divide of place, language and culture and strip us back to the essence of sharing our experience of being human. I would go further and say that I think that this is why people seek therapy, and perhaps even more so when outside their birth culture. It mattered nothing to me whether my counsellor understood what it means to be an American. In fact, I would have greatly resented the idea that my native culture somehow defined me, though if I were my therapist I'd be pretty interested in why I felt this so strongly.

Perhaps in a roundabout way my experience argues for some kind of cultural collective unconscious and the possibility that I was simply born in the wrong geographical place. Regardless of where we are on the planet, we bring our past to wherever we go and inevitably will engage with whatever the new place confronts us with through the lens of our past experience. For me, the country of my birth has no meaning for me beyond plain fact. I have a much stronger resonance with where I live now, and a deep sense of joy and belonging that I never felt in the country that most would assume I call 'home'.

26 The effects of a South American heritage

Tiane Corso Graziottin

Introduction

To explore the impact of a South American heritage in the field of counselling and psychotherapy, we need to first visit the characteristics of this unique region, which is itself constituted by peoples of various origins. The first inhabitants to influence the south of the American continent, according to the most recent historical and anthropological findings, are believed to belong to the late Pleistocene ice ages, a period corresponding to about 12,500 BC. They are believed to have come either via the north, from modern-day Siberia (Cook 2003), or from the Ancient Middle East through the Eastern Asian myriad islands of the Pacific Ocean (Kearsley 2003). Gradually, over several thousand years, many tribes emerged and human settlements arose, resulting in the development of the first civilizations in the north-west of the subcontinent,[1] including the advanced and great Inca Empire (Roberts 1998; Kearsley 2003).

The native communities developed independently until the late fifteenth century when Europeans were advancing their colonial expeditions towards other regions of the world. Christopher Columbus, a Genoese sailor financed by the Spanish monarchy (Roberts 1998), accidentally reached the region of what is currently known as the Caribbean in 1492, having aimed to arrive in East India (Saunders 2004). In the following years, Spain continued its expeditions and was joined by Portugal, whose sailors landed on the coast of present-day Brazil in 1500. Two years later, another Portuguese vessel, commanded by the Italian Amerigo Vesputti, sailed southward and officially recognized the new land as an unknown continent to the Europeans, rather than an island as was initially thought. The whole continent was subsequently named 'America' in honour of this particular navigator (Roberts 1998: 284).

The Europeans were immediately enthralled with the exotic and fertile qualities of the land and soon commenced its occupation and the exploitation of its resources. From that point onward, a new and long process was started, which shaped the lives of many people and influenced, to a great extent, the geographic,

---

[1]The word 'subcontinent' is occasionally used to describe South America based on the concept that the continent America is divided into three 'subcontinents': North, Central and South.

social and political context of today. The native inhabitants gradually lost the right for their land and the conquerors radically implemented their habits, beliefs, culture and religions (Ribeiro 1971; Guardiola-Rivera 2010). Initially, the Spanish and Portuguese were the main exploiters, but later came the Dutch, French and English. With colonial interests in mind, respect towards the native inhabitants was not a priority for the invaders since the main focus was the exploitation of natural assets, such as metals and minerals, for their own ends. The result was a great deal of human mistreatment, initially towards the native inhabitants and later focused for three centuries on African slavery. According to Galeano (1971), Brazil alone received an estimated 10 million African slaves between the middle of the sixteenth century and the official abolition of slavery in 1888.

The colonies of South America slowly became well established and by 1830 most provinces were independent, named (in chronological order): Paraguay, Argentine, Chile, Peru, Brazil, Ecuador, Colombia, Venezuela, Bolivia and Uruguay (Vizentine 2006). Guyana gained its independence from the UK in 1966 and Suriname from the Netherlands in 1975. French Guiana and the Falkland Islands remain a part of the French and British territories respectively to the present day.

After this wave of independence in the large majority of the territory at the beginning of the nineteenth century, the new empires and nations started their struggle for increased political and economic liberation. The path was difficult and suffered the heavy interference of external powers such as the UK and later the USA (Galeano 1971; Guardiola-Rivera 2010). Throughout those years, South America also experienced a second significant period of colonization (Roberts 1998). This time, however, the immigration process was prompted by national governments, which, no longer relying on slavery, required more people to work in their developing countries and growing economies. The majority of immigrants were Italians, Spanish and Germans but also included other European and Asian peoples such as Portuguese, Polish, Slovakian, Ukrainian, Russian, Palestinian, Lebanese, Syrian, Japanese, Chinese, Indian and Korean.

From 1950 to 1980, the rates of immigration slowed down as several South American nations experienced military dictatorships, bringing about yet again conflicts, struggles and injustices for the people. After long years of oppression, resulting in thousands of political exiles and executions, the dictatorial structures were defeated and gradually replaced by democratic governments (Cardoso 2006).

In the most recent decades, mostly from the late 1990s, the region started a move towards the political left, with a more social-inclusive and pro-South America agenda (see Balch 2009; Guardiola-Rivera 2010). This new political context resulted in 2008 in the official formation of the UNASUR (*Unión de Naciones Suramericanas*), which for the first time assembled the 12 independent nations of the subcontinent with the aim of building a stronger and more self-sustained South America, free of heavy external influences (see www.unasur.org). After more than five centuries of political and economic reliance, UNASUR respresents the hope of a fresh beginning for the region.

The characteristics of South American people

Given the above chain of events, it is evident that the people of South America are individuals whose identities have been formed in an essentially multi-ethnic context and, very often, from a variety of ancestries. This combination makes South America a society of vibrant and unique qualities. There is no homogeny in the subcontinent as a whole or within individual nations, making it one of the most diverse ethnic regions of the world (Cardoso 2006; Corral-Verdugo and Pinheiro 2009). The single largest ethnic group remains persons of European descent but there is a majority of mixed-race groups in countries like Brazil, Colombia and Venezuela, including *mulato* (African and European), *caboclo* or *mameluco* (indigenous and European), *cafuzo* or *zambo* (indigenous and African).

The struggles, exploitations, wars and crises experienced throughout the centuries also shaped the identity of the people from one generation to the next (Cardoso 2006; Guardiola-Rivera 2010). The mixture of strength and passiveness that might be perceived in South Americans is indicative of this pattern. There is the necessity of surviving, in both a micro and a macro context, that often feels unfair and unchangeable and yet there is also an obligation and responsibility to rebel, challenge the oppressiveness and break the 'culture of silence' (Freire 2007: 82). In this process, the people tend to learn from an early age to 'always find ways' to endure the transformations and uncertainties of life. This attribute brings in itself an inherent flexibility, which is helpful to creatively deal with the challenges and problems of social and economic inequality, both typical characteristics of South American societies. Nonetheless, it is also an unfortunate consequence of long centuries of exploitation, instability and abuse.

In the last decades, however, with the slow but significant move towards respect for social and ethnic identity and economic independence, some South American nations have begin to experience increasing stability. In Brazil, the biggest country in the subcontinent, for example, 35.87 per cent of the population were below the poverty line in 1992 and in 2006 this figure dropped to 19.31 per cent (Fundação Getúlio Vargas 2007). These statistics may seem encouraging but they do not mask the intrinsic and continual layers of historical injustice in South America. The poorest are still of African, native and/or mixed-race backgrounds. This social and economic disparity is also directly linked to educational inequality. Access to education in South America, although demonstrating gradual improvements, is still one of the lowest in the world (UNESCO 2009).

Paulo Freire, a Brazilian educator who also experienced the reality of other South American countries while in exile during the military dictatorship years, spent his professional life pointing to the inevitable correlation between popular passiveness and lack of access to education and critical learning (see Freire and Horton 1990; Freire 1996, 2007). This is an unfortunate reality that still affects millions of South Americans, from the youth to the elderly, and contributes to the continuing ideological and pragmatic power dynamics between oppressor and oppressed groups in everyday life. To face and deal with the daily struggles, the large majority of South Americans tend to rely on faith-based belief systems, which are a traditional source of strength for many people. Roman Catholicism is the single largest religious denomination resulting from the Spanish and Portuguese influence of the colonial years (Cardoso 2006). However, there is also a wide presence of other creeds and spiritual traditions, including, among others, several Protestant churches, Islam, Judaism, Buddhism, Spiritism (mostly in Brazil and followers of Allan Kardec's doctrine), Afro-American traditions (e.g. *Umbanda* and *Candomblé*), and various indigenous rituals. Regarding the African and indigenous spiritual practices, many of them also contain Christian influences because, in the past, the native and slave communities had to use aspects of Christianity to communicate their faith in order to survive the oppression of the Catholic missionary system.

Another source of strength for South American people is music, which has historically been a way to communicate and deal with individual and social experiences. As with all the other aspects of the subcontinent, the musical genres are various and influenced by diverse backgrounds, the main ones being European, African, native and, in the last century, North American. Some of these musical genres have a political focus and aim to challenge the status quo. Others are pure entertainment but still have a social impact since they bring enjoyment for the people, contributing to ameliorate the harshness of life (see Savigliano 1995; Veloso 2002; Morales 2003).

Cultural implications in South American therapeutic contexts[2]

South American clients

The client who comes for therapy[3] brings the above influences in various degrees. The social and psychological characteristics of the unique South American context can be implicitly and explicitly observed in the person's search for self-awareness and self-development. The relationships between person, others and environment tends to result in complex experiences, including high levels of 'conditions of worth', as defined by Rogers (1959: 209, 210, 224–6), which engender values and beliefs influenced by traditional ideologies and praxis. These 'conditions' are observed in persons from all social groups and classes and inevitably interfere with the client's perception of 'self' (1951: 497, 498) and 'self-ideal' (1959: 200). Even though South Americans develop in a multicultural environment, their relationships remain influenced by their individual contexts. It is not unusual to experience clients struggling in the therapeutic setting to identify and overcome the conditioning resulting from numerous external forces.

---

[2]The aspects addressed in this section relate to South America as a whole, although there is greater focus on Brazil, my home country, since I have more familiarity with its professional context.
[3]To remain respectful to diverse training and professional backgrounds, the word 'therapy' is used in the present text as a general term denoting both counselling and psychotherapy.

Nevertheless, although the client is imbedded in complex cultural and social patterns, there are factors within and without the therapeutic settings that can prompt the questioning of deterministic dynamics and engender authentic self-development. From a humanistic therapeutic perspective, for example, this process tends to be enhanced in therapy when in the presence of attitudes like 'unconditional positive regard' and 'empathic understanding' (Rogers 1978: 10, 11). These therapeutic attitudes offer the client the opportunity to feel respected and understood in their own terms, breaking the cycle of powerful external conditioning. As a consequence, the level of a client's 'congruence' (Rogers 1959: 205, 206, 230, 231) tends to increase, the degrees of experiential distortion diminish and the person becomes more autonomous from the deterministic dynamics. This psychological growth, however, may take time to occur. The person who is used to experiencing control and oppression normally struggles when psychological freedom is offered, even if in a deliberately protected environment. The safety will only be perceived after legitimately experiencing trust, which is an additional challenge for a self that has been constructed and is anchored in instability and insecurity. Yet, despite all this, South American clients tend to strive for self-independence[4] once in a consistent and genuine safe therapeutic environment.

Other aspects that might facilitate the client's search for self-awareness can be found outside the therapy room and might include, among others, increased access to critical education, social and political awareness, musical influences that facilitate greater consciousness, access to worldwide information through the internet and globalization processes and growing per capita and economic stability, which also contribute to an increase in the number of South Americans being exposed to other ways of life as they are gradually more able to travel inside and outside the subcontinent. The mental and social openness that may result from these experiences can help clients to increase their levels of critical thinking, while decreasing levels of passiveness, and improving proactivity on both personal and social levels.

The above openness is, however, often present on a small social scale, given that many South American clients come to therapy addressing difficulties associated with basic human rights such as food, safety and education. These clients are often situated in the lower two levels of Maslow's hierarchy of needs, which are concerned with physiological and safety needs (Maslow 1954). Social needs, the third layer of the pyramid, on the other hand, are normally met even in limited contexts such as those described, resulting in an interesting characteristic of South America: it is common to find clients from the poorest areas of the region without enough food to eat and living in extremely unsafe and dangerous contexts

---

[4]'Self-independence' here means the search for a higher level of congruence between *self* (perceptual field) and *organism* (the entire experiential field) that embraces biological, psychological, social and spiritual experiences. Hence, this 'independence' is one that does not deny *the other* but includes it in the process of becoming *oneself*. The main difference is the role *the other* plays, going from an authoritarian and deterministic force to an interactive or dialogical element in the process of identifying 'who I am'. The therapist, in this perspective, can be understood also as a representation of this *facilitative other*.

and yet presenting feelings of 'belongingness' (Maslow 1954: 89) and a high degree of emotional connection with family members, friends and their social environment. This level of emotional warmth and openness or 'emotional attachment to places and other individuals' (Corral-Verdugo and Pinheiro 2009: 372) is a quality commonly portrayed as 'friendly' by foreigners but is in fact a way to maintain high spirits by cooperating with each other to survive the everyday challenges of life.

This emotional attachment can be a sign of strength in some clients but might also be a weakness when it comes to striving for independence. Many of the communities in the subcontinent are still of a conservative nature and, although there are high levels of social diversity, there are also high levels of segregation and psychological rigidity. The search for self-development and liberation often clashes with the invisible walls that seize the individual within familiar social, political, economic, racial and religiously strict conventions. These processes can be a great emotional and cognitive challenge, since breaking from the values and beliefs held by the respective groups often means losing one's 'identity' and emotional safety.

In this multifaceted context, another aspect that can be observed in South Americans is the tendency to seek self-development in alternative rather than traditional therapeutic ways, given that therapy may be seen as unnecessary or as an intervention for people experiencing severe mental health problems. This tendency is a consequence of cultural dynamics and/or a lack of information for the general population about the meaning and purpose of therapy, which is often a service more accessible to the affluent classes (i.e. the minority of the population). Another factor is that many South Americans prefer to deal with their emotional needs within trusted friendships or using, among others, religion and/or recreational aspects of the natural environment, which is an essential feature of many regions. This may well be related to economic factors but it may also be simply a matter of personal and cultural preference.

South American therapists and the context of therapy

The South American therapist,[5] like the client, is influenced by the historical, multicultural, social and political elements already discussed and, consequently, learns to deal with complex demands from the early stages of professional life. The therapist's academic and practical training, unlike the North American and several European contexts, is predominantly a component of psychology programmes. As a result, 'psychotherapy' tends to be part of or even synonymous with clinical psychology and the notion of 'counselling' is not commonly applied. In some countries such as Argentina, though, there are distinctions between these terms, with the profession of counselling having its own training programmes (see *Asociación Argentina de Counselors* at www.aacounselors.org.uk and Grinblatt 2008).

As a result, the majority of South American therapists develop their professional identity within the field of psychology, which has, accordingly, ample academic

---

[5]Similar to 'therapy', the terms 'therapist' and 'practitioner' appear in the text as a general definition for both counsellor and psychotherapist.

programmes and practical applications. In Brazil, for example, a qualified practitioner will have completed a five-year psychology degree that involves extensive coursework related to theory, research and supervised practice and generally includes the disciplines of philosophy, neurophysiology, psychobiology, developmental psychology and psychopathology along with clinical psychology, health psychology, social psychology, organizational psychology and educational psychology (Hutz and Gomes 2006). The theoretical and practical approaches of the above disciplines are mostly associated with psychoanalysis, humanistic psychology, cognitive and behavioural psychologies. The greater or lesser influence of these and other theoretical tendencies depends on the priorities defined by national guidelines, although each university programme has some level of autonomy in terms of its curriculum. The decisions about textbooks, for instance, are commonly left to the discretion of the professors responsible for the disciplines (Hutz and Gomes 2006). During the five-year training, the therapists have the opportunity to experience the broad prospectus offered and identify what is their professional preference. Having completed the programme, a therapist will agree to comply with the ethical framework of the National Council of Psychology (CFP 2005) – the professional body that regulates the academic and practical exercise of the profession in accordance with guidelines stipulated by the Brazilian Ministry of Education – and is then officially qualified to work in any of the fields of psychology, including psychotherapy and counselling as it is universally known.

The broad nature of the academic programmes of a yet young profession in South America (see Hall 1946), along with the subcontinent's idiosyncratic historical, cultural, social, political and economic background provide a fertile terrain for the therapist in which to work. Within a responsible and ethical professional framework, there is freedom to practise in order to address problems such as the extensive degrees of social injustice and economic inequality. Examples of this effort are found in several parts of the subcontinent where therapists have set up creative projects to meet local needs. The *Plantão Psicológico* ('Psychological Emergency Service') in Brazil is one of these projects. It started in São Paulo during the military dictatorship years as a place for people in need of urgent emotional support (see Rosenthal 1999) and has been implemented in other cities in Brazil such as in Fortaleza since 2007 (F. Cavalcante, personal communication, February 2010). In this particular service, the clients arriving at the *Plantão Psicológico* are seen by internship students or professional practitioners and receive person-centred therapy. There are no working contracts, formal procedures or time structures for these sessions, which are based entirely on the clients' emotional needs. The client may attend a one-off session, which might last 30 minutes or several hours, or may return to see the practitioner again for up to two further sessions after a few days or weeks (see Vasconcelos 2009).

This ability to develop original ways to meet individual and social needs is one of the greatest advantages and qualities of the South American professional field. Although many of the therapeutic traditions are of a structured and determinist nature, there is, in general, scope within those approaches for flexibility and creativeness.

Some final thoughts on cultural heritage and responsible practice

Corral-Verdugo and Pinheiro (2009: 368) point to the multifaceted identity of South America and place it between the western cultures associated with an 'individualistic, post-modernist, dualistic, pragmatic, and analytic worldview', and eastern traditions related to 'collectivist, modernistic, and non-dualistic traditions, as well as biospheric and holistic views of the world'. Hutz and Gomes (2006) also express this eclecticism when they point to the frequent combination of phenomenological and experimental theory and research. According to these authors, in Brazil (and similarly in other regions) the 'pragmatism, humour, social consciousness, and ability to adapt, born of past political experiences ... enriches the critical thinking and creativity necessary for scientific advancement in the field' (p. 15).

South American therapists, like the therapeutic profession, ought to be resourceful enough to meet the contextual and individual demands of their clients in humanitarian and holistic ways. Within the four walls of a therapy room or outside in the community, therapists and clients are in various degrees experiencing the challenges of both the inner and external developing worlds. In this process, the hardness and scarcity of the cultural and societal context, when it does not turn the professional and the profession into one more passive tool of the oppressive system, prompts the promotion of constructive psychological and social change. To ensure the latter rather than the former, every therapist in South America has an ethical obligation to become aware of historical, social and political interferences, to identify her or his weakness and strengths and to challenge their own passiveness if necessary. In this sense, three of the biggest challenges for the practitioner can be identified as:

- the responsibility to remain connected to the warmth, spontaneity and creativity inherent in the core of one's cultural identity;
- the commitment to personal and professional awakening to facilitate the genuine development of others; and
- the responsibility to produce more research and writings about the remarkable work being carried out in many South American countries, which will not only strengthen the practice but will also help to develop the field within the subcontinent and beyond.

Conclusion: some reflections regarding cross-cultural perspectives

Being a therapist who grew up, trained and worked in South America, practising outside the continent is an experience that has taught me many lessons. The cultural and professional contrasts are at times extreme and prompt questions about the priorities of our societies and the helping professions as a whole.

When I left Brazil, I was a 24-year-old qualified psychologist, had completed a year of work as an educational psychologist in three local schools in a small town next to Porto Alegre, the capital of my home-state in the south of Brazil, and was actively practising in the institute of psychology that I founded with other colleagues from the same field. In both places, I had the freedom to implement projects to meet the needs of the respective contexts. In the schools, I used to provide support to the local council, pupils, parents, teachers and senior educators. There were not many practical restrictions to the work but there were clear injustices in the community due to local government's misuse of power, benefiting those who obeyed and taking away opportunities from those who did not; a typical example of the corruption that is often seen in local and national governments in the subcontinent.

In the institute of psychology, I also had a broad scope of practice. I used to provide counselling (or psychotherapy or work in clinical psychology – all being synonymous) for adults and children; teach client-centred therapy and the person-centred approach to psychology students; and develop with my colleagues a range of activities related to promoting humanistic principles in diverse contexts. By that time, I had also worked as a supervised student in, among others, psychiatric settings, social psychology and organizational psychology. Even though some of these experiences were set within a directive and deterministic system, I had sufficient autonomy to explore my beliefs and develop my own ways of working.

Those years of internship and early professional practice in South America helped to sow the seeds of the realizations that I reach today, when I reflect upon almost eight years living in the UK, being in diverse contexts and experiencing relationships with clients and colleagues from a range of nationalities and cultural backgrounds. One of the intriguing aspects identified in this process is related to the distinct levels of control found in our different societies and the ways in which they impact on who we are and how we practise. In Brazil, like several other South American countries, there is the inner and outer control resulting from colonial and conservative traditions; economic, racial, social and educational inequality; and the insecurity and fear associated with complex problems like poverty, corruption and criminality. Nonetheless, out of these ongoing challenges, therapists tend to have the flexibility and freedom to develop creative ways to meet the needs of individuals and communities.

In cultures like the UK, in contrast, the control is associated with other matters. The economic and social disparity is much less and the level of stability is much greater. The problems experienced by individuals are not linked to the denial of basic human rights as we see in South America. The inner and outer controls emerge from what seems to be an intrinsic need to maintain and increase safety and stability. This necessity, however, has evolved into a kind of greediness for control within a culture of fear. In this context, there is little scope for creativity and freedom to practise. Therapy and therapists increasingly turn into instruments of bureaucratic and controlling systems, not necessarily because of real problems but due to fear and anticipation of *potential* problems. While we in South America struggle to find ways to deal with extreme deprivation and lack of resources, practitioners in the so-called 'developed' countries have greater stability, financial and service resources, but regularly struggle to simply be a therapist due to the amount of rules and bureaucracy they face.

In these idiosyncratic yet stimulating environments, we may see highly qualified therapists who practise in one country not being able to equally practise in another as a result of incompatible professional policies. The quantity and quality of the regulations in different parts of the world, instead of facilitating constructive exchange and development of the profession, can prove most difficult and often serve to eliminate such exchange and development altogether. What to do then? I find myself with more questions than answers about the complexity of our cross-cultural fields. However, being a typical South American, I believe that it is possible to find creative ways to respect our differences, joining their strength for the benefit of clients, practitioners and the helping professions as a whole. For this to happen, however, we have to challenge the colonialism within the realm of our own profession. This is a responsibility that lies on each one of us. If we meet the idiosyncrasy of our cultures and profession with the ethical elements of trust and freedom, we will become more united and will progress much further. This path may be more challenging but it is undoubtedly a journey worth taking from both ethical and humanitarian perspectives. South American heritage is a good example of the necessity and value of this effort.

Acknowledgement

I would like to thank Colin Lago for inviting me to write this chapter and giving me the opportunity to revisit my heritage at this stage of my life. Colin was the facilitator of the first person-centred workshop that I attended in the UK. This was in 2005, in Oxford, and I was then working in London as a nanny to learn English in order to continue developing my career outside Brazil. That first meeting with Colin is still fresh in my mind along with the joy I felt to reconnect with my profession.

References

Balch, O. (2009) *Viva South America! A Journey Through a Restless Continent*. London: Faber & Faber.

Cardoso, F.H. (2006) *The Accidental President of Brazil: A Memoir*. New York: PublicAffairs.

CFP (Conselho Federal de Psicologia) (2005) *Código de Ética Profissional do Psicólogo*. Brasília: CFP.

Cook, M. (2003) *A Brief History of the Human Race*. London: Granta Books.

Corral-Verdugo, V. and Pinheiro, J.Q. (2009) Environmental psychology with a Latin American taste, *Journal of Environmental Psychology*, 29: 366–74.

Freire, P. (1996) *Pedagogy of the Oppressed*. London: Penguin.

Freire, P. (2007) *Ação cultural para a liberdade e outros escritos*, 12th edn. São Paulo: Paz e Terra.

Freire, P. and Horton, M. (1990) *We Make the Road by Walking: Conversations on Education and Social Change*. Philadelphia, PA: Temple University Press.

Fundação Getúlio Vargas (FGV) (2007) *Poverty, Inequality and Income Policies: Lula's Real – Executive Summary*. Rio de Janeiro: Fundação Getúlio Vargas.

Galeano, E. (1971) *Open Veins of Latin America: Five Centuries of the Pillage of a Continent*. London: Serpent's Tail.

Grinblatt, A. (ed.) (2008) *Practica del counseling en Argentina*. Buenos Aires: Georges Zanun.

Guardiola-Rivera, O. (2010) *What if Latin America Ruled the World? How the South will Take the North into the 22nd Century*. London: Bloomsbury.

Hall, M.E. (1946) The present status of psychology in South America, *Psychological Bulletin*, 43: 441–76.

Hutz, C. and Gomes, W. (2006) Teaching psychology in Brazil, *International Journal of Psychology*, 41: 10–16.

Kearsley, G.R. (2003) *Inca Origins: Asian Influences in Early South America in Myth, Migration and History*. UK: Yelsraek Publishing.

Maslow, A. (1954) *Motivation and Personality*. New York: Harper & Row.

Morales, E. (2003) *The Latin Beat: The Rhythms and Roots of Latin Music, from Bossa Nova to Salsa and Beyond*. Cambridge, MA: Da Capo Press.

Ribeiro, D. (1971) *The Americas and Civilization*. New York: E.P. Dutton & Co.

Roberts, J.M. (1998) *Short Illustrated History of the World*. Oxford: Helicon Publishing.

Rogers, C.R. (1951) *Client-Centered Therapy*. London: Constable.

Rogers, C.R. (1959) A theory of therapy, personality, and interpersonal relationships, as developed in the client-centered framework, in S. Kock (ed.) *Psychology: The Study of a Science, Vol. 3: Formulations of the Person and the Social Context*. New York: McGraw-Hill.

Rogers, C.R. (1978) *Carl Rogers on Personal Power: Inner Strength and its Revolutionary Impact*. London: Constable.

Rosenthal, R.W. (1999) O plantão de psicólogos no Instituto Sedes Sapientiae: Uma proposta de atendimento aberto à comunidade, in M. Mahfoud, *Plantão Psicológico: Novos Horizontes*. São Paulo: Companhia Ilimitada.

Saunders, N.J. (2004) *Ancient Americas*. Phoenix Mill: Sutton Publishing.

Savigliano, M.E. (1995) *Tango and the Political Economy of Passion*. Boulder, CO: Westview Press.

UNESCO (2009) Enrolment of pupils of the official age in pre-primary, primary and secondary education, Table 3B, retrieved from UNESCO Institute for Statistics, Global Educational Digest, www.uis.unesco.org/ev.php?ID=7628_201& ID2=DO_TOPIC.

Vasconcelos, T.P. (2009) A atitude clínica no plantão psicológico: composição da fotografia experimental do terapeuta-sherpa, unpublished masters dissertation, Universidade de Fortaleza, Pós-Graduação, Mestrado em Psicologia, www.unifor.br/tede//tde_busca/arquivo.php?codArquivo=827661.

Veloso, C. (2002) *Tropical Truth: A Story of Music and Revolution in Brazil*. New York: Alfred A. Knopf.

Vizentine, P.F. (2006) *História mundial contemporanea*. Brasília: FUNAG.

27   The effects of a Pakistani heritage

Neelam Zahid

Introduction

'*Assalam-ailakum*'. This is the Arabic greeting spoken by most Pakistani Muslims and it translates into 'peace be upon you'. These are the words from a country proud to fly the symbolic Pakistani flag representing progress, light, knowledge, peace and prosperity. An extraordinary place, Pakistan has landscapes from arid deserts to lush green valleys and snow-covered mountains. With a population of nearly 200 million people, Pakistan has borders with India, Iran, Afghanistan and China. It contains the famous Karakorum Highway and the Karakorum mountain range, home to K2, the second highest mountain in the world. Pakistan is also famous for its excellent sporting ability, with world-class cricketers such as Imran Khan and boxers such as Amir Khan. Pakistan hosted Benazir Bhutto, the first female prime minister of a Muslim country and gave a home to Taliban supporters, for which it has become known worldwide. Loved and hated simultaneously by many, Pakistan is certainly not a dull country.

As a child, my fantasy of Pakistan was of a romantic nation, with mystery and intrigue. My mother would tell me stories of love, witches and Jinn.[1] A journal extract from when I was 15 years old (in 1990), demonstrates how my fantasy of Pakistan was quickly quashed:

> It's so hot here! The heat intensifies the smell of industrial dust and smog. The police look scary, with their unkempt moustaches and huge rifles. The Pakistanis look different here than in London. They stare with their penetrating eyes...people get so close up and personal...I hate it...The sounds of fast moving rickshaws, car horns and the Azaan[2] are deafening. The bright-coloured clothes and bangles, mixed with the smell of barbequed sweet potato makes it feel so surreal.

My connection with Pakistan has always been a strenuous one. Although I was born and brought up in London, the country of my parents' heritage has evoked strong feelings of love, irritation and a sense of belonging. Growing up, I never felt at home in Britain or in Pakistan, always feeling torn between the two cultures.

---

[1]Jinn (plural) are spirits made of fire created by Allah to worship him like humans. They have supernatural powers of good and evil, and can take on human or animal forms.
[2]The Azaan is the call for prayer which takes place five times a day.

I have noticed my feeling of loyalty to Pakistan, experiencing a glimpse of the camaraderie Pakistani Muslims feel towards this country and their historical fight for being an independent state – the journey to form an identity, mirroring my own internal struggle to find a space where I feel I belong.

Pakistani history

Pre-independence

Pakistan is steeped in ancient history. To fully appreciate Pakistani heritage, one only has to examine its ancient history to gain an insight into the plethora of cultural influences. Pakistan was at the heart of the Indus Valley civilization, and was invaded by Aryans, Persians, Greeks, Arabs, Turks, Afghans, Mongols and the British. From the first revolution of agricultural life, people moved to another great revolution in their social, cultural and economic life and established trade with Turkmenistan, Uzbekistan, Iran and the Arab world, who in return imparted their cultures. One can see the many Hindu influences during the Vedic period (2000 BC to AD 600) when the hymns of Rigdeva were composed and the foundations of Hinduism laid. During the Ghandhara period (200 BC to AD 1,000), Pakistan attracted Alexander the Great from Macedonia (in 326 BC), and the resulting Greek influence. Finally, Islam came to Pakistan in the seventh century AD via the Arabs and Turks, replacing the worship of idols and introducing monotheism. Islam gradually dominated the South Asian region until the collapse of the Mughal Empire in the eighteenth century. In 1707 the Sikhs established their empire within the Punjab, which quickly came to an end after the British East India Company seized power in 1849. Thereafter, the British Raj ruled until freedom was granted in 1947. The British first appeared around 1612, when the East India Company established its first factories in Bombay, Calcutta and Madras, trading spices, cotton, silk, indigo dye, tea and opium. The company began to formally extend its power, and by the mid nineteenth century had evolved into a powerful political and military force within the subcontinent, entrusted to the British Crown.

Independence

Pakistan was created as a refuge for the Muslim world, after its declaration as an independent state on 14 August 1947. Perhaps the word 'Pakistan', derived from two Persian words, *pak* meaning pure and *stan* meaning country or land, is a reflection of the thought behind the country's envisaged future – a land blessed by God. The vision for Pakistan was mainly initiated by Mahatma Ghandi, Jawaharlal Nehru and Muhammad Ali Jinnah. In 1885 the National India Congress was founded, enabling Indians to have a legitimate share in the government. In 1906 the Muslim League, another anti-colonial organization, was founded, formed to protect the rights and liberties of Muslims in a multi-religious country, but later changing its political bent towards independence from the British.

The partition of India led to huge ethnic conflicts across the Indian-Pakistani border. Ten million Hindus and Sikhs were expelled from Pakistan, and approximately 7 million Muslims crossed the border to Pakistan. Roshida Razzaq, a Pakistani, recounts her memories as a child during the partition:

> My worst memory was watching a convoy of huge open trucks...loaded with slaughtered bodies of men, women and children, stacked on top of one another, like sacks...I could see the heavily blood-stained, scarcely clothed dead bodies, and the stiff faces of some women...I woke up, startled by the sound of the bullets and shrieks in the distance, which sounded loud and incredibly close in the stillness of the night.
>
> (personal communication)

Experiencing such horrors perpetrated by both Pakistanis and Indians has left considerable tensions between both countries, as well as with Bangladesh, which parted from Pakistan in 1971. Gilani (2001) suggests that Murd Mujahid, the 'righteous fighter', is a representation of the Jungian archetype of the *hero* within Pakistanis. Hence, combined with the myth the British left of martial races, the Pakistanis self-identity as a warrior surfaced. More recently, this archetype is reflected in militant Islamic organizations.

Modern-day Pakistan

Modern-day Pakistan is made up of four provinces: Sindh, Punjab, North-West Frontier Province (NWFP) and Balochistan. Balochistan has the largest area but the smallest population. The Punjab has a little more than half the country's population, and the second largest area. Sindh does not have as large a population as the Punjab but is home to Karachi, which is the hub of industry. NWFP and Balochistan are tribal societies with designated self-administered 'tribal territories', ruled by customary laws and with distinct subcultures.

There are two official languages in Pakistan, Urdu and English, with an additional five provincial languages. Urdu developed during the Islamic conquests of the Mughal Empire and although it is spoken by only 8 per cent of the population there has been an increase in its use among new urbanized Pakistanis as their main language.

Religion

Religion has been the seed from which Pakistan has grown, and unfortunately Islamic extremism has become strongly associated with the country. The Zia government of 1978 was pivotal in promoting extremism and reinforced some of the ideals of the Muslim League which argued for a state based on Sharia Law.[3] The events of the Iranian Revolution of 1979 and the Afghan *jihad* against Soviet occupation in 1980 accelerated the Islamization process. General Zia gave

---

[3]Sharia Law refers both to the Islamic system of law and the totality of the Islamic way of life.

Afghanistan's Mugahadins a home to train and fight for their country, and thus the political battle between Muslims and non-Muslims has since spilt worldwide.

Having the second largest Muslim population in the world, Pakistan is home to over 97 per cent Muslims (as of 2008). The remaining 3 per cent of the population are other non-Muslim religious groups such as Christians, Hindus, Sikhs, Jews, Buddhists, Parsi, Baha'i, Kalash, and atheists. There are a number of different factions of the Islamic faith, the most popular being Sunnis, Shiats, Ahmadiyyas[4] and Sufis (Sunnis being the leading majority). Over the years, tensions have arisen between the different sects, all claiming to be the correct path of Islam. Sunnis are traditionalists, following the teachings of the prophet Muhammad. Shiats follow the teachings of Ali ibn Abi Talib, the prophet Muhammad's cousin and son-in-law, believed to be the designated successor of the prophet. Sufism is the spiritual branch of Islam. The Ahmadiyya movement, founded in 1889 by Mirza Ghulam Ahmad is the most controversial sect and raises the most anger within the Islamic world. Ahmad declared himself a prophet and the 'promised messiah' of all religions. Since all sects believe that the prophet Muhammad was the last, Ahmadiyyas have been exposed to extreme violence and discrimination within Pakistan and worldwide.

All religions have equal status under the Pakistani constitution, although non-Muslims cannot become president. The Pakistani government is ruled by Islam, and hence the dominance over minorities and non-Muslims is filtered through to society. The largest minorities within Pakistan are Hindus and Christians, the majority of Christians being converted Hindus from the lower castes during the colonial period. Unfortunately they are faced with the reality of social prejudice, which is reinforced by the social hereditary structure. This structure among families in Pakistan is partially rooted in Islam and also arises from the common heritage of the Indus Valley civilization. Muslim dynasties of Persian and Afghan origins created a new elite class, from which *Zaats* were formed. *Zaat* refers to one's tribal identity and *Zaats* in Pakistan include Ashrafs (noble born), who embody the privileged status of conquerors. The former high-class Hindus kept their castes after conversion, reflecting their hereditary occupations and identities; the lower classes or 'untouchables' also remained at the bottom of the hierarchy even after they changed their religion. However, whichever *Zaat*, caste or religion one is from, Pakistanis share one common theme: the bond to one's family and the hierarchy within the family.

Family

The two most important messages at birth are the belief in Allah and the bond with one's family. From birth, the emotional tie to one's family is repeatedly reinforced by various rituals and rules. For example, my siblings and I were given honey after birth, symbolically strengthening the baby's bond with the caregiver and to allow

---

[4]Zulfiqar Ali Bhutto stipulated that Ahmadiyyas were constitutionally non-Muslim and in 1984 General Zia passed an ordinance to declare that Ahmadiyyas were not permitted to call themselves Muslim.

the baby to take on characteristics of the person giving it (Hirani 2008). Another ritual performed after the birth of a child is the giving of 'Azaan'[5] in the right ear. As children we were constantly told stories about the prophet Muhammad (*hadiths*),[6] which reinforced the godly act of serving one's parents until they die. One of the *hadiths* states that 'heaven is under your mother's right foot' and another states, 'your father is the gate to heaven'.

Pakistani society is based on strong family ties and kinship. Kinship refers to the family, extended family, members tied into bonds of mutual support, obligation, common identity and endogamy. The joint family system is the key to all emotional ties and has been described as a family in which the man is head of the household and lives with his wife, married and/or unmarried children (Chakraborty 2002). Hence, multi-storey dwellings (*havelis*) have been constructed to accommodate large extended families and it is common for one nuclear family to live in one or two rooms on each floor. In recent years, the joint family system has evolved, and there is a greater presence of nuclear families in central Punjab, urban Sindh and the Peshawar Valley, yet places like rural Sindh, southern Punjab and Balochistan still retain their traditional family structures. Since mobility has increased within Pakistan, family members are moving further for work, while still having strong links to the family home. Hence, in more recent times, older people have become *symbolic* heads of the family, which is reflected in Pakistani families all over the world.

Since independence, the agrarian economy of villages has weakened and there has been a loss of a self-contained social life. Modern housing, developed after colonialism, has also changed, and house design discourages neighbours from dropping by (Naveed-i-Rahat 1990). Similarly, marriage was about forming new families, solidarity and affirming kinship, but is now more about networking and social status – 50 per cent of marriages are between cousins (Zaidi 1998) and marriage is more common in rural areas: this ensures that wealth is kept within the family (through paying a dowry by the daughter's family) and family bonds are kept strong. However, in places like Karachi, families tend to be more dispersed, forcing some Pakistanis to marry outside their family. The majority of marriages are still arranged by parents in Pakistan, and are seen by parents and children to be better than 'love' marriages (*Herald* 1997). A belief in unrequited love is strong and is reflected in the media and in folklore. Only in places like Lahore, Karachi and Islamabad will one find a tendency towards 'love' marriages.

The main perceptions of men and women in Pakistan are that women are subordinate to men, and that the man's family honour resides in the actions of the woman of the household. To preserve this honour, society restricts women's behaviour and activities, limiting contact with the opposite sex. Some women live under *purdah* (a Persian word for 'curtain', referring to veiling). *Purdah* may take the form of wearing a burqa (a fitted body veil) or a chador (a loosely draped cloth used to cover the head and body). *Purdah* is practised in various ways, depending on family tradition, region and class, the most extreme restraints being found

---

[5]The Azaan in this case states in Arabic: 'There is only one Allah, and Muhammad is his messenger'.
[6]*Hadiths* are collections of stories about the prophet Muhammad, his sayings and actions.

in parts of North-West Frontier Province and Balochistan, where women almost never leave their homes and may not meet unrelated men except when they marry. In the Punjab and Sindh, where gender relations are more relaxed, poor rural women have greater mobility and are more likely to work. This also includes wealthier Pakistanis who are more influenced by family tradition. However, when a woman becomes a mother or a mother-in-law, the power dynamics within the family shift (Qadeer 2006). Becoming a mother brings with it a certain amount of power, and one only has to look at the relationship between mother-in-laws and their daughter-in-laws to understand that the oppressed (woman) becomes the oppressor (mother-in-law). For example, in my family I always thought my father was head of the household, but after my mother died I realized that *she* was the head of the family, the force that kept us together as a symbolic unit.

Mothers tend to take care of the children, and when women work children are cared for by their grandmother, aunt, sister or a maid. Observing child-rearing practices in Pakistan is a good indication of emotional development. For example, Hirani (2008) has highlighted that many mothers believe a baby should only be fed when they cry and awake from sleep, and a baby who is cuddled too much will produce a demanding child. Fathers do not usually take on the caring role and are the decision-makers in terms of health care, education and finances (Hirani 2008).

Women's roles changed after British rule, when the British encouraged education to support the labour force. The attempts at social and legal reform aimed at improving Muslim women's lives have been related to the social reform movement in British India and the growing Muslim nationalist movement. Currently, women's groups are supporting small-scale projects throughout the country that focus on empowering women. However, with more rights for women, incidents of violence towards them have increased since the 1990s and the Human Rights Commission of Pakistan (1995) recorded an increase in honour killings, bride burning (bride not bringing home the expected dowry) and *Karo Kari* (a Sindh tribal custom of a family murdering a women who has had 'illicit' sex).

In modern-day Pakistan, many more women are working and, in 1990, females officially made up 13 per cent of the labour force. Family dynamics and gender roles are changing and it is important to reflect on the effects of this on society at large and the impact on Pakistanis' mental health.

Mental health

In the Name of God, the Compassionate, the Merciful

DAYBREAK

Say: I seek refuge in the Lord of daybreak from the mischief of His creation; from the mischief of the night when she spreads her darkness; from the mischief of conjuring witches; from the mischief of the envier, when he envies.

(Koran 113: 1–5)

This is a verse from the Koran often recited to alleviate *jadoo* (magic), reinforcing the belief that prayer will heal 'demonic' behaviour. Many in Pakistan have misconceptions about mental health and think it has supernatural causes (Karim *et al.* 2004), seeking assistance from *hakims* (Muslim physicians) and *pir* (holy men) (Mubbashar and Saeed 2001). There is a tendency to believe in possession by ghosts or jinn, magic or the evil eye. When I was growing up, I was told that my uncle had gone mad – *pagaal* – due to being affected by industrial gases. I now understand that he was schizophrenic. As I grew up, the term *pagaal* seemed to encompass a whole range of bizarre behaviour. In families where children would not conform to traditional behaviour, parents sought cures from holy men. Thus, a vast number of families take care of the mentally ill family member in their own home, which allows them to protect themselves from the shame they feel.

Mental health awareness is determined by the general literacy rate (Suhail 2005) and a UNICEF report (2007) showed that only 55 per cent of the Pakistani population are literate. An estimated 15–24 million people suffer from mental health problems, and 1 per cent of this number suffers from severe mental illness. Between 30 and 50 per cent of these people suffer from depression. Mental health problems within Pakistan are not widely accepted, which may be a reflection of the residues of the Lunacy Act of 1912, a legacy of the colonial government. A lunatic was described as an 'idiot or person of unsound mind' (section 4). Although in 2001 the Act was replaced by the Pakistan Mental Health Ordinance, which stipulated better care and recognition of those with a mental illness, the belief that the mentally ill are lunatics did not shift.

Depression and anxiety are the main psychological diagnoses within Pakistani culture and are four times more likely to be diagnosed than psychosis (Suhail 2005). Causal effects are explained by low self-esteem, early marriage, hostile in-laws and a lack of good relationships with spouses for women (Naeem 1990). Parasuicide or self-harm is prominent in Pakistan although it is a criminal offence and Islam prohibits it. Interestingly, housewives, students and businessmen are the largest groups that attempt parasuicide (Khan *et al.* 1996), the main cause being relationship problems for both sexes. Married females under the age of 30 are found to be the largest group who self-harm in Pakistan (Khan and Reza 1996) and Zakiullah *et al.* (2008) reported that types of self-injury included throat cutting, slashing wrists, burning and jumping from high places. Self-poisoning with organophosphates and drug overdose are the most common methods of suicidal attempts.(Khan and Reza, 1996). Unfortunately, under-reporting and misdiagnosis are common (Ahmed 1983), with many families paying the police to avoid prosecution.

Treatment for mental health issues appears to be problematic within Pakistan. Gradit and Khalid (2002) estimate that there are only 3,500 psychiatric inpatient beds in private, public and teaching psychiatric hospitals throughout the country. There are four psychiatric hospitals in Pakistan and another 20 are attached to government medical colleges. Basic health units providing primary care to a rural population do not have mental health professionals attached to them. The number

of trained mental health professionals is small in comparison to population demand. There are no specialist services existing for drug/alcohol misuse (Karim
et al. 2004), which seems extraordinary in a country which has become the largest
heroin consumer market in the South-West Asia region.

The main methods of treatment for mental health conditions are medication,
electro-convulsive therapy (ECT) and psychotherapy, and only young educated
and financially independent females prefer psychotherapy (Zafar *et al.* 2009). Psychiatric training in Pakistan is in its infancy and, as Farooq (2001) suggests, a
major change in psychiatric training is needed for psychiatrists to effectively work
with other disciplines. Lack of appropriate and specialist training is due to a poorly
resourced and underdeveloped health system.

In summary, high rates of mental health problems may be due to inter-family
marriages, economic decline and high rates of unemployment, rapidly changing
social and cultural norms, fragmentation of the family system and loss of religious
values. How the symptoms are interpreted and expressed is influenced not only by
the country's culture, but also by the specific regional culture. If one pays attention
to the expression of emotions and symptoms, one may gain a better understanding
of the core mental health issues for Pakistanis.

Pakistanis in Britain

'Curry and chips don't mix' – something said to me while having a drink with
a white male. It was an ironic statement since the man I was having a drink
with was Welsh, another race exposed to discrimination. My response to this was,
'How do you know unless you've tried it!' Few people appreciate that Pakistanis
fought alongside the British in World Wars I and II. Pakistanis are associated with
the Taliban, suicide bombers and honour killings. This is covertly and overtly
reinforced by the media and the public. With 747,285 Pakistanis in the UK (as
of 2001) and more recently estimated at well over 1 million, it is inevitable that
tensions will arise between the second largest ethnic group in Britain and the rest
of the population. Within the last 10 years, Islam has taken on a different guise and
has become ever more feared and despised. With the reality of Pakistani suicide
bombers, Pakistanis in general have encompassed the negative traits of a Pakistani
and of a fanatical Muslim.

Being part of the Commonwealth, Pakistanis first came to Britain in the 1950s
and 1960s, after the collapse of the British Empire following World War II, entering
the country as legitimate workers. Many Punjabis, like my family, came to Britain
in the 1960s from cities and towns, many being qualified teachers, doctors and
engineers. Some Punjabis from the rural areas of Pakistan migrated to the English
Midlands, working mainly in the foundries. Manual workers were recruited for the
labour shortage during the 1950s, as a consequence of World War II. They found
work in the steel and textile industries of Yorkshire, Lancashire and the West
Midlands and in the light industry of Luton and Slough. The Commonwealth

Immigrants Act 1967 and the Immigration Act 1971 largely restricted any further primary immigration, although family members of already settled migrants were still allowed to enter the country.

Growing up, the tales of hell fire and damnation from my father were enough to keep me away from other religions. From an early age, we were told that *kaafir* (unbelievers) were not to be mixed with and to hold onto our Muslim Pakistani identity. At home, our Pakistani identity was preserved by wearing *salwar qameez*,[7] speaking Punjabi and eating Pakistani food. Outside the home, life was the polar opposite, as we wore English clothes, spoke English and mixed with different cultures. There was a split between east and west when I stepped outside the front door. Over the years, the split became more pronounced as I began to learn of all the 'pleasures' I was forbidden to part take in. Similarly, more western influences entered the home: we would wear English clothes more freely and had an evening a week when we would enjoy an 'English dinner'. However, the core beliefs remained the same. Although we were given tentative permission to find our own husbands if we wished, we were not allowed to marry a non-Muslim, or even marry across the sects.

I soon became aware that when my parents were looking for prospective husbands, Pakistanis living outside London appeared more traditional than our family. My mother said that some of these people came from specific regions of Pakistan and had a different mentality from ours; she described them as having 'small town' mentalities, which referred to people from Mirpur and other small rural towns. With Pakistanis making up 43 per cent of the Muslims in Britain, it is important to look at their distribution across Britain, and the specific region they have come from in Pakistan. It is inevitable that those from the more rural areas will hold more traditional values. From the total, 21.5 per cent of Pakistani Muslims reside in London, which has the most diverse Pakistani community in Britain, with a mix of 163,000 Punjabis, Pathans, Mirpuris and Sindhis. The largest populations of Pakistani Muslims resides in Yorkshire and the Humber (163,000), and the West Midlands (172,000), Mirpuris being the majority there. The 2001 census stated that Pakistanis in the North and the Midlands had the second highest rates of poverty in the country, significantly differing from those living in the South. This has major implications for access to education and mental health services, and although those based in larger cities are making progress towards professional middle-class status, migration histories should not be overlooked.

Interestingly, Nazroo and King (2002) state that Pakistanis in Britain (and Bangladeshis) have the lowest rates of admission for psychosis, yet Weich and McManus (2002) state that there are high rates of depressive episodes within Pakistani and Indian women. Soni-Raleigh and Balarajan (1992) show that British Asian women are at high risk of self-harming when it comes to stress and social

---

[7] *Salwar qameez* is a traditional costume worn by both women and men consisting of loose pajama-like trousers (*salwar*) worn with a long shirt or tunic (*qameez*).

isolation, associated with marital conflicts arising from restrictive relationships and pressures to conform to traditional expectations. When one refers back to the mental health problems within Pakistan, there appears to be a parallel: Pakistanis experience difficulties in their marital or intimate relationships. With suicide rates elevated for British Pakistani women aged between 25 and 34 (Soni-Raleigh 1996), it is questionable whether Pakistanis are receiving or are able to access the appropriate support, and perhaps a relational type of therapy is more apt in dealing with the dominant issues presented by British Pakistanis.

Conclusion

In this chapter I have outlined important factors contributing to the cultural heritage of Pakistan. An understanding of Pakistan's struggle for independence gives an insight into why British Pakistanis hold onto their heritage with such passion. The British have only been one part of the Pakistani cultural heritage, and observing other cultural influences that preceded colonialism gives an indication of the tensions existing within other cultures. The relationship with the British has always been a difficult one. They have historically been Pakistanis' oppressors and the power struggle between the two still remains. The horrific 7/7 London bombings could be seen as a re-enactment of rage from an oppressive past, where the victim becomes the persecutor.

The reality is that the Pakistani consciousness is evolving. With the joint family system devolving, another kind of support is needed. Adapting to a society which has historically been our persecutor is a difficult journey, and is heightened within the confines of the therapy room. However, learning about mental health within Pakistan is a good start in understanding the mental health of British Pakistanis. More comprehensive cross-cultural studies need to be completed on child-rearing practices as this may be key to understanding the difficulties arising developmentally within Pakistani clients. It is important to recognize that Pakistanis in Britain are different from those living in Pakistan. Pakistani culture in Britain is more preserved than in Pakistan for fear of losing its identity and arising from the need to feel safe in a contained community.

However, being part of the Pakistani community and family poses a struggle for some second generation British Pakistanis and thus the thought that Asians are better suited for family therapy is becoming obsolete. The empowerment of Pakistani women has left them more vulnerable than ever before, which in turn has changed the dynamics within Pakistani culture.

Pakistanis are forming new identities, embracing both Pakistani and British values. As we become more confident holding two cultures, we are allowing ourselves to create a new, more suitable culture influenced by different lifestyles. As with the complexity of translation, it is difficult to find a balance allowing emotions and choices to be expressed safely and to be understood by someone of a different culture.

References

Ahmed, S.H. (1983) Pakistan, in L.A. Headley (ed.) *Suicide in Asia and the Near East*. Berkeley, CA: University of California Press.

Chakraborty, K. (2002) *Family in India*. Jaipur: Rawat Publications.

Farooq, S. (2001) Psychiatric training in developing countries, *British Journal of Psychology*, 179: 464.

Gilani, S. (2001) Personal and social power in Pakistan, in A. Weiss and S. Gilani (eds) *Power and Civil Society in Pakistan*. Oxford: Oxford University Press.

Gradit, A.A. and Khalid, N. (2002) *State of Mental Health in Pakistan: Service, Education and Research*. Karachi: Hamdard University Hospital.

Herald (1997) What do Pakistanis really want? Fifty years, fifty questions, January, p. 182.

Hirani, S.A.L. (2008) Child rearing practices in Pakistan and associated challenges for health care professionals, *Coinn Newsletter*.

Human Rights Commission of Pakistan (1995) *State of Human Rights 1995*. Lahore: Human Rights Commission of Pakistan.

Karim, S. *et al.* (2004) Pakistan mental health country profile, *International Review of Psychiatry*, 16: 83–92.

Khan, M.M. and Reza, H. (1996) Methods of deliberate self-harm in Pakistan, *Psychiatric Bulletin*, 20: 367–8.

Khan, M.M., Islam, S. and Kundi, A.K. (1996) Parasuicide in Pakistan: experience at a university hospital, *Acta Psychiatrica Scandinavica*, 93(4): 264–7.

Koran (1997) Translated with notes by N.J. Dawood. London: Penguin.

Mubbashar, M.H. and Saeed, K. (2001) Development of mental health services in Pakistan, *Eastern Mediterranean Health Journal*, 7(3): 292–6.

Naeem, S. (1990) Psychosocial risk factors for depression in Pakistani women, dissertation for FCPS, College of Physicians and Surgeons of Pakistan.

Naveed-i-Rahat (1990) *Male Outmigration and Matri Weighted Households*. Delhi: Hindustan Publishing.

Nazroo, J. and King, M. (2002) Psychosis – symptoms and estimated rates, in K. Sproston and J. Nazroo (eds) *Ethnic Minority Illness Rates in the Community*. London: National Centre for Social Research, TSO.

Qadeer, M.A. (2006) *Pakistan: Social and Cultural Transformations in a Muslim Nation*. London: Routledge.

Soni-Raleigh, V. (1996) Suicide patterns and trends in people of Indian subcontinent and Caribbean origin in England and Wales, *Ethnicity and Health*, 1(1): 55–63.

Soni-Raleigh, V. and Balarajan, R. (1992) Suicide and self-burning among Indians and West Indians in England and Wales, *British Journal of Psychiatry*, 156: 46–50.

Suhail, K. (2005) A study investigating mental health literacy in Pakistan, *Journal of Mental Health*, 14(2): 167–81.

UNICEF (2007) *Pakistan Annual Report*. Islamabad: UNICEF.

Weich, S. and McManus, S. (2002) Common mental disorders, in K. Sproston and J. Nazroo (eds) *Ethnic Minority Illness Rates in the Community*. London: National Centre for Social Research, TSO.

Zafar, A.M. *et al.* (2009) Psychotherapy as a treatment modality for psychiatric disorders: perceptions of general public of Karachi, Pakistan, *BMC Psychiatry*, 9: 37.

Zaidi, S. (1998) Puppi ki beti, Mamoom ka beta, Chowk, www.chowk.com/universityAve/azaidi_march6.

28 The effects of a Bangladeshi heritage: the smell of spice

Anita Chakraborty

Introduction

It was often noisy at my home. The television would blare and a low bassy beat seeped from my brother's bedroom. There was clattering and always the smell of spice from the kitchen. This provided the backdrop to my childhood. It was the childhood of a British-Bangladeshi,[1] Hindu girl, brought up in London suburbia.

My father came to England from Bangladesh in the 1960s to study law, and my mother joined him in 1971 during the war for independence. They worked hard to forge a path for me and my brother in the UK, especially given the relative scarcity of brown faces at that time. Thanks to their endeavours, my brother and I received a good education, and we grew up as Bangladeshi children with South-East London accents.

Early on in our lives we were encouraged by our parents to pursue both Asian and western interests. For example, as a child I studied both Indian and classical dance and ballet for many years. I feel that these foundations, laid in childhood, equipped me with the ability and desire to move fluidly between different cultural contexts. As a result I am able to maintain aspects of my Bangladeshi and British identities, as well as many others, side by side.

With regard to culture, I think that history, tradition, folklore, national and regional customs all play their part in the make-up of a person's background, as do economics, politics and geography. Subcultures also develop, bringing about changes in the original culture as a whole.

It is important to state that I have no desire to imply a sense of uniformity across any one ethnic or cultural group. I believe that Bangladeshi culture is not static and therefore it is vital to resist essentialist modes of expression. However, I feel it is possible to identify broad themes regarding the effects of a Bangladeshi heritage on someone living in a host society. In this chapter I draw upon my reading, conversations with friends and family, personal experiences and research to explore such themes, and imagine how they might affect therapy with a Bangladeshi client.

---

[1] In this chapter the terms 'Bangladeshi' and 'Bengali' have been used interchangeably to refer to someone or something that is from Bangladesh.

Family

The importance of the family is particularly prominent in Bangladeshi culture and this feature sets it apart from a typically western standpoint. Parekh (1986: 2) captures this when he describes Indian society, although the same could be said of Bangladeshi society: 'Indian society is not a bourgeoisie-liberal society, for not the individual but the family is its basic unit'. In its essence, Bangladeshi culture encourages a collective identity and interdependence, whereas western culture encourages personal autonomy and individualism. In addition to this, the child-rearing practices of South Asian parents stress the importance of obedience and respect for elders (Dosanjh and Ghuman 1996), which serves to reinforce the importance of the family as a hub.

Hence, there are some potential issues regarding family to consider when working with a Bangladeshi client. One of the fundamental tenets of western psychotherapy highlights the importance of individuation and separation from one's parents (Dwairy 1998). However, where the individual is seen as secondary to the group, as is the case in Bangladeshi culture, there is the potential for a clash of perspectives. To use an example from my personal experience, my cousin, who lives in India, recently got married. Since the wedding, he has been living with his wife and his parents, together, peacefully under one roof. This arrangement is fairly commonplace among Bengali families in India, Bangladesh and even in the West. However, the same situation is almost unheard of in western families. As such, it would be important in therapy to reserve judgement regarding seemingly unorthodox family arrangements, as there are clearly different cultural standards. Also, traditionally, decision-making is left to the entire family, even after marriage. Therefore, a therapist who is working with a Bangladeshi client would need to be open minded to a different baseline of familial contact and involvement in the client's life.

Alongside the principle of respect comes the notion of honour. The honour of a Bangladeshi family is paramount, and it is each individual's duty to maintain the family's honour and good name (Ballard 1979). A family's honour can be brought into question in countless ways, with varying degrees of severity. This can range from, for example, when a family member is in trouble with the police, to a family member's unfavourable choice of partner. When a family's honour comes into question, members of the family can react in a number of ways dependent on the felt severity of the transgression. In certain families, when the 'offence' has been deemed grave, the 'offender' may be cut off from the family altogether. This will obviously have huge implications for the member of the family who has been cast out, as well as for the family dynamic.

The Bangladeshi client may feel torn between a sense of obligation towards the family and the demand for more autonomy and independence that typically comes in adolescence and early adulthood. If relevant, this will require gentle exploration and empathy from the therapist.

Research has suggested that ethnic minority groups tend to rely on the family for help with difficulties rather than use mental health services (Robbins and

Greenley 1983). A viewpoint has been identified within certain ethnic minority groups whereby the family is felt to share responsibility for an individual's problems (Sabogal *et al.* 1987). Other researchers have also found that within particular ethnic groups, it is felt that mental illness is best treated within the family (Edgerton and Karno 1971). Therefore, a Bangladeshi individual might feel more inclined to talk to their family if they need support, and the therapist may face some form of resistance.

There has also been evidence to suggest that psychiatric disorders may have a greater stigma attached to them in ethnic minority populations. Silva de Crane and Spielberger (1981) found that in a student sample, compared to white students, the black and Hispanic students held more negative views of mental illness — for example, that mentally ill individuals should be isolated from others and were morally inferior. There has also been some evidence to suggest that stigma and family shame may be particularly important within British South Asian cultures (Jacob *et al.* 1998). This may be crucial when considering attitudes towards mental health problems and help-seeking within this group. Therefore, it is possible that a Bangladeshi person seeking help may be experiencing a greater degree of stigma and shame than, for example, a white client.

Food

Food is one of the cornerstones of Bangladeshi culture. It is the glue that holds families together and a vehicle for the communication of myriad emotions. For example, in Bangladeshi circles the act of cooking for someone can be likened to the offering of love. As such, if the food is declined it is akin to rejecting the host's love and can be taken with great offence. Consequently, the everyday occurrence of mealtimes is never straightforward.

Most Bengali occasions for celebration are centred on a meal where friends and family gather to eat. I can remember the well-rehearsed routine whenever guests came to visit my parents' house for such an event. My mother deemed it essential to have some food prepared, and this often took the form of a feast. A polite refusal of food was always met with a repeated steadfast offer, the assumption being that the guests were embarrassed to accept food on their first offer and needed further encouragement. Hence, during mealtimes there was a subtle dance between the cook and the recipient, where the recipient's enjoyment, whether they finished their plate or left some food, and whether they asked for more, became critical.

When food becomes so tied up in emotion, the two things can be difficult to untangle. For example, if working with a Bangladeshi client who presents with an eating disorder it may be necessary to explore in some depth the nature of the client's, as well as their family's, relationship to food. It could be pertinent to spend some time looking at memories of how food and mealtimes were treated during childhood to tease out the effects of the client's culture.

Sex and sexuality

Sex is one of the biggest taboos in Bangladeshi culture. It is hardly ever talked about, nor is it deemed permissible before marriage in most traditional families from the Indian subcontinent (Sapru 1999). If a young Bangladeshi were to become pregnant as a result of premarital sex, this could be a source of great shock and humiliation to their entire family. This ties in with the collectivist philosophy that underpins traditional Bangladeshi family units, whereby a family's honour is carried forward by the next generation. Consequently, any actions carried out by individual family members reflects on the image of the family as a whole.

In certain Bangladeshi families, attitudes to dating can be conservative. This means that young people are often forced to date in secret or not at all. Homosexual partnerships are widely frowned upon. As a result, many gay Bangladeshi men and women will never come out to their families for fear of rejection. Those who do decide to come out face the real possibility of exclusion and alienation. Therefore, any discussions in therapy that pertain to sex or sexuality should be approached with caution and a strong degree of sensitivity to the client's cultural and familial standpoint.

Discrimination

One of the most challenging handicaps faced by migrant Bangladeshis is racial discrimination and exclusion. It has been well documented in the USA by Suarez-Orozco (2001) and Portes and Rumbaut (2001), and in the UK by Modood and his colleagues (1997), that black and Asian people face racial discrimination in housing, employment and health services as well as in other areas of life. There are still some in the host population who harbour post-colonial attitudes towards migrants and migrant culture. As such, those from migrant communities can be deemed 'inferior or at best, exotic' (Ghuman 2005: 621).

Researchers have also found elements of discrimination at school in the form of negative stereotyping and racial prejudice by teachers towards South Asian pupils (Anwar 1998; Bhatti 1999). For example, when Basit (1997) explored the situation for a group of Muslim girls in a London school, she found that many teachers showed inadvertent racism and were unintentionally prejudiced. Basit revealed that some of the Muslim values of home were being misinterpreted: 'Respectfulness is seen as shyness or submissiveness, protectiveness is viewed as oppression and modesty is construed as traditionalism' (Basit 1997). Studies in Norwegian schools have also highlighted the disapproving attitudes of teachers towards their Muslim students' beliefs and religious practices (Ostberg 2003).

Researchers have highlighted the negative impacts of racism on ethnic minority clients and the importance of acknowledging it in the therapeutic work (Clark *et al.* 1999). However, Kareem (1992) asserts that white therapists will find it easy to dismiss racism as it has not happened to them and is beyond their internal and external experience. Bhugra and Bhui (1998) suggest that this kind of insensitive therapeutic encounter may be experienced by the client as a repetition of racial oppression and its accompanying power dynamics. Therefore, issues such as the under-acknowledgment of racism in therapy can exacerbate problems for Bangladeshi clients and should be given serious attention.

Hierarchy

Traditionally, Bangladeshi family units are patriarchal. As such, there are different gender-role expectations within the family, which can lead to a kind of gender inequality (Anwar 1998). Generally, this takes the form of favouritism towards boys over girls (Sapru 1999) and can express itself in a number of ways. For example, as a child I used to help my mother tidy up after meals, while my older brother was excused from all such chores.

In some Bangladeshi families, sons are more valued and are seen as having important obligations towards their parents (Messent 1992). This is sometimes accompanied by an expectation that the son will eventually take over the running of the household and provide for the family.

The sense of hierarchy becomes clear when looking at the Bengali language. For example, in Bengali, there are different ways of addressing your siblings or peers dependent on whether they are older or younger than you – i.e. an older brother would be referred to as *dada*, whereas a younger brother would be referred to by name. The difference pertains to a higher level of respect that is due to one's elders. Owing to this sense of respect and hierarchy, there may be a tendency for a Bangladeshi client to expect a more authoritative voice from their therapist, or indeed an older therapist! As such, it may be useful in the therapy to bear in mind that the client may be looking for something more advisory than exploratory.

Many Bangladeshi parents feel strongly that their daughters carry the honour of the family and that they need 'protection and extra care in their schooling and socialisation' (Ghuman 2005: 620). This can place additional pressure on a Bangladeshi girl to be seen to succeed in the eyes of her family and uphold the family name. This will require careful consideration when working with a Bangladeshi woman in a therapeutic setting.

Religion

The most popular religion in Bangladesh is Islam and 89.7 per cent of the population are Muslims. Of the remaining population, 9.2 per cent are Hindus and the other predominant religions include Buddhism and Christianity (Bangladesh Bureau of Statistics 2006). A survey of literature on South Asian communities living in the UK showed that religion had a strong impact on the lives of first generation immigrants, and more so on Muslims than Hindus (Nesbitt 1995). The presence of mosques and temples in western cities around the world is evidence that religion has crossed country borders and in doing so has helped migrants to maintain aspects of their cultural identity and faith in their new homes.

With regard to Islam, it is important to acknowledge that events across the globe have impacted upon social, political and cultural developments among Muslim communities throughout the West. Conflicts in Afghanistan, the Middle East, Iraq and Chechnya have been followed by Muslims across the length and breadth of Britain (see Abbas 2005). Also, following the events of September 11 and a rise in Islamophobia, many Bangladeshi Muslims have been angered by attacks on the Islamic faith. As such, people's feelings about their religion as well as towards the majority group have been affected.

With regard to Hinduism, Hindus have a fairly rigid class system called 'caste'. It is based on the Hindu belief in rebirth and reincarnation and is often associated with a person's occupation. Every Hindu is born into a caste, and depending on the strength of their beliefs, as well as their family's standpoint, they must accept that caste, marry someone from the same caste and not associate with those from another caste. Consequently, dependent on the strength of these views, a Bangladeshi Hindu may or may not live their life in accordance with these rules.

A therapist working with a Bangladeshi client needs to pay careful attention to the client's religion, as well as the importance they place upon it. Dependent on their religious affiliations, the client may have specific expectations of the therapeutic encounter. For example, they may want to use prayer or consult with a religious leader before or after coming to therapy. In certain circumstances, there may be a preference for alternative forms of treatment – for example, consulting a shaman or holy person, or using yoga/meditation for therapeutic purposes. There are a multitude of differences between the dominant religions in Bangladesh, and given the history of feuding between Muslims and Hindus in the country it is imperative that the therapist is mindful of this.

Education

Many Bangladeshis who migrated to the West were sojourners who had strong motivations to improve their economic and social status and to offer their children better opportunities than they were party to. Education played a large part in this and therefore many Bangladeshi parents place great importance on the education of their children and the notion of becoming qualified.

When I was at school, there was a large expectation (from my parents and no doubt myself) that I should do well. While this level of pressure can be encouraging, stretching a child to realize their potential, it can sometimes become a burden. Parental and familial expectations can weigh down on the individual and cause anxiety, and therapists should be mindful of this when working with Bangladeshi clients.

Appearance

When considering cultural differences in clothing, it is important to think about attitudes to modesty. Bengali girls are taught from an early age to behave with modesty and decorum at all times, or they will bring dishonour to the family name. The Bengali word *lajja*, meaning 'shame', springs to mind when I think about the stance taken by some parents towards their children dressing in western clothes. For example, as a teenager I can remember my father casting disapproving glances in my direction when he deemed my clothes to be 'too revealing'. However, it would be safe to assume that this is not a phenomenon linked solely to Bangladeshi families. It may also be related to generational standards and expectations regarding dress and modesty.

In adulthood, many Bangladeshi women are extremely modest, and they are accustomed to being clothed from head to foot all the time. Of course, this varies with religious affiliation and familial stance, etc. There are also plenty of Bangladeshi women who have adopted a more liberal stance to clothing, and who are free to dress as they choose. As a therapist working with a Bangladeshi woman, it is important to remain open to the individual client without making too many assumptions, but 'listening' for any cues regarding their cultural stance on appearance, modesty and shame.

Marriage

Bangladeshi parents in the West will have different wishes regarding their children's choice of partner, depending on the family's perspective. Some will prefer them to have a partner who is also Bangladeshi, and of a similar religion. Others will not mind if their children choose a partner from a different ethnic or religious group, while yet other families deem it important for their children to marry someone from a similar caste (see section on religion).

Arranged marriages are commonplace in certain Bangladeshi families. Sometimes potential marriage candidates are sought out and brought over from Bangladesh to marry British Bangladeshi youngsters. In other cases Bangladeshis opt for a 'love marriage', where, as the name would suggest, the individual chooses a partner and decides to marry on the basis of love. Given the inherent differences between arranged marriage and the western approach to finding a partner, it is vital for therapists to be aware of their own feelings towards the different types of union. If a client senses that their therapist is at all judgemental of their situation, this could be extremely detrimental for the working alliance, and hence damaging for the therapy itself.

Touch

There are various unspoken rules regarding touch and physical proximity in Bangladeshi culture. Physical contact between couples in public – for example, kissing – tends to be deemed inappropriate. Similarly, some Bangladeshis feel that hand-holding is also inappropriate in public. With regard to greetings between people, among friends and family hugging tends to be permissible. However, when a young person greets an elder it is sometimes fitting for the youngster to touch the feet of the older person as a sign of respect.

Generally speaking, the experience of interpersonal space is such that Bangladeshi people require less personal space than their western counterparts. This will inevitably impact upon the therapeutic dialogue and as such it is important for the therapist to pay attention to the minutiae of communication via body language, in particular when greeting a Bangladeshi client.

Identity

One of the problems unique to growing up in multicultural societies relates to the construction of dual or multiple social and personal identities. Second and third generation Bangladeshis brought up in the West, especially those whose parents emigrated from rural villages in Bangladesh, may find it difficult to reconcile the beliefs and values of their homeland with the differing (and sometimes contrasting) ones of western society. In addition to this, their values, customs and beliefs may be in a state of flux. The individual's life at work or school may differ wildly from that at home and in the midst of this difference they may be striving towards a fusion of two cultures into which they can anchor themselves.

If there is a discontinuity of values and practices between the Bangladeshi person's home and wider society, this can place psychological strain on the individual. Most ethnic minorities learn to cope reasonably successfully with the demands of two cultures, but some studies have linked this phenomenon to suicide (Hoberman and Garfinkel 1988), suicidal ideation (Hovey and King 1996), conduct disorder (Apter *et al.* 1988), post-traumatic stress disorder (Bagheri 1992) and anger and aggression (Myers *et al.* 1991).

In contrast, other researchers have reached different conclusions. For example, Berry *et al.* (2006) refer to the 'immigrant paradox' whereby, they discovered, children with immigrant backgrounds exhibited *better* mental health and did as well or better than their non-immigrant peers with respect to academic achievement and psychological well-being. This research highlights the possible beneficial aspects of having more than one culture influencing one's development.

Conclusion

In this chapter, I have attempted to provide a general perspective on the effects of a Bangladeshi heritage on the individual. I have tried to offer a transgenerational slant by consulting with people from my parents' generation, as well as those younger than me. However, there are differences in the experiences of first, second and third generation immigrants, as well as countless other experiential differences – for example, depending on the individual's religious, political or geographic origins etc. – which have not been tackled in this chapter.

The importance of cultural awareness when counselling people of Bangladeshi origin cannot be overstated. It requires a level of understanding without becoming reliant on stereotypes. Indeed, therapeutic work in general requires an antidote to stereotypes and ultimately an open stance rather than one that closes opportunities down by making assumptions. In the process of writing this chapter, I have been aware of a tension to maintain a personal style while keeping some semblance of balance. While this has sometimes been possible, it is important to note that whatever is presented, however well referenced, researched or balanced, it is still a particular slant on the cultural heritage brought to it by the author. As such, the general knowledge gained from this chapter must always be held in mind by therapists as *background* knowledge. The difficult task of the therapist is to listen deeply to the client's individual experience and not to gainsay it.

References

Abbas, T. (2005) *British Muslims and September 11*. London: Zed Press.

Anwar, M. (1998) *Between Cultures – Young Muslims in Britain: Attitudes, Educational Needs and Policy Implementation*. Leicester: The Islamic Foundation.

Apter, A. *et al.* (1988) Suicidal behaviour, depression and conduct disorder in hospitalised adolescents, *Journal of American Academy of Child and Adolescent Psychiatry*, 27: 696–9.

Bagheri, A. (1992) Psychiatric problems among Iranian immigrants in Canada, *Canadian Journal of Psychiatry*, 37: 7–11.

Ballard, C. (1979) Culture, continuity and change – second generation South Asians, in V.S. Khan (ed.) *Migration and Social Stress*. London: Macmillan.

Bangladesh Bureau of Statistics (2006) *Statistics Bangladesh*. Publication for BBS, www.bbs.gov.bd.

Basit, N.T. (1997) *Eastern Values, Western Milieu: Identities and Aspirations of Adolescent British Muslim Girls*. Aldershot: Ashgate.

Berry, J., Phinney, J., Sam, D. and Vedder, P. (2006) *Immigrant Youth in Cultural Transition: Acculturation, Identity, and Adaptation across National Contexts*. Mahwah, NJ: Lawrence Erlbaum.

Bhatti, G. (1999). *Asian Children at Home and School*. London: Routledge.

Bhugra, D. and Bhui, K. (1998) Psychotherapy for ethnic minorities: issues, context and practice, *British Journal of Psychotherapy*, 14: 311–26.

Clark, R., Anderson, N.B., Clark, V.R. and Williams, D.R. (1999) Racism as a stressor for African Americans: a biopsychosocial model, *American Psychologist*, 54: 805–16.

Dosanjh, J.S. and Ghuman, P.A.S. (1996) *Child-Rearing in Ethnic Minorities*. Clevedon: Multilingual Matters.

Dwairy, M.A. (1998) *Cross-Cultural Counselling: The Arab-Palestinian Case*. New York: Hayworth Press.

Edgerton, R.B. and Karno, M. (1971) Mexican-American bilingualism and the perception of mental illness, *Archives of General Psychiatry*, 24: 286–90.

Ghuman, P.A.S. (2005) Daughters of tradition: Asian girls in the West, *The Psychologist*, 18: 620–2.

Hoberman, H. and Garfinkel, B. (1988) Completed suicide in children and adolescents, *Journal of American Academy of Child and Adolescent Psychiatry*, 27: 689–95.

Hovey, J. and King, C. (1996) Acculturative stress, depression and suicidal ideation among second-generation Latino adolescents, *Journal of American Academy of Child and Adolescent Psychiatry*, 35: 1183–92.

Jacob, K.S., Bhugra, D., Lloyd, K.R. and Mann, A.H. (1998) Common mental disorders, explanatory models and consultation behaviour among Indian women living in the UK, *Journal of the Royal Society of Medicine*, 91: 66–71.

Kareem, J. (1992) The Nafsiyat intercultural therapy centre: ideas and experience in intercultural therapy, in J. Kareem and R. Littlewood (eds.) *Intercultural Therapy: Themes, Interpretations and Practice*. London: Blackwell Scientific Publications.

Messent, P. (1992) Working with Bangladeshi families in the East End of London, *Journal of Family Therapy*, 14: 287–304.

Modood, T. *et al.* (1997) *Ethnic Minorities in Britain: Diversity and Disadvantage – Fourth National Survey of Ethnic Minorities*. London: Policy Studies Institute.

Myers, K. *et al.* (1991) Risks of suicidality in major depressive disorder, *Journal of American Academy of Child and Adolescent Psychiatry*, 30: 86–94.

Nesbitt, E. (1995) Punjabis in Britain: cultural history and cultural choices, *South Asia Research*, 15: 221–40.

Ostberg, S. (2003) *Pakistani Children in Norway: Islamic Nurture in a Secular Context*, monograph series, 'Community Religions Project'. Leeds: University of Leeds.

Parekh, B. (1986) The structure of authority within the Indian family, in A.K. Brah (ed.) *Working with Asian Young People*. London: National Association for Asian Youth.

Portes, A. and Rumbaut, G.R. (2001) *Legacies: The Story of the Immigrant Second Generation*. New York: Russell Sage Foundation.

Robbins, J.M. and Greenley, J.R. (1983) Thinking about what's wrong: attributions of severity, cause, and duration in the problem definition stage of psychiatric help seeking, *Research in Community and Mental Helath*, 3: 209–32.

Sabogal, F. *et al.* (1987) Hispanic familism and acculturation: what changes and what doesn't? *Hispanic Journal of Behavioural Sciences*, 9: 397–412.

Sapru, S. (1999) *Parental Practices and the Identity Development of Indian Families in Delhi and Geneva*, thesis presented to the Faulty of Psychology and Education, University of Geneva.

Silva de Crane, R., and Spielberger, C.D. (1981) Attitudes of Hispanic, Black and Caucasian university students toward mental illness, *Hispanic Journal of Behavioural Sciences*, 3: 241–55.

Suarez-Orozco, M.M. (2001) Globalization, immigration and education: the research agenda, *Harvard Educational Review*, 71: 345–66.

29 The effects of an Indian heritage: cultural reminiscences

Indu Khurana

Introduction

In this chapter I have collected some memories, thoughts and personal journeys I have experienced within the Indian culture. I am originally from the Indian subcontinent, and more specifically from the Punjabi, Sikh culture within that, and I have lived in England since the age of 7.

India is host to numerous cultures as well as languages. Cultural issues are not the easiest of subjects to address or discuss, and there is the added complexity of the multiplicity of cultures that reside in one land mass, that share similarities as well as some very clear differences. India is a land that has been invaded many times over the centuries and its culture has changed direction many times also – much like the river that meanders. This has resulted in a multi-layered and multi-coloured backdrop to my country of origin.

There are generalizations as well as specifics presented here, and I acknowledge that this chapter may give you more of an insight into the mix of Indian and English cultures than into a purely Indian one. The chapter is also full of my personal value systems precisely because it is derived from my personal experience.

So where to start? Feeling unsure of where the right introduction lay to my view of the Indian culture, I waited for inspiration. I was not disappointed. It came to me one morning, as I slipped from slumber towards wakefulness, that my *name* is the ideal starting point. This is at once narcissistic and yet appropriate, for therapy is the examination of oneself in the pursuit of self-knowledge. I decided to focus on myself as your storyteller, using myself as an instrument, much as I do in the therapeutic setting, to see what emerges (Mearns and Thorne 1993: 22).

The bridge between reality and mythology

My name was chosen in the way that Sikh names are traditionally chosen: the first letter of the first word read from the Sikh holy book Guru Granth Sahib, on the day that the baby is presented at the temple, is the letter that the family use to find a name for the newborn. My given name is Inderjit: 'Inder' or 'Indra' is the god of the heavens, of storms and of rain. He is a great warrior and represents courage and strength. *Jit* means 'victory' in Hindi. The two parts combined mean victory (or triumph) of the Lord (God). I adopted the name 'Indu' many years ago because it irritated me that so many English people got my name wrong, both in writing and in pronunciation. 'Indu' also felt more appropriate for the me that was beginning to emerge as I opened up to the world and formed a new identity – that of 'young adult in two cultures'. I chose this variation because it retained some of my original name, was easier to pronounce and reminded me of the Indus tributary of the Ganges. Now I find that it, in itself, means 'a bright drop of the moon' and is Sanskrit in origin.

Let's celebrate!

Many, if not all, of our festivals continue the link with mythology, nature and everyday life. One of my favourite Indian festivals is Diwali, which celebrates the destruction of the demon god Ravana, and thus safety for Ram and Sita, in Hindu mythology. As Indians, most of us tend to celebrate this festival, whether in India or elsewhere, and it is linked in to our New Year (we have a different calendar from the western calendar). I have a lasting memory of one particular Diwali that I attended as a child, where within the milieu of fireworks and people, what stood out for me as a little girl was the raging fire that enveloped the giant, colourful yet fearful effigy of Ravana. Fire was, and still is, closely associated with death: to this day, we burn our bodies at the time of death and this is considered cleaner for the earth and the general environment. It also releases the physical vessel that carried us in this lifetime back to the earth from whence it stemmed.

Another of my favourite festivals, slightly less well known in the western world, is Holi. My childhood memory is of being out in sparkling white clothes, under a glorious sun, spending the day spraying coloured water or throwing coloured powder over strangers as well as friends. Holi heralds the season of spring, and reflects the coming burgeoning of nature's colourful frock. At its roots, however, lies the mythical story of Holika, whose burning is replicated the evening before (known as Chotti Holi or Little Holi) the day of Holi by having a bonfire. Holika was a demoness who sat within a bonfire with the child god Prahlad so that he might be devoured by the fire (Holika herself being immune to fire). But Prahlad survived through his immense devotion to the god Vishnu, while Holika herself was destroyed.

The river Ganges provides a link between mythology, religion, nature, culture and tradition. She has a gender (a very human quality), is revered like a god (the god Bhagiratha brought Ganga down from the heavens via a lock of Shiva's hair), and is a torrent in her physical earthly manifestation.

When attending school in India (prior to the age of 7), I remember being taught the main tributaries of the Ganges in my school in New Delhi. The only ones that remain in my memory now are the Indus, the Jamuna (or Yamuna) and the Mahananda. Although I am not a religious person in practice, the sense of importance around the Ganges remains within me, and I am aware that while part of this might be due to its worldwide fame, part of it may also be due to the subtle cultural inscription within me from my first seven years of life in India. Although the best known part of the Ganges is the sedate section that is used by India's mass population for ceremonies of one sort or another, there are other parts of this immense river that are much more fierce. The raging furore of Nanda Devi, Trisul and Kamet slow down to eventually form the calmer Ganga River, within the Ganges Delta.

Mythology plays a substantial role in Indian life and may be one of the few things that creates a bridge across the numerous cultures that flourish within the subcontinent. As the above indicates, the elements of nature are finely intertwined with mythology and so have a substantial impact on Indian daily life.

We Indians also pay a lot of attention to the earth and call it Mother Earth or *Dharthi Maa*, because it provides for us. It is easy to forget sometimes that the industrial and technological age is relatively new and India's economy was until recently agriculturally based. Thus, in a very real way, India's land provided for its population. One of the most famous Bollywood films is the epic *Mother India*, which at one level is about poverty. But it also depicts the qualities of provision and the smallness of mankind in the vision of nature. It also depicts themes of good versus evil; the family as a strong unit; hard work reaping spiritual rewards; respect for parents and elders ... all of which constitute some of the values I was imbued with as a child. I remember watching the film with my family and feeling in every cell of my body the toil and betrayal that was depicted on the screen. I found it a tiring film, and can only now, as an adult, see the subliminal messages within it.

When I visit India, we buy our fresh food from street stalls or markets. All the fruit and vegetables are fresh and local, and the variety is vast. Some years ago, I was visiting my grandmother and she bought some purple carrots from a street stall. I exclaimed at the carrots being purple, and my grandmother reminded me that when I used to live with her I had loved to drink the juice from these dark carrots. I had no memory of this and so she made some juice for me there and then. The taste was familiar and jogged my memory: I remembered having had this juice before and loving the taste.

Living in the UK

Here in the UK I make a conscious decision to buy organic foods as often as I can. I am highly conscious that organic food is the nearest we can get to really fresh and seasonal food in this country (until, of course, I can start my own vegetable garden). I also know that for true health I need to eat food that still contains natural nutrients. Through my interest in natural health, I have learned that food in supermarkets is inevitably modified and consequently lacks nutrients. However, organic food is relatively limited in terms of variety and I am keen to find lesser-known types of food for my forthcoming vegetable garden. All this rumination about food is linked to the fact that in India food, and its abundance, is viewed as a sign of wealth: fat is regarded as the indicator of health, because in order to have health, you must have wealth (or so the belief goes). This is in great contrast to western culture (a culture that is also starting to permeate Indian society), wherein to be fat is considered unhealthy. When I visit India, I notice that I still receive questions and comments about how thin I am.

I also have an interest in natural medicine and the healing powers of food and flowers. This in turn links to Ayurvedic medicine, a subject I hope to study in the future in more depth. Ayurveda is not only a medicinal doctrine, it is a philosophy that is intrinsically holistic, and it originates in India. Although my parents have, to a large degree, relinquished care of their health to the expertise of a doctor, they still use natural remedies, including some that are Ayurvedic. Another connection in my path of cultural reclamation! All of this contributes to what nourishes my soul and I have learned that true nourishment is not only of the belly but also of the soul.

A nod to non-verbal behaviour

Something that piqued my interest some years ago was a particular and unique head movement and its meaning. In India, people move their head from side to side (ear to shoulder) to signify acquiescence, agreement or understanding, rather than the nodding of the head in the western world. This can be a difficult aspect of body language to interpret unless you know what it means. I find myself doing it in India or in the UK when talking in Indian to other Indians of an older generation, but quickly revert to the western nodding when communicating in English. So what is the significance of this head gesture? There is no right answer, but broadly speaking the side to side movement means 'I understand you but I do not (necessarily) agree with you'.

Reflections on respect

Respect for parents and elders is something we grew up with and I never questioned it until I was in therapy. It was inscribed into our psyche that as a child or an adult one should not speak loudly or rudely to parents or elders. Their expertise and experience are things to be learned from as well as being unquestionable. In this country, the culture of freedom enables us to question everyone, and the culture of therapy promotes questioning of the self. Many people hold no sense of respect for their elders, and the elderly are certainly not held in much esteem on a societal level. It was in relation to these differences and how I might or might not challenge older people (including my parents) that this issue of respect arose on numerous occasions. In one sense, the person-centred approach works very well in relation to this ideology, because the notion of congruence (Chantler 2006) enables a challenge to be made but with respect for the other's position. It enabled me to learn ways of challenging my own thinking while holding onto respect for the other.

Symbolism in culture

Symbolism is rife in Indian culture – in religious texts and in the more modern realm of 'Bollywood'. I didn't understand this until, as an adult in my middle years, I started to reclaim some of my original heritage. Prior to this stage of my life, I viewed Bollywood films only as a vehicle for badly edited, crass storylines that pounded the streets of love in a culture that did not allow romantic love within its society. This type of hypocrisy was difficult for me to accept, and played some part in my rejecting my original cultural heritage. At the same time, I adopted a monochromatic lens and accepted my second cultural heritage of the UK that symbolized freedom, openness and seemed to satisfy my soul. Now I have acquired a more balanced set of lenses that allows the various shades of grey to be visible in both cultures, and I am able to appeciate the subtext of Bollywood films as well as the multifaceted meanings of the word 'love'.

The other side of the coin to love is hate and this can sometimes be related to the concept of *difference*. Some people experience racism in a very overt way. For example, my sister, seven and a half years my junior, was subjected to being called rude names by some of her English peers when at school and college. She has told stories about how she and other Indian children were kept back at the end of a school day, or let out early when the staff were made aware of the possibility that National Front supporters or other known racist gangs would congregate outside the school at the end of the day.

My brother, two years my junior, wore a turban as a child and a young man. My parents are Sikhs and as children none of us ever had our hair cut: this is one of the marks of being a Sikh. My brother would often get called names and was frequently beaten up for 'having a bun' on his head. Even now, in recalling these incidents, I feel appalled and shameful. Perhaps this explains something about why my brother turned out to be the tough guy he has become – a persona he was perhaps forced to develop in part at least because of these experiences.

I, on the other hand, had no such experiences. Perhaps I was too caught up in my own world in a bid to go unnoticed during that phase of my life (adolescence), or I was just truly fortunate. When I talk to my sister about the issue, she tells me that our father was also subjected to racism. He too wore a turban, and I certainly remember him talking of being passed over for promotion. He also talked about how friends of his had cut their hair in order to get jobs, or to avoid being bullied at work.

From a therapeutic perspective, it is interesting to ponder why I was not affected by such issues. Perhaps I colluded with my young unconscious desire to be accepted into the British culture when I came to this country unable to speak a word of English. Ironically, my brother had been taught English at his school in India and so was not as disadvantaged, and yet racism found him instead of me. I am aware now that when I was young I perceived myself as colourless, which fitted rather well with my lack of identity that became a big issue for me in later life, and I think may have resulted, in part at least, in my total rejection of my original cultural heritage.

Luck or destiny? The formative nature and impact of cultural transition

In the light of these experiences as well as others, I have at times wondered why my father brought his family (at that time consisting of my mother, myself and my brother) here to the UK. Rationally I know that he did so for 'a better life'. But I also know that at times he regretted his decision as we turned our backs on our culture and our religion. I, on the other hand, am forever grateful that he brought us to the UK. I am very aware of how different my life would have been if I had been raised in India, even though our family lived in the relatively modern New Delhi. Our parents as children had moved to New Delhi with their parents at partition, from a part of India that became Pakistan. Had I stayed in India, I can virtually guarantee that my true self would not have seen the light of day, and I would have spent my whole life in a temple of 'conditions of worth' (Mearns and Thorne 1993). I may have been able to study to degree level (as my mother had done), but then would have had to comply with these 'conditions of worth': I would have been expected to marry and bear children. I would have been a housewife and I would not know my own feelings or myself.

On becoming a therapist

Instead, I came to the UK and ended as a therapist. I came to this line of work relatively late in life – or so it felt for me at the time. But I can appreciate the 'opening of the flower' that resulted and the adventures I have had in studying and continuing to study when the mood takes me. I enjoy having discussions and putting the world to rights and I love the philosophy and art that I have been exposed to. I am able to work and write: to follow my passions essentially. Even more fundamentally, I have been able to *connect* with my passions, which may not have happened in the alternative life I would have lived in India. I appreciate the free and rich life I lead compared to my cousins and the wives of my cousins.

So at one level I have fought for my gender and the freedoms that this country has allowed. But simultaneously, I am aware that although we as a family have been in the UK for almost half a century, I as a female have been treated differently from my brothers. I know it is not a personal persecution, but being a female and the eldest has meant that at times I have not been as celebrated or as free as my brothers have been. When it was time to select universities, they were allowed to move away from home. When they graduated, Indian sweets were handed out to mark the occasion. I, on the other hand, was brought up to be a quiet and obedient girl. Partly this was because I was the first child and my parents were learning – not only to be parents but also to be parents in a different culture from their peers. Outwardly I have accommodated many of these infringements. Inwardly I have seethed or rebelled. Even studying a subject such as therapy could be seen as a rebellion for it was unheard of as a career in our community. Literally, people did not know what it was.

It is only in recent years that I have been able to find my identity, which to my own surprise (but perhaps to no one else's) has turned out to be a mixture of Indian and British cultures. This process has occurred as I have worked on myself over the years, and has peaked (to date) within the masters programme that I undertook about five years ago – a training that encompassed Sufi spiritualism as well as many western therapeutic philosophies. It was through this time and process that I was enabled to return to, and understand, symbolism. I felt I connected with something that felt like home, and now hold it to be an essential and joyful part of me. I see it within everything in my combined culture as well as within my everyday life. I am able to further appreciate aspects of my original heritage, which was outside of my grasp or indeed interest, until I began this training. Self-acceptance, or my 'internal locus of evaluation' (Mearns and Thorne 1993) has become easier through this process and I can now see that I am in the process of making my own hybrid culture.

My greatest revelations have come through the pursuit of therapy. I have learned about myself: who I am (still evolving); what I am; what I like; what I am like *with* conditions of worth; and what I am like *without* them. What I am materially, philosophically and passionately. I have learned to question, and that curiosity is a quality to be enjoyed. I have wondered, within the therapy room, how and whether western philosophies or theories can be applied to a person of Indian origin. At times I have thought they cannot, but then realized that I am not totally Indian: genetically yes, holistically no, for I am not just a pool of genes. I have always chosen a white therapist and in recent times I have wondered why. Initially this tied in with my rejection of my culture, and the fact that some Indians I had come into contact with had proved to be judgemental and hypocritical. Plus of course, on a practical level, there were very few Asian therapists in existence.

Now I have met other Asian therapists and have found that some are able to truly espouse the qualities taught by most therapies as being fundamental: truth, non-judgement and caring, without the gossip and the disorganized mayhem that one finds still in many Indian organizations. For me these factors of honesty, acceptance and care are important as they fit better within the value base I was given and have chosen to keep hold of.

My experiences in training and therapy

My first therapy relationship was before I started studying therapy myself. It was with someone who worked in a style that I found austere, cold and aloof. I left that relationship abruptly and later discovered that the therapy in question was of the classical, analytical form. It created a fear of therapy in me, but also inspired me to seek a different approach when I because a therapist.

As a result I found myself at the person-centred 'door', which felt more welcoming and humane and more in keeping with my, as yet unconscious and unverbalized, values. As I started my studies and my personal therapeutic journey, I found myself a therapist who (thankfully) turned out to be human, caring and robust. She accompanied me at the start of my personal journey. Later, I needed to find a theory-specific therapist and I found a person-centred therapist who provided me with the softest, fleeciest blanket of her own being I have ever known, and within that containment I started to unravel. With hindsight, I can see that she espoused caring, honesty and warmth that accepted me enough to allow the necessary unravelling to take place sufficiently before she challenged me with her congruence. Yet, when it was needed, she was gently directive and that gave me the strength (as well as a role model) to develop my own self-worth.

Both of these relationships were unfocused in any specific and conscious culture overtly, and that suited me as I had a foundation to build before I could consciously know that culture, as an entity, existed. Because of this, I assume that they worked from a British cultural viewpoint – both therapists were of this background and society was not so interested in cultural issues at large at that time. At one level, the person-centred approach can be seen as *acultural* because it aims to stay alongside the client whatever their background.

After a considerable break, I engaged in a short-term therapeutic relationship which I found limited in its helpfulness because of the time-limited aspect. This was also a more directive experience for me, which at the time I did not enjoy. With hindsight I am able to wonder about other factors at play.

My most recent experience of a therapeutic relationship was with an integrative therapist who utilized the person-centred stance as a foundation for her practice. This suited me as I felt that I too was moving in this direction. What this gave me was an experience of knitting together some creative methodologies to connect to the unconscious, while remaining within the ethos of the person-centred approach as my fundamental springboard. In this relationship, I was truly able to question my cultural stance and what came from which culture. It was here that I connected with my hybrid culture in a tangible manner and had enough 'internal locus of evaluation' (Mearns and Thorne 1993) to be able to question things like the culture of India that I live in and am part of, and the Indian culture experienced by the western visitor.

Conclusion

I have shared here some aspects of Indian cultural heritage 'according to Indu', as well as hints of the impact of transition and the impact of an adopted culture. It is a personal story, but one that I hope might help you to think about things previously not contemplated, perhaps even providing you with one or two 'aha' moments as you gain a new understanding or perspective. I hope that what I have written may perhaps provide another dimension to your work with clients from the Indian culture.

I would however emphasize that, as with anything else, we cannot paste these experiences onto others. We need to be questioning – of ourselves and of the client's specific experiences – so that we learn to create an ever-growing composite jigsaw from which we can extract principles which then might have implications for practice. But the individual must be held in mind, above all – whatever their cultural background in the present and in the past.

References

Chantler, K. (2006) Rethinking person-centred therapy, in G. Proctor, M. Cooper, P. Sanders and B. Malcolm (eds) *Politicising the Person-Centred Approach*. Bristol: PCCS Books.

Mearns D. and Thorne B. (1993) *Person-Centred Counselling in Action*. London: Sage.

30 The effects of a Chinese heritage

Jin Wu

Introduction

> The Chinese have been described as possessing a national character of
> social orientation, which had been defined as a somewhat complex be-
> havioral syndrome. This syndrome comprises such features as conform-
> ing to social norms, adopting inoffensive strategies in interpersonal deal-
> ings, submitting to social expectations, and submitting to authority.
> When Chinese people are compared with those from other cultures, they
> have been found to be lacking in autonomy, aggression, and extrover-
> sion, and to exhibit excessive submissiveness, conformity, subservience
> to authority, and susceptibility to the influences of those more powerful
> than themselves.
>
> (Sun 2008: 50)

The above paragraph seems to describe only what is on the surface, not the
live Chinese person underneath. As Wong (quoted in Bond and Hwang 1986:
218) pointed out, 'What is involved in Chinese conformity and acquiescence
may only be a prudent and expedient motive to avoid disrupting the present
relationships. It has nothing to do with a lack of autonomy or self-assertion'.
Although there has been a body of solid scholarly information in the literature on
Chinese culture in the West, it seems quite easy to run into misunderstandings
of that culture, including in writings about cultural diversity. For example, in his
book *Culture-Centered Counseling Interventions: Striving for Accuracy*, Pedersen (1997:
81) stated:

> The Chinese concept of *jen*, which translates as 'person' but emphasizes
> the person's transactions with fellow human beings...Both Confucius
> and Mencius emphasized the universal principles of *jen*, and both were
> adamant that morality based on fear of public censure was not only not
> 'true' morality but also contemptible behavior.

Here there is a confusion between two Chinese characters that are pronounced the
same (which happens much more often in the Chinese language than some others): the character for 'person' is 人, while the character for the universal principles
both Confucius and Mencius emphasized is 仁.

Another somewhat amusing example has to do with the Chinese greeting 'Have you eaten?' Some, including Chinese authors (e.g. Chao 2004), thought its origin had to do with the scarcity of food in the old days. This interpretation is not quite accurate. For the Chinese, having a meal is a very important daily activity, and the meal schedule is not easily interrupted. So greeting others with 'Have you eaten?' right after the expected mealtime is a way to say 'Has your day gone smoothly?' Chinese people may greet others in their community with other routine matters. For example, in some communities, in the early evening during the summer, people might ask each other 'Have you bathed?' Out of context it might sound offensive to some outsiders, but since bathing is the last chore at the end of a long busy day, this greeting is a caring gesture, saying 'Has your day gone smoothly? And have you had a chance to relax?'

Historical background

Ancient China was an agricultural society (Fung 1948). People lived as extended families on the same pieces of land for many generations. As a nation, China was unified as one country before 200 BC, and the bureaucratic structure established then was adopted by all later dynasties until the beginning of the twentieth century. After being defeated by the western powers in the mid-nineteenth century, China entered the biggest historical transition in 3,000 years and today is still in the middle of this transition. This is the background against which traditional Chinese culture has developed.

Religion

The ancient Chinese were not so concerned with religion; ethics provided the spiritual basis of Chinese civilization, and philosophy was the tool dealing with 'values higher than moral ones' (Fung 1948: 4). China has never had a national religion. Traditionally, the Chinese worshipped heaven as the origin of everything in the material world. Ancestor worship was probably the most important ritual that gave people a sense of connection to something larger than their individual lives. Ordinary people also believed in gods and spirits.

Today, the main organized religions in China are Buddhism, Taoism, Islam and Christianity. Taoist religion is the only indigenous belief system, the rest having been introduced to China at different historical points, and then modified to suit Chinese culture. The vast majority of Chinese do not identify themselves as members of a particular religion. Some Chinese people may visit a Buddhist or Taoist temple to ask for 'prediction' or blessing, but they may or may not see themselves as being religious; some may see little conflict in worshiping in both Buddhist and Taoist temples. By contrast, there are some Chinese people who are deeply committed to religious beliefs.

Philosophy

Superficially, the main concern in traditional Chinese philosophy is human society, not the universe; but the ultimate ideal for Chinese philosophy is to achieve 'the identification of the individual with the universe' (Fung 1948: 6). There are many schools of philosophy dating back to ancient China, but the two main trends are Taoism and Confucianism. Both endorse the following concepts. First is that 'reversal is the movement of Tao'. This refers to how things begin to reverse when moving towards an extreme. It was probably 'inspired by the movements of the sun and moon and the successions of the four seasons in order to carry on their own work' (Fung 1948: 19). Because of their conviction about this theory, Chinese people remain cautious even in times of prosperity, and hopeful even in times of extreme danger. Second is the doctrine of the golden mean, which is based on the aforementioned theory. The doctrine of the mean implies 'just right, neither too much nor to little' (Fung 1948: 172). Doing too much is more dangerous than doing too little because it brings the risk of achieving the opposite of what one wants.

Confucianism

Confucius believed that

> If benevolence was highly valued by all, there was a clearly defined hierarchy of power, authority, and positions, and if each person was fully cognizant of his roles and rules of conduct, then order and harmony would naturally ensue and the Way of Humanity would prevail.
>
> (Sun 2008: 6)

Confucius emphasized the moral cultivation of men. Self-cultivation for the ordinary people begins with understanding the common good and being willing to submit one's needs and desires to it. A person should strive to maintain 'psychosocial homeostasis by accommodating one's behavior to the preordained standards of one's in-groups, society, and culture' (Sun 2008: 9–10). Scholars were also encouraged to 'unify their families, govern their countries, and bring peace to the world' (Sun 2008: 10).

Taoism

Taoism as a philosophy advocates following the rhythms of nature rather than the human will, valuing naturalness over artificiality. In human conduct, Taoism advocates that people should stay humble and easily content; they should do only what is necessary and never push too far to avoid going to an extreme which would reverse things to their opposite. In politics, Taoism advocates 'government through non-government' because the more one governs the less one achieves desirable results, and imposing human will on what is natural causes misery and suffering. Regarding human emotions, Taoism advocates that the sage who has completely understood the nature of things will no longer be disturbed by emotions (Fung 1948: 107).

Traditional Chinese society

The importance of family

Family was the central unifying system within traditional Chinese society (Cheung 1986). Fung (1948: 21) describes the Chinese family system as one of the most complex and well-organized in the world:

> The family system was the social system of China. Out of the five traditional social relationships, which were those between sovereign and subject, father and son, elder and younger brother, husband and wife, and friend and friend, three are family relationships. The remaining two, though not family relationships, can be conceived of in terms of the family. Thus the relationships between sovereign and subject can be conceived of in terms of that between father and son, and that between friend and friend in terms of the one between elder and younger brother.

These five relationships were called *wu lun*, or 'the five cardinal relationships' (Sun 2008: 11).

Unlike in tribal systems, where the entire village is a social unit, traditional Chinese farmers were quite self-reliant (Liang 1987). Although neighbours helped each other out, ultimately, for fundamental survival, it was the belief in the role of family against nature that dominated. Most Chinese are very close to their families. There may be conflict within the family, but the family will not abandon its members, and when necessary it will fight against outsiders as a whole. People may need to behave in certain ways outside the family, but they are accepted in the family. Today, for most Chinese people, family is still the most important social support system.

Social relationships

Yang's social orientation model (Sun 2008) describes the Chinese as having a 'social orientation' (p. 51) which appears in four different modalities: familistic orientation, relationship orientation, other orientation and authoritarian orientation, which in turn embraces 'authority sensitization', 'authority worship' and 'authority dependence'. *Guanxi* (relationship), *renqing* (favour) and *mianzi* (face) are consequently very important for the Chinese.

The Chinese consider people with group-enhancing qualities such as kindness and consideration as more socially attractive (Bond and Hwang 1986), but in close relationships, having others' best interests in mind is the most important asset. The closer the relationship, the more informal it should be. There is an old saying, 'no thanks should be uttered between the closest kin' (至亲不言谢). Couples often relate to each other even more casually. Parent–child relationships, however, may depend on how traditional the parents are. In some families, children are required to behave respectfully towards their parents.

The Chinese self

'The Chinese self cannot be sufficiently understood without reference to his/her interpersonal relations, including relations to ingroups and to society at large' (Sun 2008: 55). Traditionally, in Chinese society, one is defined by who one is related to more than the personality attributes one possesses, and one completes one's personality through interpersonal relating. A Chinese scholar once said, 'Westerners think "the individual and the group", while we Chinese think "the individual in the group"' (Liu 2008, personal communication). In the former view, the interests of the person and the group may inherently be in conflict; one can only try to balance them. In the latter view, the person may be a part of a group and an individual at the same time. By their social behavior, the Chinese may be more submissive, conformist, etc., but most of them do not lose their sense of self and individuality in the group.

'Emotional moderation'

To some westerners, the Chinese seem to be inscrutable, emotionally unexpressive, or even repressed; some westerners think the Chinese are a group who do not smile. There is some truth in 'the notion of emotional moderation in the Chinese' (Sun 2008: 168), which is rooted in several traditional sources. For example, traditional Chinese medicine believed that excessive emotions hurt the inner organs, Confucianism promoted self-control for social harmony and Taoist philosophy believed that a transcended person would not be disturbed by emotions. Nonetheless, in China and other Chinese societies, there are plenty of people who are quite emotionally expressive, especially in their own communities.

In public, especially when interacting with outsiders, the Chinese tend to pay more attention to other people's feelings, and strive not to embarrass themselves (not to lose face). Appearing to be emotionally uninhibited or too expressive may be seen as either immature or being insincere and manipulative. On the other hand, being emotional with understandable cause is very acceptable, such as when receiving shocking news or being injured. Others tend to be quite responsive in such cases, so people in turn tend to restrain their emotional expressions in these types of situations with the intention of not making others worry too much.

The Chinese emphasize subtlety over explicitness. Part of the Chinese way of communication is not to say everything explicitly, but to expect the other to understand what is unspoken (尽在不言中). The ideal of all Chinese art is suggestiveness, not articulation.

Relationship with authority

Chinese people have complicated relationships with their authority figures. The authorities are deemed to have absolute power, disobeying them might be very costly, and for most of the time ordinary people only have to mind their own business. The Chinese believe that somebody has to be in charge. Historically, ordinary Chinese prefer to leave the job of governance to their rulers (Liang 1987).

From both Confucianist and Taoist perspectives, maintaining one's dignity is an internal process that one can cultivate. One of the Confucian scholars specifically advocated that the way to achieve inner peace in the face of insult is not to consider insults as humiliation (Liu 1986: 7). So the Chinese do appear to submit to their authorities but they are not acquiescent internally; instead, they maintain their inner freedom in allowing themselves to feel and think whatever they want (Zheng and Liu 2001). They may be submissive, but they are not subjugated. There is a saying in modern China: 'When the higher-ups issue policies, subordinates come up with strategies' (上有政策, 下有对策).

Ideally, according to Confucianism, both parties in a hierarchical relationship should be kind towards the other, and take responsibility according to their position. However, in reality, the parties with power may abuse it, requiring others to make sacrifices under the guise of the 'collective'. Confucianism has been used to justify power, and Taoism has been used as a manipulation tool in power struggles.

Modernization

The ancient Chinese believed that their nation was at the centre of the world, and considered their culture to be much more advanced than others, calling outsiders 'barbarians' (Fung 1948). This confidence was brutally shaken after defeat and invasion by western powers in the nineteenth century. From that point on, Chinese society has been going through the most significant historical transition in several thousand years. Many phenomena in Chinese life have to be understood in the context of this historical transition. On the one hand, Chinese people are pragmatic and always believe in adaptation; on the other hand, the changes in social structure and the value clash between the old and the new are currently so huge and play out in such complex ways that few can fully comprehend or adapt totally.

Some aspects of modern Chinese life

Marriage

Arranged marriages are part of the past, but parental approval for marriage is still expected. Married couples now tend to live in nuclear families, even in rural areas (Liu 2003). Divorce is a fairly new phenomenon in Chinese societies. Taiwan has the highest divorce rate in Asia, but society has not been compassionate to divorced women (Miller and Yang 1997). In Hong Kong, research has shown that divorce was more upsetting for Hong Kong Chinese than Americans (Cheung 1986). The divorce rate was very low in China up to the early 1980s, but has increased since then, more rapidly in recent years after the government changed the requirements for filing a divorce, which made the process much easier. The blended family, comprising stepfathers, stepmothers and stepchildren, is another new challenge for the Chinese.

Filial piety

Family tradition remains strong in China, but filial piety and family obligations have to compete for resources with the demands of a modern society and the needs for personal achievement in family members (Sun 2008). Liu (2003) found that adult children in urban areas seem to be more filial towards their parents than those in rural areas, and speculated that this might be due to the fact that ageing parents in urban areas hold more access to resources that their adult children need than in rural areas. Elder abuse and elder suicide have also increased in China in recent decades.

Research on Chinese Americans has showed that adult children are more willing to provide financial support and keep emotional ties with their parents, but are less willing to accommodate their parents' wishes in areas related to personal freedom and development (Sun 2008).

Gender equality

The concept of 'men for the exterior and women for the interior' determined the traditional gender role for women, which was as a devoted wife, dutiful spouse and good mother, expected to give and sacrifice. Traditionally, Chinese women's self-esteem derives from the norms of chastity and the importance placed on the family (Sun 2008). Sons were preferred because they carry the family lineage, while daughters were given away when they got married.

In China, women's social status began to increase significantly in 1950s partly owing to government efforts in promoting gender equality and partly due to the fact that women entered the workforce in large numbers for the first time in history. In 2001, approximately 41 per cent of all the professional and technical personnel in China were women (Sun 2008). Sadly, they have lost their employment security in the new market economy. Meanwhile, there has been little challenge of the traditional expectations of male social roles, which are even reinforced by some government policies, the educational system and the media. Today, a sizeable number of Chinese women do not find premarital sex objectionable, they initiate divorce and sometimes remarry, and some even become unwed mothers.

Research has shown that Chinese men are more satisfied with life than women, while exhibiting a significantly larger number of psychiatric symptoms and scoring significantly lower on psychometric measurements of positive mental health (Sun 2008).

Parenting

The traditional notion of parenting in China has been 'stern father and nurturing mother'. In modern times more Chinese mothers take on the role of disciplinarian (Ho 1986). Research suggests that Chinese parents tend to be attentive to and protective of very young children, but become strict when the child reaches a certain age, when they consider the child to be old enough to be taught to obey the parents and be prepared for the fulfilment of social and filial obligations in adulthood (Ho 1986). Traditional Chinese parents are more concerned with impulse control than are western parents, but not universally. For example, Mitchell and Lo (cited in Ho 1986: 9) found that

> independent and assertive Chinese children tend to have mothers who are permissive (for example, allowing the child to participate in adult conversation), less harsh or punitive in the disciplinary techniques they use, setting high standards of achievement for their children, and also encouraging them to compete with other children.

The traditional extended family may lend additional hands to parenting, but many Chinese immigrant parents do not have access to their extended family and at the same time they have to make a living in their host country. They may also face the competition in terms of the values of the host culture. Some immigrant parents, because they have to work long hours, send their very young children back to China to be raised by extended family members, and then take the children back when they reach preschool age. Such major separations may cause complications in the parent–child relationship that the parents may or may not understand.

The push for achievement can be a source of pressure for Chinese children (Cheung 1986). In the old days, following one's father's footsteps was one of the common ways for a man to make a living. Only in recent decades has success in school had so much determining power in one's prospect of success.

Sex education tends to be a taboo for most Chinese parents. Traditionally, masturbation was severely discouraged in infants (Ho 1986). Although adult sexual activities outside marriage are more or less acceptable in China today, the vast majority of parents hold very strict views on teenage dating and sex (Sun and Zhang 2004). Sun and Zhang found that even parents who are otherwise permissive of their children do not talk with them about sexuality.

Mental health

Traditional Chinese medicine (TCM)

TCM is a holistic system involving external and internal conditions, and physical and psychological factors (Cheung 1986). It integrates psychological and physiological functions as the major sources of imbalance and disease. Behavioural and somatic observations are equally important for diagnosis and treatment. In the classical tradition, illnesses are discussed in terms of the balance of the *yin* and *yang* forces, the five fundamental elements (metal, wood, water, fire and earth), the *ching-lo* (meridian) system, and the circulation of *chi* (vital energy). The aetiology of illnesses is attributed to three groups of factors, six seasonal influences (wind, heat, fire, cold, moisture and dryness) and seven internal emotions (joy, grief, fear, anger, love, hatred and desire) (Cheung, 1986: 171).

The aetiology of mental illness in TCM follows the same principles as other forms of illness. The five elements can generate or attenuate each other (Sun 2008) and they correspond to the human lungs, liver, kidneys, heart and spleen (or pancreas) respectively, and in turn are associated with the five emotions of grief/sadness, anger, fear, joy/overexcitement and over-thinking/obsession. Excessive emotions are said to damage the functions of the organs and upset the balance of the body, causing disease.

Modern beliefs

Chinese people with lower social status may continue to hold folk beliefs in divination and sorcery, and believe that spirits and ghosts can cause illnesses (Cheng 1986). They may use fortune-telling, astrology, physiognomy, geomancy and shamanism as indigenous forms of healing. In China, beliefs regarding the causes of mental ill health have evolved over the latter half of the twentieth century, from having physiological origins to politicized beliefs, from the medical model to a biosocial-psychological model. However, 'China has been targeted by Western pharmaceutical conglomerates as an extremely lucrative market. This is perhaps one of the enduring forces behind China's ongoing attempts to meet international standards for the classification of mental disorders' (Sun 2008: 200). Sun points out that 'China seems to be moving towards both increasingly accepting the demarcation of body and mind, and psychologizing mental distress, rather than taking the traditional holistic stance towards health' (p. 192), while 'practitioners in the West have recognized the logic in adopting a holistic view toward health' (p. 200).

Patterns of help-seeking behaviour

Chinese and Chinese Americans tend to consult with their family and friends first before visiting a professional for psychological help, and they tend to visit physicians rather than psychiatrists or counsellors (Cheung 1986). Counseling is still a new profession in Chinese societies (Miller and Yang 1997) and the Chinese do not accord counselling the same level of importance as do Americans (Page and Cheng 2004). Chinese people with lower socioeconomic status tend to seek more indigenous means of help.

Trust

Although for most Chinese, family members are the most trusted, not all Chinese are very close to their immediate families. They may also not want to talk to their family members about their problems because they wish to spare them from worry. In addition there may be concern about certain information being spread in the family or community. An understanding counsellor who is bound by confidentiality can thereore be a good alternative. The Chinese are used to having confidants, including strangers on occasion.

Somatization

Somatization of psychological symptoms among Chinese and Chinese Americans has been observed in clinical practice (Cheung 1986; Mak and Zane 2004) but research on somatization has yielded mixed results. Some found stronger tendencies for the somatization of emotional distresses among Asians (Lin *et al.* 1985; Le *et al.* 2002), while others did not (Mackinnon *et al.* 1989). Three tendencies may explain this phenomenon. First, due to the traditional belief in mind–body integration, the Chinese are naturally aware of both physical and psychological discomfort, while westerners tend to overly emphasize psychological symptoms as psychological distress. Secondly, traditionally, Chinese people seek support from their families and other trusted individuals for emotional distress and visit a physician when they are sick; they do not perceive a physician's job as alleviating emotional pain. In addition, some Chinese see negative emotions as a sign of weakness, so may be hesitant to share them with others.

Selected mental health issues

Depression and suicide

Rates of depression have been consistently lower in China than most other countries, but there is evidence of under-reporting due to cultural and circumstantial factors (Sun 2008). Despite this, China has one of the highest suicide rates in the world (Xie 2007). China is the only country where female suicides exceed male suicides, and rural rates much higher than those in urban areas (Sun 2008). In addition, 'Particularly high rates were found in two age groups: young rural females age 15–24 and elderly men' (Sun 2008: 193). Suicide is the leading cause of death among young people aged 15–34 (Sun 2008; Hou *et al.* 2009). According to Sun (2008: 194), 'From a cultural point of view … Chinese people have a higher proclivity towards suicide'. This proclivity is supported by the Confucian belief that suicide is appropriate in certain situations of great suffering, by Buddhist beliefs in relation to speeding up the process of reincarnation, and by religious Taoist beliefs in becoming ghosts capable of returning for vengeance. However, Sun warns that this proclivity has to be modified by psychological and socioeconomic factors.

Alcoholism and drug abuse

Although alcohol consumption has long been a part of Chinese social life, alcohol-related problems in China were very low compared with those in western countries up to the 1980s (Sun 2008). With globalization and modernization, substance abuse, including drug addiction and alcohol dependence, has skyrocketed in China.

> In 2001, a survey sponsored by the World Health Organization showed that although ethanol consumption in China was still low compared with that in industrialized countries, the trend was an upward one. This was corroborated by the fact that there was a fourfold increase in alcohol-related admissions to psychiatric hospitals between 1980 and 1993 ... and alcohol dependence was ranked as the third most prevalent cause of mental illness. Amongst adolescents, a startling 78% of boys and 61% of girls reported consuming alcohol in the previous year. In terms of gender differences, more men (6.6%) than women (3.4%) were found to be alcohol-dependent.
>
> (Sun 2008: 198)

Trauma

In Chinese societies, child abuse was not recognized as a social problem until recently and wife abuse was culturally sanctioned as part of men's control over women. Public opinion now condemns domestic violence, although legally it is still treated as a domestic affair and the police refuse to get involved (Liu 2003). Rape is rarely reported (Gil and Anderson 1999). Recent surveys have found that over 10 per cent of children had unwanted sexual experiences before age 16, and 70 per cent of school age children reported family violence. Xiao *et al.* (2006: 32) reported that 27 out of 158 Chinese men in a clinical practice described childhood sexual abuse. Interestingly, in a non-clinical sample of adults used for epidemiological study, only one person reported childhood physical abuse, and none reported sexual abuse, while almost a third responded 'yes' to the question 'Are there large parts of your childhood after age 5 which you cannot remember?' Of this sample, 8.8 per cent reported hearing voices talking to them and 1.8 per cent responded 'yes' to the question 'Do you ever have memories come back to you all of a sudden, in a flood or like flashbacks?' (Xiao *et al.* 2006: 34). These authors have discussed the under-reporting of child abuse in China.

Some counselling-related issues

Suicidal clients

Since the Chinese endorse 'harmless' conflict-avoiding lies, I recommend that a counsellor never ask a suicidal Chinese client to sign a suicide prevention contract. A desperate Chinese may be even more ready to say whatever their counsellor wants to hear. Such a contract from a Chinese point of view lacks any common sense (who on earth would take their promise seriously when they want to die?).

Letting the client know that you really care and that they can contact you when feeling suicidal is more helpful.

What the Chinese client prefers in counselling

Leong (cited in Mau and Jepsen 1988: 189) states that when seeking counselling, Asian Americans tend to: '(a) have a lower tolerance of ambiguity, (b) prefer a structured situation, (c) prefer problem-solving over insight-oriented psychotherapy, and (d) exhibit a lower level of verbal and emotional expressiveness'. Since counselling is fairly new to most Chinese, some of the observations of their behaviour at the beginning of counselling may reflect their apprehension in encountering outgroups. However, when trust is built, the Chinese client may switch their way of relating to the counsellor to their way of relating to trusted in-group substitutes, although this is not widely acknowledged in counselling literature. Sue and Sue (1972) observed that Chinese American clients initially might need a lot of reassurance, but after they developed their trust in their counsellors, they did open up.

What types of counselling work best with the Chinese clients?

Although different authors have different opinions on what counselling modalities work better with, or are not suitable for, the Chinese, there seems to be no conclusive data to date. The current understanding that the therapeutic relationship is the most important factor in counselling is also applicable to the Chinese, especially if one considers that they are even more relational than westerners. As noted earlier, the Chinese are not familiar with counselling as a profession, but they are familiar with confiding their problems in trusted persons.

Today, all major western psychotherapy approaches can be found in China: cognitive behavioural therapy, psychodynamic approaches, humanistic approaches, family system approaches, brief therapy and more, plus some newly developed indigenous approaches, such as Taoist cognitive psychotherapy (Hou *et al.* 2009). There seems to be a belief in the literature that Chinese clients prefer directive approaches (Lin 2002; Page and Cheng 2004). However, Cheng and Wu (cited in Cheung 1986: 210) found that the non-directive approach was superior in long-term counselling, and refuted the belief that, 'given the "authoritarian personality" of the Chinese, the directive approach to counselling would be preferred'.

Relationship maintenance versus personal growth

Traditionally, the goal for counselling in the West has been to facilitate the client's independence, and this view has been challenged and recognized as 'more western in orientation...than universal' (Kobayashi 1989: 653). While recognizing that Chinese people's well-being is significantly determined by a harmonious relationship with others in the social and cultural context, Hsiao *et al.* (2006: 998) suggest that 'Psychotherapy emphasizing an individual's growth and autonomy may ignore the importance of maintaining interpersonal harmony in Chinese culture'. Their conclusion seems to imply that the client's personal growth is at odds with the maintenance of his or her interpersonal harmony. This does not necessarily have to be the case. The counselling relationship is another interpersonal relationship in the client's life (as temporary as it is), in which the client can unload stress, receive understanding, and re-examine important relationships in their life without disturbing those relationships.

Conclusion

Chinese culture is collectivistic, with the emphasis on the importance of family and social relationships, but the Chinese people do experience themselves as individuals in their social groups, it is just that the manifestation of their way of protecting their individual interests and expressing their individuality may differ drastically from that of the West.

With a civilization lasting for 5,000 years without interruption, in recent centuries China has experienced the biggest historical transition in 3,000 years, and all Chinese societies are moving at various paces towards modernization. These societies and those of Chinese immigrants can only be adequately understood in this historical context.

In traditional Chinese medicine, the mind and body are integrated as a whole – there is no distinction between physical health and mental health. This belief system may be part of the observed phenomenon of 'somatization' of emotional distress among the Chinese, while at the same time some Chinese societies are moving towards adopting a western view on the separation of the mind and the body.

Counselling is reatively new in all Chinese societies, and some Chinese people are used to seeking help from conventional physicians for psychological distress – however, they may open up to their mental health providers once they trust them. The counselling relationship is essential here, because the Chinese cultural tradition is more relational than the western tradition.

References

Bond, M.H. and Hwang, K.K. (1986) The social psychology of Chinese people, in M.H. Bond (ed.) *The Psychology of the Chinese People*. Hong Kong: Oxford University Press.

Chao, H. (2004) *Lao zhong lao mei dabutong* [*The Chinese and the American Differ Significantly*]. Taipei: INK Publishing.

Cheung, F.M. (1986) Psychopathology among Chinese people, in M.H. Bond (ed.) *The Psychology of the Chinese People*. Hong Kong: Oxford University Press.

Fung, Y. (1948) *A Short History of Chinese Philosophy*. New York: Macmillan.

Gil, W.E. and Anderson, A.F. (1999) Case study of rape in contemporary China: a cultural-historical analysis of gender and power differentials, *Journal of Interpersonal Violence*, 14: 1151–71.

Ho, D.Y. (1986) Chinese patterns of socialization: a critical review, in M.H. Bond (ed.) *The Psychology of the Chinese People*. Hong Kong: Oxford University Press.

Hou, Z., Leung, S.A. and Duan, C. (2009) Counseling in China: fast moving, but what is the destination? in L.H. Gerstein *et al.* (eds) *International Handbook of Cross-Cultural Counseling: Cultural Assumptions and Practices Worldwide*. Thousand Oaks, CA: Sage.

Hsiao, F., Klimidis, S., Minas, H. and Tan, E. (2006) Cultural attribution of mental health suffering in Chinese societies: the views of Chinese patients with mental illness and their caregivers, *Journal of Clinical Nursing*, 15: 998–1006.

Kobayashi, Y.S. (1989) Depathologizing dependency: two perspectives, *Psychiatric Annals*, 19: 653–8.

Le, H., Berenbaum, H. and Raghavan, C. (2002) Culture and alexithymia: mean levels, correlates, and the role of parental socialization of emotions, *Emotion*, 2: 341–60.

Liang, S. (1987) *The Essence of the Chinese Culture*. Hong Kong: Joint Publishing.

Lin, E.H., Carter, W.B. and Kleinman, A.M. (1985) An exploration of somatization among Asian refugees and immigrants in primary care, *American Journal of Public Health*, 75: 1080–4.

Lin, Y.Y. (2002) The application of cognitive-behavioral therapy to counseling Chinese, *American Journal of Psychotherapy*, 56(1): 46.

Liu, M. (2003) *Spousal Violence in China*. Beijing: The Commercial Press.

Liu, Z. (1986) Guanyu wenhuashi yanjiu de chubu shexiang [Preliminary vision on cultural history research], in N. Xiang (ed.) *Zhongguo Gudai Wenhuashi Lun* [*On the History of Antique Chinese Culture*]. Beijing: Beijing University Press.

Mackinnon, A., McCallum, J., Andrews, G. and Anderson, I. (1989) The Center for Epidemiological Studies Depression Scale in older community samples in Indonesia, North Korea, Myanmar, Sri Lanka, and Thailand, *Journals of Gerontology, Series B: Psychological Sciences and Social Sciences*, 53B: P343–52.

Mak, W.W. and Zane, N.W. (2004) The phenomenon of somatization among community Chinese Americans, *Psychiatric Epidemiology*, 39: 967–74.

Mau, W. and Jepsen, D. (1988) Attitudes toward counselors and counseling processes: a comparison of Chinese and American graduate students, *Journal of Counseling and Development*, 67(3): 189–92.

Miller, G. and Yang, J. (1997) Counseling Taiwan Chinese in America: training issues for counselors, *Counselor Education and Supervision*, 37(1): 22.

Page, R.C. and Cheng, H. (2004) A comparison of American and Chinese counseling students' perceptions of counseling, *The Person-Centered Journal*, 11.

Pedersen, P.B. (1997) *Culture-Centered Counseling Interventions: Striving for Accuracy*. Thousand Oaks, CA: Sage.

Sue, D. and Sue, S. (1972) Counseling Chinese-Americans, *Personnel and Guidance Journal*, 50: 637–44.

Sun, C.T. (2008) *Themes in Chinese Psychology*. Singapore: Cengage Learning.

Sun, Y. and Zhang, Y. (2004) *Cang zai shubao lid meigui* [*The Roles Hidden in School-bags: Interviews on Sexual Activities in High School*]. Beijing: Beijing Press.

Xiao, Z. *et al.* (2006) Dissociative experiences in China, *Journal of Trauma and Dissociation*, 7: 23–38.

Xie, C. (2007) China's suicide rate among world's highest, *China Daily*, www.chinadaily.com.cn, accessed 24 January 2011.

Zheng, S. and Liu, J. (2001) *Shen yiceng renshi zhongguoren* [*Knowing the Chinese on a Deeper Level*]. Taipei: Baishun Information Management Consultation.

31 The effects of a Japanese heritage

Yuko Nippoda

Introduction

Japan has developed as a high-tech country and has largely adopted elements of western culture. Japanese products are everywhere and Japan has created a strong presence in the world. The lifestyle has become westernized, but deep-rooted eastern tradition is still important. The eastern tradition can cause a sense of mystery in western societies, which leads British people to describe Japan as 'inscrutable'. Although Japan is westernized, the vast cultural differences make living in the UK and adapting to British society difficult for Japanese people. On the one hand, many Japanese people feel that living in the UK causes stress, producing negative effects. On the other hand, this opportunity can be a blessing in disguise for some people, giving them an opportunity to find and develop a sense of self, which can benefit their current and future life. Adams (1976) explored how people can use their experience to shape their future lives by means of cross-cultural transition. This chapter presents a view of cross-cultural adaptation between a collectivistic society and an individualistic one. Some Japanese cultural features are introduced along with issues that Japanese people living in the UK have had to address. The meaning of life in the UK for the Japanese is examined, and therapeutic implications are explored.

Japanese people living in the UK

There were 59,431 Japanese people living in the UK as of 1 October 2008, according to the statistics of the Japanese Embassy (2010). This number consists of sub-groups such as expatriates and their families, students, intercultural spouses and immigrants. Immigrants who think that they will make the UK their home constitute 22.9 per cent of the total. The majority however are short-time sojourners, whose stay in the UK ranges from a few months to around 10 years. One of the reasons for the short-term sojourn is the British government's immigration policy. Japan belongs to neither the EU nor the Commonwealth, and aside from tourists most Japanese people require a visa to stay in the UK. This leads to many of them going back to Japan after a relatively short stay.

Although Japan is westernized, there are substantial numbers of Japanese people who have difficulty adapting to British society. Research has shown that two-thirds of Japanese people living in the UK do so under tremendous stress and a quarter believe that this stress is detrimental to their life in this country (Nippoda 1999).

Influences on Japanese people's adaptation to life in the UK

The language barrier

The majority of Japanese people find communication using the English language extremely difficult and stressful. March (1992) suggests that nearly two-thirds of Japanese people have a complex regarding non-Japanese individuals primarily because they speak a foreign language. Research by Nippoda (1999) revealed that nearly 60 per cent of the participants answered that the language barrier had contributed to their maladaptation to British society. Japan is largely homogeneous and most Japanese people do not mix with non-Japanese in Japan. Although Japanese people learn English at school, there is no need to have a conversation in a language other than Japanese and they find it difficult to speak English on a practical level. In addition, the Japanese language is very different from English, and uses a completely different alphabet, grammar and structure.

Of course, if one cannot communicate with others, one cannot understand them, and this can affect daily life. When one cannot express oneself, a sense of frustration and irritation is engendered. When one does not feel understood, a sense of isolation arises. Also, many Japanese come to the UK expecting to improve their English language ability. If this does not happen, they can lose confidence. DeVos (1985) explains that in Japanese culture failure reflects an *internal* shortcoming of the self, whereas success is attributed to *external* forces. Japanese people tend to take failure personally and blame themselves rather than accepting that the language problem was bound to happen to those who do not have a chance to speak English in Japan.

Another issue is that when people speak to others using their second language, they can be treated as a child, since the language they use is grammatically incorrect and their accent is far from standard. This can result in unequal relationships. Power dynamics arise which can leave the Japanese with feelings of inferiority and a sense of discrimination. Lago (1996) refers to language and power, and asserts that these kinds of dynamics can occur in the relationship between therapist and client, and that clients can be intimidated into silence or self-doubt.

Communication style

Another difficulty the Japanese encounter is the difference in communication style. Due to the attributes of a rather homogeneous society, Japan represents a 'high context culture' (Hall 1976); this means that Japanese people have shared meanings in many aspects of their life. An aspect of the communication style entails trying to understand what others mean without words and instead conveying meaning through innuendo and subtleties (Nippoda 2001). As Tezuka (1995) explains, Japanese people try to understand what others say without frequently checking the assumption with others. Also, due to the collectivist nature of Japanese society, group needs are emphasized and individual views, which may deviate from the mainstream, tend not to be welcomed. Therefore, avoiding conflict is a high priority and Japanese people are not culturally encouraged to express strong personal views on a wide range of issues. Japanese people are lacking in assertiveness and do not in general stand up for their own needs. They avoid showing off and are self-effacing. Rather, reticence or silence is welcomed in society (Araki 1995). When Japanese people are modest about their achievements, this can sometimes be seen by British people as a lack of self-confidence (Nippoda 2002b).

Some Japanese people feel stressed when they encounter the western communication style that leads people to exchange opinions in a vigorous fashion. Sometimes western people talk over others and start their own comments before others have finished. In Japanese, the conclusion which is presented in the verb comes at the end of the sentence, whereas the verb normally comes in the middle of the sentence in English. Therefore, in Japanese, it is important to hear the sentence to the end in order to understand what others mean. Japanese people can feel left out and may seem sidelined when they try to participate in a discussion in English. They feel pushed into silence and become concerned about how others evaluate them. This can be a big cause of stress for students at school or for employees when they have meetings at work.

Another element which plays an important role in communication style is hierarchy (Nippoda 2002a). As Matsumoto *et al.* (1996) suggest, the hierarchical rubric of collectivism in Japan is represented as obedience to elders and others of higher status, and hierarchy is established depending mainly on seniority, social roles and gender. Communication is adjusted accordingly rather than on a more equal basis. When it comes to a teacher–student relationship, hierarchy is reflected more obviously than would be the case in the UK. Teachers talk and students listen. When the teacher asks questions, students hardly ever answer. Students play a passive role, which shows respect to people of higher position and status. These different interpersonal and communication dynamics make it difficult for Japanese people to participate in communication with British people.

Collectivism – group-oriented nature

Japan is a highly organized society that values neat presentation and a high level of service. In restaurants, food is presented in an organized fashion, and in keeping with the nature of a gift-giving society, goods are wrapped carefully to look attractive. Trains arrive punctually and there are many 24-hour grocery shops. Life is very convenient. Someone visiting Japan will notice excellent customer service. One Briton was surprised to see that when he went to the garage for petrol, Japanese staff came to the car, filled his tank and wiped the windows. When they finished, they escorted the car to the exit and directed other cars passing in the street to stop to let the car out smoothly and the staff bowed to the car. Good service results from the nature of a collectivistic society. Japan is a very group-oriented society and, as Hofstede (1991) suggests, people are integrated into cohesive in-groups, which protect themselves in exchange for ultimate loyalty; Japanese society looks after people. However, certain rules of behaviour are required by society, and individuals are required to live up to group needs. Group needs in general come first, before individual needs. Japanese people learn how to agree with the group or other group members and try not to deviate from the social norm, thus maintaining 'harmony'. In English, 'harmony' means the co-existence of differences, but in Japanese it means sameness and conformity. Therefore, difference is not welcomed in society in Japan. There is an expression in Japanese, which translates as 'The nail which sticks up is hammered'.

Japanese people view their sense of self differently from westerners. In Japan, the primary sense of self is represented by the role of the person in society, such as father, mother, teacher, doctor and so on, whereas in the UK the sense of self is represented by 'who you are'. The notions of 'self-actualization' or 'individuation' are quite unthinkable for people from a collectivist society (Nippoda 2001). In fact, as Markus and Kitayama (1991) describe, Japanese behaviour is based on the needs and reactions of others, as meeting others' expectations is essential for achieving personal goals.

When one is used to this kind of lifestyle, it is difficult to take responsibility for oneself and to have autonomy. In the UK, one has to be autonomous and proactive to obtain what one wishes. This is a big challenge for the Japanese, particularly when services are not as good as those in Japan. For example, in the UK, public transport can be cancelled or can fail to turn up on time. It can change the destination suddenly and break down. When one orders goods from a shop or a service from a utility company, delay might be experienced. Life in the UK can be quite unpredictable for the Japanese, and this can be disorienting and cause frustration.

As a matter of fact, many Japanese students often express their dissatisfaction with their tutors, academic staff or schools, as they do not feel supported enough and experience a lack of sensitivity to overseas students' needs. Many students feel that they are not getting what they pay for. In Japan, everything is offered and students do not have to make an effort to receive what they want. However, in the UK, they have to be proactive and ask for what they need. Pedersen (1979) explains that dependency does not have the negative implication of immaturity in non-western cultures. British academic staff indicate that they are willing to help Japanese students and invite them to come and talk to them when they have problems. However, Japanese students do not ask for help because they are 'waiting to be served'. This kind of misunderstanding often occurs due to cultural differences.

Another difference between Japanese and British students is apparent when it comes to note-taking in classes at university. Japanese students try to copy down what is written very neatly, whereas British students make notes in their own words, using their creativity. The former would comes across as rather childlike for British university lecturers.

Japanese people feel that they cannot form an equal relationship with British people. They are worried that they might not be taken seriously or they might not be heard, because they play a passive role (e.g. in class, as described above). Their passive attitude, determined by their cultural norms, may result in a childlike image being created from the perspective of westerners and this can lead Japanese students, for example, to be treated like children.

Motivation for sojourn

The motivation of immigrants coming to live in another culture has an enormous effect on their cross-cultural adaptation (Nippoda 1993). Some Japanese people who live in the UK have chosen to come freely, but for others it may not be their choice. Expatriates and their families often do not have a strong desire to live here, but may have been ordered to do so by their employer. Some Japanese who are married to non-Japanese come here because of their spouse's circumstances, needs or wishes. Students might come here via grants or scholarship schemes and this country may not be their first choice. When people stay in the UK through a sense of obligation, their unwillingness can affect their cultural adaptation detrimentally.

Racism

As the Japanese community is rather segregated and less exposed to other populations in the UK, Japanese people's experience of racism can be more subtle than other ethnic communities. Also, I have come across views that some British people consider Japan as a part of the West due to the advancement of Japanese technologies and the dominance of its economy. However, Japanese people still experience racial discrimination from members of the majority population. Some Japanese children experience bullying and isolation from the mainstream white group in primary and secondary schools in the UK.

Lack of support

Japan is a secular society and people do not talk about religion in their daily lives, although Buddhism, Shintoism and Confucianism have culturally affected their thoughts and behaviour. The majority of Japanese people do not belong to a particular religious group, and they do not seek support from religious organizations. Eleftheriadou (1994) notes that many ethnic minorities have their own way of working on their emotional issues. Japanese people have rituals to make wishes, and superstitions are widespread. For example, at the beginning of the year, many Japanese visit Shinto shrines or Buddhist temples and make wishes for their welfare and happiness; for instance, passing the entrance exam for university or high school, or to find a life partner. Such rituals are an important source of support. Also, the Japanese experience support by belonging to a social network and becoming acknowledged as a member of the group. Living in another country can bring about a loss of such support systems, and this can seriously affect their adaptation.

Kobori (2009) also raises other possible causes of maladaptation, such as the weather, food, financial matters and housing.

The meaning of life in the UK for the Japanese people

Against this backdrop, many Japanese people carry anxiety about their lives in the UK, which leads to life itself becoming very stressful. Even if they were doing well in Japan, they experience 'weaknesses' during their sojourn. In the end, many start to blame themselves and withdraw from society. Inevitably, some return to Japan without finishing their planned sojourn in the UK.

By contrast, some are able to transform their difficulties for their own development and growth. Britain is a good place to explore a sense of self, particularly for the Japanese, whose sense of self is represented by their role rather than by who they are. Such opportunities are less common in Japan.

The case of Soseki Natsume

I would like to introduce a Japanese man who experienced transformation through maladaptation to his life in London. He was a very gifted and celebrated early twentieth-century novelist, Soseki Natsume, whose face appeared on a Japanese currency note from 1984 to 2004. He came to London in 1900, funded by the Japanese government, to conduct research into English literature, and stayed for two years. However, he could not adapt to British society. He stayed at his bedsit most of the time and hardly ever mixed with fellow Japanese students. At a later stage in his life, after going back to Japan, he became one of the most popular Japanese novelists. He published a speech he gave two years before he died, entitled 'Watashino konjinshugi' which translates as 'My individualism' (Natsume 1914), which reflected on his life in London. It was acknowledged that his transformation and success were rooted in the suffering he experienced there.

Although he studied English literature at Tokyo University, which is the top university in Japan, and became an English teacher, he was feeling empty as he felt that he did not understand literature. He felt pushed into the job by a third party, a job which he thought was unsuitable for him and he did not enjoy it. He was thinking that he had a vocation for something else, but he did not know how he could find it. He experienced anxiety and insecurity in his life. After he came to London, he expected to find something more satisfying. He studied at college, trying to take in what he learned; however, the more he tried, the more he found himself getting lost in the direction of his life. There were many causes that resulted in his maladaptation but one of them was internalized racism. He felt he was an ugly yellow man from the Far East (Suenobu 2004). It is a well-known story that one day he thought an ugly man was walking beside him, but it turned out to be himself in the reflection of a window in the street. He described his life in London as extremely miserable. He read many books searching for answers. One day he realized something that empowered him. This was the concept of *Jiko-Hon'i*, which translates from a negative perspective as 'self-centredness' but from a positive point of view as 'self-autonomy'. For example, he realized that he had to make his own meaning regarding what literature was about rather than accepting other people's ideas. He believed that when people imitate others and pretend to be strong, it can provoke insecurity. He had thought that he must take in western ideas and pretend to be a westerner, but he realized that he did not need to. He felt fine about being himself. He did not need to live up to others' expectations, and he could be self-reliant in terms of what he wanted pursue. His life in the UK offered the opportunity of finding himself through a process of individuation.

He demonstrated how people can change and grow through experiencing another culture, particularly through the experience of transition from a collectivistic society to an individualistic one, and how people can use this experience for self-actualization.

The case of a Japanese student

A similar process was found in one of the case studies I conducted with a Japanese student (Nippoda 1993). She was in her mid-thirties when she came to the UK, having being sent by her employer to study and experience life in the Midlands. Right from the beginning, she was under tremendous pressure since she felt she had to bring good results back home. It was very difficult for her to communicate with others and make herself understood in English. She started to lose confidence. Life using the English language traumatized her and she even felt like breaking the TV while she was watching it. She felt trapped in the environment – for example, when she had to submit an essay she did not even think about asking for help or negotiating to extend the deadline. She felt as if everything was a dead end and there was no exit. One day it was snowing. She wanted to open the window, but it was frozen shut. Then she experienced a panic attack. The next day the same thing happened, and she finally managed to get out of the room.

What changed her was when she travelled to London and Paris. She felt it was quite important for her to change her environment. She arranged the travel by herself and did not rely on other people. She started to regain confidence by experiencing autonomy. After she went through the transformation, she felt empowered and in touch with her inner strength.

The process of individuation and therapeutic implications

Counselling and psychotherapy are not familiar in Japanese society and are thus understood differently. Not only lay people but also those in the medical profession express ignorance of this field. Psychological and emotional issues are dealt with via a medical model, and people think that the therapeutic relationship is similar to the relationship between, say, a doctor and a patient or a teacher and a student. In this kind of relationship, fostering autonomy and a sense of self can be difficult (Nippoda 2007). Murase (2000) explains that a therapist ought to have certain attributes. This indicates 'shoulds' and 'oughts' which reflect conformity rather than locating him or herself in the process of professional development.

One of the purposes of counselling and psychotherapy from a western perspective is fostering autonomy and the exploration of a sense of self. For the Japanese, who try to meet others' expectations, therapy can be a good opportunity to find their self and achieve their own individuation, particularly when living in an individualistic society.

Managing the cross-cultural transition

A client I saw came to the UK because of her husband's job. She used to have a highly skilled job in Japan, but could not obtain the same job in the UK as the qualification she had was not accepted as equivalent. Since being a child, she had studied very hard and had tried to live up to her parents' expectations. She went to a reputable university and obtained a professional qualification which her parents were proud of. When living in the UK, she did not have a job. Consequently, she felt lost as she did not know how she could pursue a career in this country. Through therapy, she realized how difficult it was for her to stand up for herself and pursue a new career, even using the experience and qualifications she had gained for a similar purpose. She experienced a fear of being challenged by others, particularly when she did something different from them. She used to tell me in the sessions that she wanted to say 'I'm sorry, it's my fault', as she felt other people criticized her. She felt awkward entering the new world of British society. She only felt good about herself through the recognition of others. The change in her outlook occurred when she got in touch with the vulnerable and weak side of herself, and started to learn how to accept herself even when she was not recognized by others. She also began to feel that she did not need to become somebody else in order to exist in the UK. Through this process, she found what she wanted to do and subsequently acquired a job in her professional field that was not exactly the same role, but was in fact more fruitful for her future.

Through therapy to choice

Finding a sense of self does not mean mastering individualism and becoming a westerner. Another client had a similar background: she came to the UK because of her husband's job and tried to live up to her parents' expectations. She was a housewife in the UK as well. Her agony was that she felt that she was not a successful housewife. She always felt criticized by her husband and parents-in-law (who were not even in the UK), and she was angry with the pressure she experienced from the family. However, what changed for her, through therapy, was that she became aware that she had chosen to be a housewife because she liked looking after people. She started to take responsibility for her choice and it became her strength. She had children and realized that she wanted to look after them as they grew up in the UK. When she became aware that she had a choice and she started to take responsibility for that choice, she was able to feel good about being a housewife.

People can find a sense of self and experience the process of individuation through the cultural transition between a collectivistic society and an individualistic one. This can come about when one starts to take responsibility for one's choices. This is a western and individualistic notion but when people from collectivistic societies such as Japan learn it and find a sense of self, it can give them the strength to be themselves. It does not necessarily mean that they become westernized or individualistic, but they have the ability to choose. Many Japanese become conscious of this process after living in the UK for some time: they realize that they can choose to please others if they want to. By contrast, in Japan, it is important to consider other people's needs all the time. Through living in the West, Japanese people have the opportunity of becoming biculturally competent.

It is very important to achieve a balance; to embrace new things from the new culture while at the same time retaining important elements of the home culture. Japanese people may work hard to adapt to western ideas and even try to forget their original identity when in fact it is important to recognize and value it (Nippoda 2003). They have to decide what they want to be for themselves and take responsibility for their own choice. However, something to which attention needs to be paid is that confusion in terms of self-identity can occur during this process. Lago (1996: 51) explains that when one lives in another culture for a certain number of years, while retaining aspects of the old one, 'subtleties of cultural identity and behaviour might become more obscure'. In therapeutic settings, therapists need to attend to clients in a more accepting and understanding manner.

Conclusion

Many Japanese people who live in the UK have difficulty adapting to the host culture. The main reasons are the language barrier and the difference of communication style. Also, the notion that one has to look after oneself can be tough for the Japanese, as they are used to a more collectivistic society that looks after you as long as you obey its rules. However, Japanese people can use the difficult experience of living in the UK to engage in a process of individuation. Change and growth can take place by finding a sense of self, taking responsibility for and discovering freedom of choice. Counselling and psychotherapy focus on fostering autonomy and can be very helpful in the process of individuation using cross-cultural transition between a collectivistic society and an individualistic one.

To conclude, here are some useful things to bear in mind when working with clients of Japanese heritage:

- Appreciate the enormous complexities they may face with communication.
- Always bear in mind that their cultural origins are collectivist and be aware of how such values might compare with your own.
- Due to the language barrier they experience, the power dynamics of interpersonal relationships are invoked and this could be reflected in the therapeutic relationship.

References

Adams, J. (1976) The potential for personal growth arising from intercultural experience, in J. Adams, J. Hayes and B. Hopson (eds) *Transition: Understanding and Managing Personal Change*. London: Martin Robertson.

Araki, S. (1995) Gaikokujin tono komyunikeshon, in F. Watanabe (ed.) *Ibunkasesshoku No Shinrigaku*. Tokyo: Kawashima Shoten.

DeVos, G. (1985) Dimensions of the self in Japanese culture, in E.J. Marsella, G. DeVos and F.K. Hsu (eds) *Culture and Self: Asian and Western Perspectives*. New York: Tavistock.

Eleftheriadou, Z. (1994) *Transcultural Counselling*. London: Central Books.

Hall, E.T. (1976) *Beyond Culture*. New York: Anchor Press/Doubleday.

Hofstede, G. (1991) *Cultures and Organisations: Software of the Mind*. London: McGraw-Hill.

Japanese Embassy (2010) *In Big Ben*. London: Nippon Club.

Kobori, O. (2009) Kokusaika, Kaigaiseikatsu to kokorononayami – Kenko, *Kokorono Kagaku*, 144: 101–7.

Lago, C., in collaboration with Thompson, J. (1996) *Race, Culture and Counselling*. Buckingham: Open University Press.

March, R.M. (1992) *Working for a Japanese Company*. Tokyo: Kodansha International.

Markus, H.R. and Kitayama, S. (1991) Culture and the self: implications for cognition, emotion, and motivation, *Psychological Review*, 98: 224–53.

Marsella, R., Tharp, R. and Ciborowski, T. (eds) (1979) *Perspectives on Cross-cultural Psychology*. New York: Academic Press.

Matsumoto, D., Kudoh, T. and Takeuchi, S. (1996) Changing patterns of individualist and collectivism in the Unites States and Japan, *Culture and Psychology*, 2: 77–107.

Murase, K. (2000) *Shinriryoho no kiso*. Tokyo: Kongo Shuppan.

Natsume, S. (1914) *Watashino Kojinshugi*. Tokyo: Kodansha (republished 1978).

Nippoda, Y. (1993) Cross-cultural counselling and personal development in another culture: how the Japanese adapt to Britain, unpublished MA dissertation, University of Keele.

Nippoda, Y. (1999) *Psychotherapy and Mental Health Issues for the Japanese Community in the UK: Report of Research Support*, Vol. 11. Osaka: The Mental Health Okamoto Memorial Foundation.

Nippoda, Y. (2001) On working with Japanese clients living in the United Kingdom, *Cross-Cultural Psychology Bulletin*, 35(1): 4–13.

Nippoda. Y. (2002a) Japanese culture and therapeutic relationship, in W.J. Lonner, D.L. Dinnel, S.A. Hayes and D.N. Sattler (eds) *OnLine Readings in Psychology and Culture*. Washington, DC: Western Washington University, Department of Psychology, Center for Cross-Cultural Research, http://orpc.iaccp.org.

Nippoda. Y. (2002b) Japanese students' experience of adaptation and acculturation of the UK, in W.J. Lonner, D.L. Dinnel, S.A. Hayes and D.N. Sattler (eds) *OnLine Readings in Psychology and Culture*, Washington, DC: Western Washington University, Department of Psychology, Center for Cross-Cultural Research, http://orpc.iaccp.org.

Nippoda, Y. (2003) Establishing mental health services for the Japanese community in the United Kingdom, *International Journal for the Advancement of Counselling*, 25(2/3).

Nippoda. Y. (2007) The British medical system and Japan, *Sogo Rinsho*, 56(12).

Pedersen, P. (1979) Non-western psychologies: the search for alternatives, in A. Marsella, R. Tharp and T. Ciborowski (eds) *Perspectives in Cross-cultural Psychology*. New York: Academic Press.

Suenobu, Y. (2004) *Natsume Kinnosuke London ni Kyoseri*. Tokyo: Seidosha.

Tezuka, C. (1995) Ibunka taijin kankei, in F. Watanabe (ed.) *Ibunkasesshoku No Shinrigaku*. Tokyo: Kawashima Shoten.

Index

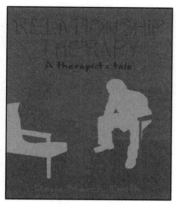

RELATIONSHIP THERAPY
A Therapist's Tale

Rosie March-Smith

9780335238927 (Paperback)
2011

eBook also available

"Rosie March-Smith has provided an insightful and rewarding journey into an area that we would all like to be better at – our relationships to others."
David Hamilton, Counselling student at South Kent College, UK

This fascinating book reveals what goes on in therapy sessions. It shows you how getting to the core of a painful issue or a relationship problem can be achieved within the first few sessions.

Key features:

- Offers invaluable learning tools for mental health professionals and trainees
- Contains case studies of different scenarios
- Includes post-therapy interviews

With a foreword by Michael Jacobs.

www.openup.co.uk

 **OPEN UNIVERSITY PRESS**
McGraw - Hill Education

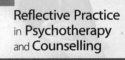

Reflective Practice in Psychotherapy and Counselling
First Edition

Jacqui Stedmon and Rudi Dallos

9780335233618 (Paperback)
2009

eBook also available

"This is a rigorously edited book that maintains consistency throughout, I found the concluding chapter 'reflections on reflections' particularly useful. This book captures what is current in reflective practice neatly charting its dissemination from education theory into the different therapy schools. Reflective practice is effectively illustrated within the different therapeutic schools. I will be recommending this book to other members of the multidisciplinary team where I work." BMA Medical Book Awards 2010 - Highly Commended in the Psychiatry Section

This book draws together conceptual and ethical issues regarding reflective practice, including the meaning and development of the orientation. More importantly, it connects theory to day-to-day practice in psychotherapy and counselling, addressing issues such as "What does reflective practice look like, in practice?", "How do we develop the skills in carrying it out?" and "What ways does it assist practice?"

www.openup.co.uk

 OPEN UNIVERSITY PRESS
McGraw - Hill Education